Museum Management

Leicester Readers in Museum Studies
Series editor: Professor Susan M. Pearce

Care of Collections
Simon Knell

Collections Management
Anne Fahy

The Educational Role of the Museum
Eilean Hooper-Greenhill

Interpreting Objects and Collections
Susan M. Pearce

Museum Management
Kevin Moore

Museum Provision and Professionalism
Gaynor Kavanagh

Museum Management

Edited by Kevin Moore

London and New York

First published 1994
by Routledge
11 New Fetter Lane, London EC4P 4EE

Simultaneously published in the USA and Canada
by Routledge
29 West 35th Street, New York, NY 10001

Editorial matter © 1994 Kevin Moore

Individual contributions © 1994 Individual contributors

Typeset in Sabon by Florencetype Ltd, Stoodleigh, Devon

Printed and bound in Great Britain by T J Press Ltd, Padstow, Cornwall

British Library Cataloguing in Publication Data

A catalogue record for this book is available from the British Library

Library of Congress Cataloging in Publication Data

A catalogue record for this book has been requested

ISBN 0–415–11278–8 (hbk)
ISBN 0–415–11279–6 (pbk)

Contents

Figures

Tables

Series preface

Museums are established institutions, but they exist in a changing world. The modern notion of a museum and its collections runs back into the sixteenth or even fifteenth centuries, and the origins of the earliest surviving museums belong to the period soon after. Museums have subsequently been and continue to be founded along these well-understood lines. But the end of the second millennium AD and the advent of the third point up the new needs and preoccupations of contemporary society. These are many, but some can be picked out as particularly significant here. Access is crucially important: access to information, the decision-making process and resources like gallery space, and access by children, ethnic minorities, women and the disadvantaged and underprivileged. Similarly, the nature of museum work itself needs to be examined, so that we can come to a clearer idea of the nature of the institution and its material, of what museum professionalism means, and how the issues of management and collection management affect outcomes. Running across all these debates is the recurrent theme of the relationship between theory and practice in what is, in the final analysis, an important area of work.

New needs require fresh efforts at information gathering and understanding, and the best possible access to important literature for teaching and study. It is this need which the Leicester Readers in Museum Studies series addresses. The series as a whole breaks new ground by bringing together, for the first time, an important body of published work, much of it very recent, much of it taken from journals which few libraries carry, and all of it representing fresh approaches to the study of the museum operation.

The series has been divided into six volumes, each of which covers a significant aspect of museum studies. These six topics bear a generic relationship to the modular arrangement of the Leicester Department of Museum Studies postgraduate course in Museum Studies, but, more fundamentally, they reflect current thinking about museums and their study. Within each volume, each editor has been responsible for his or her choice of papers. Each volume reflects the approach of its own editor, and the different feel of the various traditions and discourses upon which it draws. The range of individual emphases and the diversity of points of view is as important as the overarching theme in which each volume finds its place.

It is our intention to produce a new edition of the volumes in the series every three years, so that the selection of papers for inclusion is a continuing process and the contemporary stance of the series is maintained. All the editors of the series are happy to receive suggestions for inclusions (or exclusions), and details of newly published material.

Acknowledgements

The publishers and editors would like to thank the following people and organizations for permission to reproduce copyright material:

Peter J. Ames, 'A challenge to modern museum management: meshing mission and market'. This article was first published in *International Journal of Museum Management and Curatorship* 7 (1988), pp. 151–7, and is reproduced here by permission of Butterworth-Heinemann Ltd, Oxford, UK. Peter J. Ames, 'Measuring museums' merits', reproduced from G. Kavanagh (ed.) (1991) *The Museums Profession: Internal and External Relations*, by permission of Leicester University Press (a division of Pinter Publishers Ltd, London). All rights reserved. Valorie Beer, 'The problem and promise of museum goals', *Curator* 33(1) (1990), pp. 5–18. Copyright © the American Museum of Natural History 1990. Hugh Bradford, 'A new framework for museum marketing', reproduced from G. Kavanagh (ed.) (1991) *The Museums Profession: Internal and External Relations*, by permission of Leicester University Press (a division of Pinter Publishers Ltd, London). All rights reserved. Stuart Davies, 'Strategic planning in local authority museums', *Leeds Research Paper* (1993), School of Business and Economic Studies, University of Leeds, reproduced by permission of the author. Roger Davis and Christopher H. Lovelock, 'Museum Wharf', reproduced from C. H. Lovelock and C. B. Weinberg (eds) (1984) *Public and Nonprofit Marketing: Cases and Readings*, Palo Alto, CA: Scientific Press and John Wiley and Sons. Copyright © 1984 by the President and Fellows of Harvard College. Reprinted by permission. Suzanne De Borhegyi, 'Museum brainstorming: a creative approach to exhibit planning' reproduced from *Curator* 21(3) (1978), pp. 217–24. Copyright © the American Museum of Natural History. Victoria Dickenson, 'An inquiry into the relationship between museum boards and management' reproduced from *Curator* 34(4) (1991), pp. 291–303. Copyright © the American Museum of Natural History. Victoria Dickenson, 'The economics of museum admission charges', reproduced from *Curator* 36(3) (1993), pp. 220–34. Copyright © 1993 the American Museum of Natural History. Peter Drucker, 'The university art museum: defining purpose and mission', reproduced from P. F. Drucker (1977) *Management Cases*, London: Butterworth-Heinemann, by permission of the author. Renée Friedman, 'Museum people. The special problems of personnel management in museums and historical agencies'. Reprinted by permission of the publisher, from HISTORY NEWS, Vol. 37/No. 3, March 1982, pp. 14–18. Copyright © by the American Association for State and Local History. Rosalinda M. C. Hardiman, 'Some more equal than others', reproduced from *Museums Journal* (Nov. 1990), pp. 28–30, by permission of the Museums Association. Andy Leon Harney, 'Money changers in the temple? Museums and the financial mission', reproduced from *Museum News* (Nov./Dec. 1992), pp. 38–43, 62–3. Copyright 1992 the American Association of Museums. All rights reserved. Alf Hatton, 'Museum planning and museum plans', reproduced from *Museum Development* (Jan. 1992), pp. 32–9 by permission of the author and the Museum Development Company. Alf Hatton, 'Current issues in museum training in the United

Kingdom'. This article was first published in *International Journal of Museum Management and Curatorship* 8 (1989), pp. 149–56, and is reproduced here by permission of Butterworth-Heinemann, Oxford, UK. Peter M. Jackson, 'Performance indicators: promises and pitfalls', in S. Pearce (ed.) (1991) *Museum Economics and the Community*, London: Athlone, pp. 41–64. Copyright © the Athlone Press 1991. Peter Johnson and Barry Thomas, 'The development of Beamish: an assessment'. This article first appeared in *Museum Management and Curatorship*, Volume 9 (1990), pp. 5–24 and is reproduced here by permission of Butterworth-Heinemann, Oxford, UK. Howard Kahn and Sally Garden, 'Job attitudes and occupational stress in the United Kingdom museum sector. A pilot study'. This article was first published in *Museum Management and Curatorship*, Volume 12 (1993), pp. 285–302 and is reproduced here by permission of Butterworth-Heinemann Ltd, Oxford, UK. Marista Leishman, 'Image and self-image', reproduced from *Museums Journal* (June 1993), pp. 30–2, by permission of the Museums Association. Peter Lewis, 'Museums and marketing', reproduced from J. M. A. Thompson *et al.* (eds) (1992) *Manual of Curatorship: A Guide to Museum Practice*, London: Museums Association/Butterworth-Heinemann, pp. 148–58, by permission of Butterworth–Heinemann Ltd, Oxford, UK. Fiona Combe McLean, 'Marketing in museums: a contextual analysis'. This article was first published in *Museum Management and Curatorship*, Volume 12 (1993), pp. 11–27, and is reproduced here by permission of Butterworth-Heinemann Ltd, Oxford, UK. Victor Middleton, 'Irresistible demand forces', reproduced from *Museums Journal* (Feb. 1990), pp. 31–4, by permission of the Museums Association. Roger Miles, 'Exhibitions: management for a change' reproduced from N. Cossons (ed.) (1985) *The Management of Change in Museums*, London: National Maritime Museum, pp. 31–4, by kind permission of the editor and the author. William M. Sukel, 'Museums as organisations', reproduced from *Curator* 17(4) (1974), pp. 299–301. Copyright © 1974 the American Museum of Natural History. Kendall Taylor and Tracey Linton Craig, 'Risking it: women as museum leaders'. Reprinted, with permission, from *Museum News* (Feb. 1985, pp. 20–6). Copyright 1985, the American Association of Museums. All rights reserved. Stephen E. Weil, 'The more effective director: specialist or generalist?', reproduced from S. Weil (1985) *Rethinking the Museum and other Meditations*, Washington, DC: Smithsonian Institution, pp. 95–103, by permission of the author and the Smithsonian Institution. Stephen E. Weil, 'MGR: a conspectus of museum management', in S. Weil (1985) *Beauty and the Beasts. On Museums, Art, the Law and the Market*, Washington, DC: Smithsonian Institution, pp. 69–80, by permission of the author and the Smithsonian Institution. Stephen E. Weil and Earl F. Cheit, 'The well-managed museum', in S. Weil (1985) *Rethinking the Museum and other Meditations*, Washington, DC: Smithsonian Institution, pp. 69–72, by permission of the authors and the J. Paul Getty Trust.

Introduction: museum management

Kevin Moore

Management in museums, according to a recent journal article, is 'the flavour of the month', the most high-profile aspect of museum activity at present. Every facet of the management of museums is being examined and re-evaluated as never before. This will not, however, be a short-lived fashion, a passing fad of interest before another area of museum work is placed under the microscope. As a result of a combination of factors, management is likely to remain one of the key issues for museums into the next millennium.

Museums, in the currently rapidly changing environment in which they operate, face perhaps a greater range of pressures and challenges than they have ever previously experienced. These pressures and challenges can usefully, if schematically, be divided into the political, the economic and the social. Since the late 1970s government policies, principally in Britain but also elsewhere, have radically altered the environment in which museums operate. Since 1979 successive British Conservative administrations have sought to cut perceived waste in public funding. As most museums in this country depend either directly or indirectly on funding from central government, the sector as a whole has felt the impact of policies such as the poll tax in terms of cutbacks and emphasis on efficiency in management. The policies to encourage competition for the provision of public services have also led to the 'contracting out' of many services in museums to private companies. In at least one extreme case this has resulted in the effective 'privatization' of an entire museum service. The wider international perspective has been a similar process of cuts in direct public funding, pushing museums 'into the marketplace', with a consequent need to emphasize income generation and marketing as never before.

Museums have been pushed into the marketplace, only to find that this market is a rapidly changing and increasingly challenging milieu. Museums have always competed for visitors with each other, and with other heritage and leisure attractions, even if no charge was made for admission. This competition now has a much keener edge, with the survival of institutions ultimately at stake. Yet survival has become much more difficult, due to significant developments in the market. There has been a rapid increase in the number of museums since the 1960s, leading to the possibility that the museum market is now overstocked. Many museums now appear to be neither economically nor politically viable. Competition from without is also much more intense, both from a broader range of attractive leisure pursuits, and from the 'heritage industry' style of attractions, which arguably offer more sophisticated and entertaining displays to an ever more discerning public. Museums, with all the concomitant costs of their primary resource and *raison d'être* – their collections – struggle to compete with the appeal of the heritage centres. When the current worldwide recession is brought into this equation, it is understandable that in Britain in particular this combination of factors has been literally fatal for some museums, resulting in complete closure rather than simply cuts in services.

Museums are also increasingly having to respond to a further set of what can loosely be termed social pressures, to respond more effectively to the needs of a plural society. There is pressure from lobbying groups for museums to provide access in its broadest sense to their needs, or to represent more fully their histories in a multicultural society. Perhaps as much if not more pressure for change in these senses is coming from within, from junior members of staff. Such social pressures do not hit the headlines as much, but are a key current challenge to museum management.

If all of this appears unduly gloomy, it is important to fully recognize the challenges that museums currently face. At the same time, museums must increasingly seize the initiative, not simply passively responding to events but actively seeking to shape them as far as is possible. Museums have tended to be reactive rather than proactive. The current focus on management can enable museums to grasp more firmly why they exist, what they aim to achieve, and how this can most effectively be realized. From a management perspective, the current challenges are as much an opportunity as a threat. While most museums will always be dependent to some extent on public funding, and cutbacks are having a devastating impact, the emphasis on increased efficiency and accountability in the use of public funds, through more effective management practice, is to be welcomed. Similarly, the contracting out of services can have benefits in terms of improvements in quality and price to the customer. In any case, the move towards a contract culture is not so much a result of political change as of economic forces, reflecting much wider changes in the world of work, which will inevitably have an impact on museums. If the marketplace is initially a hostile environment for museums, the resultant improvements in income generation and marketing are to be welcomed. And while it is 'heresy' in some quarters, the creation of a leaner, fitter museum sector through market forces may be a blessing in disguise. The fashion to establish so many museums, particularly in Britain, is clearly not tenable in the long term. Finally, museums should also see the social pressures as an opportunity and not a threat. A more community-oriented and relevant role for museums will be a safeguard to their survival, and not a burden to carry and respond to. Indeed, it is a rather sad comment on the current relatively marginal role of many museums that the pressure for a pluralist perspective is much greater from within the profession than from lobbying groups without. Much remains to be done to convince all sections of society that museums are worthy of their interest.

The right kind of management can enable museums to seize these opportunities, and not only survive in these currently troubled times, but prosper in the future. Do we have the most effective management at present to take these chances; and if not, how can this be developed? To answer these questions, it would be valuable first to consider the development of management in museums.

Museums were traditionally not 'managed' at all, but were 'administered'. It is indicative that the word 'manager', until very recently, was rarely if ever used in museum job titles. Yet curators and keepers were managers in all but name. In Britain, this reflects a cultural aversion to management and management theory, reflecting a broader empiricism, and manifested in the almost negative connotations of the word 'manage', as in the sense of 'I will manage', meaning 'I will cope'. But this also reflects a wider, international distrust of the application of management theory in museums. This is not to say that many museums in the past were not effectively managed in an empirical, common-sense way. Nor does it mean that no thought was given to how museums could best be 'administered'. G. Browne Goode, Assistant Secretary of the Smithsonian

Institution, Washington, USA, outlined the following 'Cardinal Necessities in Museum Administration', in a paper to the British Museums Association conference in 1895:

> A museum cannot be established and creditably maintained without adequate provision in five [*sic*] directions:
> A. A stable organization and adequate means of support.
> B. A definite plan, wisely framed in accordance with the opportunities of the institution and the needs of the community for whose benefit it is to be maintained.
> C. Material to work upon – good collections or facilities for creating them.
> D. Men to do the work – a staff of competent curators.
> E. A place to work in – a suitable building.
> F. Appliances to work with – proper accessories, installation materials, tools, and mechanical assistance.
>
> (Goode 1895: 79)

There is much that anticipates current management thinking in these sensible if very basic principles (apart from a lack of equal opportunities!). How far further thought was given to the issue over the next sixty or seventy years or so is uncertain; the history of the development of management in museums remains to be written. However, it is indicative that Sir Roy Strong, formerly director of the Victoria and Albert Museum in London, has recalled that 'Planning, targeting and long-term strategies were never really a part of museum life as I remember it in the 1950s and 1960s. On the whole it was a piecemeal, pragmatic approach' (Strong 1988: 17). This lack of emphasis on management was not, it appears, peculiar to Britain. A review of museum management in the United States in the 1970s considered that 'The well-run museum is an accident. Most trustees and directors are either unfamiliar with modern management principles or have never thought to apply them to a museum' (Kittleman 1976: 44). While in the 1970s and 1980s museums began to experience a range of new challenges, the reaction of many was to ignore them, almost until it was too late. Sir Roy Strong commented in 1988 that 'Up until now museums have stood outside the mainstream of management professionalism. The result of this has, in many cases, been almost fatal. It has certainly left us very ill equipped to deal with the present crisis' (Strong 1988: 20).

Some museum services in Britain had begun to respond to management thinking from the 1960s, particularly the larger local government-run services such as Liverpool, for example. The impetus, however, in most cases, came from the wider move to managerialism in the local authorities as a whole, and many other museums appear to have ignored or even positively resisted such developments. The large independent museums that developed in Britain in the 1970s, such as Ironbridge, being partly commercial operations, recognized from the outset the need to adopt and adapt current management practices. However, it can be argued that throughout the 1980s, museum workers on the whole remained distrustful of management. Even into the 1990s, 'many curators and administrators remain sceptical about the motivation behind – and appropriateness of – the introduction of mission statements, management information systems . . . output indicators and performance measures . . . the brave new world of planning, budgeting and control' (Allden and Ellis 1990: 35).

It is not surprising, therefore, that when current management practice in museums in Britain has been evaluated, it has been found wanting to a degree. There is both excellence and poor performance in management, but reports have highlighted overall weaknesses. A report on local authority museums by the Audit Commission, the government body that examines the efficiency of the expenditure of public funds in Britain, published in 1991, found that 'Curators have sometimes concentrated on professional issues related to the collection rather than managerial ones such as marketing. As a result some local authority museums are worthy but dull' (Audit Commission 1991: 6). Further, there was a recognition that museum services lacked clear direction and planning: 'museum services have tended to evolve in a piecemeal way, often without clear objectives. . . . Authorities need first to be clear about why they are supporting museums, to set objectives for them and then to devise a business or development plan for the service' (Audit Commission 1991: 5–6). Victor Middleton, a leisure management consultant, was commissioned by the British Association of Independent Museums (AIM) to examine the management of independents and their future prospects. His report, published in 1990, identified 'Management creativity and flair' in many museums, but a more general 'frailty of management in the 1980s', and disturbingly concluded that 'management skills are identified as a major weakness for museums both in absolute terms and in comparison with competitors for leisure visitors' (Middleton 1990: 44, 48, 56). The national museums in Britain have also not escaped specific criticism of aspects of their management (for example, National Audit Office 1988). None of these reports has been as critical of current museum management as they perhaps could or should have been. Victor Middleton has reached a more damning general conclusion: 'As a consultant with some years' experience of museums, I have to say that . . . belief in the general management capabilities of museums is completely outside my experience' (see chapter 22 in this volume).

There have been significant steps forward in management practice in museums since Middleton made this comment in 1990. Though there is still much room for development, there is much to build upon. But how can things be improved? What can museum workers learn from wider management theory? Are some strands more relevant to museums than others? Can management techniques developed in the business world in reality be usefully applied to museums?

To answer these fundamental questions, it is necessary to briefly consider how management theory has developed. Management as a set of ideas about how organizations and businesses can be most effectively run is a twentieth-century development. In simple terms, there have been two main traditions in management thought: scientific management and the human relations approach. It was Frederick Taylor, an apprentice machinist from the United States who became a foreman and then a management consultant, who coined the term 'scientific management'. Taylor, in his *Principles of Scientific Management*, first published in 1911, contended that 'The principal object of management should be to secure the maximum prosperity for the employer, coupled with the maximum prosperity of each employee' (quoted in Pugh and Hickson 1989: 90). Though apparently contradictory, Taylor argued that through the four main principles of a 'scientific' approach to management – division of labour, scientific selection and training, time and motion studies, and payment by results – this could be achieved. Taylor remains perhaps the most influential of all management theorists, his concepts becoming common currency, scientific management remaining the dominant theoretical tradition into the 1980s. The weaknesses of this approach – its assumptions about motivation, its deskilling and dehumanization of workers, and its tendency to actually produce rather than limit industrial conflict – were brilliantly satirized by Charlie Chaplin in his film *Modern Times*, released in 1936. Yet Taylor's vision of the workplace arguably predominated, at least in factory work, for much of the century.

The inherent problems of scientific management were first challenged by management theorists in the early 1930s. Elton Mayo, an academic at Harvard University in the United States, began as an acolyte of the scientific management school, but found through five years of studies at an electrical company in Chicago, USA, that many of the principles of scientific management broke down in practice, and that human relations and workplace culture were crucial: 'In any department that continues to operate, the workers have – whether aware of it or not – formed themselves into a group with appropriate customs, duties, routines, even rituals: and management succeeds (or fails) in proportion as it is accepted without reservation by the group as authority and leader' (Pugh 1990: 355). Mayo's work spawned an alternative, 'minor' tradition of human relations studies.

Since the Second World War there has been a massive expansion in the number of managers in the economies of the developed countries, matched by the development of management theory into an industry in its own right. Particularly from the 1960s onwards there has been a plethora of publications in the field, and innumerable strands and developments, to the point where it is almost impossible to keep up with all the litera-ture and debates. Some commentators argue that management theory has splintered into a mass of conflicting views, with fads and fashions coming and going with increasing regularity, which has been referred to as the 'Management Theory Jungle'. It has led to confusion rather than clarity for practising managers, failing to deliver solutions or advice in handling everyday management issues. This has led to the view that the management theory bubble has burst – that theorists are making something far more elaborate of management than it needs to be. The academic study of management is an industry in the United States and Britain, but not in Japan or the former West Germany, which developed far more successful economies in the post-war years. This milieu has created a market for a host of books that all claim to have the one right approach, the 'quick fix' to answer all management problems. Often these are accounts of one successful individual or company, but offer no analysis of how far such successful practice is applicable outside that particular set of circumstances.

This confusion in management theory led to a 'back to basics' movement in the 1980s, which explains the extraordinary popularity of the book *In Search of Excellence* by two management consultants from the United States, Tom Peters and Robert Waterman, which has sold over five million copies worldwide to date (Peters and Waterman 1982). Though heavily criticized by theorists, practising managers have responded positively to the book's practical insights and recommendations. Peters and Waterman studied the top-performing companies in the United States, and found that they shared a simple management approach, which stressed certain basic concepts, such as having a bias for action (avoiding 'paralysis through analysis'), keeping close to the customer, and productivity through people. The popularity of this work reinvigorated the human-relations approach, with a renewed emphasis on the central role of relationships and workplace culture in management, but in a simple and digestible form.

This regeneration of the human-relations approach has also led to attempts to relate management theories developed in the business context to non-profit-making organiza-tions. Charles Handy has been both an important theorist in this field, and also an invaluable interpreter and popularizer of organization theory to a wider audience. His *Understanding Organizations*, first published in 1976, remains a landmark in this field (Handy 1993). Handy began his career as someone schooled in scientific management, but has done more than anyone to develop the study of organizations through the human-relations approach:

> I came to the study of people in organizations expecting certainty and absolute knowledge in the behavioural sciences. I anticipated that I would find laws gov-erning the behaviour of people and of organizations as sure and as immutable as the laws of the physical sciences. I was disappointed . . .

Organizational phenomena, I realized, should be explained by the kind of contextual interpretation used by an historian. Such interpretation would allow us to predict 'trends' with some degree of confidence. To add precise quantities to those trends, as in the physical sciences, would, however, be inappropriate and unrealistic.

(Handy 1993: 13)

It is apparent, however, that many do not accept such forms of interpretation and continue to bring a pseudo-scientific rigour to organizational analysis. This is indicated, for example, by the development of the term HRM (Human Resources Management), a theoretical perspective which accepts the importance of people in organizations, but argues that 'human resources' must be considered and evaluated in similar terms to other resources at the disposal of management. The essentially ideological battle here has led further to the development of 'soft' and 'hard' versions of HRM. Managerial and organizational theory is still divided between those who see management as a science and those who see it as an art.

What are the implications of all of this for museums? Management is not a value-free concept and differences in theory ultimately reflect differing ideological and political perspectives, concerning the role of individuals not only in organizations but in society as a whole. Museum managers thus cannot simply pick out ready-made solutions to managerial problems from among the varying theoretical perspectives. The application of management theory in museums from the 1970s has not therefore been without problems. First, not enough thought has been given as to whether approaches developed in the business world can simply be transferred to museums. There have been successes, but also notable failures where management techniques have been inappropriately applied. Second, the management approaches being brought to museums have tended to be outmoded by the time they have filtered through from the business world. As Hatton has commented, 'museums as social institutions, tend more to reflect social changes than predict or catalyse them. So, need we worry that museum management is only some twenty-odd years behind the rest?' (see chapter 15 in this volume). It means that museum management in the 1990s is only just catching up with the concepts and mores of the 1980s. According to a recent report on museum finance in Britain,

the 1990s already seem to have developed their own distinct identity as a less financially-oriented decade, with values and standards in marked contrast to the commercial excesses of the aggressive 1980s – they are already being referred to as 'the caring '90s'. Yet in certain respects the reverse seems to be the case in the museums world. The development of performance statistics and corporate business plans, and the emphasis placed on self-generated income for the national museums, is evidence of the fact that quantitative assessments of sound business practice are increasingly being placed alongside qualitative assessments of curatorship and scholarship as key indicators of a museum's success.

(Eckstein 1993: 60)

Museum managers are busy applying some of the scientific-style approaches of the 1970s and 1980s, ignoring the renewed emphasis on human relations, and the development of management theories specific to non-profit-making organizations. This becomes even more of a problem when, as theorists such as Tom Peters stress, the environment is changing quickly, and managers must increasingly 'thrive on chaos' (Peters 1987; see also Handy 1989).

Some management approaches are clearly more valuable than others to museums, to enable them to flourish within the current maelstrom. Museums rely heavily on the knowledge and experiences of highly skilled staff; they seek to engage with and involve all sections of society; and they remain non-profit-making organizations. For all these reasons the human-relations approach, applied to the non-profit context, is the most fertile ground for management ideas that museums can use and develop. Museum management would be significantly improved if Charles Handy's *Understanding Organizations* was more widely read.

This, however, is only the starting point. Ideally, a museum-specific organizational theory needs to be developed, derived from wider management studies, which would inform training at all levels in the museum workforce. The management of a museum shares much in common with managing other kinds of organizations, whether they be schools, factories or supermarkets, but the specificities also need to be recognized and accounted for. Some contributions have been made, but these remain little more than fragments at present. Much remains to be done in what is relatively a very much neglected area of museum studies. This volume brings together some of the key writings on museum management to date, which have begun this process of adopting and adapting organizational theory to the specific needs of museums. Such work is invaluable, indeed, perhaps even a prerequisite, if museums are to adapt, survive and flourish in the future.

Current management training in the Department of Museum Studies at the University of Leicester is based on this perspective. The basic management course divides the subject into nine key units. First, an introduction to management in museums highlights the questions and issues that have been raised in this paper thus far. Museums need a vision or mission, and a second focus is therefore the formulation of an overall policy. If policies are to become realities, a detailed plan is required. The third key area considers the formulation and implementation of corporate plans and strategic management issues. Fourth, to assess how far planning is being successfully implemented, careful performance measurement and evaluation is required. To achieve the aims of the corporate plan, managers bring three key resources to bear: people, money and the museum site (the building, collections and facilities); these resources are considered in detail in the next three units. A corporate plan will inevitably be made up of a number of varied and discrete projects, and the eighth unit considers the best approaches to project management. Finally, marketing is now a key part of management strategy and practice, reflecting the increased emphasis in recent years on visitor needs and services.

One of the most welcome developments in museum management in recent years has been the recognition that museums need to define an overall policy. Museums need a sense of purpose and a sense of direction. They cannot fall back on the generally accepted definitions of museums and their functions (for example, 'an institution which collects, documents, preserves, exhibits and interprets material evidence and associated information for the public benefit' according to the Museums Association in Britain), since these are both too general and lacking in vision. Each individual museum needs to define its unique contribution, which should be ultimately reducible to a short, fifteen- to twenty-word 'mission statement'. This should then be developed by a number of more specific goals or aims. Mission statements have proved invaluable in focusing the activities of museums and helping to ensure that all staff are working in one direction, rather than to individual and often competing missions.

Despite the welcome development of mission statements and overall policy objectives, a key issue remains unresolved: by whom, and through what process, these should be formulated. Whose vision should guide a museum, and how can this best be established? This raises issues of the relationship between museum staff and governing bodies, and the question of the broader democratic accountability of museums. In theory, the responsibility for establishing the mission statement resides with the governing body. As the Museums Association Code of Practice for Museum Authorities in the UK states, 'the governing body or other controlling authority of a museum should prepare and publicise a clear statement of the aims, objectives and policies of the museum'. Whether governing bodies should do so might be challenged on the grounds of their composition (in terms of gender, ethnicity, social class or other factors), their competence, and their commitment. In reality, the latter factor means that governing bodies usually do not fulfil this responsibility, and this falls to the museum director and her or his staff. Stephen Weil makes a powerful argument in favour of museums being guided by the vision of their directors rather than their governing bodies (see chapter 26 in this volume). However, this view in turn can be challenged on several grounds, not least in terms of problems of continuity when a director moves on. Furthermore, though directors are often left to provide the museum's vision by their boards, all too often when this does not match the board's unformulated perceptions, this leads to conflict. The article by Dickenson examines the extent of conflict between boards and professional managers in general, and she concludes that such tensions tend to revolve around different perceptions of the goals of museums (see chapter 8 in this volume). The case study developed by Peter Drucker neatly summarizes the kind of impasse that too often develops, and makes a convincing case that boards must take a degree of responsibility for policy (see chapter 10). Dickenson, however, also highlights the problem that boards are neither socially representative nor necessarily either competent or committed enough for the task. Valorie Beer usefully broadens the debate by arguing that policy formulation should be neither a responsibility of governing bodies in isolation, nor the museum director (with or without their staff), or a combination of these (see chapter 3). Beer convincingly argues that representatives of all stakeholders in the museum – including its various publics – should be involved in the process. Through an analysis of the Japanese American National Museum in Los Angeles, USA, she also makes a valuable contribution to the debate as to how museum goals can best be established, stressing a creative process involving group work and brainstorming. Much remains to be done in this field, in terms of both theory and practice. Greater public control over a museum's policy formulation is likely to be a key issue in the future. This will be crucial if museums are to fully attract the support of the communities that ultimately maintain them.

Policies need plans to turn them into realities. A mission statement and a set of goals are only the starting point. A 'corporate' plan is required to establish defined objectives for a museum over usually the next three or sometimes five years. Corporate planning, as Sir Roy Strong's comments quoted above demonstrate, was traditionally not a recognized element of museum management, but since the late 1980s it has become almost ubiquitous. (There is a significant confusion over terminology in this field, but corporate, forward, development, business or simply 'museum' plans are largely the same.) This has been a welcome development in museum management, aided by being an integral part of the Museum Assessment Program in the United States, and encouraged by the Museums and Galleries Commission in Britain through the publication of the handbook of *Forward Planning* (Ambrose and Runyard 1991). While museum managers are increasingly aware of the value of corporate planning, and of the process involved, some important issues still need to be debated. Too often planning seems to have taken on a life of its own, becoming a process in and for itself. Carefully crafted plans can sit gathering dust on shelves because planning was almost seen as the end, rather than the beginning, of the process. This all too common failure to fully consider the implementation process tends to reflect the way that plans are formulated. As with policies, plans can only be successfully implemented where all interested parties have been involved in some form of consultation process, so that there is a wide sense of ownership and commitment. Davies considers the relative lack of such broader consultation, particularly in terms of visitors and non-visitors, as part of his invaluable survey of planning in local authority museums in Britain (see chapter 5 in this volume). This provides a 'snapshot' of current practice in, and attitudes towards, corporate planning, which has wider significance. The survey also highlights a further key issue – the concern that there is an over-emphasis on planning in such a rapidly changing environment. As Davies's survey demonstrates, the scepticism with which many museum managers view corporate planning is largely a reaction to the mounting crises they face. In the words of one museum manager, 'In the present financial climate . . . it is all very well planning for the future and setting targets – but what's the point when we cannot achieve even the most modest goals. Things now evolve through opportunism as opposed to planned strategies!' (see p. 54).

Planning in museums may have become too formal and rigid in the face of such challenges, but this reflects a degree of shallowness in the level to which it is currently pursued. As Davies's survey shows, museum managers have only a very sketchy understanding of strategic planning, and are unaware of the degree to which such a fuller understanding would provide the flexibility and ability to respond creatively to challenges and opportunities which is currently lacking. Strategic planning is not the straitjacket that the level of planning so far established in museums, no matter how welcome this is, has tended to become. Hatton has begun the attempt to make museum managers more aware of strategic management concepts and clearly senior management training in this field is a key issue for the future (see chapter 14 in this volume). The major research project undertaken by Johnson and Thomas on Beamish, the North of England Open Air Museum, is a very welcome development in this respect, and will hopefully be the first of a number of major strategic studies of this kind (Johnson and Thomas 1992). Their historical analysis of the development of Beamish is included in this volume (see chapter 17).

We may know what we wish to achieve, and how we intend to achieve it; as part of the process, we also need some means of measuring or evaluating how successfully this is being done. This provides both a sense of achievement, and also an 'early warning system' if performance is not matching up to requirements. Performance measurement has become a key issue in museum management in recent years and is one of the few areas that has received serious academic study. Seminal papers by Ames and Jackson are included here (see chapters 2 and 16). Museums have always carried out some form of performance measurement, even if only visitor numbers or expenditure per visitor. The recent emphasis on establishing whether or not museums provide value for money has been the impetus behind the development of thorough systems of measurement, linked to corporate objectives, particularly at the British national museums. While this is a welcome development, it is not without its problems. Some systems appear to verge on over-complexity, providing too much information for this to be used effectively, and draining resources from other activities. Above all, the danger is that the focus is largely on measuring quantity at the expense of quality, simply because the latter is much more difficult to do. Particularly in museums, the quality of what is achieved is as important as the quantity of work done. In framing systems of measurement managers need to get to grips with the evaluation techniques being developed by communication and education specialists. Indeed, perhaps it is time to abandon the use of the term performance measurement in favour of evaluation, which inherently encompasses both quantity and quality.

The current fashion for corporate plans and performance measurement among museum managers reflects how slowly museums react to wider trends in management practice.

The renewed emphasis on the human relations approach from the 1980s has yet to have a major impact in museums. Yet this approach has so much to offer, particularly with the current emphasis on a community orientation to museum work. Of the three key resources that museum managers bring together to achieve the established objectives of the organization, 'human resources' appear to be especially valuable in the museum context. Museums rely on highly skilled professional staff, working on creative projects, in an increasingly close relationship with all kinds of community groups and individuals. But as yet insufficient management training has been provided to enable museum staff to develop more effective inter-personal skills and working relationships. An understanding of the human-relations approach to management and its application to museums is likely to be both the greatest opportunity and challenge over the next decade. Little of any great value has been written on the subject as yet, though the article by Friedman remains a useful introduction to the key issues (see chapter 11 in this volume).

The skewed composition of the museum workforce, particularly in terms of ethnicity, gender, disability and class, and the need to develop effective equal opportunities policies and practices in the light of this, is perhaps the most significant of these. Little has been published in this respect despite the developments taking place in practice; the article by Hardiman is included as a polemic, to highlight some of the responsibilities of all museum managers and staff in this respect (see chapter 12). Recruitment and selection practices in museums would be a particularly useful topic for future research. The training and development of staff has received more attention. The article by Alf Hatton reflects on the British experience of inadequacy and confusion in training provision and career structure, but again his discussion has a wider international resonance (see chapter 15). Perhaps the most welcome development in human resource management practice in recent years in museums has been the concern for the development of 'non-professional' staff, through job enrichment and rotation schemes, and the provision of training and promotion opportunities. The paper by Leishman is a useful introduction to such developments, which are certainly worthy of more intensive analysis, as the entire role of attendant staff is re-evaluated (see chapter 19). The motivation and development of professional staff also needs consideration in both theory and practice, as the traditional reliance on a sense of vocation is being eroded by increasingly poor salary levels and conditions of employment. Indeed, the reasons why museum salaries lag so far behind comparable occupations has never been adequately explained. The study by Kahn and Garden in this volume on job attitudes and occupational stress in museums in the United Kingdom, at a time of rapid change in the sector for its workforce, is a most welcome and timely piece of research (see chapter 18). It is a model for further studies in museum personnel management. More attention has been given to the role of volunteers in museums, perhaps not surprisingly, given their crucial role. Some valuable studies and guides to good practice have been published. What is lacking so far is an attempt to relate to the museum context concepts of organizational analysis developed for the voluntary sector as a whole.

Museums, like all organizations, have both a formal organizational structure and an informal workplace culture. Museum management tends to place undue significance on staff structures, all too often seeing a restructuring as almost a panacea for any problems. Managers also lack sufficient awareness of the broader move towards more task- and project-oriented structures. Similarly, workplace culture is an unexamined aspect of museums as organizations. Such cultures develop as much through the informal initiatives of staff as through management policies; managers must develop an awareness of this to both minimize conflict in the workplace and establish more effective working relationships. The need for research in these areas is therefore particularly acute, in order to provide a basis for the development of adequate management training.

Leadership might seem to have a dated air about it, smacking of elitism or even authoritarianism. Yet after being out of fashion as a topic of study in management for some time, 'leadership' has returned as one of the buzz-words of the 1990s. All organizations, even co-operatives, seem to require some form of leadership, but of what kind? Schematically, leadership theories have developed from 'trait' theories, which argue that leaders are 'born', through 'style' theories, which argue that leaders are 'made', to the current 'contingency' approach, which emphasizes that a range of variables determines the most appropriate form of leadership for a particular organization or situation. This stresses a 'post-heroic' role for leadership – the leader as enabler, team-builder and co-ordinator, rather than power-broker or controller. Leadership is fashionable also in museums at present, but more in a 'heroic' than a 'post-heroic' mould. Museum directors are currently cult figures, portrayed as rescuing and revitalizing moribund museum services, in the image of successful business entrepreneurs. Yet museum leadership has received little serious scrutiny. What kind of leadership is most appropriate to museums? Museums, traditionally, unconsciously adopted a trait theory approach, that leaders were born – they were simply the curators with the best academic qualifications. In the 1970s and 1980s this was increasingly turned on its head. Academic curators tended to be seen as unsuited, and instead managers with the right 'traits' were brought in, often inappropriately, from the business world. By the late 1980s it was recognized that leaders could be developed through training from within the profession – a version of style theory. However, too often the style developed has not matched the needs of the organization, and hence the often controversial role of the museum director today. The 1990s will hopefully see a move towards a post-heroic contingency approach to leadership. At the same time, the white, male, higher social class dominance of museum leadership must also be addressed. The article by Taylor and Craig (see chapter 25) is included here to raise awareness in terms of gender in museum leadership, and further valuable research in this field has recently been carried out in Britain (Blake 1993). Further research leading to positive strategies and action for change in this respect remains a priority.

The second key resource for museum managers – finance – has been a source of both threat and opportunity in recent years. In broad terms public funding sources have tended to be frozen or even cut, and partly as a result new sources of private finance have been opened up, through income generation, fund-raising and sponsorship. Basic financial management skills, in terms of day-to-day budgeting and control, is one area of museum practice that still needs to be significantly improved through training initiatives and museum-specific publications. The development of private funding could also be further enhanced through more coherent training. The British journal *Museum Development* is devoted to the issue of expanding private sources of income, and much practical advice is available, but there is no key manual or manuals of museum-specific practice in this respect. Similarly, there has been little academic study of these highly significant developments in museum funding, which have had widespread repercussions, not just in financial management terms, over the last decade. The article by Harney is a useful overview and introduction (see chapter 13). Dickenson has recently published an important piece of research specifically on admission charges (see chapter 9). The work of Johnson and Thomas has opened up future areas of research regarding the wider economic role of museums (Johnson and Thomas 1991, 1992).

The third key resource of management is the museum site – its buildings, facilities and collections. The management of collections is the subject of further volumes in this series, though the inter-relationship with broader management activities should always be kept in mind. Responsibility for aspects of site management falls to curatorial staff at an early stage in their careers, though increasingly specialist posts are being established. A variety of literature exists to inform those responsible for day-to-day management of museum buildings and facilities, but this could usefully be drawn together into a manual of good practice. What has been written about site management tends to focus on the negative rather than the positive aspects of the role, in terms of managerial responsibilities relating to legal constraints, health and safety regulations, or restrictions regarding the use of historic buildings. What is lacking is an analysis of the opportunities and potentialities in the development of both new and existing museum buildings and sites. Site managers need to develop a holistic approach to their role, with a concern for the creative use of space and the creation of atmosphere and ambience.

A corporate plan will be broken down into a number of discrete projects, which could range from a small temporary exhibition, to a complete redisplay of a gallery, to an entirely new building or redevelopment. Project management, however, appears to be an area of notable weakness in museums. Curators in particular find difficulty in keeping to exhibition deadlines, perhaps a reflection of the relative timelessness of the collections they work with. Skills in this field are improving, and there is an increasing literature of a practical nature to draw upon (see particularly Lord and Lord 1992). Such literature provides a thorough grounding in project planning and the control measures required to keep a project on course. It does not, however, adequately relate such processes to the increasingly rapidly changing political and economic environment in which museums are having to operate. No amount of critical path analysis can prepare a project manager for the kind of challenges and changes that undermine the planning and execution of any major long-term development at present. Political bargaining and marketing skills are increasingly important aspects of project management.

Human relations management in projects is also a relatively neglected area. Successful projects depend on a diverse range of highly skilled and creative people working together to tight budgets and deadlines. Managers seem increasingly able to keep control, but not necessarily to get the best out of, the project team. How often do the more creative initial ideas in an exhibition seem to get lost somewhere in the process? Project management is as much about managing creativity as anything else, fostering the conditions for creative ideas to develop in the first place, and ensuring that these are workable and achieved in the end result. Striking the delicate balance between creative anarchy and management control is the secret of successful exhibitions. The contribution by Miles is an invaluable starting point to what needs to be a fruitful area of debate and discussion (see chapter 23 in this volume).

Marketing is even more anathema to many museum workers than management. The suspicion is that it will lead museums to give the public 'exactly what they want', turning them into heritage theme parks geared to the lowest common denominator. As marketing departments have developed dramatically in museums since the mid-1980s, some curatorial staff have come to recognize the importance of marketing skills and techniques, but remain fearful of marketing gaining too much influence over the museum 'product'.

Museums traditionally held that they had a good and unique product which the public would need little encouragement to come and enjoy. In the 1970s, in response to declining interest, museums adopted a 'hard sell' approach, using blockbuster exhibitions, which perhaps inevitably failed to live up to their billing. The marketing techniques utilized since the 1980s have enabled museums to identify their current and potential users, and the needs and wants of these target 'markets'. It is in this context that concern has arisen that marketing has begun to dictate, rather than simply to inform and enact, the missions of museums. The paper in this volume by Peter Ames discusses this conflict, and offers a way forward, outlining a role for marketing in relation to the mission (see chapter 1). In reality, marketing staff in most museums have rarely had the power to even begin to influence the curatorially defined mission. Marketing is too often confined to low-key promotional and public relations activities, rarely informed by detailed research and strategic analysis. Too much scaremongering about marketing has clouded how little influence it has in most museums, which lack specialist marketing staff, other staff with any expertise, or adequate resources.

Far from needing to be controlled, marketing must be given a much more prominent role in museums. In the business world, marketing is increasingly seen as a vital element in the strategic management process. It is a central function of senior management, and not an add-on, low-grade activity. All managers must develop an awareness and understanding of key marketing concepts, even if much of the practice would still be undertaken by specialists in this field. It is for this reason that marketing is included in this volume. The innovative study by Davis and Lovelock demonstrates the strategic importance of marketing for museum management, even before it had become a recognized part of museum work (see chapter 6 in this volume).

It has been objected, however, that marketing techniques developed in the commercial sector are inappropriate to the museum context. As with management, the application of marketing practices without an awareness of the specificities of museums has been partly responsible for the unpopularity of marketing in museum circles. Too much museum marketing to date has involved employing, through trial and error, often inapt practices. Lewis's paper provides an excellent introduction to the attempt to develop a museum-specific form of marketing (see chapter 20 in this volume). Bradford's research highlights how commercial marketing activities fail to take account of the institutional politics of museums (see chapter 4); McLean builds on this to offer both a deeper and broader analysis of the specific character of marketing in museums (see chapter 21). A healthy debate of this kind will facilitate the development of a more informed and effective marketing practice in museums.

Important strides forward have been made in recent years in the quality of management in museums, but there remains much room for improvement. The development of museum-specific training, literature and manuals of good practice is crucial to ensure this. This work in turn must be based on academic research, which draws on existing excellence in museum management practice, together with an understanding and appreciation of organizational theory, to develop a body of management thought tailored specifically to museums. This volume is offered as a contribution towards that process by bringing together some of the most important contributions made in this field to date. It is hoped that this reader will convince any of those in museums who remain sceptical about management or even hostile towards it, that it is not a threat but a defence, not a dull, dry science but a people-centred art, and not an interference, but a catalyst for change. Above all, management is crucial to ensure that museums will survive and prosper in a rapidly changing world.

REFERENCES

(All books are published in the UK unless otherwise stated)
Allden, A. and Ellis A. (1990) 'Management: the flavour of the month', *Museum Development*, November: 35–9.

Ambrose, T. and Runyard, S. (eds) (1991) *Forward Planning*, London: Routledge.
Audit Commission (1991) *The Road to Wigan Pier? Managing Local Authority Museums and Art Galleries*, London: HMSO.
Blake, M. (1993) 'Why are there not more women museum directors? The underlying reasons and suggested solutions', unpublished MA thesis, University of Leicester.
Eckstein, J. (ed.) (1993) *Cultural Trends 1993. 14. Museums and Galleries: Funding and Finance*, London: Policy Studies Institute.
Goode, G. B. (1985) 'The principles of museum administration', *Museums Association. Report of Proceedings . . . Sixth Annual General Meeting*, London: Dulau & Co.
Handy, C. (1989) *The Age of Unreason*, London: Business Books.
—— (1993) *Understanding Organizations*, Harmondsworth: Penguin.
Johnson, P. and Thomas, B. (1991) 'Museums: an economic perspective', in Pearce, S. (ed.) (1991) *Museum Economics and the Community*, London: Athlone.
—— (1992) *Tourism, Museums and the Local Economy: The Economic Impact of the North of England Open Air Museum at Beamish*, Aldershot: Edward Elgar.
Kittleman, J. (1976) 'Museum mismanagement', *Museum News*, March/April: 44–6.
Lord, G. D. and Lord B., (eds) (1992) *The Manual of Museum Planning*, Manchester: Museum of Science and Industry/HMSO.
Middleton, V. (1990) *New Visions for Independent Museums in the UK*, Chichester: Association of Independent Museums (AIM).
National Audit Office (1988) *Management of the Collections of the English National Museums and Galleries. Report by the Comptroller and Auditor General*, London: HMSO.
Peters, T. (1987) *Thriving on Chaos: Handbook for a Management Revolution*, New York: Harper & Row.
Peters, T. J. and Waterman, R. A. (1982) *In Search of Excellence: Lessons from America's Best-Run Companies*, New York: Harper & Row.
Pugh, D. S., (ed.) (1990) *Organisation Theory. Selected Readings* Harmondsworth: Penguin.
Pugh, D. S. and Hickson, D. J. (eds) (1989) *Writers on Organisations*, Harmondsworth: Penguin.
Strong, R. (1988) 'Scholar or salesman? The curator of the future', *Muse*, Summer: 16–20.

1

A challenge to modern museum management: meshing mission and market

Peter J. Ames

Is marketing in any sense a threat to museums? Peter Ames, in this perceptive paper, considers the conditions in which marketing, despite its invaluable contribution, may come to conflict with a museum's mission. He concludes by proffering a strategy to ensure that marketing enhances the mission, rather than imposing its own agenda.

Mature museums, in advancing their missions, have often had to reconcile them with some incongruous interests of their most important assets. Staff have often wanted more time to pursue their own interests than employment in a subsidized, public service institution warranted. Large donors have wanted more attention devoted to their particular collection interests than the breadth of the mission would permit. Financial means in general have never measured up to the dreams, and the reconciliation of the ideal with the financially feasible has, as with most endeavours in life, always consumed considerable energy. But it is the interests and forces of the market, the recent arrival of which have benefited museums so much, that are now most to be reckoned with. They can provide almost as much tension with, as support for, the mission, and in the outcome of that tension is many a modern museum's soul distilled. To understand and manage the mix, we must examine the nature of mission and market strength and how the two relate to each other, in theory and in recent practice.

In theory, a museum's mission emanates from its charter (usually quite broad), its role as a museum (to collect, preserve and educate), and its tax exemption (based entirely, in the United States of America, on its educational function). It falls in theory to trustees, some of whom are expected to be philosopher-kings, and senior staff to determine the current needs of their community in their institution's field; to articulate the best focus for its mission in their time; and to limit its scope sufficiently to give the resources available to advance it a fair chance of being used effectively. In addition, as stewards of an institution required to benefit the public, the trustees are expected to monitor such issues as reasonable access, the concerns of future generations, non-discrimination, and general integrity of purpose and practice. While sources of the mission are relatively few, its interpretation over time is difficult, and its qualified and committed supporters relatively scarce.

The workings of the market's forces are complex and increasingly more forceful. In a healthy museum, there are two primary rationales for its influence. First, in order to educate effectively, particularly in short stints, it is critical to know the age, education level, motivations and interests of the audience. Second, in order to attract the largest possible audience, and thereby increase operating support, one must have profiles of one's current and potential audiences. That second rationale is the stronger in practice in most museums, and its strength is dependent on at least four factors – the absolute size of the audience, the degree to which the museum's budget is covered by admissions-based operating income, the museum's overall financial health and prospects, and how clearly the current and potential audience's desires are perceived or interpreted. Marketing departments, almost non-existent in museums fifteen years ago, have today in many large museums become divisions, and media budgets that approach five per cent of their museum's total budget are not uncommon.

Even in theory, conflicts between a museum's mission and its marketing seem inevitable. In determining when it should be open to the public, a staff-driven museum might opt for week-days, so that nobody has to work on weekends or in the evening. A market-driven one might choose evenings and weekends, when most of the public has its leisure time. A mission-driven one would have both but would insist on whatever measures were neces-sary to ensure that attendance was spread out and large crowds did not interfere with the educational experience. These measures might include the imposition of peak period surcharges and the limitation of free passes to off-peak periods. The ideal mission-driven plan incorporates studies of the museum's actual and potential audience's desires and interests, but is based primarily on the concerns of future generations and on what its experts in the field believe its current audience needs to, or should, know. A market-driven museum will focus most sharply on what its contemporary market wants and, to a lesser extent, what that market, as opposed to education experts, thinks it needs. From a market point of view, the more the merrier; from a mission perspective, when an audience becomes a crowd, educational potential declines. Marketing staff will want a well-known personality with a recognizable voice as the narrator for a popular exhibition; programme staff will want someone with expertise and credibility in the field. A mission-oriented exhi-bition respects the dignity of its objects and speaks at a fairly professional level, assuming its audience is highly motivated. A market-oriented exhibition may be more concerned with attracting an audience than with the quality of the message they will receive from it. While each has elements of the other, mission is concerned primarily with education; market, given human nature, leans toward entertainment, stimulation and making learn-ing fun. Striking the proper balance between education and entertainment is extremely difficult, and while the latter can be very useful to the former, some believe that, when the two are combined, entertainment will usually prevail.[1] So, in summary, while fulfilment of its mission's and market's needs are essential to a museum's well-being, doing both reasonably well, if not to the satisfaction of all, is a constant challenge. How are museums faring and what are the risks that the new order is bringing?

Large museums that have had marketing departments or divisions for a few years or more usually experience many, if not most, of the following developments. Based on marketing studies which find that the public perceives the institution as static, considerable emphasis is put on increasing the pace and size of temporary exhibitions. An effort is made at least every few years to stage a very large exhibition that will appeal to a broad audience. New wings have a larger percentage of space devoted to auxiliary activities than the rest of the museum. Marketing budgets, rising to between 5 and 8 per cent of total institutional budgets, are used to profile, target and reach audiences, and often result in large increases in attendance. Physical capacity, i.e. the number of visitors the museum can effectively accommodate at a given time, becomes an issue. Hitherto relatively unrepresented audiences are in evidence. The revenue and usually the surpluses of ancillary activities such as restaurants, shops and the sale of space for functions grow dramatically. What would appeal most to the public becomes a major factor in a wide variety of decisions. Significantly, market-driven income – that generated by admission and ancillary income – also almost always increases substantially as a percentage of the overall operating budget.

Those developments, and the resultant wonderful unrestricted income, have usually led to greater vitality and visibility and better economic health for the institution, but often at some cost, the immeasurability of which delays recognition of their impact, to the mission and the integrity of the institution. Many small risks are encountered. A reasonably contemplative environment may be compromised either by temporary shops or food services in the middle of galleries, or crowds so thick that any sense of communion with an exhibition or a particular object is impossible. Public access during normal hours may be limited by private functions that require closing part of the museum. Walk-up access to 'blockbuster' exhibitions may be denied because cash flow and crowd-control considerations limit admission to those who have purchased tickets in advance. Educational quantity may be reduced by the displacement of educational facilities to provide space for large exhibitions or the crowds they attract. Educational quality may suffer when the drive to stimulate the audience's senses loses sight of the educational purpose, or a programme's medium is either inappropriate for its message or so overwhelms it that the memory of the 'experience' overshadows that of the message.

A museum's integrity may be eroded by advertising that hypes an exhibition so much that disappointment is almost inevitable, or by advertising, not reviewed by a subject matter expert, that gives inaccurate information, or even a message contrary to that which the exhibition it supports intends to convey. The emphasis on temporary exhibitions may result in the serious neglect of the permanent collection or permanent exhibits, either physically or in terms of scholarly publications or programmes. The content parameters of a museum's mission, to the extent it has them, may be frequently breached by the content of exhibitions or special events chosen more for their popular appeal than their relevance to the presumed, but often unarticulated, mission. Integrity may be questioned if corporate sponsorships constitute bartering rather than philanthropy, with cash exchanged for publicity and, in some cases, editorial influence.[2] The same can be said of corporate and individual memberships when the value of benefits offered equals or, in some cases, exceeds the cash provided. The ever-changing logistics of frequent turnover of large exhibitions, combined with the sheer mass of ancillary activities and the increasing number of means and marketing issues, may effectively pre-empt the informal, even leisurely, discussion of mission and programmes so vital to their health. There is hardly a museum that has built up a large marketing effort that has not experienced a culture clash with the programme staff.

If mission and market forces are not meshed well, a goodly number of those compromises and corrosions occur, and are not mitigated. The entire tone and culture of the museum may become unbalanced, with decidedly deleterious consequences. Psychic income – the sense of institutional pride, of advancing a meaningful mission, of making a difference – so important to attract the best people and so necessary to make most of the salaries supportable, may diminish to such an extent that turnover becomes excessive, productivity declines, and the quality of staff suffers. Education can be seen as a process that starts with having one's curiosity stimulated, then receiving and digesting relevant information, and finally, sometimes, achieving understanding (the aha! effect). If museum programmes, as a whole, are intended to work to some degree at all three levels, then exhibits and exhibitions that do almost nothing but stimulate are not, unless they are supplemented by programmes that advance the process at least to the second level doing the job. But if many of the 'new' audiences, as opposed to the committed 'hard core' audience of earlier days, are quite ambivalent about the subject matter, the temptation to choose exhibitions for their stimulating subject matter, and to present them in a way that emphasizes stimulation, is overwhelming. Engaged in frequently enough, blockbusters and 'entry-level' exhibitions may result in people leaving with little more than a sense that 'I was there'. While there are few studies on the subject,[3] and education and entertainment have both been present to some degree in most people's motivation in visiting a museum, the central thrust of most motivations may shift in favour of entertainment and an experience. With those changes, the museum may lose one of its foremost educational tools – an expectation of learning and a contemplative environment. The percentage of the actual audience that is receptive or can be motivated[4] may decline. Marketing, rather than serving as an important means to a museum's mission, may become its master.

There is a growing number of museums – they tend to be relatively large ones – where those developments prevail. Combined with the number of museums where the pendulum is swinging quite far in the market-dominated direction, the order of magnitude warrants an analysis of the roots of these growths wherein the remedies may lie. Two factors – the absence of which characterizes institutions at the extreme of the marketing pendulum, and are conditions to be guarded against for those which want to keep a shorter swing on theirs – are vital to the successful meshing of mission and market in a museum. They are clarity of, and commitment to, a meaningful mission statement, and a relative balance of mission and market financing.

A museum, in order to be true to its mission, must have a strong sense of what that mission is. But writing a meaningful mission statement, one that focuses a museum's purpose and gives some sense of its priorities and primary methodologies, is difficult and time-consuming. Developing one that has the support of the community, the respect of the board, and the commitment of the staff, is even harder. More challenging still is the forging of mission-driven criteria to guide an art museum in ensuring that the subjects covered in ten years of temporary exhibitions are not haphazard, or a science centre in ensuring that the subjects represented in its permanent displays are based on criteria more meaningful than that as a whole they represent the field. Equally difficult is the development of mission-based criteria for selecting the specific subject matter, size and media of temporary exhibitions, and the measuring of their educational effectiveness. These difficulties are compounded, if not caused, by senior staff members who often have no prior museum experience, programme committees composed more of advisory members than trustees, programme committees that meet infrequently and/or do not report regularly to the full board, and boards less than ten to twenty per cent of the members of which have any expertise in the mission.

Yet the only governmental office charged with monitoring the board's compliance with the public trust, the charities office of each state's attorney general, does not have the resources to investigate anything but clearly criminal activities. Given, among other factors, human nature and the uncompensated nature of board membership, self-regulation of adherence to the mission is often lacking. Mission guardianship often falls to staff and, depending on the values of the executive director not always senior staff. The result, understandably yet too often, is a mission vacuum, a situation where, despite insufficient resources for the almost insurmountable challenge of a focused mission, the mission statement, usually only in the form of the language of an unpublished charter, provides little guidance and vague boundaries. Resources are dissipated in all sorts of activities by an institution willing or trying to be all things to all people. The vacuum, particularly where the marketing function is well developed and in strong hands, is easily filled by the measurable (and readily understood and appreciated by the board), needs of, and criteria for, marketing success. What the well-crafted marketing studies show the public wants influences more and more what the institution ends up providing.

A recent, thoughtful and popular, if somewhat densely written, book, which attributes a large number of the failures it perceives in higher education to unwillingness or inability to determine what its graduates should have learned there, ascribes a similar strength and impact to market forces. Would someone, it asks, reading just the Bible, Shakespeare, and Euclid be 'really worse off than those who try to find their way through the technical smorgasbord of the current school system, with its utter inability to distinguish between important and unimportant in any way other than by the demands of the market?'[5] Later it states 'the value crisis made the university prey to whatever intense passion moved the masses'.[6] The author of another best-seller, believing that our current citizenry is more culturally illiterate than the previous generation, attributes a good deal of the problem to his perception that school curricula have been based largely on what interested the students and not enough on what their teacher thought they should know, with the result that the amount and level of knowledge transmitted has often sunk to the lowest common denominator.[7] The informally educational purpose on which the tax exemption of museums is largely based certainly does not require the rigour of institutions of more formal learning, but the impact of market forces on mission vacuums has been almost as significant in some museums.

While mission vacuums may have existed for some time without much detrimental effect, the increasing imbalance in some museums in market/mission financing in favour of the former has occurred in the last ten years and had significant effect. It could be argued that the financial strength of a mission derives from endowment income, governmental subsidies, donations, and individual and corporate memberships (if the memberships are primarily gifts and not bartering). Although it would take considerable research to prove it, the overwhelming majority of American museums, twenty plus years ago, probably covered at least 40, if not 50, per cent of their operating expenses from those sources. That percentage is now in many cases less than 35, and, in more than a few important institutions, 25 per cent. Several factors, interacting in several ways, may account for the decline.

Operating expenses inflated in the 1970s. Marketing professionals from the private sector were added to the staff. Large new wings, featuring ancillary enterprises and exhibition space where an image of change could be projected, were added, sometimes largely debt-financed for the first time. Operating budgets increased considerably, sometimes doubling. Endowments, despite a rising stock market, did not increase nearly as fast and endowment/operating budget ratios declined significantly. While federal grants, small to begin with, rose, city and state subsidies, relatively large, levelled off or declined. At the same time, museum attendance grew dramatically. 'Blockbuster' exhibitions attracted new audiences and put museums on their region's maps. Many museums with operating deficits converted them to surpluses. But with the increase to 70 and 80 per cent of the operating budget financed by the market have come, particularly in institutions with mission vacuums, numerous compromises in educational effectiveness, and even integrity.

Who can doubt the corrosive effect on educational quality of market-based financing where it comes to dominate an educational, or potentially educational, organization? Is regular television, despite its vastly greater resources, as educational as public television? Are private colleges dependent on tuitions for eighty per cent or more of their income as effective educationally as those that are less than seventy per cent dependent? The reverse is equally true. In Europe, except in England and France where conservative governments are 'privatizing' parts of the charitable sector by reducing subsidies to museums and forcing them to develop more support from their markets, most museums have eighty per cent or more of their expenses covered by their governments. Shops often run at a loss. Comment books for visitors do not exist and letters from them are often ignored. An ivory tower mentality often prevails and service to the public is not part of the staff culture.

Marketing forces have clearly contributed much to American museums – visibility, vitality, viability, and a spirit of service to their publics – but in some institutions the pendulum has swung too far and in many others, here and in England, it is heading that way. Entertainment and fun are crucial to learning in museums – you have to reach them to preach to them, and they have to sense the sizzle to seek the steak – but some museums are stimulating a lot and educating a little. Stimulating, motivating – affective education generally – many museums and science centres do not want to do more, are not expected by their communities to do more, and may believe that their tax exemptions do not require them to do more. Others may disagree. Here are some indicators for you and your institution to watch, and efforts to undertake, if you would have the best of both worlds.

Ensure the existence, understanding, and honouring of a meaningful mission statement. In developing that statement, some agreement should be reached on the content priorities. What are the target audiences and should any have priority? What major ways of advancing the missions are authorized? Proponents of new activities or programmes should be asked how they would advance the mission. Encourage the development of mission-based criteria for selecting and evaluating exhibitions and programmes *vis-à-vis* their subject, size, and medium. This effort will be facilitated if the board membership includes a goodly number of mission experts and is exposed to educational literature on museology and the museum's content field.

Ensure a reasonable balance between mission and market financial forces. Meshing the two is difficult enough on a reasonably level field; make sure the financing of both is not inordinately unbalanced. Determine what financial sources in your institution most support its mission (generally, endowment income, donations and governmental subsidies or grants that support operations) and those which finance its market forces (generally, all sales). Try to have each group cover at least thirty-five per cent of the operating budget, and consider anything less than twenty-five per cent very unhealthy. If market forces appear to be dominating, work hard to increase governmental support, the endowment and donations.

Ensure marketing support of the mission beyond attracting a broader audience. Marketing may be able to help with the evaluation, if not the content, of educational programmes. It should go beyond testing popularity and experiential impact in exit interviews to attempting to ascertain their cognitive effect. It might sample the entertainment/education expectations of visitors every few years. It might use advertising to encourage visiting during relatively uncrowded times, or even recommend peak/off-peak pricing to reduce the midday crunch on weekends. Have all exhibit advertising reviewed by a subject matter expert. Be sure someone is charged with marketing specific education programmes as opposed to just the institution as a whole and major exhibitions. Consider putting marketing and some programmatic functions in the same division.

Ensure depth is available to those who want it. If the primary virtue of a film, event, or particular exhibition, in terms of the mission, is to attract a broader, larger audience, ensure that greater depth and different media (i.e. bibliographies, catalogues, lectures, field trips and dramatic presentations) in the same subject are available, easily accessible and well publicized. Provide ways, for example through visiting times exclusively for members, for those who seek a thoughtful visit in a contemplative atmosphere to have it.

Develop a data bank of performance criteria and urge your national museum association to develop one nationally. What are the norms for the ratios of endowments to operating budgets for institutions of various ages, and for the ratio of education to marketing budgets? What are the advertising media costs per visitor, and as a percentage of the whole budget? Individual efforts will both contribute to the national pool and benefit from knowing their position *vis-à-vis* the norm.

The democratization of museums in the last fifteen years has benefited museums and their public tremendously, capitalizing on the assets and increasing the vitality and economic well-being of the former while broadening the horizon and stimulating the curiosity of the latter. But it would be unfortunate if, just when the nation needs more education and higher standards in every corner, museums were to compromise their educational roles and settle for popularity.[8] To paraphrase de Tocqueville, who admired America and democracy greatly, the danger of democracy taken to the extreme is that everything sinks to the lowest common denominator. For museums, as with most educational non-profits, meshing and balancing mission and market forces is the best way to maintain standards yet be intelligible, to educate on the most complex subjects yet be relevant, to meet the needs of our communities yet attract new audiences, in short, to advance their missions.

This article first appeared in the International Journal of Museum Management, *1988 (7), pp. 151–7.*

ACKNOWLEDGEMENT

This article has benefited substantially from the comments of Roger Miles, head of public services at the British Museum of Natural History; Ned Pearce, head of the library at the Boston Museum of Science; Steven Weil, deputy director of the Hirshhorn Museum and Sculpture Garden; and Brent Jackson, head of courses and lectures at the Boston Museum of Science. Indeed, the ideas explored in this article have been based on consultations with a wide range of concerned professional colleagues, and are intended to open a debate.

NOTES

1 'There is surely a lesson here for all science centres. When education and entertainment are brought together under the same roof, education will be the loser.' (Shortland 1987.)
2 'There is a danger you'll gear what you're doing towards something you can find sponsorship for, not something that really needs doing.' (Lobbett 1987.)
3 For one, see Borun 1977.
4 Cf. Miles 1986.
5 Bloom 1987: 59.
6 Ibid 314.
7 See, generally, Hirsch, E. D. Jr., *Cultural Literacy, What Every American Needs to Know* (Houghton Mifflin) 1987.
8 'Museums should be rewarding learning environments, and any attempt to settle for mass popularity alone is to sell museums short.' ('Science Museums on the Move', *New Scientist*, 12 May 1983, 381.)

REFERENCES

Bloom, A. (1987) *The Closing of the American Mind*, New York: Simon & Schuster.
Borun, M. (1977) *Measuring the Immeasurable*, Philadelphia: Franklin Institute.
Hirsch, E. D., Jr (1987) *Cultural Literacy, What Every American Needs to Know*, Boston, MA: Houghton Mifflin.
Lobbett, A. (1987) 'Talking sponsors' language', *Financial Times*, 9 November: 34.
Miles, R. (1986) 'Museum audiences', *International Journal of Museum Management and Curatorship* 5: 73–80.
—— *New Scientist* (1983) 'Science museums on the move', *New Scientist*, 12 May: 381.
Shortland, M. (1987) 'No business like show business', *Nature* 328, 16 July: 213.

2

Measuring museums' merits

Peter J. Ames

How should museums measure their performance and achievements? Peter Ames's paper offers a valuable and concise introduction to the subject, and in proposing a systematic and well-considered range of measures, provides the basis for a thorough and fruitful debate on the issue.

Performance indicators, and the data to compare results, are quite common in the 'for-profit' sector and in many fields in the 'not-for-profit' (for example, debt/equity and price/earnings ratios, occupancy ratios in hospitals, and admit/apply ones in colleges). With the exception of measurements such as annual attendance, budget size, and staff size, which speak only to quantity, the museum field globally has almost no such measures. Moreover, a survey of the literature in the United States and discussions with museologists in several other countries have not, with a few unpublished exceptions (such as Wehle 1978), yielded any article even suggesting the development of such indicators for the museum field, never mind proposing specific ones. This chapter will attempt, as a message and a manual, to do both.

Does such an effort to encourage quantitative and qualitative measures of a museum's merits ignore the silence on the subject at its peril, or is it timely and perhaps overdue? On both advisability and feasibility levels, it is not hard to see why caution has been appropriate. There is still little agreement even within a subject sector, such as history, art or science, as to what definable or measurable goals museums do, or should, have in common. To the extent such goals or values are concerned with quality and intangibles, they will always be difficult or impossible to measure.

People who choose to devote their careers to the museum field are often, by learning style or temperament, not inclined toward such a methodical and meticulous exercise. Those who think their institutions might not bear comparisons or meet standards easily, or do not care if they do, might be even less inclined. The appropriate data, whether at the individual institution, museum sector or national level, has usually not been available. Perhaps most critically on the feasibility level, the variables which could skew the data, such as nationality, subject matter, size, age, differing accounting practices, location and stage of development are, at first glance, daunting. The case for pressing on is perhaps best made on the advisability level by describing the recommendation, its benefits, and its potential beneficiaries, and on the feasibility level by offering solutions to the known obstacles.

An effort should be made first to reach some consensus in a given country's museum community on which areas of a museum's performance are of significant interest, for reasons of integrity, accountability, and/or efficiency, to its managers, stewards, funders, regulators and/or accreditors. Then, measurable indicators of performance in each of those areas should be determined. Third, subject-based museum associations should consider the advisability of determining actual, and perhaps ideal, ranges of performance in terms of those indicators. Finally, individual museums should be encouraged to develop the ability to determine and report on their own performances, and to consider developing their own minimum standards.

The process of determining which areas and indicators can and should be monitored, and to what standards, could encourage healthy discussion of what a particular museum should be and what attributes all museums in the same sector should strive to have. To the extent that some consensus is reached, those sectors in the museum field will be united and strengthened by common goals. Institutions that may be adrift will have some signs to guide the way. The process of developing target ranges and the ability to monitor performance should clarify the mission and improve the management information systems of a committed institution.

Monitoring the results, for example staff attrition rates or operating costs per visitor, should provide several management tools to an individual institution: a warning system if there are significant negative variances from the norm or trend without apparent justification; proof of progress to interested parties if the trend is positive; a way of measuring responsible staff capability; and a clearer sense of purpose for the museum and proof of its commitment to excellence.

Lastly, numerical performance indicators, particularly ratios, to the extent they are accurate and valid, may provide the best indicators, that is true and easy, to busy trustees, accreditors, donors and others concerned with the integrity and accountability of museums. They are true in the sense that audited numbers rarely lie and, if they involve expenses, because 'expenditure ratios are a much truer indicator of institutional priorities than any strategic plan, speech, or press release' (Chabotar 1989: 189). Ratios, in particular, can pinpoint the state of critical relationships. They are easy because they are quickly understood, particularly as the consensus on the indicators widens and their definitions are clarified and standardized.

On the feasibility level, the picture for measurable performance indicators has brightened. Museum associations in both England and the United States, and at least one subject-based museum association in the latter, have recently collected, tabulated and disseminated fairly comprehensive data on their members (Prince and Higgins-McLouglin 1987; American Association of Museums 1989; Association of Science-Technology Centres 1989). The number of museums with reasonably sophisticated management information systems seems to be increasing. While the types of museums are growing, and the very definition of a museum may be in flux, communication and co-operation between similar museums also seem to be growing. Differences due to size, age and subject matter, serious and ever-present obstacles, can be reduced to the extent that data are grouped and norms developed down to subsections with similarities in at least three areas of variation (such as nationality, subject matter and size).

Before suggesting some measurable performance indicators, a review of the risks of using them may be healthy. First, it cannot be over-emphasized that many, if not most of the critical qualities of good museums cannot be measured numerically. Ratios cannot measure the importance of a museum's purpose or the quality of its educational programmes. A collection of ratios for a given museum should never be intended, nor be read, as more than a partial portrait. At best, such a collection may, in time, pinpoint those qualities of integrity and characteristics of efficiency that prove susceptible

23

to analysis by ratio and give some indication of whether a museum is well managed. Second, it will be hard to determine what the ideal range for a given ratio, if any, should be. Third, the need to confirm comparability of one institution's ratio with the norm for its sector is ever present. Are the definitions of the numerator and denominator, the units of measure, and the pertinent accounting rules exactly the same? Last, 'a performance measurement system must be kept in perspective . . . otherwise the primary focus of museum management may switch from actual mission accomplishment to the system itself' (Wehle 1978: 19).

With that wary preamble in mind, let us look at the ratios themselves (Table 2.1). There are any number of categories in which they could be grouped. The categorization chosen, by functions as they tend to or reasonably might be clustered in the organizational structure of museums, reflects the belief that the best indicators will be developed, the definitions tightened and more use made of the indicators, if curators and administrators can focus easily on those that concern them the most. Priority has been given to those indicators that speak more to mission integrity and accountability than efficiency, and those 'mission monitors' have been starred (*). Relatively mature management information systems were assumed, but consideration was given in the selection of indicators to the relative ease of assimilating the relevant data. The sector range column could include the norm for an individual museum's chosen sector, if determinable. The target range column could include whatever goal or acceptable range an individual museum sets for itself. Whatever entries appear here are offered as possible targets. Last, every effort has been made to select only the most important indicators and to keep the total under fifty. They are presented in a form that, it is hoped, can be adapted by individual institutions.

These indicators should be considered just a start. Ideally, in the near future:

•   Function specialists, that is curators, fundraisers and others, will gather to determine if there are better indicators and if the definitions should be tightened.

•   Individual institutions will determine what target ranges they want to set for which indicators.

•   National and subject matter museum associations will report existing ranges at least by subject matter, size, and perhaps age.

Many in the museum field would like to know how our institutions are doing in advancing their missions and striving for efficiency. Indicators such as these, used co-operatively and constructively, might help enough to be worth the effort.

This paper first appeared in G. Kavanagh (ed.) (1991) The Museums Profession: Internal and External Relations, *Leicester: Leicester University Press, pp. 59–68.*

REFERENCES

American Association of Museums (1989) *Survey of Museums 1989*, Washington: AAM.
Association of Science-Technology Centers (1989) *The ASTC Science Center Survey*, Administration, Education and Exhibits Reports, ASTC.
Chabotar, K. J. (1989) 'Financial ratio analysis comes to non-profits', *Journal of Higher Education* 60(2): 198.
Prince, D. and Higgins-McLouglin, B. (1987) *Museums in the UK: The Findings of the Museums Association Data-Base Project*, London: Museums Association.
Wehle, M. (1978) *Museum Management Tools*, Boston: Management Analysis Center.

Table 2.1 Annual performance criteria/results

Museum function: access/admission/security

Performance measure/purpose	Formula/ratio	Sector range/norm	Target range	For year: Comments
Attendance trend *	This year's total attendance / Avg. of last 3 yrs. attendance			
Capacity utilization *	Total annual attendance / Sq. ft. accessible to the public[1]			Best way to measure underutilization/overcrowding.
Low income accessibility *	Hrs. per week avail. for free / Total hours per week accessible during minimum 3-month period of maximum public accessibility		Minimum 7%	Should be an important component of every museum's mission, and is not sufficiently appreciated as such.
Minority attendance *	Annual minority attendance / Total attendance			Very difficult to measure minority attendance and depends on community, but solid efforts must be made.
General accessibility	Avg. no. of hrs. open: per week/per week other than 9–5 on Mon.–Fri.		Minimum 40/10	
Admissions financial efficiency	Admissions budget[2] / Total attendance		$0.30–040/ visitor	Generally, the admissions cost per visitor should not exceed 8% of the highest admissions price.
Admissions staff efficiency	Admissions FTE staff[3] / Total attendance			
Security efficiency	Security cost / Total sq. ft./attendance			An area that very much needs some effectiveness measures and for which little data is available.

Notes:
1 Excluding any garage   2 Including visitor assistants, but not guards   3 Ibid

Table 2.1 Annual performance criteria/results

Museum function: fundraising

For year:

Performance measure/purpose	Formula/ratio	Sector range/norm	Target range	Comments
Balance of mission/market financing *	$\dfrac{\text{Sales income}}{\text{Total income.applied to operations}}$		30–70%	Best bearing on the lines between indifference to public-mission–market balance/entertainment.[1]
Financial strength *	$\dfrac{\text{Total endowment mkt. value}}{\text{Operating budget}}$		Minimum 2/1	This minimum applies to institutions at least 50 yrs old.
Fundraising for operations *	$\dfrac{\text{Gifts restricted to oper. (GRO)}}{\text{Operating budget}}$ GROs: closed/reported to donor/outstanding		Minimum 15%	More difficult to raise than capital, but critical to the mission.
Fundraising financial efficiency *	$\dfrac{\text{Fundraising costs}}{\text{Fundraising income}}$	18–23%		These costs should include all expenses in the development/fundraising budget.
Sponsorship philanthropy *	$\dfrac{\text{\$ value of services rendered to sponsors}}{\text{Total sponsorship}}$		Maximum 15%	Difficult, but important, to measure. Include only svcs that are appraisable, i.e. don't include publicity.
Fundraising staff efficiency	$\dfrac{\text{Fundraising staff FTE}}{\text{Fundraising income}}$	1 $250–400,000		
Realization of membership potential	$\dfrac{\text{Total individual/family membership}}{\text{Total annual attendance}}$	1–5%		Assumes that $ value of membership benefits does not exceed their price.
Membership renewal rate	$\dfrac{\text{No. of members who renewed}}{\text{Total membership last yr.}}$	60–75%		Good measure of perceived value of exhibits/programmes.

Notes:
1 For full discussion, see Ames 'Challenge to modern museum management: meshing mission and market' chapter 1 in this volume. Sales income includes admissions, shops, function sales, membership up to the value of the benefits they confer, and education fees.

Table 2.1 Annual performance criteria/results

Museum function: human resources (paid staff and volunteers)

For year:

Performance measure/purpose	Formula/ratio	Sector range/norm	Target range	Comments
Role of human resources *	$\dfrac{\text{Staff salaries and benefits}^1}{\text{Total budget}}$	60–75%		
Staff attrition rate *	$\dfrac{\text{Exempt FTE departures}}{\text{Exempt FTE staff}}$ $\dfrac{\text{Non-exempt FTE departures}}{\text{Non-exempt FTE staff}}$		10–15% 18–25%	Good measure of staff morale. High rates decrease productivity tremendously.
Staff intellect/ contribution to field *	$\dfrac{\text{No. of advanced degrees/ No. of external publ. this year}}{\text{Total staff FTE}}$	$\dfrac{1}{20\text{--}30}$ $\dfrac{1}{50\text{--}75}$		Needs help and may not be worth it. Of greater interest to institutions with research in their missions.
Benefits equity	$\dfrac{\text{Staff benefits (\$)}^2}{\text{Staff payroll (\$)}}$	18–25%		The numerator must be defined carefully.
Staff efficiency: personnel volunteer services	$\dfrac{\text{Personnel staff FTE}}{\text{Staff FTE}}$ $\dfrac{\text{Volunteer services staff FTE}}{\text{Volunteer FTE}}$	$\dfrac{1}{50\text{--}70}$ $\dfrac{1}{10\text{--}15}$		
Volunteer contribution	$\dfrac{\text{Volunteer FTE}}{\text{Staff FTE}}$		7–12%	Good measure of community support.
Commitment to staff training	$\dfrac{\text{Staff training expenses}}{\text{Staff FTE}}$			Numerator should be carefully defined and should probably include attendance at conferences.
Volunteer/ exempt staff tenure	$\dfrac{\text{Volunteer/exempt staff FTE with 2+ yrs longevity}}{\text{Volunteer FTE}}$		40–50% 70–80%	Measures staff treatment of volunteers and vitality of institution. High rates increase effectiveness considerably.

Notes:

1 Includes only regular salaries. i.e. permanent part-time and overtime, but not contractors and temporary help.

2 Includes institutional payment for social security, pension, life/health/ and disability insurance, and not vacation/sick leave.

Table 2.1 Annual performance criteria/results

Museum function: marketing/ancillary activities

Performance measure/purpose	Formula/ratio	Sector range/norm	Target range	Comments	For year:
Per visitor gross sales income (in UK spend per head) *	$\dfrac{\text{Gross admissions, shops, food income}^1}{\text{Total annual attendance}}$			Useful to compare with finance-operating cost per visitor ratio.	
Marketing efficiency *	$\dfrac{\text{Total mktg budget}^2}{\text{Total admissions income}}$	12–15%			
Publicity effectiveness	$\dfrac{\text{No. of unpaid media exposures}}{\text{Total publicity budget}}$				
Shop efficiency: Sales per a) square foot b) buyer c) visitor	$\dfrac{\text{Shop net income}}{\text{a) public square feet}}$ b) No. of transactions c) No. of admissions	a) \$3–500 b) varies c) varies			
Shop/food surplus margin	$\dfrac{\text{Shop income}}{\text{Shop expenses}}$ $\dfrac{\text{Food income}}{\text{Food expenses}}$				
Food sales efficiency: sales per square foot and buyer	$\dfrac{\text{Food sales gross income}}{\text{Public sq ft/ No. of sales}}$				
Parking surplus margin/income per visitor	$\dfrac{\text{Garage income}}{\text{Garage expenses/users}}$				
Shop inventory turnover	$\dfrac{\text{Total shop sales}}{\text{Average retail value of inventory}^3}$	2.5–3 1		Generally, the higher the average sales per buyer, the lower the inventory turnover.	

Notes:
1 For more widespread comparability, exclude parking income.
2 Should include all internal, as well as external, costs, but not publicity costs.
3 Based on averaging beginning and end of year retail value of inventory.

Table 2.1 Annual performance criteria/results

Museum function: finance/facilities

For year:

Performance measure/purpose	Formula/ratio	Sector range/norm	Target range	Comments
Operations surplus/deficit *	$\dfrac{\text{Operating net income}}{\text{Operating expenditures}}$		0–5%	Could be compared to stock and bond indexes.
Investment acumen *	$\dfrac{\text{Endowment income and capital appreciation}}{\text{Endowment market value at end of last year}}$			
Commitment to maintenance *	$\dfrac{\text{Building maint. expense}}{\text{Total square feet}}$			Maintenance deferral is among the biggest problems in museums. Norms will vary enormously with sectors.
Borrowing capacity *	$\dfrac{\text{Debt service costs}}{\text{Total income applied to operations}}$		0–5%	
Capital asset replacement funding	$\dfrac{\text{Reserve for accumulated depreciation}}{\text{Accumulated depreciation}}$			
Financial staff efficiency	$\dfrac{\text{Financial staff FTE}}{\text{Total operating budget[1]}}$	$\dfrac{1}{\$2\text{–}3 \text{ million}}$		Assumes computerization. Includes CFO. Comparisons may be more useful for museums with large budgets. The individual institution's track record will be more relevant than norms here.
Energy efficiency	$\dfrac{\text{Energy costs}}{\text{Total sq. ft.[2]}}$			
Operating cost per visitor	$\dfrac{\text{Total operating expenses[3]}}{\text{Total attendance}}$			Highly useful if norms for comparable museums are available. Higher for museums with substantial research or conservation functions.

Notes:
1 Excluding capital costs, but note when they are high.
2 Excluding garage.
3 Excluding those of ancillary services and off-site activities.

Table 2.1 Annual performance criteria/results

Museum function: programme (exhibits, collection, education)   For year:

Performance measure/purpose	Formula/ratio	Sector range/norm	Target range	Comments
Collection use *	$\dfrac{\text{No. of collection objects exhibited}}{\text{No. of objects in collection}}$			'Exhibited' should include objects used in educational programmes.
Collecting/ conservation commitment *	$\dfrac{\text{Additions to collection/ conservation budget}}{\text{No. of objects in collection}}$			
Commitment to evaluation *	$\dfrac{\text{No. of evaluations performed}[1]}{\text{No. of educational programmes offered}[2]}$		$\dfrac{1}{7\text{--}10}$	
Commitment to education *	$\dfrac{\text{Education staff payroll}[3]}{\text{Total staff payroll}}$		Minimum 10%	
Exhibit maintenance capability	$\dfrac{\text{Exhibit maint. staff FTE}}{\text{Exhibit square feet}}$		$\dfrac{1}{10\text{--}12{,}000}$	Most relevant to science museums and those with moving, electric or interactive exhibits.
Exhibit/ exhibition balance	$\dfrac{\text{Temporary exhibit space (square feet)}}{\text{Total exhibit/exhibition space (sq.ft.)}}$		10--20%	
Average exhibit maintenance results	$\dfrac{\text{Exhibits out of order}}{\text{Total no. of moving part exhibits}}$		5--8%	Numerator should be the average of 3 spot checks during the year.
Financial self-reliance of education	$\dfrac{\text{Educ. fees, grants + restricted endowment income}}{\text{Education budget}}$		Minimum 70%	

Notes:

1 To qualify, an evaluation should have at least 200 responses, the process and conclusions should be in writing, and the results responded to by the programme administrator.

2 To qualify, a programme's annual audience should exceed 250 and its length 2.5 hours.

3 All staff who spend at least 50% of their time either relating educationally with the public/or planning and managing their own or others' educational interaction. Include only regular (see Human resource footnote 1) salaries for both payrolls.

3

The problem and promise of museum goals

Valorie Beer

Who should formulate the mission and goals of a museum? Valorie Beer reviews the approach adopted at her own museum, the Japanese American National Museum, Los Angeles, California, USA, and makes a powerful case for the widest possible community involvement in the process.

Museums need goals

That notion, and complaints about why museums have such trouble with goals, is not new. In 1930, the Carnegie Commission found that museums had unclear goals and were not organized to achieve the goals they did have. The Commission's report concluded that this lack of direction meant that museums were unable to achieve, or show achievement of, any consistent results (Smith, Aker and Kidd 1970). A half-century of reflection has done little to resolve the problem. 'The museum's role in society today is very indefinite. Neither the public nor the museum community is certain of its path' (Hancocks 1987: 184).

At first glance, the problem appears to be rooted in a disagreement over content: upon which topics or issues should museum goals focus? Specific content is the secondary problem, however; the goals themselves come first – but how to decide on them? Reconciling and integrating the desires of myriad constituencies, each with its own agenda for the museum, can be daunting. Yet, lack of a *process* for creating and articulating goals may contribute more to the persistence of 'mission vacuum' (Ames 1989: 10) than does the more visible debate over what those goals should be.

To substantiate such a premise, this chapter will briefly review the evolution of thought on museum goals – not to advocate any goal in particular, but to highlight the literature's preoccupation with goal content. A process for establishing museum goals then will be described. An expanded typology of museum goals (with examples) will be suggested to help museum goal-setters through those uncomfortable early moments when the question 'What kinds of goals do we need?' threatens to derail the entire process. The chapter concludes with the benefits of using a systematic process to establish museum goals, not the least of which is to alleviate the 'confusion both on the part of the public and on the part of the museums themselves about the role of museums' (Hendon, quoted in Hancocks 1988: 258).

WHAT ARE MUSEUMS' GOALS?

Despite the confusion over goals, there seems to be some agreement that they fall into four main categories – acquisition, conservation, research and education (Ames 1988) – and that education has eclipsed the others as museums' primary goal. Yet, even within this consensus of museum-as-educator, there remains debate over the details of the goal. In one scenario, the educational goal does not belong to the museum at all, but to the schools. The museum's part in achieving the goal is to be a 'visual extension of the text-book' or to 'elaborate on related topics not covered by the text' (Baker and Sellar 1983: 71–2). Thus, museums can illustrate, but not initiate, educational goals.

The difficulty with this approach to museum goals is that it does little to define the museum as an independent institution. However (to continue the education example), museums are not schools, nor are they subordinate to them: 'museum work should not be regarded as just another visual aid' (Cook and Gerard 1969: 118). Museums make their own unique contribution to educational goals by providing opportunities for direct learning from objects, stimulation of curiosity and interest, promotion of sensory and perceptual learning through hands-on experiences, and support for independent learning projects (Borun 1977; Miller 1983; Neill 1978; Newsom and Silver 1978; Pitman-Gelles 1979).

The 'learners' themselves present yet another challenge to museum goal-setters. Museum visitors have diverse motives and interests, and anticipating their goals is tricky business. They certainly cannot be approached in a school-like manner, even if learning is their goal. Although over half of museum visitors indicate that learning is one reason for their visit (Beer 1987), other goals may surpass education in importance. To have fun, entertain guests, participate in a family excursion, or escape from the daily routine may be primary goals for the trip to the museum (Borun 1977). Visitors also use museums as detours on the way to other institutions or businesses in the museum's neighbourhood (*Lifelong Learning* 1978). Setting goals with visitors in mind can be difficult. 'No one has ever been able to decide what the public wishes to see in a museum' (Ripley 1969: 112).

If the visitors are not sure that they want to be educated, neither are museums themselves in complete agreement on the primacy of educational goals. Although over 90 per cent of museum personnel believe that educational goals are important (*Museums USA* 1975), they also want their museums to focus on other aspects that have nothing to do with acquiring knowledge and changing behaviour. 'Exhibit designers . . . can't understand why visitors should learn anything as long as they enjoy their visit and are impressed with the exhibits' (Linn 1983: 123). Museums exist to entertain, provide enjoyment and encourage play, and if they are not attending to these goals, in addition to educating, they are remiss (Neill 1978; Newsom and Silver 1978). 'If a visitor does not have a good time in a modern museum, something is wrong, and it is wrong with the museum, not with the visitor' (Neal 1976: 2).

Neal's comment foreshadows a recent development in the museum goal debate: that museums should 'add entertainment elements for revenue generation and in order to compete for customers with other attractions' (MacDonald 1988: 71). A mission vs. market dilemma has emerged in which museums' traditional goals are perceived as being in conflict with market necessities, i.e., the entertainment and fun that bring in visitors and revenue (Ames 1989). Another controversy surrounds the proposal that museums should serve national and social goals by providing overviews of social issues, helping citizens and foreign visitors to understand the local culture, and preserving *in situ* living or archaeological history (Hancocks 1987; MacDonald 1988).

Thus, despite Alexander's reassurance that 'education definitely has become the prime objective of American museums' (1988: 77), the goal debate continues. (If any additional evidence were necessary, one need look no further than this journal. The articles in which Alexander, Ames and Hancocks proposed different primary goals for museums all appeared within the past two years.) And the consequences are evident. In addition to the problem of 'mission vacuum' already noted, lack of consensus on goals leads to museum personnel working at cross-purposes, to vague to misplaced notions of accountability (Conaway 1989), to an identity crisis (are museums schools? amusements?), to a preoccupation with the past and a concomitant unwillingness or inability to tackle more relevant goals (Hancocks 1987), and to the more general problem of justifying the existence of the institution.

In summary, lack of agreed-upon and specific goals makes it difficult to determine what, if anything, museums are or should be accomplishing.

ESTABLISHING MUSEUM GOALS

Given the preceding discussion and the diverse nature of museums, it seems worthwhile to propose a process that museums can use to systematically think about, articulate and communicate their goals – and to let the debate over goal content be settled by each museum as it works through the process. The goal-setting procedure described here was used successfully by the Japanese American National Museum (JANM) in Los Angeles, California, during a year-long process to define the mission and goals of the museum. A couple of caveats must be noted: JANM had the luxury of seeing the process to conclusion *before* opening day. In addition, the process did in fact take *one year* of frequent meetings involving various constituencies. However, the resulting document (Makinodan 1987) constitutes the 'road map' that guides the museum's development and operation.

The process has five phases: (1) identifying groups to include in the goal-setting endeavour; (2) brainstorming goals; (3) prioritizing goals; (4) categorizing goals; and (5) translating goals into action plans. The process is more iterative than linear, and probably has no exact 'end point', given the evolving nature of most museums. (The analogy used at JANM was that the process resembled wet concrete: gooey and not too pretty in the beginning but a solid foundation when completed.) The goal-setting process takes no special training to use, although JANM invited a neutral facilitator (a volunteer with museum research experience who was committed to the process but detached from the politics and subject matter of the museum) to help the goal-setters stay on track. A description of each phase of the process follows, illustrated by examples from the JANM experience.

Identify groups to involve in goal-setting

The joy and pain of dealing with a museum's numerous constituencies have been amply documented elsewhere (see for example Linn 1983). The problem seems to be that responsibility and accountability are 'defined without regard to the museum's clients' (Conaway 1989: 77). Diverse agendas of, for example, boards (financial solvency), docents (education), visitors (learning, recreation, diversion), local leaders (enhanced status and visibility for the community), researchers (quality primary source material), museum staff (enhancement of the profession) and patrons (prestige and social contribution) threaten to overwhelm fledgeling goal-setters. Yet all of these groups must 'buy in' to a unified mission so that the museum can get its work done.

A frightening, but ultimately productive, way to begin is to involve everyone. Inviting representatives from several constituencies to the first few goal-setting sessions has a couple of major benefits: early commitment to the importance of goals and to the success of the goal-setting process, and strategic visibility for each group's agenda (which may lead to supportive coalitions instead of 'turf wars' later on). After the whole group has reached consensus on the major goals, each group may decide to repeat the process for its own function. Communication among groups should continue so that goal lists are shared (both to encourage intergroup synergy and to mitigate parochialism).

JANM started its goal-setting almost two years before opening day. At the time, the 'museum' consisted of a fledgeling board of trustees, a skeleton staff, and an unrenovated building in the Little Tokyo section of Los Angeles. Collections and fund-raising had just begun, and a research project, sponsored by the National Endowment for the Humanities, was under way. The goal-setting began with a mixed group of board members, staff, and volunteer scholars and community leaders in large (but not unwieldy) meetings. After the 'top layer' of goals had been set, smaller groups met to decide on the more specific goals.

Brainstorm goals

Most of the time and effort involved in establishing museum goals should occur in this phase; rushing this part of the process may result in a limited set of fuzzy goals that have little support outside the group that 'owns' them. The great strength of brainstorming is that everyone has a chance to be heard – and constituencies who feel that they have been heard are more likely to listen to, even support, the ideas of others.

Brainstorming requires some equipment and assistance: several large chart pads or pieces of newsprint, marking pens in colours that can be seen from a distance, pins or tape to hang the newsprint, and 'scribes' to write down the ideas. The cardinal rule of brainstorming – that every idea is valid and may be built upon but not criticized – should be visibly posted and reviewed by the facilitator as often as necessary to keep the group in a creative mode. The group also may wish to establish a particular format for goals, e.g., vague, one-word goals ('education') will need to be expanded into a complete thought ('To educate visitors on the Japanese American experience as it relates to the US Constitution'). Finally, goals should be stated in neutral terms to 'resist any temptation to submit to advocacy or lobbying' (Hancocks 1987: 188). (A neutral goal does not suggest a particular point of view. For example, the JANM goal-setters selected the neutral goal 'to describe racial attitudes encountered' over the more negative goal 'to describe racism and discriminating'.)

The brainstorming session proceeds in a free-wheeling manner with participants calling out their goal ideas at will. For larger groups, however, this unstructured approach makes it difficult for the scribes to keep up with the flood of ideas. Alternatives include the round-robin method (in which participants give their ideas in turn) and the brain-writing method (in which everyone writes down ideas first, and then presents them in a round-robin format). With any of these methods, the facilitator must not end the session prematurely when it appears that no more goals are forthcoming; silent pauses give the brainstormers time to review and build upon the list. Allowing the participants to get away from the list (perhaps during lunch or coffee breaks) will help them return with fresh ideas or with additions to and refinements of the ideas already presented. In the end, as many goals as possible (even 'wild' ones) should be listed so that the resulting 'goal bank' is richly representative of all constituencies involved.

At this point, the brainstormed list of goals is fertile ground, but not for immediate action. In this raw state, the ideas are undifferentiated, overlapping and imprecisely stated – in short, they are not yet the guiding banner under which the museum's various constituencies can rally for concerted action. The goal-setters now need to revisit the brainstormed list and trim it by:

- Combining into one goal statement all goals that seem to have the same intent and interpretation.
- Removing goals (such as 'to achieve world peace') that, although worthwhile, are beyond the scope of the museum.
- Refining vague or poorly-worded goals into concise goal statements.

The danger in condensing the brainstormed lists is that, in the rush to get on with it, ideas treasured by certain constituencies may be overridden. (Perhaps a particular group firmly believes that the museum should contribute to world peace efforts.) The rule in such situations is: When in doubt, leave it in. Later discussions, when other goals are in place and when participants have had an opportunity to reflect on the mission of their museum, will clarify what should be done with the disputed goals.

At the conclusion of their first morning session, the JANM brainstormers (board members, researchers, community leaders and staff members) had listed and refined over one hundred goals for their museum. They were in a position to begin planning to achieve the goals.

Fig. 3.1 JANM goals (sample brainstorm list)

understand and appreciate the diversity of experience within Japanese American community

give access to different and diverse views of the Japanese American experience

provide balanced content on general public perceptions of Japanese Americans

foster accurate, complete perceptions

build, maintain collection to support short-term and long-term research, exhibits, programmes

(be a) depository for future research

(be a) catalyst/stimulus of Japanese American studies

work in an interdisciplinary way

be a centre for ethnic studies

serve national, local and international audiences

communicate to the largest possible audience

Prioritize goals

But where to begin? Given museums' finite resources, every goal cannot be equally important. Neither can one goal dominate, lest constituencies feel slighted. Further, one goal may become the responsibility of more than one group (see Categorize goals). Prioritizing goals as a group prevents the subgroups who will later share responsibility for the same goal from giving it conflicting priorities.

With a clean list of goals for reference, participants begin with a general discussion of priorities. Factors that might affect prioritization (e.g., financial and human resources, nature of the surrounding community, space and facilities considerations) are recorded and posted as the session proceeds; however, the facilitator should discourage 'politicking' for or against specific goals. (In the JANM situation, for example, the facilitator cut short a few long digressions regarding a Second World War emphasis for the museum.)

If the group of goal-setters is small, it may be possible to establish goal priorities by consensus following the general discussion. Larger groups will need a method of weighting the priorities. If the list is short (fewer than twenty goals), the group can use the paired-comparison method. Taking two goals at a time, the group decides which is the more important. For example, the group might compare the goal 'to show Japanese American contributions to American agriculture' with 'to present the Japanese American experience as it relates to the US Constitution'. Having decided that the latter was more important, the group then might compare it to another goal, 'to describe the immigrant experience'. If the latter is more important, then it has top priority among the three, followed by the 'Constitution' goal and then the 'agriculture' goal. (It helps to have each goal written on a separate slip of paper so that the slips can be moved up or down after each comparison.)

For larger lists, weighted voting is more feasible. Participants agree on a certain number of votes that they each can distribute among their favourite goals. A limit may be placed on the number of votes that one participant can expend on any one goal. The JANM goal-setters decided to use weighted voting and agreed that the number of votes per participant would be 75 per cent of the number of goals (to force at least some choice among the goals), and that each voter could place no more than six votes on any one goal. The results of the voting showed a clear distinction between a few 'priority' goals for the museum and the remaining secondary goals. Table 3.1 shows a partial list of the prioritized goals.

Categorize goals

When consensus has been reached on the compacted, prioritized goal list, the next step is to look for patterns or categories that broadly describe the goals. The intent is to differentiate the goals according to their purpose and their target (for whom or what they will be done) and to make some tentative assignments regarding the group(s) that will have responsibility for the goals. For example, the traditional goal-categorization scheme – acquisition, preservation, education, research – suggests that different departments in the museum are responsible for each goal type and that the results of their activities vary according to that goal type.

In addition to the traditional four, other categories for the goals may be implied in the organizational divisions of the staff or board of trustees (administration, finance, community outreach), in the type of museum (art, history, science), or in the museum's subject matter ('Japanese Americans'). The purpose is *not* to force each goal into only one category (unless it clearly belongs in just one) but to reduce the set of goals for any one constituency to a manageable number and to highlight goals on which intergroup collaboration will be necessary.

Table 3.2 shows the goal typology, including definitions and examples, devised by the JANM brainstormers. (The goal types and definitions may apply to museums in general; the examples reflect JANM's focus on a particular ethnic history.)

Table 3.1 Prioritized goals for JANM (partial list)

Priority	Weighted votes	Goals
High	16–20	To provide valid, research-based content for the permanent exhibit process To foster understanding and appreciation of the diversity of experience within the Japanese American community To present the Japanese American experience as it relates to the Constitution To promote better race and inter-ethnic relations
Medium	9–14	To serve national, local and international audiences To foster accurate, complete perceptions To be a catalyst and stimulus for Japanese American studies To provide a stimulating environment to educate and entertain To be a centre for ethnic studies
Low	0–8	To communicate to the largest possible audience To show the continuity of Japanese social institutions and customs To define 'ethnicity' and its role and importance through the Japanese American experience

Translate goals into action plans

Goals represent a desired state, a future condition, that the museum hopes to attain. Reaching the goals requires strategic and tactical plans. So as not to lose the momentum of the goal-setting effort, the session should end with participants agreeing on specific, short-term actions that will result in progress (however small) towards the goals. The components of the action item list include:

- The specific action ('hire a director')
- The goal that the action supports ('to attract the best people')
- Who is responsible for the action ('Vice President for Administration')
- Other groups/individuals who should be involved in the action or who will be affected by it ('other Board members and staff')
- Timeline for completion, including milestones for major substeps ('all final interviews completed by March')
- Criteria for measuring the successful completion of the action ('qualified director hired by April')

These components also can be used to make long-term goals ('conduct succession planning for Board positions') amenable to immediate action.

The goal-setting and action planning yielded immediate, specific results for JANM: a new board position covering docents and other volunteers was created to address some of the human-resources goals, and a set of guidelines for research proposals was drafted in

Table 3.2 A typology of museum goals

Goal type	Definition	JANM examples
Educational/ interpretive	Goals for exhibits, publications, lectures, and other programmes to promote learning by visitors (including knowledge acquisition and changes in attitude, awareness or feeling)	To communicate with children about the immigrant experience; to define 'ethnicity'
Social purpose	Goals to promote positive changes in society	To ensure continuity of social institutions and customs; to promote better race and inter-ethnic group relations.
Curatorial	Goals for acquisition and preservation of collections and for research on the collections	To build and maintain a collection that will support short-term and long-term exhibits and programmes; to be a depository for future research
Professional	Goals for contributing to the museum profession (including networking with other museums, historical societies and academia)	To be a centre for ethnic studies; to work with other similar institutions worldwide
Environmental	Goals for the museum's relationship with the local retail and residential communities (including outreach to non-museum organizations and community groups)	To merit the respect and support of the community; to be a museum without walls
Organizational/ administrative	Goals for the internal affairs of the museum (including staff and volunteer organization)	To attract the best people; to evaluate progress towards the goals at least twice each year
Financial	Goals for maintaining and enhancing the museum's endowments with other fiscal supports	To develop a large membership base; to achieve financial independence
Marketing	Goals for promoting and advertising the museum (public relations)	To be a commercial success; to create and develop communication media (e.g. newsletters, ads) to inform people about the museum
Logistics	Goals for the effective and efficient use of museum property and facilities (including internal and external traffic flow and use of non-exhibit space)	To provide adequate space to support programmes and exhibits; to provide adequate parking and traffic flow for tour and school buses

response to the goal of providing 'valid, research-based content'. In the longer view, JANM's goals are providing the benchmarks for collections, exhibits, research and curricula.

The process of establishing museum goals is now complete – but it never ends. Each constituency repeats the process to create its own specific goals within the framework of goals that have been established for the museum. As the museum grows and matures, the process can be used again to revisit and revise goals in light of changes in philosophy, audience, subject matter, funding requirements or other factors.

PITFALLS AND BENEFITS

Using a systematic process for establishing goals may help a museum to articulate and communicate its mission; however, plenty of pitfalls await the goal-setters. As the process begins, discussions on (broad) museum goals may be side-tracked into (narrow) content or topics. At the end of the process, translating goals into actions can be difficult. Statements of goals often sit on the shelf and are not seen as the 'living document' or 'road map' that guides all actions taken on behalf of the museum. New constituencies (such as additional staff, trustees or departments) that arise to augment or replace the original goal-setters may not be committed to the existing goals or to the process by which they were established.

However, the most persistent road-block that goal-setters will face is that not all constituencies (old or new) will be convinced of the need for goals. They may participate in the goal-setting exercise but later follow their own agendas or the status quo (in museums where some goals already exist), especially if the proposed goals involve issues that the group does not support.

These problems are likely to occur whether or not the museum follows a systematic process for establishing goals. The secret is to view the process as a long-term strategy for creating, modifying and communicating a coherent rationale for the museum's existence. Thoughtful, well-stated goals that have broad support among the museum's constituencies will:

1. Broadcast the museum's message. Goals are good for public relations. They provide a foundation for communicating the major themes and topics through which the museum will illustrate the significant aspects of its subject matter. Goals allow the museum to explain its existence and to advertise that it is seriously committed to being a major contributor to the community and to the museum profession.

2. Focus research and acquisition on aspects of the subject matter that are most important to the museum. Goals provide an outline for preplanned, systematic investigation and collection of facts and artefacts. Goals also can focus grant proposals for research and other museum work.

3. Ensure that constituencies are all guided by a common philosophy for the museum. Shared goals mean a unified approach to the museum's mission and help to ensure that parochial interests, biases and 'hidden agendas' do not dominate.

4. Allow the museum to present various points of view on its subject matter. Neutral goals, in particular, allow topics to be presented from a variety of perspectives. Such goals empower the visitors to decide for themselves the meaning of the museum experience.

39

5 Promote agreement and collaboration among the museum's internal departments. Each department will find it easier to support the activities of others if goals are communicated interdepartmentally and if each group is involved in goal creation.

6 Support strategic planning. The long-term health of the museum depends on a clear vision of where the museum is going and how it intends to get there. Goals and action items provide the grist for strategic planning.

Some of the polemics reviewed earlier over the content of museum goals may be symptomatic of a lack of a *process* for establishing those goals. Museums are at once bombarded by various opinions on what they should be doing and bereft of any method for resolving the issue. *What* a museum is – its goals as an institution – is a decision best left to the constituencies involved. *How* that decision is made will benefit from a process for establishing a set of comprehensive and comprehensible goals that clearly indicates the museum's position on (if not resolution of) the great museum goal debate.

This paper first appeared in Curator 33(1) (1990), pp. 5–18.

ACKNOWLEDGEMENTS

The author wishes to thank the Board of Trustees Scholars' Committee and staff of the Japanese American National Museum for their tenacity and dedication throughout the goal-setting process.

REFERENCES

Alexander, E. P. (1988) 'The American museum chooses education', *Curator* 31(1): 61–80.
Ames, P. (1988) 'To realize museums' educational potential', *Curator* 31(1): 20–5.
—— (1989) 'Marketing in museums: means or master of the mission?' *Curator* 32(1): 5–15.
Baker, B. and Sellar, J. (1983) 'Science comes alive in the Natural History Museum', *Curriculum Review* 22(5): 71–4.
Beer, V. (1987) 'Great expectations: do museums know what visitors are doing?' *Curator* 30(3): 206–15.
Borun, M. (1977) *Measuring the Immeasurable: A Pilot Study of Museum Effectiveness*, Philadelphia, PA: Franklin Institute (ERIC Document Reproduction Service No. ED 160 499).
Conaway, M. E. (1989) 'We must remain accountable to *all* our varied clients', *Museum News* 68(4): 76–7.
Cook, J. M. and Gerard, D. E. (1969) 'Libraries and museums', in Jessup, F. W. (ed.) *Lifelong Learning*, New York, NY: Pergamon Press.
Hancocks, A. (1987) 'Museum exhibition as a tool for social awareness', *Curator* 30(3): 181–92.
—— (1988) 'Art museums in contemporary society', *Curator* 31(4): 257–66.
Lifelong Learning/Adult Audiences: Sourcebook #1 (1978) Washington, DC: Center for Museum Education, The George Washington University (ERIC Document Reproduction Service No. ED 191 754).
Linn, M. C. (1983) 'Evaluation in the museum: focus on expectations', *Educational Evaluation and Policy Analysis* 5(1): 119–27.
MacDonald, G. F. (1988) 'The future of museums in the global village', *Museum News* 67(1): 69–71.
Makinodan, T. (1987) *The Themes and Goals of the Japanese American National Museum*, Los Angeles, CA: Japanese American National Museum.
Miller, H. G. (1983) *Adult Education in Museums and Public Libraries*, Carbondale, IL: Southern Illinois University (ERIC Document Reproduction Service No. ED 231 986).
Museums USA: A Survey Report (1975) Washington, DC: National Research Center for the Arts.
Neal, A. (1976) *Exhibits for the Small Museum*, Nashville, TN: American Association for State and Local History.
Neill, S. (1978) 'Exploring the exploratorium', *American Education* 14(10): 6–13.
Newsom, B. Y. and Silver, A. (eds) (1978) *The Art Museum as Educator*, Berkeley, CA: University of California Press.
Pitman-Gelles, B. (1979) 'United States of America', in Olofsson, U.K. (ed.) *Museums and Children*, Paris: UNESCO.
Ripley, D. (1969) *The Sacred Grove*, New York, NY: Simon & Schuster.
Smith, R. M., Aker, G. F. and Kidd, J. R. (eds) (1970) *Handbook of Adult Education*, New York, NY: Macmillan.

4

A *new framework for museum marketing*

Hugh Bradford

Are marketing concepts and techniques developed in the commercial world appropriate to the non-profit making museum environment? Hugh Bradford's research offers a persuasive critique of the unquestioning application of commercial marketing in museums, and outlines a museum-specific theory of marketing.

In this chapter, I outline a new framework for museum marketing in the light of doctoral research carried out in Scotland. The theoretical background of marketing in general and museum marketing in particular is drawn on, and I examine the choices facing researchers within this field. The problems to be found in the existing concepts of marketing and the difficulties of applying general marketing theory direct to museums are considered. The documentation of existing good practice and the fieldwork and analysis employed to investigate more fully the marketing of Scottish museums are discussed.

The findings of the research undertaken have led to proposals for a framework for the marketing of museums. This largely arose from an interpretative model of how successful curators actually operate. It identified three important, often shared areas: the management of the museum; the management of the museum's reputation; and the management of the relationship with the museum's patron groups.

I conclude with a discussion of some of the identifiable characteristics of successful curators, and observations on the implications of the research findings.

MARKETING THEORY; CONTENT, CONTEXT AND CRITICISM

The images and ideals of marketing are relatively recent in origin. The principal components of general marketing theory are contained in a range of literature dating from the 1960s (for example, Ansoff 1965; Borden 1965; Levitt 1960, 1965; Sheth and Garrett 1986). A significant proportion of marketing theory appears to have been deductively derived and based on speculation rather than observation. Where empirical testing has taken place, it has usually occurred in specific environments: for example, in North America rather than Europe; within large corporations rather than small businesses; centring on goods rather than services; profit-making rather than non-profit companies; and concerned with homogeneous rather than heterogeneous markets. Certain areas of marketing theories, if subjected to empirical testing, are supported only at the point where they become tautologous, or where selective hindsight is used. Alternatively, they cease to be theories at all. They may be useful as definitional schemata, but cannot be used to explain or predict (for example, Borden 1965).

Marketing theory has also been criticized as reflecting marketing's identity crisis (Bartels 1974). This has caused: an emphasis on quantitative methodologies rather than the usefulness of findings; the development of an esoteric and abstract marketing literature; and a concern for increasingly sophisticated methods of data analysis rather than problem solving.

One of the dominant marketing theories is the 'marketing mix' (Borden 1965). In its abbreviated '4 Ps' form (price, product, promotion, place), the marketing mix concept has played a significant part in the development of the study of marketing. As Hunt puts it: 'for over two decades the closest thing to an accepted taxonomic paradigm of the nature of marketing has been the "4 Ps" model' (Hunt 1983: 31). Borden's original list was not restricted to four items, but was presented in two parts, the elements of the marketing mix of manufacturers and the market forces bearing on them. These classifications arose from earlier studies that tried to produce evidence of uniformity of marketing costs among US companies engaged in similar businesses. This effort was unsuccessful and Borden concluded that a company's marketing spending was influenced by a combination of factors, and was subject to the overall availability of resources, and the tactics and strategy that the company employed.

There is an element of confusion here, since if one needs to know the strategy before the marketing mix can be decided upon, how can the marketing mix help to formulate the strategy? As a definitional schema the marketing mix may be useful, but it is similar to other marketing concepts in that it is difficult to translate it into a theory capable of being empirically tested and employed.

Many marketing theories could more accurately be described as metaphors. The problem with such metaphors is that they are treated as though they are models. Data that do not appear to contribute to the model are disregarded. Conversely 'proof' is provided by the use of selective examples of past events. This will inevitably lead to problems when applying the theory outside the specific environment in which it was developed. The commercial context in which marketing theory developed is very different from that of museums and galleries. Under these circumstances, direct transfer of marketing theories to a museum and gallery context will not be appropriate.

The concept of museum marketing is even more recent, particularly in the United Kingdom. An examination of the available literature shows that one of the earliest references to museum marketing is contained in Kotler and Levy (1969). Owing to the frequency with which it is cited by writers on museum marketing, it is worth quoting the passage that relates to museums:

> Most museum directors interpret their primary responsibility as 'the proper presentation of an artistic heritage for prosperity'. (This is the view of Sherman Lee, Director of the Cleveland Museum, quoted in *Newsweek*, Vol 71, April 1, 1968, p. 55). As a result, for many people museums are cold marble mausoleums that house miles of relics that soon give way to yawns and tired feet. Although museum attendance in the United States advances each year, a large number of citizens are uninterested in museums. Is the indifference due to failure in the manner of presenting what museums have to offer? This nagging question led the new director of the Metropolitan Museum of Art to broaden the museum's appeal through sponsoring contemporary art shows and 'happenings'. His marketing philosophy of museum management led to sustained increases in the Met's attendance.
>
> (Kotler and Levy 1969: 11)

It is arguable whether the 'sustained increases' brought about by the 'marketing philosophy of museums management' can be distinguished from the 'advances each year' in museum attendance that were already taking place. Leaving this particular point to one side, the article is important because it sets a pattern for the treatment of non-profit marketing (Kotler 1975; Rados 1981). This approach has a number of features. First, a marketing concept or technique is drawn from mainstream marketing. Second, an assertion is made that this is applicable to non-profit areas. Last, a case study is provided in support of this assertion. Where an actual case is not immediately obvious, a hypothetical case is invented to illustrate how a transfer can take place. Such justification could be regarded as basically flawed, since by carefully selecting or inventing aspects of supporting cases, one could support virtually any argument.

In writing about the marketing of museums, Hoyt (1986) and Fronville (1985) have asserted the transferability of marketing concepts to the museum context. Where there is a clear difference. such as museums that do not charge for admission, ways are found to make the concepts fit. Rodger comments that he regards public subsidies as 'the price the public is paying, albeit indirectly' (Rodger 1987: 30). It is difficult to see how such a concept of pricing can be reconciled with the more usual view of it as a part of the marketing mix, over which an organization has virtually complete control.

Foxall questioned the whole basis on which such transfers take place (1984). In criticizing a description of the provision of social workers as a 'typical social marketing exchange' he comments that

> this rules out all the principles on which marketing-oriented management is founded: the 'customer' has no discretion because he has choice of supply; he cannot withdraw his taxes; nor is he able to resist the legally-enforced ministrations of social workers. It is difficult to perceive exchange relationships in (this) example, let alone identify the freely-entered, invariable mutually beneficial transactions which are the essence of modern marketing.
>
> (Foxall 1984: 25)

More recently writers (for example, Ames 1989) have drawn attention to some of the differences in the museum context, and the implications that these have for museum marketing.

Museum marketing theory transferred from other contexts is flawed in two ways. First, the original marketing theories tend to be deductively derived, and, if empirical testing took place, this was carried out in an environment fundamentally different from that of museums and galleries. For this reason, the chances of successful transfer are reduced. Second, the arguments put forward to support transferability contain contradictions and stretch the concept of exchange to a point where it has little meaning.

There has also been a failure to take account of the institutional politics of museums and galleries. Museum marketing literature lacks a political dimension. By contrast, the general museum and gallery literature is full of references to institutional politics. Both museum marketing and general museum literature, for example, cover the subject of admission charges. But, museum marketing writers have treated this as simply a pricing question. Such ignoring (or ignorance) of the political context decreases the validity of their findings and reduces the inclination of museum and gallery staff to adopt them.

In sum, there is a clear lack of museum marketing theory derived from studying museums and their functions. There is a need for inductively derived empirically-based studies from which to develop a more appropriate museum marketing theory. It was with this in mind that the research was conducted.

RESEARCH INTO THE MARKETING OF MUSEUMS IN SCOTLAND

Before examining the methodology used in this particular study, it is worth examining the two paradigms underpinning the research. But stating that there are two different paradigms is itself a piece of rather heavy-handed reductionism. Perhaps it would be more accurate to regard them as being two ends of a continuum along which any individual piece of research could be situated.

First, adopting a positivist approach to the study of marketing Scotland's museums and galleries has certain implications. At the researcher level, there is a need to formulate hypotheses and then test them. Such hypotheses would normally be deductively derived from the existing body of knowledge on the subject. However, as the literature review has discovered, the body of knowledge on the subject of marketing museums and galleries is neither extensive, nor well-grounded in the study of museums. Given the findings of the literature review, it is doubtful whether useful hypotheses could be derived. One could if one wished produce hypotheses for testing, such as 'the marketing of museums differs from the marketing of consumer goods' or the alternative hypothesis 'there is no difference between the marketing of museums and the marketing of consumer goods'. At a methodological level, there would then be a need to operationalize the concepts in a way that rendered them capable of being measured.

One could then set out to use the language and paradigms of consumer goods marketing to produce, for example, a questionnaire to measure some of the factors considered to be relevant. The problem, as Foxall (1984) has pointed out, is that alternative concepts are required. By only building on existing concepts, it is unlikely that more appropriate and alternative ones can emerge. Criticisms of the desire of social sciences, particularly psychology, to emulate the methodology of natural sciences are provided by Harré (1981). If one has based a questionnaire on inappropriate concepts, then it is possible not only for valuable data to be lost, but also for positively misleading data to emerge.

Questionnaires provide a closely worked mould for the data which they are intended to gather. The difficulty is that when looking at the results, one often sees the shape of the mould rather than a ready analysis of its contents. The success of this type of research depends on being able to ask the right questions. Unfortunately, if one does not have the relevant information on which to base the questions, then one may unnecessarily restrict or distort what can be discovered. Even apparently objective measures, such as attendance figures, can provide misleading information. For example, in a museum without entrance charges, how does one compare ten people who came in to get out of the rain with the one person who had a positive reason for a visit? This illustrates the problem of even the most basic quantitative measure in a museum context. Therefore, it was thought that the use of a positivist approach and quantitative techniques would not be appropriate for this particular study.

The second paradigm, a phenomenological approach, leads to the use of qualitative methods, defined by Van Maanen:

> The label qualitative methods has no precise meaning in any of the social sciences. It is at best an umbrella term covering an array of interpretive techniques which seek to describe, decode, translate and otherwise come to terms with the meaning, not the frequency, of certain more or less naturally occurring phenomena in the social world. To operate in a qualitative mode is to trade in linguistic symbols and by so doing, attempt to reduce the distance between indicated and indicator, between theory and data, between context and action. The raw materials of qualitative study

are therefore generated *in vivo*, close to the point of origin. Although the use of qualitative methods does not prohibit a researcher's use of the logic of scientific empiricism, the logic of phenomenological analysis is more likely to be assumed since qualitative researchers tend to regard social phenomena as more particular and ambiguous than replicable and clearly defined.

(Van Maanen 1987: 9)

The idea of grounded theory expounded by Glaser and Strauss (1967) and further developed by Strauss (1987) is concerned with developing theory from data obtained in the field. This is essentially about interpreting and understanding what is happening, rather than measuring and testing. It was this general approach that was adopted in this case. It was felt that there were existing examples of good marketing practice within some Scottish museums. Whether all the museums would have chosen to call what they did 'good marketing' is questionable, but the research was more concerned with establishing what they did, rather than what they called it.

A panel of experts advised on the selection of museums for the study. The objective of using an expert panel was the provision of an independent view of what constituted good practice in museums. Members of the panel were nominated by the Scottish Museums Council as being people of standing in both the museums field and other closely related areas. Each of the panel members was interviewed for their opinions on examples of good practice in Scotland and the reasoning behind their choices. They also provided a great deal of background material on Scottish museums and galleries and this helped to familiarize the researcher with the area of study.

Further discussion took place with the Director of the Scottish Museums Council. The objective of this was to choose, from the list of nominated museums, four museums suitable in the first phase for more detailed study. A factor in this choice was the need for the sample to include representative museums from a range of sizes, locations and ownership types.

Curators and directors of the selected museums were approached by telephone and an explanation was given of the objectives of the project and the likely extent of their involvement and that of their staff. There was a high level of co-operation from the curators and an initial timetable was agreed. A period of one week at each museum was chosen to allow for familiarization, without the risk of potential alienation of the participating museums by outstaying one's welcome. It was, however, recognized that further time on site might be required, but that it would not be possible to assess this until the fieldwork had started.

The objective of the fieldwork was to discover what actually happened in the museum. A questionnaire was avoided because of its rigidity and instead a topic guide was employed. It was felt that this might be useful in stimulating broad areas of discussion, without precluding other items of importance to the curators and their staff.

Data of various types were collected. The most important sources were interviews, all of which were tape-recorded. These were supported by brief field notes taken by the researcher to put each day's material in context. In two cases, curators agreed to complete diary sheets detailing their activities for one week after the researcher had left the site. Where available, the museums also provided reports, publicity material, attendance figures and other written information. In each of the museums, curators were interviewed, along with all senior staff, and as many as possible of the staff (for example, warders). Given the small number of staff employed at most of the museums, this effectively meant that almost all staff were interviewed. Interviews varied in length, although those with curators tended to be the longest, between an hour and two hours.

The interviews were transcribed and coded. This assisted analysis of the material and helped in the development of integrative diagrams and recommendations. Before the full analysis of the data from the first four museums was completed, a second group of museums was chosen from the original list of museums provided by the expert panel interviews. Because this was still essentially an exploratory exercise, the lack of a completed analysis from phase one was a positive advantage. The phase two interviews were similarly transcribed and coded. Integrative diagrams and recommendations were produced concurrently with those from phase one.

Curators who had taken part in the study were consulted over the preliminary findings of the research. They were interviewed and their reactions, suggestions and comments recorded. This further extended the research and allowed a counter-check on the researcher's analysis and conclusions.

The data collected at the museums at each stage of the research were logged on computer. They were then analysed using a procedure that broadly followed that outlined by Strauss (1987). It was possible to modify the procedure because the chosen software, Ethnograph, was sufficiently flexible to allow for changes and experiment. Curator interviews were transcribed *verbatim*. This generated a very large volume of data, but it was felt that this was desirable as it gave the research its essential richness. It is, however, recognized that the transcript itself is not the same as the interview. The very process of transcribing can destroy much of the meaning of the spoken words in terms of tone, inflection, meaningful pauses and various other non-verbal forms of communication. The transcribed data were organized and coded. Text can be categorized in a number of ways. One can either have a prepared code list and try to assign these codes to the text, or one can allow categories to emerge from the text. Due to the exploratory nature of the research, the latter approach was considered to be more appropriate.

The first type of coding referred to by Strauss (1987) is 'open coding'. This can be described as a process of reading and noticing, that is reading the transcript, noticing what a particular section is about and labelling it with an appropriate code or codes. The next stage described is that of 'axial coding', that is taking a piece of text from a single case that has been open coded, and coding it more intensively around the existing open codes.

Where the methodology in this study differs from this is that the Ethnograph software allowed the collection of similarly coded pieces of text from multiple cases. The software is a text numbering, coding and retrieval system, designed to facilitate the analysis of transcribed data (Seidl *et al.* 1988). It assigns line numbers to the text, which can then be coded by assigning codes to various sections of text. This provides a greater degree of cross-referencing and as a result a more detailed analysis of the text is possible.

When all the interviews have been transcribed and coded in this way, it is then possible to recover all similarly coded sections of text simultaneously from all interviews. This gives an immediate insight into the differing or similar opinions of the various curators on particular topics. The advantage of the Ethnograph over manual cutting and pasting is that there is no need to become attached to the first coding scheme that one uses. The next stage described by Strauss, 'selective coding', is to establish the categories that are more robust and to display the relationship between these in an integrative diagram.

The way the process has been described above may give some impression of being very linear. This, however, was not the case. The process was decidedly cyclical, that is, arriving at a first version of an integrative diagram, deciding whether or not it was a useful representation of what was taking place, and if necessary (and it was) returning to some earlier stage, even to the original raw data, and repeating the process until an appropriate diagram was produced. An example of a final diagram is shown in Fig. 4.1. Whilst this type of analysis can be regarded as having its own intrinsic validity, it was further tested by presenting the findings to the curators for their comments. Issues of validity in this type of research are explored by Reason (1981) and Heron (1988). The systematic use of feedback loops enhances the validity of research and is one of the things that helps to distinguish research from journalism.

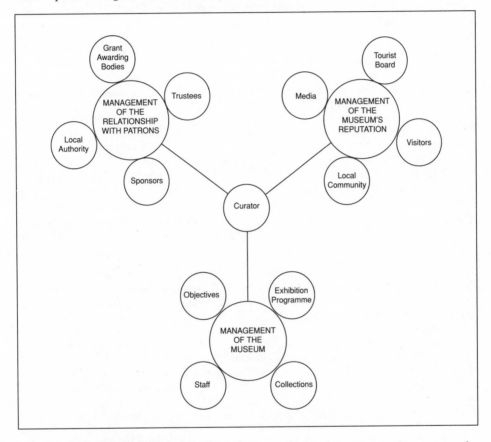

Fig. 4.1 Integrative diagram: the selective codes representing three areas of importance for curators, showing the split between maintaining reputation and attracting funds

RESEARCH FINDINGS

The findings of the research emerged in two different forms, a set of categories (the selective codes mentioned above) that appeared to be important for all the museums studied, and a set of characteristics displayed by the successful curators. The categories that emerged addressed three principal orientations within a successful museum's activities. They were the management of the museum itself, its reputation and its relationship with its patron. The term patron is used here as someone who provides funding for the museum. This could include a local authority, a grant-awarding body or a paying visitor.

One of the features of these categories is the separation of those with whom one is trying to establish the museum's reputation (the audience) from those who provide the museum's funding (government, sponsors, funding agencies and benefactors). Whilst building a reputation with one's visitors is undoubtedly highly important, it does not necessarily ensure funding and financial success, particularly in a museum that does not charge for admission. This is in direct contrast to the consumer goods sector, where a good reputation among customers and high sales are the foundations for financial success. For the museums that were studied, financial success, or at least viability, was much more dependent on patron groups. This meant that they were aware of the importance of maintaining a positive relationship with their patrons. Some of the implications of this are discussed below.

One of the three areas to which the successful museums attached importance was, not surprisingly, the management of the museum itself. In all cases the central role of the curator was emphasized. Fig. 4.1 shows the curator of one particular museum maintaining a balance between the three principal categories. The categories clustered around the three main selective codes are some of those that emerged from the analysis.

All curators agreed that the three main categories that had been identified were important. However, one curator suggested that there was a dynamic aspect to the relationship between the categories. The view was that sound management of the museum was the basis for a good reputation for the museum. This in turn enhanced the relationship with the museum and its patrons. Once this relationship was established, the funding could be secured, which in turn enabled the curator to do even more within the museum, which in turn improved the museum's reputation. Curators prepared to pay attention to all of these aspects are in a position to establish a 'spiral of success' as shown in Fig. 4.2.

Although every museum and every curator are different and individual, there are some characteristics that were shared by most studied. What follows is by no means an exhaustive list, but it does represent those characteristics which appeared to be important in the context of this research.

Most of those interviewed had a clear idea of what their museum was trying to achieve, and for whom they were doing it. As well as having this clear overall idea of the museums' objectives, the curators had also been able to communicate these objectives to their staff. This clarity of objectives was supported by a bias for action by the curators; they were proactive rather than reactive, particularly in dealing with the museum's patron groups. They were proposing projects rather than waiting to be told what to do.

The channel of communication between curator and patron was clearly assisted by direct access to the relevant committee in the case of local authority museums, and an effective trustee structure in the case of independent museums. It did, however, appear that the presence of a formal structure was not the only factor. An example of this can be shown by two curators in local authority museums both reporting to directors of leisure and recreation departments. In the one case, the Director of Leisure and Recreation played a positive supporting role, enhancing the relationship between the curator and the local authority patrons. In the second case, the Director of Leisure and Recreation occupied a central role, dealing with the local authority, but also taking responsibility for the promotion of the museum as one feature of the council's leisure and recreation provision. In this case, the curators ran the risk of being marginalized; they could influence what went on inside the museum, but were restricted in their dealings with patrons and the management of the museum's reputation.

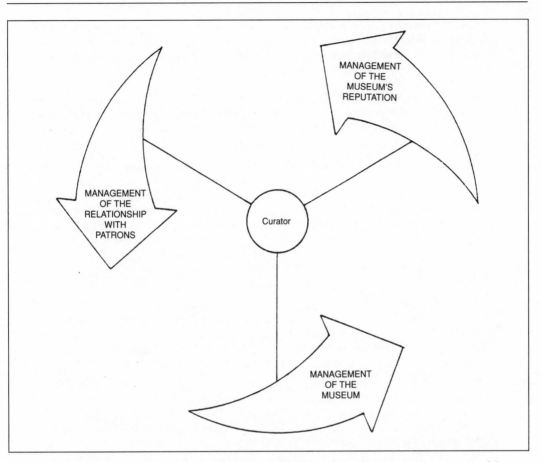

Fig. 4.2 The spiral of success: the dynamic relationship of the three categories in successful museums

The curators studied emphasized the importance of physical closeness to the visiting public and made themselves both visible and accessible to the local community. There was not, however, a great deal of importance attached to more 'formal' market research, such as questionnaire surveys. Despite (or perhaps because of) this lack of formal research, the curators were well aware of the different audiences for their museums both in terms of tourists and the local community. Such awareness appeared to inform their activities, rather than dictate what they did.

Last, but importantly, the curators were seen to be able to balance the differing requirements of managing the museum, managing its reputation and managing the relationship with the museum's patron groups.

IMPLICATIONS AND CONCLUSIONS

There are a number of issues arising from this research. It poses the question of whether museums should be ready to accept advice uncritically from a commercial context, without examination of its suitability in a museum context. The research tends to indicate that to do so would be unsound, due to the different nature of museums.

One of the characteristics of marketing in the museums studied was that it was rarely seen as a separate activity. In fact, none of the museums employed a marketing officer. This tends to support the view that it forms part of the way in which an institution is managed, rather than a bolt-on extra. If this is the case, then it certainly has implications for the way marketing advice is offered to museums. Grants given to encourage museums to 'do a bit of marketing' are unlikely to result in sustained improvement. On a more positive note, in presenting the findings thus far to museum professionals, the author has found a high degree of acceptance. As well as the actual content of the findings, this acceptance is almost certainly related to the fact that the findings were derived from a museum context.

As far as the split between relations with visitors and with patrons is concerned, clearly different approaches are required. The management of reputation with visitors and potential visitors has certain aspects in common with commercial marketing. But the relationship with patrons is rather different and has more of a public relations aspect to it. Using the three categories model as a paradigm for museum marketing should help to identify the areas requiring most attention. Therefore, it is intended that the integrative diagram should be developed into a diagnostic tool. This should, it is hoped, assist museums in targeting their activities more effectively, rather than responding to the blanket encouragement to do more marketing.

Some curators have commented that the spiral of success can just as easily become a vortex of despair. When one of the three categories is neglected it can lead to problems elsewhere. An institution may have a very good public reputation, but if it neglects its relationship with its patrons then insufficient funding may be provided for the museum to continue as it would wish. It is significant that curators in the sample did not appear to have particular problems in this area.

As far as the characteristics of curators are concerned, one is faced with the question of whether these are largely innate, or whether they can be instilled through training. It is, however, certain that people can be trained to recognize the position of their institution, and to identify the areas requiring most attention.

Every aspect of this research from the literature review to the findings suggests that museum marketing is different. Whilst this may not come as a surprise, it has certainly not permeated the thinking of many of those who write about museum marketing, or those who give marketing advice to museums.

This paper was first published in G. Kavanagh (ed.) (1991) The Museums Profession: Internal and External Relations, *Leicester: Leicester University Press, pp. 85–98.*

NOTES

1 This paper is based on recent Ph.D. research entitled 'Marketing Scotland's Museums and Galleries' carried out by the author in the Department of Marketing at Strathclyde University, under the supervision of Dr Andy Lowe. The research was conducted in conjunction with the Scottish Museums Council (for whom the author is now employed as marketing manager) and was funded principally by the Economic and Social Research Council, with some fieldwork support from the Museums and Galleries Commission.

REFERENCES

Ames, P. J. (1989) 'Marketing in museums: means or master of the mission'. *Curator* 32 (1): 5–15.
Ansoff, H. I. (1965) *Corporate Strategy*, Maidenhead: McGraw-Hill.
Bartels, R. (1974) 'The identity crisis in marketing', *Journal of Marketing* 38: 73–6.

Borden, N. H. (1965) 'The concept of the marketing mix', in Schwartz, G., *Science in Marketing*, Chichester: Wiley.

Foxall, G. (1984) 'Marketing's domain', *European Journal of Marketing* 18 (1): 25–40.

Fronville, C. L., (1985) 'Marketing for museums: for-profit techniques in the non-profit world', *Curator* 28 (3): 169–82.

Glaser, B. and Strauss, A. J. (1967) *The Discovery of Grounded Theory*, Chicago: Aldine.

Harré R. (1981) 'The positivist-empiricist approach and its alternative', in Reason, P. and Rowan, J. (eds), *Human Inquiry*, Chichester: Wiley.

Heron, J. (1988) 'Validity in co-operative enquiry', in Reason, P. (ed.), *Human Enquiry in Action*, Sage: London.

Hoyt, S. L. (1986) 'Strategic market planning for museums' *The Museologist* 49 (173): 4–9.

Hunt S. D. (1983) *Marketing Theory*, Homewood, IL: Irwin.

Kotler, P. (1975) *Marketing for Non-profit Organizations*, Englewood Cliffs, NJ: Prentice Hall.

Kotler, P. and Levy, S. J. (1969) 'Broadening the concept of marketing', *Journal of Marketing* 33: 11–13.

Levitt, T. (1960) 'Marketing myopia', *Harvard Business Review*, July/August: 45–6.

—— (1965) 'Exploit the product life cycle', *Harvard Business Review*, November/December: 81–94.

Rados, D. L. (1981) *Marketing for Non-profit Organizations*, Boston, MA: Auburn House.

Reason, P. (1981) 'Issues of validity in new paradigm research', in Reason, P. and Rowan, J. (eds), *Human Inquiry*, Chichester: Wiley.

Rodger, L. (1987) *Marketing the Visual Arts*, Edinburgh: Scottish Arts Council.

Seidl, J. V., Kjolseth, R. and Seymour, J. (1988) *The Ethnograph: A User's Guide*, Littleton, CO: Qualis Research Associates.

Sheth, J. N. and Garrett, E. G. (1986) *Marketing Theory*, Cincinatti: South-Western Publishing.

Strauss, A. J. (1987) *Qualitative Analysis for Social Scientists*, Cambridge: Cambridge University Press.

Van Maanen, J. (1987) *Qualitative Methodology*, London: Sage.

5

Strategic planning in local authority museums

Stuart Davies

Though focused on the local authority museum sector in England and Wales, Stuart Davies's analysis of the response of museums to strategic planning has much wider implications in terms of the problems and possibilities in developing a strategic approach to museum management.

INTRODUCTION

This chapter describes the findings from a postal questionnaire survey into the incidence and practice of strategic planning in local authority museums in England and Wales and the museum managers' perceptions of the usefulness of planning in their sector. The survey was carried out in October/November 1992 and was supported by a number of qualitative interviews with managers, mostly in November/December 1992. The salient conclusions from those interviews are included as supporting material to the question-naire findings.

BACKGROUND

After an initial rush of enthusiasm in the 1960s and early 1970s, strategic planning in the public sector became a rather discredited concept (Porter 1987). Recently, however, it has started to enjoy something of a revival (Caulfield and Schultz 1989) and there is certainly no shortage of instructional manuals for its close cousin, business planning (Delderfield *et al.* 1991; Puffitt 1993; Wills 1992). In the museums sector the Museums and Galleries Commission (which maintains an overview of the sector and channels central government funding into provincial museums and art galleries) has been actively promoting the virtues of 'forward planning' since the end of the 1980s, regarding it as a helpful mechanism for improving management, making the best use of existing resources and helping to attract additional funding (Ambrose and Runyard 1991).

There was, however, regardless of the level of activity, very little information available on how planning had been introduced, what form it took, what uses it was being put to and whether or not it was proving successful. This project set out to gather the necessary information and analyse it.

In many respects, of course, the conclusions have to be regarded as tentative. Because the current wave of activity is still very 'new', many of the local authority services responded on the basis of only one or two years' experience of planning, or even less.

To fully evaluate the impact of planning in museums it will be necessary to look again at this issue in two or three years' time.

THE FINDINGS

Introduction

The findings derived from a postal questionnaire sent to senior museum managers in most English local authority museum services are detailed below. The responses allow some assessment to be made of how far strategic management and strategic planning is understood by them and to what extent is it practised. The questionnaire is appended to this chapter.

Methodology

A sample of 205 English and Welsh local authority museum and art gallery services (representing 96 per cent of the population) were sent a questionnaire, to be completed by the senior museum manager. The authorities and managers' names were derived from the *1992/93 Museums Association Yearbook*. A total of 110 were returned (without any reminders), a response rate of 53.7 per cent, which is considerably higher than what might be expected for this type of survey.

Is the concept of strategic management accepted?

Museum managers were offered a definition of strategic management of which they were invited to associate with or otherwise, and then explain their response:

> Strategic management is concerned with determining the future direction of an organisation and implementing decisions aimed at achieving the organisation's objectives.

> (Clarke-Hill and Glaister 1991)

Most heads of local authority museum and art gallery services appeared to understand (and approve of) the definition of strategic management offered. As Table 5.1 shows, three-quarters of them also recognized the definition with regard to their own organization.

Table 5.1 Recognition of a definition of strategic management

How far do you recognize this definition with regard to your own organization?

n = 108	*Frequency*	*Percentage*
Not at all	1	1
Vaguely	6	5
In part	17	15
Mostly	44	41
Totally	40	37

The invitation to explain the responses to this question in part reinforces the impression that most senior museum managers are committed to at least the concept of strategic management (even if their answers to later questions cast doubt on the extent of its practice). Some related it directly to the core functions or values of museums:

> The museum needs to have a plan for change/upgrading/development in order to carry out its core responsibilities (e.g. . . . storage and documentation) and to continue to attract visitors (ideally in increasing numbers) by providing a stimulating service . . . [Also] to maintain support from the governing/authority and to maintain the motivation/interest of staff as well.

Similarly, another manager was committed to providing a successful future for its collections and saw strategic management as central to this purpose, while another emphasized the importance of strategic management in difficult times, believing that during a period of shrinking resources a clear perception of aims and objectives is the only way that one can establish the priorities of the service: 'Forward planning is a way of retreating in good order. Ultimately we are faced by unpalatable decisions . . . which will not stop.' Strategic management is usually perceived as being essentially about producing 'plans': 'Having a "PLAN" gives a framework for activity . . . I consider it an essential tool to get anything done, or even to recognise achievements!'

Some respondents were, however, concerned about the inflexibility of plans. While agreeing with the definition and concept of strategic management, one added: 'but . . . current budgetary problems can cause havoc with any forward plan. Museums also occasionally have windfalls which open up new fields of opportunity, so again plans need to be flexible.' Another manager made a similar point: 'I fully accept the need for a forward plan, and use one. It is, however, necessary to have the flexibility to snap up windfalls and cope with changes in finance and legislation.'

However, while these affirmations of the value of strategic management (or at least strategic/forward planning) are reassuring, a far greater number of the comments are sceptical of both concept and practice:

> In the current economic climate, the concept of strategic management for local authority museums is almost meaningless. The only strategies are short-term, i.e. to survive from one year to the next. Wholesale redundancies in other leisure services have demonstrated the acute vulnerability of non-statutory services (including museums).

> Strategy needs to be geared to both the short-term and long-term survival of museum services. Most local authority policy is now very short-term, i.e. a knee-jerk reaction to fluctuating central government policies. Long-term planning is almost impossible in this climate.

> . . . in the present financial climate and Local Government it is all very well planning for the future and setting targets – but what's the point when we cannot achieve even the most modest goals. Things now evolve through opportunity as opposed to planned strategies! Large museums with reasonable staff structures can devote time to strategic management, smaller organisations have neither time, staff nor resources.

> Strategic management needs within the service tend to ignore the pressures on small museums with skeleton staffing levels. Here the priority is to keep the service running smoothly and satisfying the customer. We are now increasingly

under pressure to justify our needs for the future when the prospects of achieving these are slim.

Strategic management should not be proposed as the only solution to museum problems. Nothing compares with good product and good staff. Growth by stealth and pragmatic opportunism are equally valid growth and development strategies and may work better than formal strategic management in some cases – certainly in the past they have underpinned development in my authority.

The problems of external pressures apparently beyond the manager's control and the uncertainties (especially funding) of the environment in which public museums operate are recurring themes:

Whilst in full agreement with the definition, and the desirability of employing the concept in my museum, external variables and uncertainties have also to be recognised – particularly in the current economic/political climate.

Another important consideration to museum managers was their lack of confidence in the strategic abilities of the elected members: 'Strategic plans are either shunned by the governing body or, if adopted, are superseded by crisis management to deal with unplanned cuts in revenue.' In one case, the 'problem has been getting Councillors to think "strategic management" (basically they don't)'. One manager found it difficult to recognize the virtues of strategic management 'when the political masters cannot agree on whether to support museums or not'. Elected members are also blamed for frustrating the best intentions of museum managers. While museums and the local authority may be keen on forward planning,

the Council has not made resources available to realise planned developments and political difficulties have delayed the implementation of strategies to meet the current situation facing local government.

Finally, while senior museum managers may understand strategic management this may not be the case with elected members, 'who only look at net revenue costs'. Similar criticisms are also extended to the chief officers of 'umbrella' departments (e.g. Leisure), which encompass museums.

Possibly most illuminating of all are the comments made by a few of the respondents on the definition itself. One suggested that 'the direction of an organisation should be concerned with values and attitudes. The nitty-gritty of corporate planning is not much use at the moment'. The definition is specifically criticized for containing two issues ('determining the future direction' and 'implementing decisions'), which it is claimed are distinct from each other.

Implementing decisions requires a different set of skills as they usually concern either staff or public or both. People who make policies seldom concern themselves with implementation, at least not directly. Sadly this is a trend easily observed throughout the museum world, where not enough attention is being focused on long term issues or the long term consequences of a change of direction.

The definition, for local government, seems too simplistic. 'Strategic' implies manoeuvrability according to projected situations and would need to take into account resources, priorities, timescales etc. Given that local government is subject to quite fluid projections for the future, our strategies must be capable of responding similarly. Related to this, strategic management must also refer to the management of change. Therefore although the definition is broadly right, it seems to confidently imply that all that is required is set the goal and aim for it.

Finally, one experienced manager focuses on the issue of 'future direction':

> It is not possible, currently, in the local authority/political environment to have a comprehensive, consistent, realistic view of 'where the organisation will be' in, say, 10 years' time. You can of course have an aim/mission, and you can try and predict trends and likely developments, but this falls short of '*determining* the future direction'.

Here there seems to be some confusion over what might be meant by 'determine'. Are we talking about deciding upon a course of action or what pressures an organization will have to respond to?

Table 5.2 analyses an attempt to explore the depths of scepticism about strategic planning induced by the current financial climate in the public sector.

It is perhaps encouraging that over one-half of the managers responding felt that service planning was essential. Nevertheless, there does seem to be a lack of congruence between the managers' stated principles and preferences and their confessed scepticism. This needs to be explored further.

To what extent is strategic planning practised?

This project's questionnaire offered a range of types of plan for managers to recognize. In this survey only 19 per cent of managers said that they had a business plan. However, at least two-thirds of the respondents claimed to have mission statements, aims and objectives and some form of 'plan'. The full responses are detailed in Table 5.3.

Not all of these plans are necessarily strategic in content. One-third had 'forward plans', but these may be a response to Area Museum Council initiatives and vary in their depth of analysis. One-third also had 'development plans', which may be little more than statements of aspirations. Fifteen per cent of respondents include collection management plans. Table 5.4 shows how less than one-third of respondents analysed environmental conditions or attempted to forecast the budget over the next three or more years, suggesting that whatever planning is claimed, the analytical process supporting them is not always in evidence.

Table 5.2 Responses to current political and financial problems

In the present political and financial climate do you feel that the planning of services and resource allocation beyond the next twelve months is:

n = 110	*Frequency*	*Percentage*
Futile	2	2
Futile but has to be done	5	4
Hardly worth the effort	7	6
Something that 'ought to be done'	11	10
Worth attempting	27	24
Essential	58	53

Table 5.3 Frequency of planning documents

Does your museum/museum service have any of the following documents?

n = 110	Frequency	Percentage
Forward plan	36	33
Strategic plan	17	15
Strategy	24	22
Mission statement	62	56
Aims and objectives	79	72
Policy statement	40	37
Business plan	21	19
Corporate plan	10	9
Development plan	36	33
Other	17	15
None	9	8

Table 5.4 Elements in planning documents

Does your plan/document contain any of the following elements?

n = 100	Frequency	Percentage
Forecasting budget for next 3 or more years	24	24
Analysis of environmental conditions	32	32
Schedule of objectives	85	85
Mission statement	72	72
Targets with specific deadlines	79	79

Who contributes to the strategic plan?

Establishing who is (or has been) involved in strategy formulation is a useful indicator of the attitudes of the organization (and its senior managers) to strategic management as a serious activity. It may also suggest how likely the 'plan' is to be embedded in the thinking of the organization.

It is generally accepted that the most effective 'plans' or 'strategies' are those that engage the support and confidence of all the organization's major stakeholders. The responses presented in Table 5.5 suggest that a high percentage of, but by no means all, senior museum managers involve (or at least consult) their immediate professional colleagues in the formulation of mission statements, objectives and plans. Rather fewer (a little more than half) also involved other colleagues (usually elsewhere in the local authority but interpreted by some respondents as other professional colleagues outside their own museum service) and elected members (though it is not clear at what stage). Involvement or consultation with the public has not been common. A number of respondents specifically stated that this amounted to no more than taking into account the findings of visitor surveys and other market research. Cost is usually cited as a barrier to such research.

Table 5.5 Contributors to the strategic plan

Who is consulted or contributes to the contents of the document

n = 105	*Frequency*	*Percentage*
Museum service colleagues	94	89
Other colleagues	63	60
Elected members	60	57
Visitors/users	32	30
Non-users/general public	16	15
Other: Area Museum Council	4	4
Other: Consultants	3	3

How is the strategic process monitored?

Following a similar principle, exploration of how the process is being, or is to be, monitored may indicate the relationship between the process, the organization and its stakeholders. It may also act as a surrogate measure of commitment to the process.

While many museum managers accept that it is a 'good idea' to produce some form of a strategy and most realize that a 'plan' is increasingly a requirement (especially by funding bodies), the acid test of commitment to a strategy is the monitoring of it and what use is made of it. As Table 5.6 shows, virtually all claim that they report the progress or performance of their objectives or strategy. What is perhaps a little surprising is that 23 per cent of museums do not report to the governing body (i.e. elected members). This, together with the finding that only 31 per cent publish an annual report or review, not only reflects unfavourably on the museum services but also suggests a corporate lack of commitment to performance review within local authorities.

Frequency of updating may be another indicator of commitment. It should be noted that respondents answered to this question either according to what has happened or what it is intended to happen where documents have only been very recently approved. The only significant conclusion from Table 5.7 is that nearly three-quarters of services do or expect to update their plan annually. Although the question gave the opportunity, no respondent suggested that strategic management is a continuous process.

What use is made of the planning document?

The responses in Table 5.8 reflect the fact that forward planning is seen principally as the concern of senior management and the elected members, while recognizing that a product of this, 'the plan' may also have promotional, fund-raising and staff information functions as well. But none of the respondents related the plan to performance. Its value was seen in terms of communication.

Table 5.6 How is the plan monitored?

How is your document monitored?

n = 102	Frequency	Percentage
Published annual report/review	32	31
Reports to governing body	79	77
Reports to a management team	54	53
Reports to a co-ordinating department elsewhere in the authority	14	14
None	1	1

Table 5.7 How often is the plan updated?

How often is your document updated?

n = 97	Frequency	Percentage
Bi-monthly	1	1
Quarterly	6	6
'If required'	1	1
Annually	70	72
Two years	2	2
Three years	7	7
Five years	5	5
Periodically	1	1
'Hasn't happened yet'	3	3
Never	1	1

Table 5.8 Use of planning document

What use is made of the document?

n = 104	Frequency	Percentage
Reference for senior management	89	86
Guidance for other council officers	59	57
Guidance for elected members	81	78
'Bid' document for grant-aid, sponsorship, etc.	60	58
Copied to all staff for information	63	61
Other (e.g. internal 'bids')	9	9
Proposed use only	5	5

Strategic analysis of the museum environment

Three questions were used to try and establish how far museum managers were employing the methodologies of strategic analysis. Again, the underlying purpose of these questions was to try and establish whether there is any strategic substance behind the superficial commitment to strategic planning. Table 5.9 suggests that there is little substance.

In analysing the responses, it has been assumed that no answer or answers like 'never heard of it' may be equated with 'never'.

Two characteristics of the sample have been noted. First, a number of respondents use performance indicators and nothing else. This may be the result of the considerable publicity given to the virtues of performance indicators in the museum (and local authority) press over the past five years. Second, there seems to be a clear correlation between the smaller museum services and those who never used any of the tools listed.

The statistics themselves reveal that PEST analysis is rarely used and commonly is totally unknown to respondents. Workforce planning is also little used and the concept is frequently unfamiliar. More surprisingly, trend analysis is similarly little used. Of the others, performance indicators are most regularly used but business planning and SWOT analysis techniques are also relatively common.

Table 5.9 Use of analytical techniques

Does your museum/museum service use any of the following?

n = 109	f	%	f	%	f	%	f	%	f	%
	Never		Tried it		Sometimes		Frequently		Regularly	
SWOT	37	34	18	16	32	29	10	9	12	11
PEST	97	89	5	5	4	4	2	2	1	1
Business plans	46	42	11	10	22	20	11	10	19	17
Performance indicators	34	32	3	3	16	15	16	15	40	37
Trend analysis	77	71	2	2	12	11	9	8	9	8
Workforce planning	75	69	3	3	15	14	7	6	9	8

A supplementary question was designed to explore the use of analytical techniques. Table 5.10 shows that while over three-quarters had looked at their visitor or admission patterns and about one-half had looked at the cost of their services, such techniques generally seem to be a long way from being of standard application in museum management. Table 5.11 explores whether or not this situation is a reflection of inadequate training in this sector.

Between one-third and one-half of the managers claim to have had some form of training in setting objectives, business planning, performance review and strategic management.

Table 5.10 Subjects of analysis

Has your museum/museum service carried out a formal analysis of any of the following?

n = 100	*Frequency*	*Percentage*
Projected demographic changes	20	20
Visitor/admission figures	88	88
Cost of collecting	21	21
Cost per visitor over 3 or more years	49	49
Comparison with Audit Commission profile	52	52
None	3	3

Table 5.11 Analysis of training provision

Have you received training in any of the following?

n = 90	*Frequency*	*Percentage*
Business planning	49	44
Financial forecasting	13	12
Strategic management	39	35
Setting objectives	59	54
Achieving targets	37	34
Performance review methods	44	40
Decision-making	35	32
None	7	6
No response	20	18

In part this may reflect the fact that all of the Area Museum Councils have held training seminars in 'forward planning' during 1992. The lack of training in financial forecasting was a not unexpected weakness. Two managers noted that they had a DMS, one a Dip. Public Admin., and one an MBA.

Responding to external guidance

Two questions (analysed in Tables 5.12 and 5.13) examined the museum managers' response to the Audit Commission's report *The Road to Wigan Pier?* (1991), which provided a clear strategic framework (in the Commission's style) for local authorities and the museums' community to be guided by. Its value was communicated to the profession at every opportunity and recognition was given to its sensitivity to professional issues as well as its excellent managerial advice.

Stuart Davies

Table 5.12 The response to *The Road to Wigan Pier?*

How did your museum/museum service respond to *The Road to Wigan Pier?* ?

n = 105	Frequency	Percentage
Not at all	35	33
Report to the governing body	45	43
Review the service	35	33
Other	17	16

The Road to Wigan Pier? was a major landmark in helping local authority museums to understand some of the basic concepts of strategic planning, and perhaps can claim to be the best management manual available to museum managers today. This and the following question were designed to both help assess how far these principles may have been at least considered and also to try and measure the impact of the Audit Commission's work on local authority museums. About one-third made no response at all, nearly one-half reported the document's existence (and usually assessed how their service measured up to it) and about one-third also conducted a review of the service along the lines suggested by the Audit Commission. Some managers noted that they had discussed it with their chief officers, while others had introduced performance indicators recommended in *The Road to Wigan Pier?*. In three cases it led directly to the preparing of a Development Plan an in one instance to the appointment of a Museum Services Manager.

There has been some unhappiness among museum managers about both the incidence and quality of the District Audit follow-up reports to *The Road to Wigan Pier?*. Table 5.13 reveals that over half the museums surveyed were not reported upon by the District Audit, which reduces the impact of the Audit Commission's work. Anecdotal evidence suggests that the thoroughness of the reports that have been carried out was very uneven.

Table 5.13 District Audit reports

Have the District Audit compiled a report as a result of *The Road to Wigan Pier?* ?

n = 109	Frequency	Percentage
Yes	48	44
No	61	56

Strategic positioning and choice

Museums and galleries are currently under considerable financial pressures. Many are having to make 'cuts' on an unprecedented scale, which are (or should be) forcing them to make radical strategic choices about their current and future pattern of service delivery. A range of questions was designed to elicit how far managers are prepared to seriously review what they are doing. But, also, it was hoped to achieve an indication of the strength of professional attitudes and its influence over strategic decision-making at times of organizational stress. In so doing it should also indicate some of the key cultural characteristics of museums.

Table 5.14 presents the responses. Against each possible course of action (e.g. 'reduce your opening hours'), the table indicates how many respondents ranked this as their first priority when making cuts (i.e. nine), how many their second priority (i.e. four), how many their third (i.e. six), and so on.

Table 5.14 Predicted responses to the need to make a 15 per cent budget cut

If you were asked to make a 15% cut in your budget next year, would you . . .

$n = 77$	Rank								
	1	*2*	*3*	*4*	*5*	*6*	*7*	*8*	*9*
Reduce your opening hours	9	4	6	6	12	18	14	3	4
Close one or more buildings	2	1	2	6	6	6	9	18	26
Reduce the number of professional posts	0	4	3	4	5	12	12	16	20
Cut the conservation budget	2	1	3	11	15	11	14	10	9
Increase your income (other than by admission charges)	23	27	8	7	5	3	2	1	1
Cut the exhibitions budget	0	6	16	14	14	10	6	7	3
Prioritize your activities and discontinue non-core ones	30	17	17	8	3	1	1	0	0
Introduce or increase existing admission charges	6	10	10	8	4	10	13	11	4
Cut the purchase fund	5	7	12	11	11	5	6	9	10
No response/did not rank =	33								

This was the most complex question for managers to respond to, and some assumptions and special features need to be noted. The 'close one or more buildings' option was sometimes marked as 'not available' or automatically ranked ninth because the manager only has one building, and to close it would be to effectively terminate the museum service. For a similar reason the conservation budget and purchase fund options were given a low ranking by some because either they do not exist or are already very small indeed. Two respondents stated that their service was already 'pared to the bone', a view implicit among many of the responses of the smaller local authority museums.

It is possible to produce a 'summary ranking' reflecting an overall view of how the majority of museum managers appear to respond to a financial crisis:

1 Prioritize activities and discontinue non-core ones.
2 Increase income (other than by admission charges).
3 Introduce or increase existing admission charges.
4 Cut the exhibitions budget.
5 Reduce your opening hours.
6 Cut the purchase fund.
7 Cut the conservation budget.
8 Reduce the number of professional posts.
9 Close one or more building(s).

Most managers claim to give preference to prioritizing their activities and discontinuing non-core ones. However, anecdotal evidence suggests that there would probably be more prioritizing than discontinuing. Furthermore, while more managers ranked this first than any other category, they still represent no more than 40 per cent of the sample. Almost as many (over 30 per cent) would look first to increase income from any source other than by introducing (or increasing) admission charges. Overall there seems to be a (perhaps not unreasonable) preference for finding ways of increasing income rather than reducing expenditure. Interestingly, the museum manager's traditional aversion to admission charges seems to largely collapse in the face of real financial crisis.

Therefore the preferences are difficult to disentangle and will, in any case, tend to differ according to local circumstances. Most managers will only turn to cutting expenditure when income-raising has failed, or at least shows no possibility of success. One important aspect of this process which cannot be appropriately explored by questionnaire is how realistic managers are in their assessment of how to meet 'cuts'. Many are, one suspects, prone to over-optimism when it comes to income. When it is considered necessary to cut expenditure they turn either to reducing opening hours (presumably hoping to make savings through the wages of attendants) or to cutting the exhibitions budget, the 'softest' target (being usually easily identifiable and most frequently totally under the manager's control).

Beyond that, there is a considerable reluctance to have to cut in areas that may be considered the 'professional heartland'. Purchase funds do not appear to be the 'sacred cow' that they once were, but clearly museum managers still wish to defend conservation budgets, professional (i.e. curatorial) posts and the museum buildings themselves. In the latter area, as noted above, they may feel that they have relatively little discretion over what happens, particularly in the smaller services. And even in larger services with more than one building, those museums that may be assessed as peripheral, not essential to the service or providing poor value for money, cannot be easily closed. As with branch libraries, there is often local community protests at such proposals, political vetos or an inability to come up with an alternative use for what is commonly a historic building in a less than desirable location.

The broad pattern would therefore seem to be that the more enlightened managers tend to first prioritize their activities. Most managers will seek an income-related solution to their problems, then reduce expenditure in either the 'soft' area of the operational budget or by reducing the quantity of service available to the public. Only after this will the professional core of the service be cut. Does this reveal unwritten strategies based on organization culture?

The responses in Table 5.15 reveal that museum managers will usually seek advice or discuss the options with key stakeholders when trying to arrive at difficult financial decisions. No one offered an analytical course of action and one could be left with the feeling that decisions are indeed made on the basis of museum management (or curatorial professional) values rather than analytical assessment.

Table 5.15 How do managers make difficult financial decisions?

Would you arrive at a decision by any of the following means:

n = 107	Frequency	Percentage
Report options to governing body	89	83
Discuss with colleagues in your own service	89	83
Discuss with other colleagues	62	58
Consult a management textbook	5	5
Consult your area museum service	59	55
Discuss with a finance officer	63	59
None of these	1	1

Future prospects

Two questions were set to establish how managers viewed the environment in which they are working and what help they might need to assist them.

The fact that nearly all the respondents viewed the outlook as bleak or challenging will come as no surprise. One can only speculate as to what effect this might have on managerial action or responses.

Between nearly one-third and one-half of the managers responding felt that training, more information or 'hands on' assistance would be useful, suggesting that there is an identifiable need for support in this area. The 'other' responses were very wide-ranging, with 'more time' (5) being the only significant one. There were calls for more support from elected members and chief officers, a desire for political and financial stability, a change of government, and one manager even wanted a local authority that understood strategic management. One believed that statutory status would help and another called for the implementation of the recommendations of *The Road to Wigan Pier?*. Measurable conclusions are impossible, but suffice to say that most managers felt that they needed support and assistance one way or another.

Some managers commented on the current state of training in their organizations. One described the issues covered by the questionnaire as 'less of a problem' in his museum because of the authority's 'integrated and corporate nature of management training':

> More and more demands are being put upon museum professionals outside 'core activities'. In a small museum service such as mine, I have to organise marketing/advertising, forward planning etc. but with no proper training. In fact my budget is to be cut by 15% next year and one of the victims will be training – this will have £Nil budget in 1993/94. Also . . . I have never had a conservation or purchase budget! Happy Days!

Table 5.16 The outlook for local authority museums

How would you describe the outlook for local authority museums in this country?

n = 106	Frequency	Percentage
Bleak	32	30
Challenging	68	64
Stable	2	2
Optimistic	3	3
Exciting	1	1

Table 5.17 Assistance needed to achieve effective strategic management

What sort of assistance do you think your museum/museum service needs to achieve effective strategic management?

n = 110	Frequency	Percentage
A training course in basic skills	46	42
More information about the social and economic environment	33	30
'Hands on' assistance from a specialist	42	38
None/no response	11	10
Other	25	23

Another said that 'training and action in strategic planning has helped our service to continue development momentum in a difficult economic climate. This, however, has only been possible with the support and encouragement of management and the governing body'.

Qualitative evidence

In addition to the postal questionnaire, thirty semi-structured qualitative interviews were conducted with practising museum managers and Area Museum Council directors. These revealed quite widely different understandings of what strategic planning or 'strategy' is actually about. But there was general agreement on what the benefits were of producing a 'plan' or similar document. Many managers saw its value as a 'bid' document for funding, as a method of communicating the service's 'vision' to stakeholders and as an ownership and motivating force for the staff.

There was also a great deal of scepticism about the value of planning. It is often seen as an onerous, inflexible burden not designed to meet the needs of museum managers. These seemed often to be the reactions of pragmatic managers who want maximum flexibility to be able to respond to change, and perceive strategic planning as creating an inflexible document which either prevents them from doing that or increases the risk of having their (unwritten) plans 'torpedoed' by others. On the other hand, those managers who understood the principles of strategic management and the benefits of 'strategic thinking' recognized its value as a tool, albeit only one among the many, which they might use in pursuit of securing their organization's objective.

CONCLUSION

'Strategic management' is almost automatically equated with 'strategic planning' by the majority of museum managers. Many of them recognize the need to 'plan', but scepticism and resistance runs deep. They stress the dangers of inflexibility; the inadequacy of written plans when dealing with a turbulent environment and unsympathetic stakeholders; the importance of opportunism, good staff and good product. It is not always recognized that 'strategic management' can embrace all of these issues.

Despite this, two-thirds claimed to have some form of a 'plan', which usually included reference to targets. However, internal and external environment analysis appears to be weak; stakeholder consultation is limited and formal monitoring is not common. Plans are seen as communication tools rather than analytical tools. The traditional values of a professional organization culture appears to be strong. Training opportunities have not materialized and at a time when managers consider the sector outlook not to be good, they themselves are indicating that they need support and assistance to act strategically in the future.

Three key strategic issues were identified by managers: resources, managerial competencies and stakeholders (all those individuals or organizations that have a legitimate interest in your organization). They realized that it is important to address these, but were clearly not convinced that strategic planning was the best way of doing it.

They concluded that strategic planning may help with the planning of resources but of equal value is the framework that it provides to ensure that managers have addressed all the key issues relevant to their organization and have thoroughly thought through all the options available to them for action. Stakeholder management is more strategically central to the future success and development of public museums. In this respect the best strategic managers use plans (and planning) to communicate with stakeholders, while less experienced managers need the discipline of planning to ensure that their organizations do not lose the confidence of external stakeholders.

This paper was first published as a Research Paper, School of Business and Economic Studies, University of Leeds, 1993.

REFERENCES

Ambrose, T. and Runyard, S. (eds) (1991) *Forward Planning: A Handbook of Business, Corporate and Development Planning for Museums and Galleries*, London: Routledge.
Audit Commission (1991) *The Road to Wigan Pier?*, London: HMSO.
Caulfield, I. and Schultz, J. (1989) *Planning for Change: Strategic Planning in Local Government*, London: Longman.
Clarke-Hill, C. and Glaister, K. (1991) *Cases in Strategic Management*, Harlow: Pitman.
Delderfield, J., Puffitt, R.R. and Watts, G. (1991) *Business Planning in Local Government*. Longman.
Porter, M.E. (1987) 'The state of strategic thinking', *The Economist*, 23 May.
Puffitt, R. (1993), *Business Planning and Marketing: A Guide for the Local Government Cost Centre Manager*, Longman.
Wills, N. (1992) *The Application of Business Planning*, Local Government Management Board.

APPENDIX: POSTAL QUESTIONNAIRE

Strategic management in the museums sector: current practice and future development

Name of institution/service ....

Your name ....

Your position ....

Q1 This is one accepted definition of 'strategic management':

> Strategic management is concerned with determining the future direction of an organization and implementing decisions aimed at achieving the organization's objectives.

How far do you recognize this *with regard to your own organization*:
(Please tick one)

... Not at all
... Vaguely
... In part
... Mostly
... Totally

Q2 Would you like to explain your answer?

Q3 Does your museum/museum service have any of the following documents?
(Please tick)

... Forward plan
... Strategic plan
... Strategy
... Mission statement
... Aims and objectives
... Policy statement
... Business plan
... Corporate plan
... Development plan
... Other (please specify)

Q4 If you have got a document listed in Q3, please indicate (tick) if it contains any of the following elements:

    ... Forecasted budget for next three or more years
    ... Analysis of environmental conditions
    ... Schedule of objectives
    ... Mission statement
    ... Targets with specific deadlines

Q5 Who is consulted or contributes to the contents of the document?
(Please tick)

    ... Museum service colleagues
    ... Other colleagues
    ... Elected members
    ... Visitors/users
    ... Non-users/general public
    ... Other (please specify)

Q6 How is your document monitored?

    ... Published annual report/review
    ... Reports to governing body
    ... Reports to a management team
    ... Reports to a co-ordinating department elsewhere in your authority
    ... Other (please specify)

Q7 How often is it updated?

    ... More than once a year (please specify)
    ... Annually
    ... Other (please specify)

Q8 Who is involved in the updating?

Q9 What *use* is made of the document?

    ... Reference for senior management
    ... Guidance for other council officers
    ... Guidance for elected members
    ... 'Bid' document for grant-aid, sponsorship, etc.
    ... Copied to all staff for information
    ... Other (please specify)

Q10   Does your museum/museum service use any of the following?
(Please indicate by the appropriate number)

        SWOT analysis   . . .
        PEST analysis   . . .
        Business plans   . . .
        Performance indicators . . .
        Trend analysis   . . .
        Workforce planning . . .

        1 Never
        2 Tried it once
        3 Sometimes
        4 Frequently
        5 Regularly

Q11   Has your museum/museum service carried out a formal analysis of any of the following
(Please tick if 'yes')

        . . . Projected demographic changes
        . . . Visitor/admission figures
        . . . Cost of collecting
        . . . Cost per visitor over three or more years
        . . . Comparison with Audit Commission profile

Q12   Have you received training in any of the following (please tick if 'yes'). Please note any formal management qualification you may possess.

        . . . Business planning
        . . . Financial forecasting
        . . . Strategic management
        . . . Setting objectives
        . . . Achieving targets
        . . . Performance review methods
        . . . Decision-making

Q13   In the present political and financial climate do you feel that the planning of services and resource allocation beyond the next twelve months is:
(Please tick)

        . . . Futile
        . . . Hardly worth the effort
        . . . Something that 'ought to be done'
        . . . Worth attempting
        . . . Essential

Q14   How did your museum/museum service respond to *The Road to Wigan Pier?* ?
(Please tick)

        . . . Not at all
        . . . Report to the governing body
        . . . Review the service
        . . . Other (please specify)

Q15 Have the District Audit compiled a report as a result of *The Road to Wigan Pier?* ?
(Please tick)

    ... Yes
    ... No

Q16 If you were asked so make a 15 per cent cut in your budget next year, would you

    ... Reduce your opening hours
    ... Close one or more building(s)
    ... Reduce the number of professional posts
    ... Cut the conservation budget
    ... Increase your income (other than by admission charges)
    ... Cut the exhibitions budget
    ... Prioritize your activities and discontinue non-core ones
    ... Introduce or increase existing admission charges
    ... Cut the purchase fund

Please rank 1 (first thing you would do) to 9 (last thing you would do)

Q17 Would you arrive at a decision by any of the following means
(Please tick)

    ... Report options to governing body
    ... Discuss with colleagues in your own service
    ... Discuss with other colleagues
    ... Consult a management textbook
    ... Consult your Area Museums Service
    ... Discuss with a finance officer

Q18 How would you describe the outlook for local authority museums in this country?
(Please tick)

    ... Bleak
    ... Challenging
    ... Stable
    ... Optimistic
    ... Exciting

Q19 What sort of assistance do you think your museum/service needs to achieve
effective strategic management?

    ... A training course in basic skills
    ... More information about the social and economic environment
    ... 'Hands on' assistance from a specialist
    ... None
    ... Other (please specify)

Q20 Have you any other comments?

THANK YOU

Please return (using s.a.e. provided) by: *FEBRUARY 1st 1993*

6

Museum Wharf
Roger Davis and Christopher H. Lovelock

Marketing in museums may be substantially different to that in the commercial sector, as Hugh Bradford and Fiona McLean argue in their papers in this volume. However, this case study of a marketing campaign by Roger Davis, then Lecturer in Marketing, Baylor University, and Christopher Lovelock, then Associate Professor of Business Administration, Harvard University, is in many senses a model for this kind of analysis, not least by stressing that marketing should be a key part of the strategic management process.

Four yellow school buses were lined up, nose to tail, on the Congress Street bridge next to Museum Wharf. Outside the long, six-storey brick structure, flags were flying briskly in the chill March wind blowing off the harbour. In the lobby, a group of schoolchildren was pressing eagerly towards the large exterior elevator that would take them up to the Museum of Transportation. Another group of smaller children was clattering up the wide stairs leading to The Children's Museum. Several accompanying teachers were doing their best to maintain some semblance of order. It was a typical Monday morning during the school year at Museum Wharf. In the third-floor conference room, administrators of the two museums were reviewing the eight-month period since July 1979, when they had inaugurated their new joint home. Of particular concern was what relationship the museums should have in the future with respect to promotional activities. Michael Spock, director of The Children's Museum, glanced out the window towards the nearby office towers of downtown Boston. 'We both have good relations with the schools,' he said, gesturing towards the buses below. 'I think the task now is to build up attendance among tourists and local residents.' Duncan Smith, his counterpart at the Museum of Transportation, nodded agreement. 'There's so much competition in this city,' he remarked. 'Both of us need to toot this place. But the question is, do we do it jointly or separately? Frankly, I'm worried about the fuzzy image of the two museums and the way we seem to blur together in people's minds.'

A TALE OF TWO MUSEUMS

Boston was well known for its museums and other visitor attractions. These included: the paintings and art treasures of the Museum of Fine Arts (MFA) and the Gardner Museum; the eighteenth-century frigate *USS Constitution* (better known as 'Old Ironsides'); the Museum of Science with its slogan, 'It's fun to find out'; the artistic and scientific exhibits of the several Harvard University museums; and the dramatic marine exhibits of the New England Aquarium. Other local attractions included the Franklin Park Zoo, and the archives and museum of the John F. Kennedy Memorial Library, opened in late 1979. Two smaller, but growing, museums had relocated in 1979 from separate locations in the inner suburbs to a new, shared facility on the edge of downtown. These were The Children's Museum and the Museum of Transportation. Fig. 6.1 shows the location of each of these attractions on a map of the Boston area.

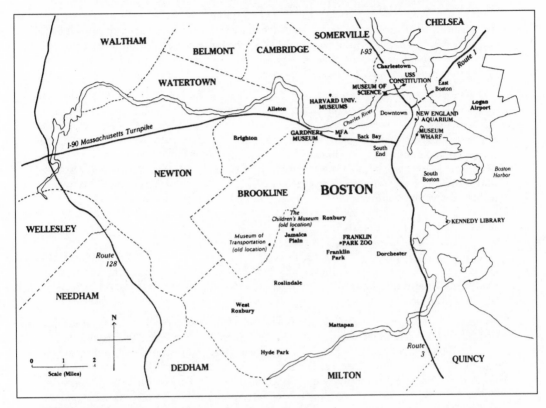

Fig 6.1   Major museums and attractions in the Boston area

The Children's Museum

In 1913, a group of university and public school science teachers in Boston founded The Children's Museum (TCM) to supplement natural science programmes in local schools. Its initial location was in the Jamaica Plain area of Boston, about four miles from the city centre. In 1936, the museum moved to a larger facility in the same area.

Michael Spock, whose graduate training was in education, was appointed director of TCM in 1962. He introduced innovative ways of extending the reach of the museum, as well as an aggressive approach to grant-seeking. TCM's offerings included participative exhibits, community-based activities, and training programmes for teachers and community workers. Spock described the museum's distinctive mission as follows:

> What makes TCM different is the commitment we have to helping everyone learn from an increasingly tough and demanding world through direct experiences with real materials. We believe in learning by doing.

The museum's Resource Center conducted workshops, developed and published educational materials, and lent or rented exhibit-related materials to students, teachers, museum members and community workers. One offering, called 'Recycle', involved objects donated by manufacturing plants (which would otherwise have discarded them). The items in question ranged from defective camera lenses to washers to pieces of shaped wood or styrofoam. They were sold by weight or measure as raw materials for children to use in arts, crafts, science and other learning projects.

The Exhibit Center accounted for most of the museum's direct contact with the public. It consisted of 'hands-on' exhibits for families, designed primarily for children from pre-school age through early teens. Overall administration of the museum and its programmes was the responsibility of the Support Services group.

The success of these innovations soon taxed the capacity of the Jamaica Plain facilities. Space problems placed a ceiling on attendance. Since more than half of TCM's operations budget came from admissions, the museum was rapidly becoming restricted in its ability to develop new programmes and exhibits. Another cause for concern was the relative inaccessibility of the Jamaica Plain location (see Fig. 6.1). It was not served by Boston's extensive rapid transit system, and the directors felt that it was hard for out-of-town visitors to find. By the early 1970s, feasibility studies were being conducted to help determine requirements for a new building in central Boston.

Museum of Transportation

Until it moved to Museum Wharf, the Museum of Transportation (MOT) was located in an old carriage house in Brookline, a suburb of Boston (see Fig. 6.1). From its beginning in 1947 as the Antique Auto Museum, it had developed into a museum of different types of transportation.

Duncan Smith, who became director of MOT in 1970, had previously been an exhibits designer for the Museum of Fine Arts. His arrival at MOT marked the beginning of a decade of change for the museum. First he added other transportation antiques, such as bicycles, to the collection. Special meets were held featuring different types of transportation. The name of the museum was changed in 1971 to reflect its new emphasis. Then, in 1978, the entire museum was renovated and a hands-on activity centre added. Special efforts were made to reach out to the schools and new educational programmes were developed. Gradually, the museum evolved into a 'museum of transportation archaeology', as Smith described it. He elaborated:

> By this I mean that the museum not only shows antique cars and bicycles, trains and ships, but also explains them in terms of their social context so visitors can see just how transportation has affected their lives. . . . It's full of folklore and myth. Someone was always mad because his horse kicked him, his bicycle had a flat tire, his car ran out of gas on the freeway, or the airline lost his luggage. We're building a museum that looks at transportation through these many perspectives.

Soon after Smith's arrival at MOT it became apparent that the Brookline location was not adequate. It did not have the space necessary to house many of the proposed exhibits. It, too, had an out-of-the-way location, which limited its attendance. Smith began to look around for a new location that would allow the museum to expand its offerings and attract more visitors. One site considered was the old Watertown Arsenal, about five miles from downtown Boston. But the sharp rise in oil prices in 1973 convinced Smith that heating costs would be prohibitive and that a central location, close to public transportation, was essential.

A new home for both museums

Smith and Spock were neighbours in private life; they often discussed with each other the problems involved in finding suitable locations for their respective museums. Though the directors had not decided that shared facilities were the solution to their relocation decisions, they had noted that sharing would be beneficial for both museums, offering some economies of scale and the opportunity to pool resources in areas such as admissions, a retail shop, parking and security.

In early 1975, Spock learned that the Atlas Terminal Warehouse, overlooking Fort Point Channel on Boston's waterfront, was for sale. Though the building was too large for TCM, its location and structural qualities were very desirable. Spock felt that this might be the opportunity to join forces which he and Smith had been thinking about. The two men saw that, with renovation, the nineteenth-century brick and timber warehouse would meet the existing space requirement of both museums and still leave room for future expansion. In December 1975, MOT and TCM jointly signed a purchase contract. Prior to its opening in July 1979, the building was renamed 'Museum Wharf'.

REDEVELOPMENT IN BOSTON

During the 1960s and 1970s, the City of Boston witnessed a dramatic rebirth of its historic central area, spurred by a series of major redevelopment and restoration efforts. Particularly noteworthy was the revival of the badly deteriorated wholesaling and warehousing sections along the waterfront, long a victim of Boston's decline in importance as a seaport.

Beginning with construction of the New England Aquarium (opened in 1969) and the Harbor Towers apartments, the waterfront started to take on a new life. Old warehouses, only a few minutes' walk from the new Government Center administrative complex and the office towers of the booming financial district, were converted into expensive apartments and condominiums. The Bicentennial saw the opening of the Faneuil Hall Marketplace. Housed in restored, historic buildings, this cluster of restaurants, small stores and professional offices quickly became immensely popular with residents and visitors alike. The Museum of Fine Arts, located two miles away, opened a 'branch' in one of these buildings. In 1978–9, the nearby Washington Street retail area, containing two major department stores, was converted into a pedestrian mall and promoted by the Mayor's Office of Cultural Affairs as the 'Downtown Crossing'. (In 1980, responsibility for joint promotional efforts was transferred to an organization of local merchants.)

The Fort Point Channel area

The directors of MOT and TCM felt that Museum Wharf was in the path of redevelopment in Boston. It was located in a several-block cluster of tall, solidly constructed brick commercial buildings just across the Fort Point Channel (an extension of Boston harbour) from South Station and the new Federal Reserve Bank tower (see Fig. 6.2). Three bridges spanned the channel.

The Wharf was about seven minutes' walk from South Station, which was served by commuter rail, Amtrak and subway. Plans were in hand to renovate the station and construct a new transportation centre there that would serve as a terminal for inter-city buses. The Central Artery, a major expressway, passed in front of South Station and had on and off slip roads within two blocks of the station. The most direct access by car to the Museum Wharf parking area was across the Northern Avenue swing bridge, an

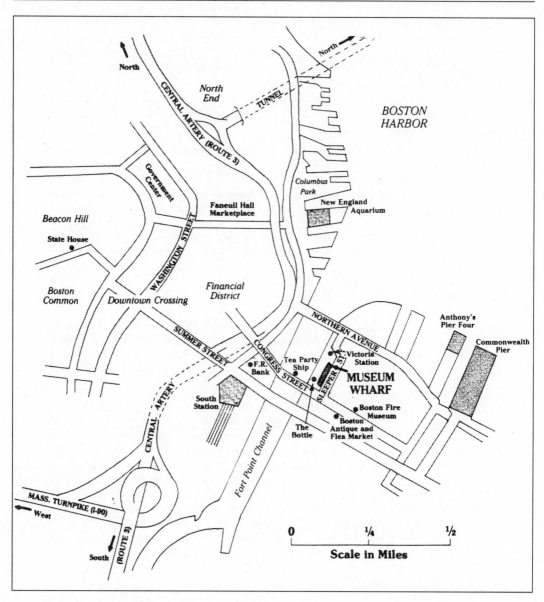

Fig. 6.2 Museum Wharf and Downtown Boston

old-fashioned structure built of a latticework of steel girders, which had railway tracks running down the median of the bridge deck.

Most of the buildings on the museum side of the channel were occupied by commercial and industrial firms, including wholesale suppliers of office equipment, linoleum and wall coverings, as well as printing firms and a manufacturer of custom furniture. Signs of a change in this mix included renovation of the second floor of one building for an art gallery, and conversion of street-level space in another into an elegant law firm office.

There were a number of other attractions nearby which the museums' directors felt would contribute to attendance at Museum Wharf. New England Aquarium, a marine life museum, was fifteen minutes' walk from Museum Wharf. The Tea Party Ship, a for-profit museum and gift shop reached from the Congress Street bridge, was moored in the Fort Point Channel directly across from Museum Wharf. The Boston Fire Museum, managed by MOT, was scheduled to open in autumn 1980 in a late nineteenth-century fire-house, one block away. The Boston Antique and Flea Market, another newcomer to the area, was open every Sunday just across the Street from the Fire Museum site. A little further away, on the edge of the harbour, were Anthony's Pier Four (a well-known seafood restaurant) and Commonwealth Pier, site of the annual New England Flower Show and other exhibitions.

MOT and TCM administrators felt that the redevelopment taking place along Boston's extensive waterfront, combined with increased accessibility, was likely to lead to further investment in the area. Private developers had recently announced plans to 'recycle' one of the commercial buildings near the Wharf and convert it into condominiums. However, in March 1980, the general tone of the immediate vicinity of the Wharf remained that of a slightly run-down commercial area.

MUSEUM WHARF

Originally constructed as a wool warehouse in 1889, the museums' new home was six storeys high, 370 feet long and 70 feet deep; it contained 144,000 square feet of space. A broad apron, suitable for development into a small urban park and display area, separated the full length of the building from the waters of the 200-yard-wide channel.

The museums shared the $5.2 million purchase, renovation and financing costs. Additional sums of $400,000 and $1 million were spent by MOT and TCM, respectively, for final preparation and installation of their exhibits. Although private donations supplied most of the funds for the project, substantial credit was provided by Boston-area banks and tax-exempt bonds. Even after major renovation, the cost per square foot was estimated at less than half that of a brand new building.

The first floor consisted of joint lobby and retail space. TCM was located in 39,000 square feet on the second, third and fourth floors, and MOT in 30,000 square feet on the fourth, fifth and sixth floors. Space was reserved for retail tenants on the ground floor; 51,000 square feet on the upper floors were set aside for future expansion of the museums.

Inside the lobby were an admission desk and entrances to both museums. Though the museums shared the desk, they charged separate admissions (see Table 6.1 for price schedule). The cash registers printed slips specifying the museum to be visited, the number and type of admissions (adults, children, discounts) and – through a link with the computer owned by TCM – stored this admissions data for later retrieval.

Visitors entered TCM by climbing a wide stairway which led from the lobby to the second floor. Smaller stairways provided access from the second floor to the third and fourth floors. Handicapped visitors could reach the exhibit areas by elevator. TCM's exhibits included the 'Giant's Desktop', where everything from a pencil to a coffee cup to a telephone was twelve times the normal size; 'Living Things', a natural history corner with small urban animals from mice to cockroaches; 'City Slice', a three-storey cross-section of a city street and Victorian house; 'Grandparents' House', including working kitchen and attic with trunks of old clothes and Victorian memorabilia; 'What

Table 6.1 Comparative price schedule for six Boston museums, March 1980[a] (US$)

	MOT	TCM[b]	Museum of Fine Arts[c]	Museum of Science[d]	New England Aquarium	Tea Party Ship
Adult	3.00	3.00	1.75	3.50	4.00	1.75
Children	2.00	2.00	Free	2.25	2.50	1.00
Senior citizens	2.00	2.00	–	2.25	3.00	–
College ID	2.00	–	–	2.25	3.00	–
School group	1.80	Free	–	Free	2.00	–
Friday night	1.00	1.00	–	1.00	2.00	–
Wednesday afternoon	–	–	–	Free	–	–
Sunday	–	–	1.25	–	–	–
Tuesday (after 5.00 p.m.)	–	–	Free	–	–	–
Civic groups	–	Free	–	–	–	–
Adult	–	–	–	–	2.00	–
Children	–	–	–	–	3.00	–
College and senior	–	–	–	–	2.50	–
Special needs	–	–	–	–	2.00	–
Adult group	–	–	–	3.00	–	–

[a] MOT and TCM planned to increase admissions prices to $3.50 for adults and $2.50 for children, effective from 15 April, 1980

[b] All non-profit Massachusetts community and school groups admitted free through a special state appropriation

[c] Admission to the MFA branch in Faneuil Hall Marketplace was free

[d] The Museum of Science, located about two miles from Museum Wharf, contained several transportation-related exhibits

If You Couldn't?', an exhibit about handicaps; 'We're Still Here', an exhibit showing how American Indians lived then and now; and 'WKID-TV', a news studio with closed-circuit television.

Visitors to MOT rode a large, glassed-in external elevator to the sixth floor, enjoying a fine view of downtown Boston and part of the harbour. The fifth and fourth floors were reached either by connecting stairs or by the elevator. MOT's main exhibit was called 'Boston – A City in Transit'. Visitors progressed through nine time periods, from 1630 to the present day, seeing and hearing the development of transportation in and around Boston. In the process, they experienced a colonial shipyard, a nineteenth-century railway station, an early subway stop, and a mid-twentieth-century automobile showroom. Other exhibits included: audio-visual presentations of the history of the shipping trade and immigration into Boston; 'Crossroads', a hands-on section where both adults and children could ride a model hovercraft, slide down a fire pole, pedal a high wheeler, or climb on board an early trolley; a film about the development of flight; and a selection of MOT's extensive antique carriage and auto collection (the balance remained in the museum's old site in Brookline).

Besides the two museums, the Wharf included two restaurants. There were also a small park and a dairy bar on the apron overlooking the channel. Antique vehicles provided outdoor rides during the warmer months.

Impact of Museum Wharf

The two commercial establishments most affected by the opening of the museums were the Victoria Station restaurant and the Boston Tea Party Ship and Museum.

Victoria Station, a unit of the national restaurant chain, was located next to Museum Wharf at Northern Avenue and Sleeper Street. Like others in the chain, the restaurant had a British railway theme. Part of the structure was housed in converted railroad boxcars. Victoria Station had been in business at that location for over six years when Museum Wharf opened. The manager thought that the overall impact of her new neighbours had been beneficial. She commented:

> It's easier now for us to identify our location. People know where Museum Wharf is. They don't know where Sleeper Street is. We've also increased our meal counts since the opening. The only real problem stemming from the museum is parking.

The manager had noticed that the customers at Victoria Station were younger and more likely to bring children than previously. She also felt that the general atmosphere of the area had changed and become more attractive. She believed that her customers felt more comfortable and secure now that there were more people visiting the immediate area.

The site for the Tea Party Ship had been designated by the City of Boston in 1972. An old wooden Danish sailing vessel was purchased, modified to resemble an eighteenth-century brig like the *Beaver*, and sailed across the Atlantic to Boston. It was moored in the Fort Point Channel next to a wooden bridge tender's house containing a gift shop. This exhibit, which commemorated the famous Boston Tea Party protest of 1773, opened in 1974. Visitors could not only learn about the incident and see what the original ship, the *Beaver*, must have looked like, but could themselves hurl tea chests (connected to the ship by lines) into the harbour.

Barbara Attianese, the director, felt that the opening of Museum Wharf had been beneficial to the area. She commented:

> When we opened, we felt a little like pioneers in this part of Boston. There were few other attractions nearby, so we had to bear the burden of attracting people to this area. With the opening of Museum Wharf, we expect that the area will get more attention from improved parking, lighting and security to more interest among business and civic leaders.

Attianese did not feel that Museum Wharf was in competition with the Tea Party Ship, but instead saw them as complementary attractions:

> Our price is lower – $1.75 for adults and $1.00 for children – and the average time spent in our museum is 30 minutes. We are a different type of attraction, from MOT and TCM. We benefit from their location here because of increased exposure resulting from more traffic over the bridge.

As further evidence of the good feelings generated between the Tea Party Ship and Museum Wharf, Attianese pointed to an arrangement between her museum and MOT, whereby a discount was given to school groups who booked visits to both MOT and the Tea Party Ship. She envisioned an even more co-operative future.

Other food service operations

The retail business located in the Museum Wharf building were a McDonald's fast-food restaurant, a medium-priced seafood restaurant called 'Trawlers', and the Museums' Shop. Outside the building stood 'The Bottle', a dairy bar within a 40-foot-high wooden replica of a milk bottle.

In 1978, the McDonald's Corporation had agreed to operate a company-owned restaurant – as opposed to a franchise – at Museum Wharf. The site appeared well suited to McDonald's strategy of appealing to families and children. Opening in December 1978, McDonald's was the first occupant of the Wharf to begin continuous operations.

Business at McDonald's for the seven months prior to the opening of the museums was described as slow. Some of the customers came from the Federal Reserve Bank across the bridge and other commercial buildings in the area, but mostly when the weather was mild. Following the grand opening of the museum, sales rose dramatically through August and then fell as museum business dropped at the beginning of the school year.

John Betts, manager of the McDonald's outlet, said that though museum-related trade was a substantial part of his business, a core of customers unrelated to the museums had developed. He estimated that 60 per cent of weekday sales were not associated with the museums. On weekends, he felt that up to 85 per cent were museum-related. Even with the museum, Betts reported that this McDonald's was a low-volume store. He attributed much of that to the early closing time of the museum (6.00 p.m. during summer months and 5.00 p.m. in winter), observing:

> Because there is little or no traffic here after the museums close, we close at 7:00 p.m., except on Fridays when the museums are open until 9:00 and we remain open until 10:00.

Betts, however, was not discouraged. He felt that as the area continued to develop and become established, the restaurant would become very successful.

Trawlers restaurant had closed in November, allegedly for renovations. Business had reportedly been good during the day, but evening traffic had apparently been poor. In early March 1980, Museum Wharf administrators learned that Trawlers had closed permanently, and began a search for a new restaurant tenant with better financing.

'The Bottle', which sold a variety of cold dairy products and salads, was closed during the winter months. An eye-catching landmark, 'The Bottle' was featured prominently in the museums' pre-opening publicity and was adopted as the symbol of Museum Wharf, appearing on maps and directional signs. Once a distinctive ice-cream stand located in Taunton, Massachusetts, it had been donated by Hood Dairy Company to Museum Wharf and shipped there by barge.

Museums' Shop

The Museums' Shop was located on the ground floor of Museum Wharf between McDonald's and the museum lobby. It was a joint operation of the two museums, which had agreed to share the profits (or losses). At their previous locations, the two museums had operated shops in cramped quarters that were out of the normal flow of visitor traffic. It was felt that these out-of-the-way locations, combined with budgeting constraints, had prevented the shops from increasing sales. With the move to Museum Wharf, serious consideration was given to franchising the shop to an outside operator. After careful study, it was concluded that the profit potential of the shop was great enough that it should be operated by the museums themselves. Further discussions led to an agreement that TCM would run the shop.

Judy Flam, manager of the Museum's Shop, felt that prior to the move to Museum Wharf neither museum had taken its shop seriously. However, she believed the new shop would prove profitable. Flam predicted sales of $300,000 for the fiscal year ending June 1980. This was five times sales of TCM's Jamaica Plain shop and over three times the combined sales of the two separate shops. By the end of December 1979, sales of the shop had exceeded $185,000 and the $300,000 goal seemed easily reachable.

The merchandise in the shop reflected the themes of both museums. It included books, models, electric trains, T-shirts with museum logos, and a wide variety of relatively inexpensive items aimed at children. Numerically, there were many more items with a children theme than with a transportation theme. However, many of the transportation-related items were higher priced, so that the disproportion was reduced when inventory values were used as the basis of comparison. Flam estimated that the volume of traffic in the shop generated by TCM was four or five times that generated by MOT. She cited the 'kid's shop' was evidence of this. 'Two-thirds of our dollar sales', she said, 'come from one-third of our floor space. In that section of the shop – we call it the "kid's shop" – all items are priced under $5.00.'

The high percentage of low-priced items sold led Flam to conclude that many of the higher priced items displayed with MOT visitors in mind would not sell in sufficient volume in the shop to merit stocking in the future.

PROMOTIONAL ACTIVITIES

Recalling the questions faced by the museum administrators prior to the opening of Museum Wharf, Duncan Smith commented:

> We actually faced two decisions. First, what should our short-term promotional strategy be and second, what should our long-term promotional strategy be? We felt that there were essentially three alternatives available. We could promote the pieces, the building, or the area.

'Pieces' were the individual units that composed Museum Wharf; this strategy would have resulted in separate promotion of each unit in Museum Wharf. The 'building' was Museum Wharf; a 'building' strategy would require promotion of Museum Wharf and tenants. Area promotion would involve Museum Wharf, its tenants and (at a minimum) Victoria Station and the Tea Party Ship.

The opening campaign

No long-term promotion strategy decisions were made prior to the opening, but directors of the two museums agreed that short-term objectives would best be accomplished through the use of a 'building' strategy.

By the time the opening date arrived, Museum Wharf had received heavy publicity throughout New England, reinforced by extensive advertising. The initial campaign was designed to publicize the relocation of the museums to Museum Wharf and to emphasize both museums' individual exhibits and programmes. Advertising, budgeted at about $20,000, consisted of ads in newspapers and special interest magazines, and display cards on buses and subway cars (see Table 6.2 and Fig. 6.3 for expenditure breakdowns

Table 6.2 Initial joint advertising expenditure breakdown, June–August 1979

The following insertion orders were executed:		Budget ($)
Where Magazine	¹/₃ page, eight weekly insertions, 7/7 through 8/25	1,193.20
Panorama Magazine	¹/₄ page, eight weekly insertions, 7/9 through 8/27	408.00
Metro Transit	250 car cards on main rapid transit lines, July and August	3,000.00
	75 bus rears, Massachusetts Pike and Downtown, July and August	6,000.00
	Additional 200 car cards on main rapid transit lines and 250 cards inside buses, July and August	no charge
	Additional 25 bus rears in surrounding towns, July and August	no charge
Boston Globe	3 columns × 115 lines opening ads – 6/22, 6/29, 7/2, 7/5	3,648.38
	2 columns × 60 lines individual exhibit ads in rotation, two per week for 7 weeks, 7/9 through 8/20	4,662.00
Metroguide	6" × 3 columns, one insertion, 6/21 Boston issue	477.70
Production Costs:	Bus rears and car cards, Wisewell	1,128.00
	Type, illustration, production, HH	not known
Total Committed to Date		$20,517.28

Source: Museum Wharf

Note: Discounts Obtained: *Where*, 5%; *Boston Globe*, standard 25% non-profit; *Metroguide*, standard 15% non-profit plus 15 insertion frequency discount; Metro Transit, $900 off car cards plus additional car cards and bus rears as noted above; *Panorama*, standard 15% non-profit.

and representative print ads.) Though some media expenditures were planned and budgeted through August, most ended in July.

Administrators of both museums expressed dissatisfaction with the initial advertising campaign. They believed that it did not reflect the reality of Museum Wharf and had confused the images and exhibits of the two museums. Duncan Smith said bluntly that the advertising had simply 'created the image of a children's amusement park', adding:

> My previous assumption was that any news is good news. Now I know that transmitting the wrong image can be damaging. We've all learned a lot about the client's responsibility to ensure that the agency develops effective advertising. In the future, we've got to face up to the issue of whether we're selling individual museums to a site with a bag of things in it.

Publicity was handled jointly for the museums by Jonathan Hyde. Prior to joining TCM as public relations director in 1977, he had had five years' experience as senior editor and writer for a university publications office. Hyde admitted that he had not been comfortable with the initial joint promotion effort:

> At the time of the opening, the two institutions had different amounts of public visibility. It's fair to say that public knowledge of MOT was much less, their admissions base was much less, and they had recently gone through fairly dramatic changes in what that institution saw as its mission. From my perspective the public had not caught up with those changes when we opened. Those issues, plus the fact that it was the 'International Year of the Child', resulted in TCM's getting the lion's share of the publicity. I was faced with trying to turn opportunities for TCM into joint pieces.

The grand opening of Museum Wharf on 1 July 1979 was the beginning of two successive record-breaking months for both museums. Though attendance was expected to drop in September, neither museum had thought that attendance would fall back as much as it actually did. Table 6.3 compares monthly attendance figures at MOT and TCM with those for the Museum of Fine Arts, Museum of Science and Aquarium. TCM's attendance was only slightly below budget for September, but MOT's was almost 50 per cent below the budgeted level. Budgeted attendance for each museum reflected financial needs as well as market analysis. The 1979–80 fiscal year budgeted attendance for MOT was 280,000, accounting for 41 per cent of total budgeted expenses of $1.3 million; but projected attendance was 216,000. At TCM, both budgeted and projected attendance were 500,000, representing 45 per cent of total budgeted expenses of $1.6 million.

Subsequent MOT promotional efforts

As October progressed, it became apparent to MOT administrators that actual attendance would remain well below target. A series of discussions at MOT led to the planning and development of an advertising campaign to begin in late November.

MOT administrators felt that a big part of the attendance problem was related to the public's expectations of MOT. They felt that though the initial advertising and publicity had successfully communicated Museum Wharf to the public, it had not been effective in communicating the breadth of MOT's exhibits. They were also concerned about a 'fuzzing' effect which they believed contributed to confusion about what Museum Wharf really was. This concern was expressed by Joan Fowler, head of marketing and development for MOT, whose previous background had been in arts administration and conference management. Said Fowler:

> I've noticed that when people refer to this place they call it 'The Children's and Transportation Museum'. I'm wondering if the joint expenditures were a good use of our money. I feel the site name is still up in the air, still fuzzing in people's minds. What we have to do is to let people know that we are separate in our products. We may both be museums, but the products are different.

Fowler believed that the best way to do this was through separate advertising to correct the misconceptions of the public about MOT and Museum Wharf. So a new advertising campaign was developed, budgeted for $18,000 and designed to run from late November 1979 through February 1980. It consisted of an initial advertisement in the *Boston Globe Calendar* and a series of smaller ads in subsequent *Calendars* emphasizing the different exhibit themes which were introduced in the initial ad. The recurring theme of these ads was, 'We're not just a bunch of old cars'.

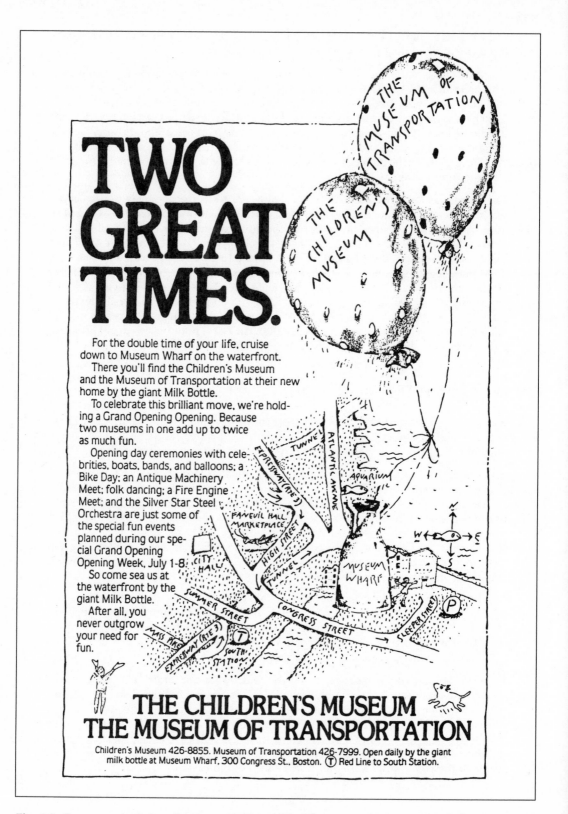

Fig. 6.3 Representative joint advertisements for grand opening

Table 6.3 Monthly attendance figures for five Boston museums[a]

1978	MOT[b]	TCM[c]	Museum of Fine Arts	Museum of Science	New England Aquarium
July	3,699	17,847	125,636	91,801	128,149
August	4,288	26,879	38,096	103,818	131,881
September	1,550	closed[c]	36,059	36,689	57,334
October	2,612	20,650	55,039	64,355	59,880
November	2,082	13,095	79,945	75,740	59,464
December	1,466	12,273	68,897	73,741	42,815
1979					
January	1.767	11,911	75,459	75,957	40,757
February	3,588	21,889	39,929	96,267	62,471
March	3,509	18,009	47,877	93,557	68,639
April	4,255	18,003	59,686	90,820	86,249
May	6,678	closed	64,986	108,670	94,085
June	4,027	closed	134,615	83,439	86,537
July	15,803	70,398	31,657	71,397	112,234
August	18,454	83,201	41,810	97,548	128,690
September	7,289	26,676	46,856	24,144	46,831
October	6,906	30,630	85,313	55,473	51,046
November	7,972	36,595	75,449	65,834	55,794
December	8,299	31,684	36,211	65,644	48,201
1980					
January	8,167	32,012	38,371	68,676	53,740

[a] Data for Boston Tea Party Ship & Museum not available
[b] School groups accounted for 35% of MOT attendance and 10% of TCM attendance in fiscal 1979/80
[c] Prior to the move to Museum Wharf, TCM had customarily been closed during the month of September

Source: Museum Wharf

In late December, MOT took another step to eliminate misconceptions about the relationship between the two museums. MOT administrators felt that the original layout of the lobby was dominated by the large stairway that led to The Children's Museum. They felt that the prominence of this stairway, coupled with the greater public visibility of TCM, left many visitors with the impression that MOT was a tenant of TCM or a less-than-equal partner. In an attempt to overcome this perception the lobby was renovated so that, as visitors entered the area by the elevator leading to MOT, their eyes would be caught by wall panels and small exhibits with a transportation theme. An information desk staffed by an MOT employee was placed in the same area. Some MOT administrators wondered whether their museum should go further and institute a separate admission counter.

MOT gained further publicity (and income) by conducting 'Gas Guzzler' auctions of large, high-gasoline-consumption automobiles. Since these cars had been donated to the museum and were transportation related, donors could deduct for tax purposes the *Blue Book* value of the vehicles. MOT had also been making an aggressive effort to expand membership. Through a series of special events, notably at weekends and during vacations, administrators sought to ensure that something new was taking place when people visited the museum. They also seized opportunities for major media coverage, including the use of MOT for functions and press conferences.

Although MOT administrators felt that their promotional efforts had helped, they concluded that initial projections of 216,000 visitors for the twelve months ending June 1980 would not be reached. So, in late February 1980, they reduced the first-year attendance projection to 180,000.

Promotional efforts by The Children's Museum

Though TCN's attendance had fallen below budget for September and October, cumulative attendance remained above budget for the year. In late February 1980, projected attendance for the first year was revised downwards from a target of 500,000 to 485,000.

Since the conclusion of the opening advertising, TCM had relied, with one exception, on publicity-generated media coverage to maintain visibility. The exception was a membership campaign that began in December. Directed at children, it consisted of public service spots and one-page flyers distributed through retail outlets in suburban neighbourhoods. The campaign was built on a spoof of a current American Express card advertising campaign ('Don't leave home without it'). There had been some internal opposition at TCM to this campaign because of its apparent upper-income theme and the possibility that there might be an adverse reaction from some segments of the population.

THE PLANNING MEETING

In mid-March 1980, administrators of the two museums met to discuss planning for the spring and summer seasons. Both groups expected to increase their promotional efforts in the coming months, but there had been much debate on whether to proceed individually or to join forces as they had the previous summer. Each group was anxious to be co-operative but felt their first responsibility was to select that approach which would most benefit their own museum.

This paper first appeared in C. H. Lovelock and C. B. Weinberg (eds) (1984) Public and Nonprofit Marketing: Cases and Readings, *Palo Alto, CA: Scientific Press and John Wiley & Sons, pp. 215–29.*

7

Museum brainstorming: a creative approach to exhibit planning

Suzanne De Borhegyi

How can managers foster an environment in which the most creative ideas for exhibitions can be nurtured? In this paper first published in 1978, Suzanne De Borhegyi considers the initial approach taken at the then new project of the Albuquerque Museum in New Mexico, USA.

How does a museum with a young, enthusiastic, but relatively small and inexperienced staff go about developing a new and dynamic approach to regional history – one that will meet the expectations and needs of a multicultural community? This is the challenge faced by the Albuquerque Museum as it prepares to move into its new four-million-dollar museum in early 1979.

Created only ten years ago as a branch of city government, the museum had a slow and difficult beginning. According to its charter, it was charged with the preservation and interpretation of the art, history and science of central New Mexico. To meet this broad and all-encompassing mandate, the trustees determined that a three-part exhibits programme should be developed consisting of: (1) temporary exhibitions of works by local and national artists, both past and contemporary, juried and invitational exhibitions and major travelling exhibits; (2) temporary exhibits of history and science interpreting current developments in the Middle Rio Grande Valley; and (3) a series of permanent exhibits relating the long and multicultured history of the Middle Rio Grande Valley.

Funded and staffed minimally by the city for the first half of its existence, the museum was located in temporary quarters in the old airport terminal and was virtually devoid of collections. The staff was hard put to develop even a portion of this programme, but a strong, community-oriented art exhibition programme was eventually started, augmented by an equally strong docent-guided education programme. Fortunately these staff efforts, and those of a small but dedicated corps of volunteers, coincided with a belated wave of cultural awareness in the community. In 1974 a sympathetic city council and administration scheduled the museum for a $2.9 million building programme – to be funded by municipal bonds, which needed voter approval.

This important breakthrough was clouded by the realization that selling the museum would be a monumental task. Few voters knew what they were voting for, since so little of the museum's programme had actually been realized. Nevertheless, a vigorous campaign was waged, and – based on the strength of the art programme and the oft-repeated promise of a high quality history programme that would preserve the cultural heritage and build pride and ethnic identity – the bond referendum passed by a narrow margin in October 1975.

In the years since, both staff and budget have grown substantially. In August 1977, the city added an additional $1 million to the building programme through the Economic Development Act. A handsome new building is going up, and community expectations have soared. Now the museum must make good its campaign promises.

No museums in the area have attempted exhibits of regional history on a large scale. Many nearby museums specialize in specific areas of American ethnology and archaeology, Spanish colonial art history, the Anglo–American West, or contemporary and recent Anglo–American art history. None pull all the fragments together to tell the story of humanity's long sojourn in the Southwest, showing the relationships through time of one culture to another or the inter-relationships of art, history and science. The Albuquerque Museum therefore not only is free to fill this vacuum but, in a very real sense, also has an obligation to do so. As the tax-supported institution serving the largest and fastest-growing segment of the state's multicultural population, it necessarily has to serve a broad educational purpose. Its youth and lack of significant collections add to its flexibility – it has no predetermined subject areas or donors to satisfy. The lack of collections obviously poses a problem but not an insurmountable one. Discussions with other museums assure us that loan material will be available as needed. Moreover, a major assumption is that collections will be drawn in once the museum begins developing and publicizing its future exhibit programme.

Freedom, however, as humans long ago discovered, is a very demanding and challenging state. It requires endless decision-making and value judgements. With a 20,000-year continuum of human activities to choose from, we faced the task of deciding what should be selected, how it should be presented, and what special purpose should be served. As director of the museum, I asked myself how we could fulfil this awesome task with the existing staff – myself, a curator of history, a curator of exhibits and a curator of education. This was the central problem we faced when we applied for a planning grant from the National Endowment for the Humanities in the summer of 1976.

Through long experience with the large and very capable staff of the Milwaukee Public Museum, I was aware of the great good to be experienced through a cross-disciplinary approach to exhibit planning. Only by involving such specialists as historians, anthropologists, educators and museum exhibit designers – and including representatives of the major local ethnic groups – could we hope to develop a really comprehensive programme of exhibits. Most of all, we hoped to focus on a theme, uniquely appropriate to the area, that could be used not only to tell the history of this region but also to say something about human nature in general.

With this in mind, we proposed bringing together an assemblage of experts in the history and cultures of this area-defined roughly as the Middle Rio Grande Valley – to help us 'brainstorm' our future programme. The proposal was submitted to NEII, and in June 1977 we were awarded a grant to pay expenses and honorariums for such a session. Bernard Lopez, executive director of the New Mexico Arts Commission, an experienced 'facilitator' of such workshops, agreed to lead the initial two-day session. Immediately afterwards, with ideas still fresh and minds attuned, the museum professionals in the group were to spend an additional two days expanding on and consolidating the results of the brainstorming session into a roughed-out script. This script and the ideas generated throughout the four-day session would be fuel for future staff development and implementation.

The group consisted of six historians, five anthropologists, two educators, three exhibit designers, a research engineer and a political journalist/poet. Represented in this gathering were eight museum professionals and three Albuquerque Museum trustees. Two members were of Hispanic background; one was a Pueblo Indian. Thirteen were men, five were women. All but four had an intimate knowledge of the area.

Before coming to the Albuquerque Museum, each person received an informational packet containing a copy of the NEH grant proposal, a background history of the museum, a statement of the goals and objectives as contained in the museum's Master Plan Phase I, a list of staff members and their credentials, and a list of the participants in the planning session. The purpose of the meeting, as adapted from the text of the grant proposal, was stated as follows:

> The purpose of this grant is to plan a series of semipermanent exhibits for the new Albuquerque Museum linking the museum's three areas of concern – history, art, and science – within a humanistic multicultural framework provided by the concept of human creativity. We wish to focus on what it is that makes us human. We believe it is the ability to create – technologically, conceptually, aesthetically. We hope to do this by showing the diversity of human creative products within a particular geographic area – the Middle Rio Grande Valley and the adjacent mountains and semiarid plains of central New Mexico – and by so doing to explore the reasons behind this creativity and the values that produce and reflect a creative environment. For our purposes we will define creativity as the ability to shape the physical and cultural environment by identifying and solving problems, with the tools and resources available, and by so doing to make life more abundant, comfortable, stimulating and aesthetically satisfying.

> We believe this particular geographic area is ideally suited to such an effort. It has as long a span of human history as any place in the New World. It has been touched by a multitude of cultures – American Indian, Spanish, and Anglo – in all its modern urban complexity. Unlike many areas of our country, the absorption concept of the 'melting pot' has not prevailed here. The earlier cultures continue to survive and with varying degrees of success preserve their lifestyles and traditions, even while interacting economically with the dominant Anglo culture. Thus, this area is a unique case study of cultural plurality. It is equally a case study of cultural diffusion.

> In spite of its long cultural history, this area has been and continues to be a cultural frontier, both in the sense of being peripheral to highly developed cultural centers (the high cultures of Middle America, Spain and Central Mexico, the eastern seaboard) and as an area where new solutions had to be found to old problems. Today it is at the forefront of both energy and environmental research. It is, in addition, one of the most productive areas for artistic creativity among all cultures.

> This is an area where living has never been easy or abundant. The challenging nature of the environment, the isolation from established centers of trade and communication, and the coexistence of different cultures have put a premium on human creative energies. It is a story that should be told.

When the group assembled, few knew each other and all shared various degrees of doubt and apprehension concerning the effectiveness of this method of exhibit planning. Bernard Lopez quickly put everyone at ease and to work. Everyone listed their first expectations of what they hoped would result from the planning session – and what they feared might occur. These lists were valuable both in establishing the guidelines of the session and later as a checklist in evaluating its effectiveness. (I might add that it was necessary at this point for me to cease to be the leader and become a participant observer – a schizophrenic situation that was interesting but anxiety-producing. While it was important that I did not direct the thinking, I did feel fully responsible for getting worthwhile results.)

Following this introductory exercise, the group was divided into four smaller units and asked to list the characteristics of an ideal museum. When the four sets of answers were compared, the results were surprisingly and gratifyingly consistent (see Appendix I).

Working again as a whole, the group listed the attributes and functions it would like to see in the Albuquerque Museum interpretation programme under ideal circumstances – an exercise that was followed immediately by a listing of appropriate exhibit topics. These provided ammunition for the next and longest exercise, attacked in smaller groups of four to five; fitting any one of the possible exhibit topics into the framework of the 'ideal' museum programme. As could be expected, the exhibit topics ranged from the conventionally 'do-able' to some so abstract that they were virtually impossible to interpret three-dimensionally.

At the end of the first day, most participants were stimulated but still somewhat sceptical. Some groups had participated in vigorous discussions that were more philosophical than concrete; others had spun their wheels in professional antagonisms. The next day, when everyone returned to the planning session refreshed and eager, an interesting change occurred. The philosophical ideas turned increasingly into 'do-able' solutions, and the antagonisms disappeared in a spirit of co-operation. By late afternoon, when the participants assembled for the last time to discuss and compare the results of their efforts, it was apparent that a general consensus had been reached that included a hierarchy of exhibit themes and topics, as well as a long list of exhibit ideas.

Part I of the planning session had clearly succeeded. Part 2, which was to involve only the visiting museologists and the Albuquerque Museum staff, took place on the succeeding two days. It was totally unstructured, with discussion developing from the concepts generated during the first two days.

The third day, like the first, ended inconclusively. As the leader/participant observer, I was near panic at the thought that nothing firm would result. But my fears abated when the final day brought additional insights and co-operation. We parted satisfied that we had found the exciting and intellectually challenging approach to regional history that we wanted (Appendix II).

A review of the successes and failures of the session reveals some points of significant interest. Unquestionably, these four days were among the most productive in the history of the museum, but, as already noted, the session was not without problems.

Almost everyone agreed that time was too short and another couple of days would have been highly desirable. But the short time introduced an element of tension that seemed to be a necessary motivation for successful problem-solving. Without a hard deadline, the discussions could have continued almost indefinitely in a nebulous, unfocused fashion.

The people in our planning group were devoting time from otherwise busy schedules, so it was necessary to make this time as short and productive as possible. Daily honorariums and living expenses were also limited, and we therefore only had the four days. I am convinced that this time pressure, this very sense of urgency, helped the discussions immensely. The timespan was obviously insufficient for us to take full advantage of the many individual talents represented in the group, but the local people volunteered to review plans and engage in further discussion and the out-of-town people agreed to do the same by mail or telephone. Through this continuing involvement, we can expect to make maximum use of everyone's knowledge and talents.

One problem inherent to any group of specialists is the matter of professional differences and conflicting personalities. These surfaced repeatedly in the early stages of discussion.

Had we known the individuals better – and been able to anticipate problem areas – we might have structured the groups. But the sense of urgency, and the fact that each individual was being paid to accomplish a set of stated objectives, brought a feeling of responsibility towards the final product that minimized conflicts. Unquestionably, the skill of the facilitator in leading the group and keeping everyone's attention riveted to the final goal was a key factor in the success of the project.

The group included some individuals with little museum experience and others with museum experience but little knowledge of local history; this was less of a problem than we had anticipated. Museum professionals should keep in touch with what non-museum people think and expect of museums, and people who know region well can benefit from perceiving it through the eyes of newcomers. Our future exhibits will be for non-museum people, many of whom will have little background in the region or its history, so the 'outsiders' at our session added to instead of detracting from the effectiveness of our planning.

In the session we established the primacy of a single theme and produced a hierarchy of topics and subtopics that provided us with a host of ideas for future temporary exhibits.

The work of exhibit planning is really only beginning. We must research, refine and develop the final script, while we identify and collect the necessary artefacts. A large segment of the New Mexican museum community now knows our artefact needs, and as we move forward in the months ahead, we will not be struggling alone. We have many friends ready to help us.

APPENDIX I

Characteristics of the ideal Albuquerque museum (exhibit design)
Summary of ideas from Part 1 of planning session

1 It should be an appealing and enjoyable educational experience.

   (a) Should stimulate the visitor's imagination, intellect and curiosity.
   (b) Should provide an environment for a total sensory experience (sound, light, motion, scale, touch).
   (c) Should encourage personal identification with the subject matter (projection and role playing).

2 It should be dynamic.

   (a) Should introduce humour, surprise and the element of play
   (b) Should introduce artefacts and ideas in new ways and associations.
   (c) Should permit 'discovery'.

3 It should minimize barriers.

   (a) Should seek to disguise necessary barriers in environmental setting.
   (b) Should be aware of visitor's physical limitations (i.e., that children can see, people with bifocals can read labels, handicapped people can function).
   (c) Should eliminate psychological barriers such as ethnic and sexist stereotypes.

4 It should appeal to a broad audience.

   (a) Should appeal to people of both limited and rich academic backgrounds.

(b) Should encourage participation from different interest, age and ethnic groups.

(c) Should emphasize universal human values.

5 It should use artefacts in many ways.

(a) In interpretive exhibits.

(b) In period settings.

(c) As isolated wonders in their own right.

6 It should extend the museum experience to localities and people beyond its walls

(a) Satellite, storefront, travelling exhibits.

(b) Historic properties.

(c) Educational 'suitcase' kits and materials.

(d) Slide and lecture programmes.

7 It should be reliable.

(a) Should take into account changing scientific and historical knowledge.

(b) Should base exhibits on thorough research.

(c) Should avoid compromising scientific or historical accuracy with overly simplified or dramatic exhibit techniques.

APPENDIX II

Conceptual approach to regional history
Summary of ideas from Parts 1 and 2 of planning session

1 It should present history within a humanistic context.

(a) Attention should be focused on the creators and users of historic artefacts rather than on the artefacts themselves ('No one was ever a Basketmaker II!').

(b) Components and themes should be based on social and economic concerns and interactions rather than political events.

(c) All cultures should be represented, but greater attention should be given to cultural relationships and interaction than to cultural differences.

(d) Themes to be explored should be:

Home and family life
Ways of making a living
Spiritual life
Trade and transportation
'Newcomers' versus 'old-timers'
The future as an extension of the past.

2 It should present history within an ecological context.

(a) Attention should be focused on the interrelation and interdependence of people, land. water and sunshine.

(b) The environment should be presented as both a benefit and a limitation of life in the Middle Rio Grande Valley.

(c) Themes to be explored should be:

Technological responses to the environment (irrigation, solar heating)
Societal responses to the environment (communal water usage, competition for natural resources, potential for population growth, limitations to population growth).

3 It should present history as something more than nostalgia and antiquarianism.

 (a) It should be a vehicle for self-knowledge and cultural identification.
 (b) It should provide information for understanding the present and making decisions concerning the future by focusing on recurring patterns and continuing themes.
 (c) It should present historical changes not as 'progress' but as a series of 'trade-offs'.
 (d) It should, as much as possible, ask questions rather than give answers in order to stimulate curiosity and a desire for further knowledge and/or education.

This article first appeared in Curator *21(3) (1978), pp. 217–24.*

8

An inquiry into the relationship between museum boards and management

Victoria Dickenson

Conflict between museum governing bodies and senior management is an all too common problem. Victoria Dickenson analyses the causes of these tensions, concluding that at heart these reflect unresolved differences in perspectives as to the goals of museums. This re-emphasizes the importance of involving all parties in the establishment of a mission statement which is then binding on all parties.

In the spring of 1988 I was asked by the Museum Branch of the federal Department of Communications to prepare a paper on museum management development. This paper was one of a series of papers written as background documents for the development of a new national museum policy for Canada. Some of the information from this paper found its way into the first policy paper, entitled *Challenges and Choices*, and into the final National Museum Policy, promulgated in 1990. In order to complete the paper, I undertook a review of relevant literature on museum management and training, as well as a telephone survey of regional and provincial museum associations and major museums across Canada. What surprised both the policy planners in the Museum Branch and me was the number of times that board–management conflict was cited as the chief problem in the area of museum management in Canada. Over and over, directors of training courses for regional museum associations and museum workers noted misunderstandings between board and director as the chief cause of concern and the principal area that management development might address.

This concern on the part of the Canadian museum community suggested that an investigation into the form of museum governance and the relationships between boards and staff might be welcome. Was this problem between board and management the result of personality conflict, or was there an underlying structural problem?

This chapter is an inquiry into the common form of governance of the museum – the board of trustees – and its relationship to the museum administration, or more precisely, the director. In the late 1960s and early 1970s conflict between museum boards and directors was, if not exactly front-page news, certainly well publicized. The firing of directors at museums like The Museum of Modern Art in the United States and the 1972 dismissal in Canada of the Royal Ontario Museum's dynamic director, Peter Swann, occasioned public debate. Swann found that the complaint of unjust or precipitate firing was common enough among arts organization administrators so that he founded the Association for Cultural Executives, a support group for beleaguered executive directors and arts administrators.

The relations between boards and directors in the 1980s would seem to have been less dramatic, though incidences of conflict between boards and directors have continued.[1] Yet the evidence of interviews and a literature review conducted during a recent study of museum management in Canada[2] identifies the number one problem in museum management today as the relationship between museum directors and museum boards. Museum directors complain that board members are either uninformed and uninterested, or interfering and amateurish. Board members, for their part, feel that museum directors are unrealistic and unbusinesslike, with little or no management skill. Can it be that there are simply many combative personalities in the museum community? Or is there some problem inherent in the structure of the board/director relationship that causes difficulties?

The board of trustees is the pre-eminent form of museum governance. In Canada, it would appear from Statistics Canada surveys that over two-thirds of all museums and historic sites are governed by some kind of board.[3] Some of these institutions are governed by the boards of other non-profit institutions, like universities, community arts agencies, or academies. For the remaining third, the status is unclear. There are public museums that operate as line departments of government. Other museums have a quasi-private, quasi-public mode of governance. They are funded by a government agency, but they also have private boards. (The four Canadian national museums have recently been restructured to operate on this model.) Given its widespread acceptance, what purpose does the board serve for the museum? And why does it continue to be the favoured form of governance despite the management problems that appear to surround it?

THE NATURE OF TRUSTEESHIP

The museum board is a board of trustees. The idea of the trust is not a recent invention. Stephen Weil notes that the American private museum is a 'direct descendant of the English charitable use or trust' developed in the Court of Chancery in the fifteenth century.[4] Trusts were seen in Britain, the United States and Canada as being particularly suited to public purposes. They were ultimately responsible to the Crown or to the Attorney General, and they supplied a mechanism of accountability that permitted the 'creation of trust' in an organization outside the family or the state. A trust, like a museum collection, an orphanage or a hospital, benefits 'an indefinite group of others'.[5] Trustees were people one could trust to take care of something from which they did not directly benefit. Thus, the fiduciary duties of a trustee came to be defined as care and loyalty. Horace Walpole gives an engaging impression of the obligations of trusteeship at the founding of the British Museum in 1753:

> You will scarce guess how I employ my time; chiefly at present in the guardianship of embryos and cockleshells. Sir Hans Sloane is dead, and has made me one of the trustees to his museum, which is to be offered for twenty thousand pounds to the King, the Parliament, the royal academies of Petersburg, Berlin, Paris and Madrid. He valued it at four score thousand and so would anybody who loves hippopotamuses, sharks with one ear, and spiders as big as geese! . . . We are a charming wise set, all philosophers, botanists, antiquarians and mathematicians; and adjourned our first meeting, because Lord Macclesfield, our chairman, was engaged to a party for finding out the longitude![6]

Luckily for Britain, the trustees managed to care for the spiders and sharks until they could persuade Parliament to purchase the collection for the nation. Care thus translates for the museum trustee as an obligation to the collections and the institution. It concerns the proper management of assets, of 'caring for' the collection in trust, making it secure, insured, and providing for its management through the selection and review of competent staff. Loyalty concerns the protection of corporate property. For example, a board member cannot appropriate such property for his or her personal gain. A board member should not sell his or her services to the trust, and conflicts of interests (such as personal collecting) must be disclosed.

The law on the 'fiduciary duty' of board members is a developing legal area, perhaps in response to the proliferation of the non-profit form and its dominance of many sectors of contemporary life (health care, education, culture, social services). In recent years, some board members have actually been taken to court for breach of trust, for not fulfilling their fiduciary duties. The celebrated case of the Harding Museum in the United States, in which the state took the governing board of the museum to court for not fulfilling the duties of their trusteeship, is one such example.[7] Suits over breaches of liability are, however, rare, since confusion exists concerning to whom trustees are accountable. Theoretically, they are accountable to the highest authority, that is, in Canada, to the Crown, or to its delegate, the attorney general. In practice, there is little effective regulation of museum trustees.[8] As Peter Dobkin Hall points out, the board of the small non-profit organization or museum can be a law unto itself: 'To the extent that it was accountable to anyone, the nonprofessional management of these organizations was accountable only to the individuals who composed them.'[9]

PROBLEMS OF ACCOUNTABILITY

It is in precisely this area of accountability that some of the conflicts between trustees and administrators have arisen. Trusteeship is the governing form of the so-called 'third sector' (the non-profit sector) in North American life, but it is intimately related to the other two sectors (government and business). Trustees derive much of their power and authority from their relationship to the private sector and, in Canada, often from their positions in the public sector. Boards of trustees tend to be self-perpetuating, in that the nominating committees will select candidates who most resemble themselves. As a result, boards are often formed of interlocking relationships, of people who went to school together, belonged to the same club, or work in the same corporations.

A historical example. The years before the First World War were very fruitful for the establishment of Canadian museums, and it was a very busy period for a relatively small group of associates. The National Gallery was founded in 1913, but its establishment had long been advocated by Sir George Drummond, a Montreal art collector, and his close associate Sir Edmund Walker, both involved in banking. Walker was also associated with his old school friend, C. T. Currelly, in the founding of the Royal Ontario Museum. Walker and his friend Sir Edmund Osler (brother of the famous doctor) approached the provincial government to support the project and he also encouraged the support of friends like Mr and Mrs H. D. Warren. The Art Gallery of Ontario also opened its doors in 1913. Its founding members included Sir Edmund Walker, Sir Edmund Osler, Mrs H. D. Warren and Chester D. Massey. When Sir Edmund Walker relinquished his management of the Gallery's fund-raising campaign, he turned it over to the Honourable Vincent Massey, under whose guidance the Massey Report on Canadian culture was produced in 1951.

A few recent studies in the United States have sought to look at the characteristics of people who serve on the boards of contemporary non-profit organizations. A 1977 study (Nason, quoted in Middleton 1987) estimated that there were at that time some

100,000 to 130,000 members of non-profit boards in the United States. They were predominantly white male Protestants, in their fifties or sixties, wealthy, and involved in business or law. Only 19 per cent of all board members were women, and only 0.3 per cent were from other ethnic groups. A 1983 study (Kohn and Mortimer) of university trustees tended to confirm. these characteristics. Of those surveyed, 85 per cent were male, 95 per cent were white, 65 per cent were over 50, 90 per cent had BAs, and 75 per cent were in business or the professions.[10] Unfortunately, no comparable Canadian studies have been done, although a recent survey by a non-profit agency indicates that Canadian and American trustees, at least in the arts, share many demographic characteristics.[11]

The authority of board members, derived from their position in the 'outside' world, has been confronted by that of the trained museum professional, who finds authority within the tenets of the profession. The phenomenon of professionalization has entered into many aspects of community life in this century, not the least into the non-profit sector. Museum workers began to see themselves as a profession around the end of the nineteenth century. The journal of the British Museum Association was first published in 1890, and the American Association followed suit with its own journal in 1900. Although the Canadian Museums Association was not founded until 1947, Canadians appeared as frequent contributors to both journals and were present at annual conferences on both sides of the Atlantic.

Professional museum directors are accountable not only to a board, but also to the professional community of which they are a part. This community imposes its own standards and ideology on its members, which they in turn carry into their work. The loyalty of the professional to the tenets of his or her profession are often central to the individual, and threat to this set of principles is not taken lightly. This external standard requires accountability, which may at times conflict with the equally strongly held ideas of the board members.

Prior to the entry of professionals into the museums, a collection of artefacts, specimens or paintings was very much the creature of its board. Often the collection had been brought together by a single individual or a small group and reflected their tastes and interests. The desire of the director to bring order into what is perceived as chaos can result in conflict over the interpretation and content of collections. The desire of a director to orient the museum to the goals valued by the profession may move the museum in directions unsanctioned by the trustees. For example, the recent concern for veracity by historians in the portrayal of violence and class conflict in the past is not always welcomed by the board members of history museums and historic sites, whose desire to view a nostalgic past that reinforces their present values is in direct conflict with 'professional' truth. Dr Jeanne Canizzo documents the way in which a museum board was remade by the government, so that the National Barbados Museum might more accurately reflect the history of all classes in Barbadian society.[12]

Canizzo's description of the situation in Barbados highlights the role of a third party that often enters into the relationship between board and director in Canada and the United States – government. Various levels of government in Canada provide almost three-quarters of all museum funding,[13] and they naturally demand some right to call a tune. Where the museum is not a line department, this means working through the boards. In return for financial support, the Ontario Government, for example, appoints members to the boards of the largest museums – the Royal Ontario Museum, the Art Gallery of Ontario, the Ontario Science Centre, Science North in Sudbury and the McMichael Canadian Collection in Kleinburg. Government-appointed representatives account for eleven out of seventeen board members on the McMichael board. Governments also have cultural objectives, and there are certain areas, like language rights and accessibility, in which they impose their will on the museums.

Government priorities may act to reinforce board priorities, or they may work to the ends of the professional community. Government granting agencies tend to be concerned with standards of operation and maintenance, often set in concert with the professional community. These can have a direct impact on the boards and the wishes of board members. At one medium-sized Canadian institution, board members have been delighted to borrow pieces of the collection to display at various non-museum functions, a practice that is taboo according to professional standards. (The agency has since developed a conservation policy in consultation with the regional museum association.)

There is another kind of accountability that has occasioned much frustration between boards and directors. Within the museum itself, the director is held accountable for the good management of the institution. Performance is not as easily measured in the museum as it is in the corporate world, where the bottom line is the clear signal of success or failure. For some board members, used to the hard data of the corporate sector, the nebulousness of the museum's goals and the intangibility of its products is unnerving. In addition, the tendency of service institutions like museums to make ends meet only with the greatest difficulty (and sometimes not at all) has been noted by W. J. Baumol.

He described, in his now classic 1957 article on the performing arts, how 'the objectives of the typical non-profit organization are by their very nature designed to keep it constantly on the brink of financial catastrophe.' Their goals can never be realized, for new projects come to replace old as audience demand changes or increases.[15] And museums, like other service agencies, find it difficult to decrease the level of service, since their rationale is based on providing programmes to all comers. The fact that many museums continue to privilege curatorial knowledge above business administration skills also reinforces the tendency of museum directors to devote more energy to the realization of museum objectives than to maintaining a strictly balanced budget. Not only are museum services in more demand, but they are also becoming increasingly expensive to provide; and to continue the level of the service the community expects, some museums have begun, like their sisters in the performing arts, to run deficits. In 1981–2, none of the thirty-one galleries surveyed by the Ontario Association of Galleries (OAAG) had a deficit. Five years later, the deficit among these galleries was over $330,000.[16]

In this area of fiscal accountability and improved management, the boards are often supported by government policy. Like recent American administrations, the conservative Mulroney government in Canada believes that museums can garner more support from their clientele if the government plays a less prominent role in funding. The federal government has urged, through its studies and policy statements, that museum directors pull up their bootstraps and do a better job at raising funds. One of the recommendations of the Bovey Commission on Funding of the Arts in Canada was that museums institute admission fees. While many museums already do charge admission, for others, charging visitors is an admission of despair. The British tradition (before Mrs Thatcher) was that museums were public institutions, like libraries, established for the common good.

The current catch-phrase, however, is 'user-pay', to which the Bovey Commission noted a 'unanimous and negative' response from the arts community.[17] Members of the Bovey Commission tended to represent, however, not the professional arts community but the community from which trustees spring. The user-pay issue has tended to polarize feelings among interest groups. Whereas user-pay makes sense to many people with a business or economics background, it is anathema to many other people who see a museum, like a library, as a public good. The artists' community was particularly vocal on this point. Greg Curnoe, a London, Ontario artist, speaking to 'The Cultural Imperative' conference, saw the user-pay concept as a reflection of the ideologies held by board members. He described board members as representative of 'middle management people and administrators – staunch believers in user-pay theories, otherwise known as double taxation'.[18]

This is not to say that all museum directors object to admission fees and are without the management skills demanded by the board. Many are highly trained administrators, and their business skills – combined with professional qualifications – make them powerful managers. It is this struggle for power within the museum that also adds to the sources of tension for museum boards and directors. Traditionally, it has been supposed that the board is responsible for setting institutional policy and evaluation goals. It is also seen to be in charge of fund raising. Martha Cohen, president of the Calgary Centre for the Performing Arts, defined the role of the Board at a 1986 conference on arts management:

> The role of the board member in a cultural institution is practically the same as for all other institutions. To formulate policies under which your management team is expected to operate. To keep a close eye on the finances of the organization. To be the body which tries to raise most of the funds to cover the operational deficits each year. And to be an extra PR interpreter to the general community, with regard to the work of your organization. And to assist in recruiting volunteers required for those efforts.[19]

The role of the director is assumed to be implementation of the policies defined by the board and management of the organization and operation of the institution. Few studies have been conducted on the functioning of boards and management in museums and other non-profit organizations, but it would appear that in fact this description represents a normative formulation of responsibilities. A 1977 US study (Fenn, quoted in Middleton 1987) indicated that policy is rarely a priority of boards, and few were concerned with long-term institutional strategy; rather, board members responded to the policy suggestions of professional management.[20] While some boards are concerned with fund-raising, others rely on professional staff to prepare grant applications to government and foundation sources or hire a development officer to seek out corporate funding opportunities. In her study of non-profit boards, Melissa Middleton points out that, despite the assumption that the relationship between board and director is a partnership based on mutual trust and effective communication, it is an essentially paradoxical situation. The board has final authority but must rely on the director for information and for policy development. The board has the power to hire and fire the director, yet the director must depend on the board for certain crucial external functions.[21]

THE PRESSURE OF CLIENTELE

The division of power within the museum and the problems of accountability can lead to a situation fraught with tensions between boards and directors. These tensions can be exacerbated by demands from community groups that are foreign to the interests of the board or downright threatening. The 'democratization' of museums espoused in the 1980s by both Canadian and American museum professionals and funding agencies is not necessarily welcome at the board level. One museum director is quoted in *Museum News* as saying that 'it is possible that the greater democratization of our museums has something to do with the waning enthusiasm of a number of former donors. In the past some wealthy people have, consciously or not, thought of the museum as a kind of aesthetic country club'.[22] The 'country club' mentality and the exclusivity it creates is now under siege in many communities.

Democratization implies an opening of the museum to diverse audiences and a sensitivity to the demands of what have been marginal audiences. Thus, blacks and Hispanics in the United States, ethnic minorities and native peoples, feminists and gay liberation advocates have begun to demand that the museum represent their art, voices and material history. Many museum professionals, particularly those educated in the 'new' social history that privileges the poor and the downtrodden, have responded with passion in creating exhibitions and programmes reflecting the needs and interests of these communities.

This new diversity of audience and programmes appears not, however, to be reflected to the same degree in museum board membership. Paul DiMaggio and other scholars have theorized on the formation of 'cultural class', a social elite that seeks hegemonic control through control of the institutions of culture. DiMaggio describes the brahmins of nineteenth-century Boston, who controlled the museum and the symphony, as a 'densely connected self-conscious social group, intensely unified by multiple ties among its members based in kinship, commerce, club life, and participation in a wide range of philanthropic associations'.[23] The brahmins wanted to ensure that the kind of culture of which they approved was not at the mercy of the waves of immigrants – particularly the Irish – then inundating Boston.

Museum board members, as has been noted in surveys, reflect the characteristics of the dominant elite of North American society – white, male and well-educated. Because of the manner in which they elect their successors, boards tend to emerge as cohesive units, sharing similar views on a number of topics. The very cohesiveness of their associations may make them unwilling or perhaps unable to respond to changes in the social and cultural environment. The issues that agitate certain more marginal sectors of the community, from which they are isolated by social position and interest, can seem like a ripple from a distant storm. Unlike politicians, who must make periodic appeals to an electorate, trustees are not required to appease the demands of the vocal minorities in an effort to keep their seats at the board table. While many museum directors may share the beliefs and interests of their boards as far as the social role of the museum is concerned, the increasing interest by the profession in serving non-traditional audiences may cause additional tension in the relationship between board and director.[24]

CONCLUSION

Much more work needs to be done, but one might be able to draw some very tentative conclusions on the nature of at least some of the disputes between museum boards and directors. Much of the tension revolves around different perspectives. Volunteer boards and professional managers tend to define the goals of the museum differently and – given the fact that there would appear to exist no canon law for museum management relations – the disparate views are often unresolved.

This inquiry began with wondering why boards of trustees constituted the dominant form of museum governance. The persistence of board governance is in part a result of historical prejudice, and in part, I think, a recognition of social necessity. Some would abolish boards altogether, following Thorstein Veblen's 1918 condemnation:

Indeed, except for a stubborn prejudice to the contrary, the fact should readily be seen that the boards are of no material use whatsoever: their sole effective function being to interfere with the management in matters that are not of the nature of business and that lie outside their competence and outside the range of their habitual interests.[25]

But there is an argument for their retention, which Middleton describes as their 'boundary spanning and control' function,[26] and Hall sees as their 'legitimation' role. For example, a board member might answer criticism of the institution without involving the whole organization. Board members can have valuable linkages to external groups. And a board can act as a buffer against and a lobby with government. A board can also serve as a curb on the passions of the professionals. Hall suggests that even in the nineteenth century, the lay board of trustees was considered as a 'rein on the tendency of institutions to go their own way'.[27] This need still exists. By its very nature, professionalization of museums tends to homogenization of purpose and story, something that a locally representative board will not or should not allow. The nature of board representation, however, is due for an overhaul, and the presence of government appointees, at least in Canada, may begin the reform. The conflicts between boards and directors that surfaced in the late 1960s are as yet unresolved. Their resolution may depend on factors beyond the control of either trustees or museum professionals – the voice of the consumer and the directives of government.

This article first appeared in Curator 34(4) (1991), pp. 291–303.

NOTES

1 Dr T. Cuyler Young, personal communication.
2 Dickenson 1988.
3 Statistics Canada (1986–7) *Survey of Heritage Institutions*, Statistics Canada: Ottawa.
4 Stephen Weil, 'Breaches of trust, remedies an standards', in Weil 1983.
5 Hall 1982.
6 Horace Walpole, in a letter to Sir Horace Mann, 14 February 1753, quoted in Atlick 1978: 25.
7 Boyd 1984.
8 Weil, op. cit.
9 P. D. Hall, 'Abandoning the rhetoric of Independence: reflections on the nonprofit sector in the post-liberal era', in Ostrander and Langdon 1987.
10 Middleton 1987.
11 Sarah Iley, unpublished personal communication regarding Council for Business and the Arts 1988 Survey of Board Members.
12 Canizzo, J. (1987) 'How sweet it is: cultural politics in Barbados', *MUSE*, Winter. Christine Miller-Marti, writing in the Summer 1987 edition of *MUSE*, examines the way in which the members of the board of a local history museum enshrine a 'history' which reflects their interests and their need for reinforcing local identity. (Miller-Marti, C. (1987) 'Local history museums and the creation of the "Past"', *MUSE*, Summer.)
13 Department of Communications (1989) *Facts about Canadian Museums*, Ottawa: Department of Communications.
14 For example, an exhibition funded by an agency of the federal government in Canada, such as Museum Assistance Programs, must have both French and English text. In order to receive an operating grant from the Government of Ontario, a community museum must meet a series of standards set by the Heritage Branch of the Ministry of Culture and Communications.
15 Baumol, W. J. 'Economics of the performing arts', in Blaug 1976: 218–25.
16 Ontario Association of Art Galleries (1987), unpublished study.
17 Task Force on Funding the Arts (1986) *Funding the Arts in Canada to the Year 2000*, Ottawa: TFFA: 63.
18 Association of Cultural Executives 1986.
19 Ibid.: 18.
20 Middleton, op. cit.

21 Ibid.
22 Shestack 1978.
23 Paul DiMaggio, 'Cultural entrepreneurship in nineteenth-century Boston', in DiMaggio 1986: 55.
24 See the recent spate of special issues of museum journals on such issues as museums and cultural diversity (*Journal of Education in Museums*, September 1987, *Museum News*, March/April 1989), women and museums (*Museum News*, July/August 1990), native people (*MUSE*, fall 1988).
25 Quoted in Middleton, op. cit.: 142.
26 Ibid.: 145.
27 Hall, op. cit.: 100.

REFERENCES

Altick, R. (1978) *The Shows of London*, Cambridge, MA: Belknap Press, Harvard University.
Association of Cultural Executives (1986) *The Cultural Imperative: Creating New Management for the Arts*, Toronto: ACE.
Blaug, M. (ed.) (1976) *Economics of the Arts*, London: Martin Robinson.
Borst, D. and Montana, P. J. (eds) (1977) *Managing Nonprofit Organizations*, New York, NY: AMA-COM (American Management Association).
Boyd, W. L. (1984) 'The case of the Harding Museum: what have we finally learned about trustee liability', in *ALIABA Course of Study Materials, Legal Problems of Museum Administration*, Philadelphia, PA: ALIABA.
Dickenson, V. (1988) *Management Development for Canadian Museums. Background Paper for Museum Policy Working Group*, Ottawa: Department of Communications.
DiMaggio, P. (ed.) (1986) *Nonprofit Enterprise in the Arts: Studies in Mission and Constraint*, New York and Oxford: Oxford University Press.
Evans, J. T. (1982) 'Third sector management: the museum in the age of introspection – survival and redefinition for the 1980s', *Public Administration Review*, September/October.
Hall, P. D. (1982) *The Organization of American Culture, 1700–1900: Private Institutions, Elites, and the Origins of American Nationality*, New York, NY: New York University Press.
Hendon, W. S., Shanahan, J. L. and MacDonald, A. J. (eds) (1980) *Economic Policy for the Arts*, Cambridge, MA: Abt Books.
McDougall, W. J. (ed.) (n.d.) *The Role of the Voluntary Trustee*, London, Ontario.
McLaughlin, C. P. (1986) *The Management of Nonprofit Organizations*, New York, NY: Wiley.
Middleton, M. (1987) 'Nonprofit boards of directors: beyond the governance function', in Powell, W. J. (ed.) *The Nonprofit Sector. A Research Handbook*, New Haven, CT: Yale University Press.
Ostrander, S. A. and Langton, S. (eds.) (1987) *Shifting the Debate: Public/Private Sector Relations in the Modern Welfare State*, New Brunswick, NJ: Transaction Books.
Powell, W. (ed.) (1987) *The Nonprofit Sector. A Research Handbook*, New Haven, CT: Yale University Press.
Rose-Ackerman, S. (ed.) (1986) *The Economics of Nonprofit Institutions: Studies in Structure and Policy*, Oxford and New York: Oxford University Press.
Shestack, A. (1978) 'The director: scholar, businessman, educator and lobbyist', *Museum News* 57(2).
Weil, S. E. (1983) *Beauty and the Beasts. On Museums, Art, the Law and the Market*, Washington, DC: Smithsonian Institution.
Zuzanek, J. (ed.) (1979) 'Social research and cultural policy', *Monographs in Leisure and Cultural Development, Monograph 1*, Waterloo, Ontario: OTIUM Publications.

Whatever the French experience, up until the 1980s, free admission was the rule at the great public museums and particularly at the national museums of Britain and North America. In the case of the Smithsonian, charging an admission fee is explicitly prohibited by legislation. In Canada, entrance to the four national museums and their branches was free from their foundation in the mid-nineteenth century up until 1988, when – in a manner very similar to their British counterparts – the national institutions began a programme of either voluntary or compulsory admission fees. In Britain, both the National Gallery and the British Museum, which were not charging entrance fees in 1989, were eloquent in defence of the principle of free admission. The National Gallery in London asserted that 'succeeding generations of Trustees have held free admission to be central to the fulfilment of the principal aim for which the Gallery was set up' (House of Commons 1989: 1). The British Museum replied to the inquiries of the parliamentary committee in a note that quoted the words of Sir Frederic Kenyon to another such committee sixty years previously:

> The question at issue is a very simple one. Is it desired to encourage the use of the museum or is it not? There is not the smallest doubt that the imposition of fees discourages attendances. . . . The question, therefore, simply is whether it is worthwhile to exclude the public (and especially, of course, the poorer members of the public) for the sake of the pecuniary return to be expected from fees.
>
> (House of Commons 1989: 50)

The appearance of admission charges at the national museums and galleries of Britain and Canada between 1984 and the present has gone against a long tradition of public policy and public expectations. The French rationale, whether sympathetic or not, is based on a strategic policy perspective. The change in British and Canadian policy, however, appears, as far as can be determined, to have been based on an economic rationale. This being the case, it is important to examine the economic basis for the decision to charge and to understand the complex relationship between the notions of revenue generation and museum mandate.

THE SEARCH FOR REVENUE

When a museum is faced with a major budget cut, as Greenwich was in 1984, there are only two alternatives. The first is to tighten the belt, and the second is to raise revenue to cover costs. The belt can only be pulled as tight as the museum's mandate will allow, and the museum mandate is intimately tied to its collection. The Royal Ontario Museum in Toronto, for example, has chiselled into stone on its façade these words: 'The works of man and the products of nature through all the ages.' A large mandate. In order to meet its mandate and increase its assets and prestige and the prestige of the staff, the collections must grow.

There is an obvious cost in acquisition, and the expenditures of art museums on Old Masters and contemporary artists are front-page news. Many acquisitions do not, however, require an expenditure of funds from the acquisition budget, coming instead as donations and bequests or as the results of field collection by museum staff. These have, nevertheless, a substantial price tag. The failure of museums to recognize the costs of assembling great collections has had major consequences for their operation. Their collections are always growing, but the space in which to display them often remains constant. They are forced to either build or rent new storage or new display space. Museum-quality storage demands complete environmental control, and museum-quality display is routinely costed at $200 to $300 per square foot.

Museums are thus asset-rich but very often revenue-poor, and raising revenues is neither simple nor straightforward. Martin Feldstein has pointed out in a recent article on American art museums that, as non-profit institutions, museums 'lack both the ability to raise financial resources in the ways that profit-making businesses can and the substantial public funding of government activities' (Feldstein 1991a: 53). An obvious means of raising revenue – liquidation of assets – is prohibited by the institutional mandate. For example, a museum's collection may be valued at many millions of dollars; and, in the case of some art museums, the sale of a single painting might fund the museum's entire annual operation. Although museums do occasionally de-accession works from the permanent collection, the sale of assets to raise capital or operating dollars is counter to the stated and accepted purposes of the institution – the collection and preservation of material heritage for future generations. Thus, museums must seek other sources of revenue, most of which are influenced by the international economic climate and market forces.

THE SOURCES OF REVENUE

Perhaps in recognition of this public mandate, in Britain, Europe and Canada, the greatest support for museum operation is derived from government. In Canada, a 1991 survey of forty-five public museums by the Council for Business and the Arts revealed that the percentage of revenue derived from government grants was almost 84 per cent. For provincial and national museums, the percentage of government-derived revenue was even higher. In Britain, the 1989–90 operating revenues of the national museums were funded primarily by government grants, with the percentage of grants to operating revenues in a similar range to the Canadian. In the United States, the Smithsonian Institution also receives over 80 per cent of its funding from the federal government, and many smaller museums receive substantial funding from other levels of government. For many non-government museums in the United States, however, a major source of revenue is interest from endowments, with varying levels of support coming from federal, state and city governments.

In recent years, all museums have turned to affiliate enterprises to raise revenue. Some museums have set up trading companies to deal in things such as museum reproductions, publications, videos, etc. Retail operations, such as shops and mail order, parking fees, rental of space for non-museum functions, fees for services (photographic, reproduction fees, lecture tours, acoustiguide rentals, etc.), and food services account for almost 9 per cent of public museum revenues in Canada. A 1988 survey of 155 large art museums in the United States showed that they earn anywhere from one-fifth to one-quarter of their revenues from these sources. Membership, which might be likened to shareholding, with the profits distributed in the form of 'psychic income' and benefits (free admission, discounts on merchandise, etc.), can also contribute substantially to net revenues. At the Museum of Science in Boston, membership fees account for $2 million in annual revenues, approximately 10 per cent of the museum's annual operating budget in 1991–2. Museums also rely on gifts and donations and the returns from fund-raising for special projects.

THE DECISION TO CHARGE AT THE DOOR

Once a museum has exploited all sources of earned revenues, received the largest grants it can muster from all levels of government, and opportuned all possible donors and benefactors, and yet still shows an operating deficit, there is only one other untapped source – the visitor. There are, however, a number of objections often raised to pricing a public good such as a museum. These include the idea of the 'merit good', the 'distributional' argument, the 'intergenerational' argument and the pragmatic argument.

Museums might be considered a merit good, like education, which is not always appreciated by the market, but which society as a whole feels it is important to support. The Smithsonian Institution has suggested a politically astute variation on the merit-good argument for retaining free admission. As one senior official put it, when visitors walk freely into one of the Smithsonian museums, they know that 'something is working in their favor', that their tax dollars have not all gone for nought. In February 1993, the Smithsonian installed donation boxes, but Secretary Robert McAdam insisted that 'this should not be regarded as getting our foot in the door for paid admissions. The sense is strong that the Smithsonian is an institution for all the people.' The distribution objection – voiced by McAdam – considers that if a good is priced, unequal access will result. Museums are also considered in the sense of a trust for future generations. Since our great-grandchildren cannot express their preference for the preservation of certain works of art or objects, then we must be willing to finance intergenerational subsidization. Finally, there is the rather prosaic argument of cost of administration. It may simply cost more than it's worth to charge people at the door. The National Gallery of Canada announced at the beginning of October 1992 that it was rescinding admission fees for the months of December, January, and February. Revenues from admissions during the same period the previous year had been so minimal that the cost of collecting the admission charge was prohibitive. (In February 1993, the gallery extended free admission for the month of March.)

The theory of marginal costs has also been cited by some authors to support free admission to museums. It suggests that a museum may as well be free since the fixed costs are so high and the variable costs so low that the costs for each additional visitor are minimal. Despite these many objections to charging, the spectre of diminishing revenues and deteriorating exhibits appears to make admission charges, as Neil Cossons put it, the lesser of two evils. But is an admission charge the solution to a museum's revenue gap? How much can a public museum expect the visitor to pay, and what are the trade-offs of the admission charge for what has been a free good?

The revenue derived from visitor admissions is highly variable, dependent on number of visitors, price of admission, attractiveness of the 'product', and competition in the market.[1] In some cases, the revenue derived from admission is essential to the operation of the institution. This is particularly the case with very popular institutions such as science centres, zoos and aquariums. The Museum of Science (Boston), for example, earned 36 per cent of its 1991–2 operating revenues from admission charges on its 1.5 million visitors. The admission charges follow a variable pricing policy common to museums, with the top charge for adults ($6.50) and the lowest for seniors and children ($4.50), with students in the middle ($5.00). The Vancouver Public Aquarium, with 800,000 visitors in 1991, earned almost two-thirds (65 per cent) of its operating costs from admission revenue. In Britain, museum heritage sites like Ironbridge and Beamish have received over three-quarters of their revenues from the gate. (One informant suggested that revenue from visitor admissions only becomes significant if visitation is in the one-million-visitors range.)

By contrast, the Council for Business and the Arts in Canada notes that, for the ninety Canadian museums and public art galleries in their survey, 'entrance fees' accounted for under 4 per cent of revenues.

For example, at the Canadian Museum of Civilization in Hull, Quebec, which is the country's largest history and ethnographic museum, admission revenues were just under 2 per cent of operating costs. The $1.4 million earned from the two museum sites it operates can only be seen as a drop in the bucket of a $46-million annual budget. The Royal Ontario Museum, the largest museum in Canada, earns just 5.7 per cent of its $26-million annual operating budget from admissions. At the Royal British Columbia Museum (which is provincially supported), admissions are far higher, at 17 per cent of operating, but the imposition of admission fees left a bitter taste in the mouth of local residents. (In 1987, 11,000 people signed a petition against the imposition of admission fees by the provincial government.) At the National Museum of Science and Technology and the National Aviation Museum, admission revenues are under 3 per cent of operating. The case is little different in the United States. Martin Feldstein suggests that only about 5 per cent of the total income of the 150 largest art museums comes from admissions revenue (Feldstein 1991a: 54). In Britain, the Victoria and Albert Museum, which has a voluntary admissions programme, received approximately 5.6 per cent from admissions in 1988–9, while the National Maritime Museum earned half of all non-public income from admissions. (The non-public income represented 40 per cent of all operating costs in 1988–9.) For the public museums, even those revenues earned are not necessarily theirs to keep. The Ontario Science Centre, for example, which recorded 887,000 visits in 1991–2, turned over its $2.5 million admissions revenue to the provincial government, its chief funder.

With the exception of the few extremely popular museums, science centres, zoos and historic sites, the revenue contributed by the visitor is not a substantial portion of museum earnings. Why are revenues so low? Is there insufficient demand? Or is the product priced too low? It is important first to understand how a museum goes about setting a price for the public use of the museum exhibits. For-profit enterprises generally use a number of techniques to set prices; these include cost-plus, 'follow the leader', product analysis and contribution targets. Conversations with museum staff and review of a report prepared in 1988 for the National Museums of Canada Corporation made it obvious that museums are generally using the modified follow-the-leader technique.

Those responsible for setting a museum's admission policy scan the environment in which they believe the museum operates. In Canada at the present time – and one suspects in both Britain and the United States – museums are classified as heritage attractions and perceived to be in competition with other 'attractions'. These other attractions range from theme parks, such as Canada's Wonderland near Toronto or Epcot Centre, to the cinema. (As one ticket seller at the Royal Ontario Museum said when queried about the price of admission: 'It's cheaper than the movies!') The price should reflect, the authors of the 1988 study said, 'fair market value', taking into consideration the difference in each museum's 'state of development of their public facilities and the characteristics of their audiences' (McFetridge 1988: 2). Thus museums rarely charge as much as a bona fide theme park, recognizing that the state of their public amenities will not allow them to compete successfully in that market.

Museum admission charges are, by many estimates, relatively low. The adult visitor will pay anywhere from $2 to $8 for a visit, which at larger museums generally lasts between one and two hours, and in many instances under one hour. Museums also recognize a fair amount of price variability in their charges. Harking back to their mandates and original missions, museums often institute discounted prices for children, senior citizens and students. They also often provide free days so that those visitors who might be unable to visit for economic reasons have an opportunity to view the collections.

Why are prices so low? As has already been noted, many museum managers are reluctant to abandon completely the idea of free public access, as shown by the variable pricing and the recent statement by the Secretary of the Smithsonian, reaffirming that the museum is an 'institution for all the people'. Price elasticity is also limited. While people may be willing to pay considerable sums for a theme-park experience, they will not pay similar amounts for a more limited museum experience. Though many larger museums see themselves as entering into the theme-park or heritage-attraction arena, few can offer the level of amenities provided by most theme parks. Given that the average museum visit lasts sixty to ninety minutes, or even less, it is obvious that without substantial changes, most museums cannot compete in this area. Cross-elasticity may also be a factor. For some potential visitors, museums may be indistinguishable, as studies undertaken at heritage sites in Wales suggest (Prentice 1988). Unless a museum can claim a highly differentiated or superior product, the 'paying punter' will simply choose the less expensive museum option.

THE EFFECT OF CHARGING ON DEMAND

Even with these modest charges, a free museum that initiates a charge feels immediate effects. The first is likely to be reduced attendance. Evidence from a number of sources points to a drop of approximately 20 per cent (in some cases as high as one-third) in attendance when museums begin to charge. Advocates of charging respond that pre-charging counts were inaccurate and inflated, but studies at the Victoria and Albert Museum and at the Science Museum in London suggest that there are actual reductions. Since museum visits are a non-essential for most people, charges do diminish the number of visits. Conversely, the recent experience at the National Gallery of Canada illustrates the effect of rescinding admission charges. From December through March, 1992–3, visitation to the gallery increased between 54 per cent and 74 per cent over the previous year (see Table 9.1). When charges were reinstituted in April, attendance fell off by 40 per cent from the previous months.

The reductions noted in attendance at the Victoria and Albert Museum and the Science Museum in London appear to be greatest among local residents and young people, which would suggest that drop-in traffic has been reduced and that charges affected those with the least discretionary income (the young). At present, numerous studies in the United Kingdom and in the United States show that what the British called the SMC (salaried middle class) and what in North America is called the professional/managerial group are already over-represented among museum visitors. Admission prices further discourage attendance by those at lower-income levels. The second result of charging, then, is likely to be a change in the distributional benefit of museums.

Table 9.1 Attendance statistics, the National Gallery of Canada

Year	December	January	February	March	April
1991–2	17,422	17,313	21,939	24,232	26,140
1992–3	26,878	30,170	35,555	39,378	23,550
% change	+54%	+74%	+62%	+63%	–10%

Finally, though the assertion has not been tested, the National Gallery in London has also argued strongly that charging would adversely affect both revenues from ancillary operations, such as the restaurant and the shop, and that donations to the collection and sponsorships would be substantially reduced. In Ottawa, the National Gallery of Canada experienced a substantial increase in revenues from shop, food services and parking during its period of free admission. In the case of donations, the National Gallery in London suggested that the imposition of a charge would constitute a betrayal of past donors, a sort of variation on the inter-generational argument.

CHARGING AT THE NATIONAL MUSEUMS

Given the facts that in most cases – and particularly in the case of national museums – the revenues collected through entrance fees are minimal and pricing of a free good leaves the institution open to serious criticism, why would the museum trustees agree to charge the visitor for viewing his or her heritage? At the most simplistic level, the answer seems to be that making the users pay is seen to be a good thing, a form of fiscal responsibility. The Treasury Board of Canada defines user fees in the following manner:

> User fees involve the recovery of a fair share of the cost of providing goods and services from those who receive a direct benefit from them. They are not another form of taxation; they actually increase the equity of the revenue system by shifting some of the burden away from general taxation borne by the taxpayer to those individuals who derive a clear benefit from specific government activities.
>
> (Treasury Board 1992: 1)

In theory, user pay abrogates the merit-good argument by assuming that there is no divergence between welfare and preference. In practice, it leaves museum managers puzzling as to which of their users should pay most. In the case of a national or provincial institution supported primarily by public subsidy, one might consider that those who benefit most from the facility are those who live close to it. If the museum is of more use to the local resident than to the visitor from out of town, then the local visitor should pay for that service. Contrarily, it is obvious that tourists are the mainstay of many museums. The visitor from out of the country, however, has not subsidized the museum through taxes; therefore, that visitor should also pay for use. The 'user-pay' notion that has become a cornerstone of conservative regimes in Europe and North America derives its authority from its connection with the market economy. What consumers want, consumers will pay for; and what they do not want, they should not be forced into supporting through public subsidy. In effect, it turns the merit-good argument on its head by assuming that there is no divergence between welfare and preference.

The assumption that society's interests are coincident with the interests of the market underlies much of the current thinking about public support for social institutions. It is assumed that the free market is basically a democratic institution that allows the individual the widest possible choice. Museums are being asked to account for their limited share of the market. Visitor and participation-rate studies have shown that museums have a fairly limited clientele. Museums have often been characterized (DiMaggio 1986; Merriman 1991) as instruments of social and cultural hegemony, supporting the interests of an elite; and support for museums as a free good is thus characterized as rent seeking, to serve the ends of members of limited special-interest groups.

111

William Grampp in his provocative 1989 study, *Pricing the Priceless*, suggests that if museums were serious about taking their chances in the market, they would drastically revise their pricing policies in line with the principles of marginal cost pricing:

> This ... means an organization – in order to do the best it can with what it has, that is, in order to operate efficiently – should engage in an amount of activity such that if it did more the additional cost would be greater than the additional activity was worth. This never can be done literally, but an organization can compare the cost and the income from different amounts of activity and choose the amount which yields the highest return.
>
> (Grampp 1989: 194)

Grampp goes on to suggest: (1) that museums should limit the amount they collect so that a reasonable portion can be exhibited; (2) change the hours of operation and the pricing structure to encourage attendance; and (3) make an effort to understand that non-profit-making need not mean unprofitable.

If museums were truly to follow Grampp's advice or the tenets of user-pay, could they charge the users anywhere near the cost of the service? To fund the Canadian Museum of Civilization from visitor revenues, for example, would require that for each visit, the 'paying punter' (as T. P. Besterman calls the visitor) would be required to lay out something in the order of $33 net. A family of four, then, might be required to spend over $130 for tickets to visit the museum.

While these figures are not unrealistic for Epcot Centre or Walt Disney World, they are shocking in the context of the museum. There has been considerable interest in the last decade in sprucing up the museums, making them into mini-Disneys – attractive, entertaining and profitable. Unfortunately or not, the mandate and mission of the museum in society is not primarily that of entertainment. A family of four required to pay over $100 would be unlikely to be able or willing to come more than once per year, no matter how great the collection or special the exhibition. Certainly this kind of cost would abrogate the educational function of the museum, which many would see as its most important social contribution.

Finally, let us return to the case of the national museum. Is user pay an adequate justification for admission charges at these public institutions? Can the users, the 'paying punters', ever hope to bear even a reasonable amount of the costs? And why must the cost per visitor be so high? Is it simple inefficiency? bureaucratization? waste? There is very likely an element of all three in the budget of every institution, but the museum by definition discharges a special mandate. Whether it does it for well or for ill, whether it is efficient or negligent, the museum has been charged by society with the collection and preservation of material heritage. In the eighteenth century, people considered it important to preserve the material remnants of the past, the artefacts of foreign peoples and the products of nature in collections for public study. The decision to subsidize these collections with public funds was hotly debated in the Houses of Parliament, when the members accepted Hans Sloane's gift to the British people, and in the Congress and Senate, when James Smithson's legacy provided the foundation of the Smithsonian Institution.

The costs of acquisition, preservation and public display are high. To place the simplest of collections on public view requires large expenditures of time and dollars. Huszar and Seckler pointed out, in a 1974 article on the institution of admission fees at the California Academy of Sciences, that 'over a broad range of attendance levels, the costs of operating the museum are relatively constant. This means that the marginal costs to the museum are approximately zero, whether many or only few visit it' (Huszar and Seckler 1974: 68). Few museums have made the calculations to determine the marginal costs of public accessibility. In many respects, it would be a futile exercise. As Huszar and Seckler pointed out almost twenty years ago, 'the social marginal benefit curve – the amount society is willing to subsidize museum attendance – is ultimately a political question. . . . Museum officials may be forced into socially and economically inefficient policies simply in order to obtain a cash flow sufficient to keep their facility operating' (Huszar and Seckler 1974: 369).

We who are the curators and directors of contemporary public museums are heirs to an institution whose social benefits were largely defined in the Victorian era. Does the museum experience still offer the same social value it once did? Is it still worthwhile to maintain large collections of art or artefacts available for research and public inspection? Is the public museum as necessary to a city or town as the public library or the public park? It has been argued that a free library card is a right of citizenship. Can we argue that free admission to our museums is an equally important right for all citizens, or is the museum of marginal importance to the majority, a resource to be used exclusively by the people who can appreciate and support it?[2]

This article first appeared in Curator *36(3) (1993), pp. 220–34. Victoria Dickenson is currently Director of Public Programmes at the National Aviation Museum in Ottawa.*

NOTES

1 The calculation of the proportion of operating costs represented by visitor admissions can be both simple and very complex. The percentages given above are based on a very simple comparison of net revenues against total operating; that is, salaries and 'O and M' (operations and maintenance). They are, and can be, only approximate, since individual institutions include varying items under O and M. As a general rule, however, operating costs include the fixed or non-discretionary cost of operation, such as rent, heat, light, paper, pencils, etc., as well as the costs of researching and maintaining collections and preparing and delivering programmes. In a more complex calculation, one might calculate net revenues against only the discretionary public programme expenditures of the museum, such as the exhibition and education programmes. I would contend, however, that all discretionary and non-discretionary costs must be included in the comparison, since all contribute to the development of the public face and public perception of the museum.

2 The views expressed here are the author's, not necessarily those of the National Museum of Science and Technology Corporation. Information for this paper was derived from two principal sources: a review of literature including the records of parliamentary inquiries, government policy documents and museum surveys, and a structured telephone interview with financial officers in ten major Canadian and American museums having diverse policies on admission fees.

REFERENCES

American Museum of National History (1874) *Annual Report*, New York, NY: AMNH.
Bazin, G. (1967) *The Museum Age*, New York, NY: Universe Books.
Besterman, T. P. (1985) 'Charging and restriction of access', *Museum News* 64(5): 4–5.
Cossons, N. (1985) 'The Greenwich experiment', *Museum News* 64(4): 2–3.
Council for Business and the Arts in Canada (1991) *Annual CBAC Survey of Public Museums and Art Galleries: Survey Analysis*, Toronto, Ont.: CBAC.
DiMaggio, P. (ed.) (1986) *Nonprofit Enterprise in the Arts: Studies in Mission and Constraint*, New York and Oxford: Oxford University Press.
Duffy, C. T. (1992) 'The rationale for public funding of a national museum', in Towse, R. and Khakee, A. (ed.) *Cultural Economics*, Berlin: Springer-Verlag.
Feldstein, M. (1991a) 'Rich and poor', *Museum News* 70(3): 53–7.
—— (1991b) *The Economics of Art Museums*, Chicago, IL: University of Chicago Press.

Goode, G. B. (1895) 'Principles of museum administration', *Smithsonian Institution Annual Report*, Pt II, Washington, DC: United States National Museum.

Grampp, W. D. (1989) *Pricing the Priceless: Art, Artists, and Economics*, New York, NY: Basic Books.

Hole, J. (1853) *An Essay on the History and Management of Literary, Scientific and Mechanics' Institutes*, London: Longman, Brown, Green & Longmans (reprint Frank Cass & Co., London, 1970).

—— (1989b) 'Rent-seeking in arts policy', *Public Choice* 60(2): 113–22.

House of Commons Education, Science and Arts Committee (1989) *Should Museums Charge?: Some Case Studies Together with the Proceedings of the Committee, Minutes of Evidence and Appendices: First Report*, London: HMSO.

Huszar, P. C. and Seckler, D. W. (1974) 'Effects of pricing a "free good": a study of the use of admission fees at the California Academy of Sciences', *Land Economics* 50(4): 364–73.

McFetridge, R. (1988) 'Report of the special group on admission fees for the national museums of Canada', unpublished, Ottawa.

Merriman, N. (1991) *Beyond the Glass Case. The Past, Heritage and the Public in Britain*, Leicester: Leicester University Press.

Prentice, R. C. (1988) 'Pricing policy at heritage sites: how much should visitors pay?' in Therbert, D. T., Prentice, R. C. and Thomas, C. J., *Heritage Sites: Strategies for Marketing and Development*, Aldershot: Avebury.

Robertson, I. G. (1987) 'Admission charges – a new policy', *Museums Bulletin* 27(3): 1–2.

Ruskin, J. (1880) 'Letters to Leicester Museum subscribers', *Art Journal*, new series, XIX.

Snow, A. (1989) 'Museum admission charges', *Museum News* 68(2) Spring: 2.

Treasury Board of Canada (1992) *Guide to User Fees*, Ottawa: Minister of Supply and Services.

Ward, J. (1913) 'The relation of schools of art to museums', *Museums Journal* XII/February.

10

The university art museum: defining purpose and mission

Peter Drucker

When one of the most popular and influential of all management writers turned his attention to the museum as an organization, the results could only have been stimulating and insightful. Peter Drucker, in this piece first published in 1977, sketches an all too familiar picture of board-management conflict, where the mission has been inadequately or only partially formulated. The questions he poses show that there are no easy solutions.

Visitors to the campus were always shown the University Art Museum, of which the large and distinguished university was very proud. A photograph of the handsome neo-classical building that housed the museum had long been used by the university for the cover of its brochures and catalogues.

The building, together with a substantial endowment, was given to the university around 1912 by an alumnus, the son of the university's first president, who had become very wealthy as an investment banker. He also gave the university his own small, but high quality, collections – one of Etruscan figurines, and one, unique in America, of English Pre-Raphaelite paintings. He then served as the museum's unpaid director until his death. During his tenure he brought a few additional collections to the museum, largely from other alumni of the university. Only rarely did the museum purchase anything. As a result, the museum housed several small collections of uneven quality. As long as the founder ran the museum, none of the collections was ever shown to anybody except a few members of the university's art history faculty, who were admitted as the founder's private guests.

After the founder's death, in the late 1920s, the university intended to bring in a professional museum director. Indeed, this had been part of the agreement under which the founder had given the museum. A search committee was to be appointed, but in the meantime a graduate student in art history who had shown interest in the museum, and who had spent a good many hours in it, took over temporarily. At first, she did not even have a title, let alone a salary. But she stayed on acting as the museum's director and over the next thirty years was promoted in stages to that title. But from the first day, whatever her title, she was in charge. She immediately set about changing the museum altogether. She catalogued the collections. She pursued new gifts, again primarily small collections from alumni and other friends of the university. She organized fund raising for the museum. But, above all, she began to integrate the museum into the work of the university. When a space problem arose in the years immediately following the Second World War, Miss Kirkhoff offered the third floor of the museum to the art

115

history faculty, which moved its offices there. She remodelled the building to include classrooms and a modern and well-appointed auditorium. She raised funds to build one of the best research and reference libraries in art history in the country. She also began to organize a series of special exhibitions built around one of the museum's own collections, complemented by loans from outside collections. For each of these exhibitions she had a distinguished member of the university's art faculty write a catalogue. These catalogues speedily became the leading scholarly texts in the fields.

Miss Kirkhoff ran the University Art Museum for almost half a century. But old age ultimately defeated her. At the age of 68 after suffering a severe stroke, she had to retire. In her letter of resignation she proudly pointed to the museum's growth and accomplishment under her stewardship. 'Our endowment', she wrote, 'now compares favourably with museums several times our size. We never have had to ask the university for any money other than for our share of the university's insurance policies. Our collections in the areas of our strength, while small, are of first-rate quality and importance. Above all, we are being used by more people than any museum of our size. Our lecture series, in which members of the university's art history faculty present a major subject to a university audience of students and faculty, attract regularly three to five hundred people; and if we had the seating capacity, we could easily have a larger audience. Our exhibitions are seen and studied by more visitors, most of them members of the university community, than all but the most highly publicized exhibitions in the very big museums ever draw. Above all, the courses and seminars offered in the museum have become one of the most popular and most rapidly growing educational features of the university. No other museum in this country or anywhere else', concluded Miss Kirkhoff, 'has so successfully integrated art into the life of a major university and a major university into the work of a museum.'

Miss Kirkhoff strongly recommended that the university bring in a professional museum director as her successor. 'The museum is much too big and much too important to be entrusted to another amateur such as I was forty-five years ago,' she wrote. 'And it needs careful thinking regarding its direction, its basis of support and its future relationship with the university.'

The university took Miss Kirkhoff's advice. A search committee was duly appointed and, after one year's work, it produced a candidate whom everybody approved. The candidate was himself a graduate of the university who had then obtained his Ph.D. in art history and in museum work from the university. Both his teaching and administrative record were sound, leading to his present museum directorship in a medium-sized city. There he converted an old, well-known, but rather sleepy museum to a lively, community-orientated museum whose exhibitions were well publicized and attracted large crowds.

The new museum director took over with great fanfare in September, 1971. Less than three years later he left – with less fanfare, but still with considerable noise. Whether he resigned or was fired was not quite clear. But that there was bitterness on both sides was only too obvious.

The new director, upon his arrival, had announced that he looked upon the museum as a 'major community resource' and intended to 'make the tremendous artistic and scholarly resources of the Museum fully available to the academic community as well as to the public'. When he said these things in an interview with the college newspaper, everybody nodded in approval. It soon became clear that what he meant by 'community resource' and what the faculty and students understood by these words were not the same. The museum had always been 'open to the public' but, in practice, it was members of the college community who used the museum and attended its lectures, its exhibitions and its frequent seminars.

The first thing the new director did, however, was to promote visits from the public schools in the area. He soon began to change the exhibition policy. Instead of organizing small shows, focused on a major collection of the museum and built around a scholarly catalogue, he began to organize 'popular exhibitions' around 'topics of general interest' such as 'Women Artists through the Ages'. He promoted these exhibitions vigorously in the newspapers, in radio and television interviews and, above all, in the local schools. As a result, what had been a busy but quiet place was soon knee-deep in schoolchildren, taken to the museum in special buses which cluttered the access roads around the museum and throughout the campus. The faculty, which was not particularly happy with the resulting noise and confusion, became thoroughly upset when the scholarly old chairman of the art history department was mobbed by fourth-graders who sprayed him with their water pistols as he tried to push his way through the main hall to his office.

Increasingly the new director did not design his own shows, but brought in travelling exhibitions from major museums, importing their catalogue as well, rather than have his own faculty produce one.

The students too were apparently unenthusiastic after the first six or eight months, during which the new director had been somewhat of a campus hero. Attendance at the classes and seminars held in the art museum fell off sharply, as did attendance at the evening lectures. When the editor of the campus newspaper interviewed students for a story on the museum, he was told again and again that the museum had become too noisy and too 'sensational' for students to enjoy the classes and to have a chance to learn.

What brought all this to a head was an Islamic art exhibit in late 1973. Since the museum had little Islamic art, nobody criticized the showing of a travelling exhibit, offered on very advantageous terms with generous financial assistance from some of the Arab governments. But then, instead of inviting one of the University's own faculty members to deliver the customary talk at the opening of the exhibit, the director brought in a cultural attaché of one of the Arab embassies in Washington. The speaker, it was reported, used the occasion to deliver a violent attack on Israel and on the American policy of supporting Israel against the Arabs. A week later, the university senate decided to appoint an advisory committee, drawn mostly from members of the art history faculty, which, in the future, would have to approve all plans for exhibits and lectures. The director thereupon, in an interview with the campus newspaper, sharply attacked the faculty as 'elitist' and 'snobbish' and as believing that 'art belongs to the rich'. Six months later, in June, 1974, his resignation was announced.

Under the by-laws of the university, the academic senate appoints a search committee. Normally, this is pure formality. The chairman of the appropriate department submits the department's nominees for the committee who are approved and appointed, usually without debate. But when the academic senate early the following semester was asked to appoint the search committee, things were far from 'normal'. The Dean who presided, sensing the tempers in the room, tried to smooth over things by saying, 'Clearly, we picked the wrong person the last time. We will have to try very hard to find the right one this time.'

He was immediately interrupted by an economist, known for his populism, who broke in and said, 'I admit that the late director was probably not the right personality. But I strongly believe that his personality was not at the root of the problem. He tried to do what needs doing and this got him in trouble with the faculty. He tried to make our museum a community resource, to bring in the community and to make art accessible to broad masses of people, to the blacks and the Puerto Ricans, to the kids from the ghetto schools and to a lay public. And this is what we really resented. Maybe his methods were not the most tactful ones – I admit I could have done without those interviews he gave. But what he tried to do was right. We had better commit ourselves to the policy he wanted to put into effect, or else we will have deserved his attacks on us as "elitist" and "Snobbish".'

'This is nonsense,' cut in the usually silent and polite senate member from the art history faculty. 'It makes absolutely no sense for our museum to try to become the kind of community resource our late director and my distinguished colleague want it to be. First, there is no need. The city has one of the world's finest and biggest museums and it does exactly that and does it very well. Second, we here have neither the artistic resources nor the financial resources to serve the community at large. We can do something different but equally important and indeed unique. Ours is the only museum in the country, and perhaps in the world, that is fully integrated with an academic community and truly a teaching institution. We are using it, or at least we used to until the last few unfortunate years, as a major educational resource for all our students. No other museum in the country, and as far as I know in the world, is bringing undergraduates into art the way we do. All of us, in addition to our scholarly and graduate work, teach undergraduate courses for people who are not going to be art majors or art historians. We work with the engineering students and show them what we do in our conservation and restoration work. We work with architecture students and show them the development of architecture through the ages. Above all, we work with liberal arts students, who often have had no exposure to art before they came here and who enjoy our courses all the more because they are scholarly and not just "art appreciation". This is unique and this is what our museum can do and should do.'

'I doubt that this is really what we should be doing,' commented the chairman of the mathematics department. 'The museum, as far as I know, is part of the graduate faculty. It should concentrate on training art historians in its Ph.D. programme, on its scholarly work and on its research. I would strongly urge that the museum be considered an adjunct to graduate and especially to Ph.D. education, confine itself to this work, and stay out of all attempts to be "popular", both on campus and outside of it. The glory of the museum is the scholarly catalogues produced by our faculty, and our Ph.D. graduates who are sought after by art history faculties throughout the country. This is the museum's mission, which can only be impaired by the attempt to be "popular", whether with students or with the public.'

'These are very interesting and important comments,' said the Dean, still trying to pacify. 'But I think this can wait until we know who the new director is going to be. Then we should raise these questions with him.'

'I beg to differ, Mr. Dean,' said one of the elder statesmen of the faculty. 'During the summer months, I discussed this question with an old friend and neighbour of mine in the country, the director of one of the nation's great museums. He said to me: "You do not have a personality problem, you have a *management* problem. You have not, as a university, taken responsibility for the mission, the direction, and the objectives of your museum. Until you do this, no director can succeed. And this is *your* decision. In fact, you cannot hope to get a good man until you can tell him what your basic objectives are. If your late director is to blame – I know him and I know that he is abrasive – it is for being willing to take on a job when you, the university, had not faced up to the basic management decisions. There is no point talking about *who* should manage until it is clear *what* it is that has to be managed and for what."'

At this point the dean realized that he had to adjourn the discussion unless he wanted the meeting to degenerate into a brawl. But he also realized that he had to identify the issues and possible decisions before the next faculty meeting a month later. Here is the list of questions he put down on paper later that evening:

1 What are the possible purposes of the University Museum:

    (a) To serve as a laboratory for the graduate art-history faculty and the doctoral students in the field?

    (b) To serve as major 'enrichment' for the undergraduate who is not an art-history student but wants both a 'liberal education' and a counterweight to the highly bookish diet fed to him in most of our courses?

    (c) To serve the metropolitan community – and especially its schools – outside the campus gates?

2 Who are or should be its customers?

    (a) The graduate students in professional training to be teachers of art history?

    (b) The undergraduate community – or rather, the entire college community?

    (c) The metropolitan community and especially the teachers and youngsters in the public schools?

    (d) Any others?

3 Which of these purposes are compatible and could be served simultaneously? Which are mutually exclusive or at the very least are likely to get into each other's way?

4 What implications for the structure of the museum, the qualifications of its director and its relationship to the university follow from each of the above purposes?

5 Do we need to find out more about the needs and wants of our various potential customers to make an intelligent policy decision? How could we go about it?

The dean distributed these questions to the members of the faculty with the request that they think them through and discuss them before the next meeting of the academic senate.

How would you tackle these questions? And are they the right questions?

This paper first appeared in P. F. Drucker (1977) Management Cases, *London: Heinemann, pp. 28–35.*

11

Museum people. The special problems of personnel management in museums and historical agencies

Renée Friedman

The literature relating to personnel management issues in museums is comparatively under-developed. Renée Friedman's article, first published in 1982, remains a useful introduction to the specific issues and factors in managing people in the museum sector.

Museums are labour intensive. The 5,000 museums in the United States employ approximately 118,000 people. The combined budget of these museums is in excess of one billion dollars, and 60 to 80 per cent of that money is allocated to personnel expenses. Regardless of this heavy reliance on human resources, museum management has rarely attempted to establish personnel policies that view employees as valuable resources. Instead, management has relied on personal commitment – to a profession, to museums in general, or to the 'treasures' of the world – to retain its staff.

The traditional relationship between museum management and staff is growing less stable as more and more employees become aware of the inequities in salaries and fringe benefits between jobs in museums and jobs in the business world. Increasingly, museum employees also recognize that management is demanding more of them in terms of on-the-job responsibility which makes the lower salaries less palatable. In addition, employees are coming to realize that management does not, in fact, regard them as valuable to the museum as a Winslow Homer seascape or an eighteenth-century soup tureen or a recently acquired onyx from Africa.

This growing awareness by museum staff members, and management's inability, (and often unwillingness) to respond adequately to it have complicated the already complex nature of non-profit personnel management. The problems related to personnel in museums, as well as in historical agencies and other cultural organizations, are specific to them. Especially when dealing with professional staff – with directors, curators and conservators, with educators and historians, even with volunteers – trying simply to transfer the problem-solving methods and techniques of corporate personnel managers to non-profit museums will not always work.

HISTORICAL PERSPECTIVE

The reasons for this are in part historical. Although museums have changed dramatically over the last ten years, their operation continues to be based on a tradition that was established nearly a century ago. Changes are still occurring, but they are slow, tortuous and groping changes. They are accompanied by many tensions. To understand personnel management in museums one must see it in the context of change from an older tradition.

Until the 1950s, museums were elitist. They were run by the monied and cultured for the monied and cultured. Genteel directors spent leisurely summers travelling about collecting rare and beautiful objects. In winter, they wined and dined the upper crust, cajoling their guests to finance operations and collections for yet another year.

If there was any staff at all, its members felt honoured to work at the museum and accepted whatever management offered them. Meanwhile, the world of business and industry was experiencing what author and management consultant Peter Drucker calls the 'management boom'. It had already fully assimilated management pioneer Frederick W. Taylor's scientific management performing time studies and task analyses. And I. E. Dupont, with the Rand Corporation, had introduced the critical path method of planning.

In the 1950s museum staffs began to realize they had a responsibility to the public. They began to develop new programmes and a new profession. Museum education emerged, and with it a rigorous professionalism in programme planning. Museum operations, however, were still managed and financed in the traditional genteel manner. By way of contrast, note that at about the same time the US military and American industry developed and began using PERT (Program Evaluation Review Technique – a sophisticated form of flow-chart devised as part of the Polaris Missile Program. A tool for scheduling, planning and allocating costs, manpower and resources, PERT proved itself effective in non-technological fields as well.)

The social turbulence of the 1960s seemed to create a cultural boom. More people visited museums than attended sporting events. The National Endowment for the Humanities and the National Endowment for the Arts were born, and with them an unprecedented level of federal financial support for museums and historical agencies. Museums meanwhile realized that while their programmes were being handled expertly by committed professionals, they were unprepared managerially to run such large organizations. Though professional management techniques had begun to filter into the museum field and individual managers were exposed to MBO (management by objectives), to critical path planning (circuitously through commercial exhibit houses) and to PERT (again, roundabout through the Head Start programme), knowledge of these techniques was in bits and pieces. Museum management generally still had little respect for or interest in the systematic procedures that had so successfully shaped corporate America.

The crisis in museum personnel management really began in the 1970s. Staffs began to organize and to speak more forcefully on employment issues. In 1971 at the Museum of Modern Art in New York, the Professional and Staff Association (PASTA) went out on strike for a 'fair contract' – the first time in history museum labour had gone out against museum management. Unionization was, of course, a reflection of social change, part of a populist/egalitarian movement that was forcing many of the elitists out of museum work and leading museum people to declare that they should be treated equally with other labourers.

The Bicentennial increased Americans' awareness of their past, and visitors poured into our historic houses and museums in the last years of the past decade, forcing museums to increase their services and enlarge their staffs. In the early 1980s those services and staffs were for the most part still in place though visitation had begun to fall off and museum incomes remained, as always, fixed or limited. Personnel problems were bound to grow tense as highly skilled labour demanded – and was refused – increased compensation and as the political climate for federal support worsened under President Reagan.

PERSONNEL PROBLEMS

With this brief and sketchy history in mind, we turn now to personnel problems that in many ways are peculiar to museums or to the non-profit sector in general. First there is the problem with recruitment.

The job market for professional employment in museums is extremely tight. A position advertised nationally in *The New York Times* or in the professional trade journals – *History News* and the American Association of Museums' *Aviso* – will garner from 100 to 150 responses. The number varies of course, with the type of position. An entry level position may attract many more than 150 applications. A middle or top management position may attract fewer than 100 applications.

Aware of the deluge of applications that will follow such an advertisement, recruiters often hesitate to begin a process that may paralyse them with paper and take upwards of six months to complete. Instead, they frequently find it tempting to 'let it be known', mostly by word of mouth, in the museum community that a position is open. Sometimes, because it is easier, they seek to fill the job with a local applicant.

At the same time, the skills necessary to perform museum work are very specialized. Because the total number of people working in museums is small, it is usually necessary to recruit on a national level. Although word of mouth has been the most popular method, recent concern with equal employment opportunity and affirmative action guidelines is beginning to change this. Advertising nationally is quickly becoming the accepted method.

The special problem then is this: the recruiting process is inefficient because it demands an excessive amount of the recruiter's time, especially since recruiters almost always handle personnel matters as just one of several job responsibilities.

Along with recruiting comes employee selection. Until recently, members of the museum community resisted any attempt to publish job descriptions for the various professional jobs within a museum. 'Curator' meant one set of responsibilities in one museum and a different set in another. Museum people felt the work was flexible and could not be defined easily or fixed by iron-clad standards. Those with highly individualistic personalities protested categorization. Recently AAM attempted to offer a first set of guidelines for selecting new employees by publishing a list of job descriptions, though it is still too early to evaluate its effect.

The museum profession has finally settled the debate over whether qualifications for employment should include a degree in a subject area or one in museum studies by deciding that either is acceptable. It is not grappling, however, with the qualifications for management positions. What should be the balance between education and experience in management and subject specialization? Can someone with a solid management background make the aesthetic judgements necessary to museum decision-making? Can someone with specialized knowledge of a discipline – art history, history, biology, botany – make qualified management decisions for the museum?

The problem is that museums operate in a long tradition borrowed from academia. That tradition assumes that expertise in a given subject qualifies one for top management positions. It does not take into account the possibility that museums are changing, are developing into big businesses that require expert management skills.

VOLUNTEERS

The 1978 AAM 'Survey of Hiring Practices and Salary and Fringe Benefits' found that the total work force – professional staff and support services – includes 41.8 per cent full-time paid workers, 17.3 per cent part-time paid workers and 40.9 per cent volunteer workers.

The dependency on volunteer labour to carry out the mission of museums creates acute personnel problems. What sort of control can management exert on the volunteer work force when that work force is present only because it chooses to be and when volunteers that constitute it receive no compensation other than self-satisfaction? What discipline measures make sense for these highly motivated workers who do not always have the skills necessary to do the job? How does management mesh the needs of these volunteers with the goals of the organization? How should management respond to the attitude of 'Anything I do as a volunteer is good in itself'? And how does an organization get rid of an ineffective volunteer?

Museums, then, are heavily dependent on a work-force over which they have little control.

EQUAL EMPLOYMENT OPPORTUNITY

The same survey revealed that 90.7 per cent of the museum work force is white, while 9.3 per cent of those working in museums belong to ethnic or racial minorities. Males constitute 57.8 per cent of the work force, females 42.2 per cent. These figures, however, do not provide a full picture. Though women are well represented in middle management as business managers, comptrollers, educators, librarians, public relations officers and registrars, only 16.7 per cent are directors. And while minorities, too, are well represented as business managers, exhibit technicians and clerical workers, only 1.1 per cent are directors.

Affirmative action programmes have had limited success. Museums have a low turnover rate. When positions open, they are often filled from within, or at least the position is posted within. And since the museum work force is not representative of the overall population, internal promotions do not create opportunities for minorities. Also, the large number of applications for nationally advertised jobs tends to overwhelm personnel staffs. Personnel managers then, find the call for a programme that brings even more applications neither reasonable nor practical. Finally, because top management jobs frequently get filled by word of mouth, those who fill the positions tend to come from the current work force.

In short, EEO and affirmative action are not well established in the museum field, and the museum community has not dealt adequately with the problem by developing plans to ensure fair and equitable searches.

COMPENSATION AND PROTECTION

The biggest personnel problems for museums concern compensation and protection, and they are problems museums find extremely difficult to solve. Traditionally, museum management has relied on an employee's personal commitment to shared goals to bridge the gap between actual salary and a fair wage. Those who worked in museums received compensations other than money. They worked for the prestige the work brought them, or in order to associate with the wealthy and cultured, or to have the opportunity to make significant contributions to history. They worked because they enjoyed the freedom of the workplace, or the magnificent surroundings, or the flexible and varied job responsibilities or the opportunity to travel. Their reward often was in what they were doing, rather than in the money they received for doing it.

Such a system is difficult to maintain as institutions grow larger, as inflation rates soar, as job responsibilities multiply and as similarly qualified workers receive disproportionately larger salaries and greater benefits in business and industry. While many individuals are, in fact, willing to accept lower salaries for work they like, they grow increasingly dissatisfied as those salaries become less and less capable of supporting a middle class style of life, especially when they realize that no matter how high they rise in their organization, they will never have even an adequate salary.

The 1978 survey showed that in fringe benefits, 81 per cent of the country's museums offered medical insurance, 18 per cent offered dental plans, 67 per cent offered retirement packages, 63 per cent made provisions for leave time, and 39 per cent provided at least a few other benefits such as life, health, accident, hospitalization, disability and automobile insurance, savings plans, tuition assistance, housing, and so on.

The same survey revealed that the median salary for museum directors was $20,525, for conservators $14,050, for curators $14,475, for development officers $17,500, for educators $12,600, for exhibit designers $12,487, for registrars $10,978.

Clearly, compensation and fringe benefits in the museum field have not kept pace with those in the rest of society. But the real problem stems from the fact that museum workers are no longer as willing as they traditionally have been to accept the intrinsic rewards of museum work as compensation for low salaries.

This problem is complicated by the fact that museums have fixed or limited sources of income with which to solve it. Since they are usually already operating on a deficit budget, museums have no 'extra' to share among their employees.

Museum boards, charged with the obligation to obtain financial support for the museum, must 'find' enough money elsewhere to make up the deficit and to cover increases in salaries and in fringe benefits. Traditionally they did so by 'tapping' a wealthy donor, but with the tremendous growth in museums and museum expenses that occurred during the 1960s, they often find this method no longer feasible.

EVALUATION

Because a museum worker's performance is very difficult to measure, rewards are separated from performance. In business, management can reward or punish its employees on the basis of sales or productivity because these accurately measure performance. The same is not true for museums. Judgements for performance tend to be subjective. For example, should an employee be rewarded or punished if he or she designs an excellent exhibit which no one attends, or if the attendance is high, but the quality of the show is poor? If an employee takes three months to do conservation work on a second-rate, but still important nineteenth-century landscape painting, what determines whether the time spent was productive?

The absence of quantitative and definable measures for performance leads museums to reward and punish, to promote and discharge, on the basis of seniority and external training. This separation of reward from performance weakens the influence of managers with subordinates.

LABOUR RELATIONS

The museum field lacks the basis for successful collective bargaining – management and labour's conflict over the division of profits. The acknowledged premises for the nego-tiating process in the museum field are that there already exists a deficit, that agreement to labour's demands will increase that deficit, that the increase will have to be made up by contributions from outside sources instead of earned income, that the board will have to find these contributions, and that the deficit will not be decreased by price increases, reduction of personnel, reduction of costs or increases in production.

Instead of collective bargaining then, most museums engage in co-operative bargaining. Management, labour and the board sit down together to formulate policy, agree upon salaries, state working conditions, determine the size of the deficit and identity potential funding sources.

The income gap always present in museum budgets leaves very little room for negotia-tion and much room for destructive frustration on the part of all involved.

TRAINING AND DEVELOPMENT

One of the more painfully and slowly changing areas of museum personnel management has been training and development. Here museum management has expounded on its traditional attitude towards salaries (that it is a privilege to work in a museum) to say that training and development benefits the employee directly but benefits the institution only peripherally. Therefore, it is the individual employee's responsibility to seek and pay for continuing professional education.

Only recently, at the 1980 and 1981 annual meetings of the American Association for State and Local History, have museum and historical agency workers spoken out on this issue. In New Orleans and in Williamsburg, these workers charged that institutions have a responsibility to improve the abilities of their human resources.

Although plans are under way to conduct a survey of institutional attitudes towards training and development programmes and to bring this issue into focus by publishing articles about it in the trade journals, at present little institutional support in terms of tuition reimbursement, leave time or encouragement is evident.

In general, museum management seems to feel no responsibility for establishing formal policies for training and development.

DISCIPLINE AND CONTROL

Museum work is a profession. Individuals who belong may have a stronger allegiance to the profession than they do to the institution they work for. Generally, museum pro-fessionals tend to view the museum simply as the place they practise their trade.

This professional commitment can affect individual attitudes within a given institution towards job enlargement and enrichment. Narrow specializations require lengthy training and lead to the development of codes of conduct and sharp delineations between what is and is not part of a particular job. Conservators, registrars, exhibit technicians, curators and museum educators are occasionally liable to respond to attempts to expand their activities through job enrichment with phrases such as 'That's not part of my job' or 'I was not hired to do that'.

Professional codes of ethics may also conflict with established policies in particular institutions. AAM's book *Museum Ethics* urges ethical conduct especially in regard to such things as royalties and copyrights, personal collecting by employees and all other areas that may involve a conflict of interest. When these ethics conflict with institutional policy, the museum worker usually abides by the professional code. If the worker is discharged because of it, the case well may end in court.

Professionalism can also hinder promotion from within. In the private sector, management and worker alike assume that as an employee gains more experience, the scope of his or her job will expand. Personnel departments seek to develop certain employees to take on more responsibility within the company. Although internal movement like this does occur in museums, professionals more typically look for promotion by moving to similar jobs in, larger, more financially sound, more prestigious institutions. Rarely will an individual step out of his or her professional role to take on new work solely in order to serve the needs of a given institution.

In addition to being professionals, museum people tend to be highly individualistic, imaginative, articulate and achievement-oriented. They are not especially co-operative. 'Teamwork' often has a negative connotation for them. Accustomed to a freedom in the workplace without parallel in the corporate world, they are not concerned with efficiency but with quality and aesthetics. They see tasks defined not by the time they take but by the care they require to be done correctly.

Sherman Lee, director of the Cleveland Museum of Art, articulated the prevailing attitude of museum professionals when he said, 'The museum is not in business to be efficient. It is in business to be the best possible art museum it can be'.

For management the problem becomes how can its professional techniques relating to efficiency and teamwork be integrated into museum operations without losing the individualism, imagination, aesthetic judgement and concern with quality that museums find essential to accomplishing their mission?

THE CHALLENGE OF PERSONNEL MANAGEMENT

Museums and historical agencies must face the challenge of personnel management. Young professionals, a larger public, shrinking federal sources, and entrenched and outmoded management attitudes do not make for a healthy mix. Some of the problems can be addressed by the more sophisticated and professional management techniques of the private sector, some cannot. Some probably cannot be solved at all, given the present state of the field. The financial situation many museums now find themselves in, for example, forces them to delay dealing with many of the personnel problems explored here. And correcting that situation may well take more than good management. It may depend on all of us finally deciding who should be responsible for the cultural resources of the country and who should pay for institutions that serve to enhance the quality of our lives.

This article first appeared in History News *37(3) (1982), pp. 14–18.*

REFERENCES

AAM (1978) *Museum Ethics*, Washington DC: American Association of Museums.

Alexander, E. P. (1973) *Museums in Motion*, Nashville: American Association for State and Local History.

Conger, J., Egherman, R. and Mallard, G. (1979) 'The museum as employer', *Museum News*, July/August: 22–8.

Economist (1976) 'The arts in deficit', *The Economist*, 25 September: 25–6.

Faine, H. R. (1973) 'Unions and the arts', *American Economic Review*, May: 70–7.

Goldsmith, J. C. (1979) 'Farewell to the volunteer fireman', *Harvard Business Review*, May/June: 14–18.

Kimche, L. 'American museums: the vital statistics', *Museum News*, October: 52–7.

Levitt, T. (1973) *The Third Sector*, New York: Amacom.

McQuade, W. (1974) 'Management problems enter the picture at art museum', *Fortune*, July: 100–3+.

Mittenhal, R. A. and Mahoney, B. W. (1977) 'Getting management help to the nonprofit sector', *Harvard Business Review*, September/October: 95–103.

Museum News (1980) 'Museum studies: a second report', *Museum News*, October: 26–40.

Newman, W. H. and Wallender, H. W. III (1978) 'Managing not-for-profit enterprises', *Academy of Management Review*, January: 24–31.

Selby, C. C. (1978) 'Better performance from nonprofits', *Harvard Business Review*, September: 92–8.

Sukel, W. M. (1978) 'Third sector organizations: a needed look at the artistic-cultural organization', *Academy of Management Review*, April: 348–53.

Towers, C. R. (1978) 'Lets be affirmative about affirmative action', *Museum News*, May/June: 5–7.

12

Some more equal than others
Rosalinda M. C. Hardiman

The need to develop effective equal opportunities policies and practice is one of, if not the most important challenge facing museum managers today. Rosalinda Hardiman's paper is a brief but forceful polemic, aimed to focus attention on this question, particularly with regard to people with some form of disability.

I write from two viewpoints: one as a female professional and as a member of the working group set up following the Museums Association's 1989 AGM to develop draft policy statements on equal opportunities.

Every reader of *Museums Journal* should be aware of the insistent statistic that 49 per cent of the Museums Association's membership is made up of women. The Association's Council acknowledges that 'women form a large and committed part of the Association, yet are under-represented on its governing body and in its public profile.'

My second viewpoint is as a disabled museum professional, but here there are no statistics even in that repository of knowledge, the database. No figures are available for what I suspect is an extremely rare breed. There may be under-representation of women at council level but as the MA again acknowledges, there are 'no representatives from disabled groups' or indeed from ethnic minorities. The working group and the Museums Association are anxious to redress the balance, stating that 'future positive measures are required'. In the field of equal opportunities some are indeed more equal than others.

Since the International Year of Disabled People in 1981, arts venues have focused attention on making provision for disabled people. In many cases, museums and art galleries have attempted to make their often intractable buildings accessible to the visitor. However, of the 1,726 venues listed in the *1989–90 Yearbook* as open to the public, only 689 stated that they had access for disabled people. Others admitted to having only partial access. The database does not yet ask for details of access to staff areas but it is unlikely that many of the 689 would qualify.

I welcome this gathering awareness of the problem and the actions taken to provide disabled access to our institutions, but I have to regret that virtually all of these approach the provision of facilities from the one-sided viewpoint of the disabled visitor. That is rightly stressed, but there is a widespread assumption that all museum staff will be able-bodied. The idea of planning for potential disabled members of staff is alien to most employers.

If the thought of provision for possible future employees is absent, the need to provide continuing employment for members of staff who become disabled while employed is rarely confronted. All too often when a member of staff becomes disabled, immediate recourse is made to the medical referee and the person is retired on grounds of ill health. Many staff, who at present are forced into early retirement through disability of whatever kind, could have continued their careers with more flexible attitudes on the part of the employers. Admittedly, in most cases some financial input will be necessary, but if the corporate will is lacking, then no attempt will be made at all.

Disability covers a wide range of conditions, but it is worth bearing in mind that someone with severe heart problems and emphysema is just as frustrated by a flight of stairs as is a paraplegic, but only the paraplegic is generally regarded as 'disabled'.

There are three main sets of legislation regarding the employment of disabled people. The Disabled Persons (Employment) Acts, 1944 and 1958; the Chronically Sick and Disabled Persons Act, 1970 and the Companies (Directors' Report) (Employment of Disabled Persons) Regulations, 1980, which is part of the Companies' Acts, 1948 to 1983. The first two, for technical reasons, do not apply to government departments (such as the national museums) although the obligations the acts impose fall equally on them. The third does not apply to public-sector employers although the obligations that the regulations (1980) impose fall equally on them.

The (in)famous quota, whereby employers with 20 or more workers have a duty to employ a quota of registered disabled people, was introduced in the 1944 Act. The standard quota is 3 per cent of an employer's total work-force. It is not an offence to be below quota, but it is an offence to engage anyone other than a registered disabled person without first obtaining an exemption permit from the local job centre. An employer must not discharge a registered disabled person without reasonable cause if the employer is below quota or would fall below quota as a result. Most local authorities are below the 3 per cent quota but have exemption certificates and in government departments there is an average of just 1.3 per cent compliance.

The 1970 Act has 29 sections, one of which requires physical access to public premises. However, a convenient get-out clause is often used, as compliance is required only 'in so far as it is in the circumstances both practicable and reasonable'. Many authorities find that it is *not* reasonable to make their buildings accessible.

The Companies Act Regulations relate to policies towards the employment of disabled workers generally, and not only, as in the quota scheme, to those who are registered as disabled under the Disabled Persons (Employment) Acts. On registration, it is worth adding a word of personal experience here. Many disabled people choose not to register, so that in employment terms they can cheerfully fill in an application form and put 'no' in the box that asks 'are you registered disabled?', as I did when I applied for my present post. Within two weeks of taking up my post, considerable pressure was placed on me to register, so that my registration would help towards the quota. Newly in post and less militant than I am now, I agreed, although unhappy at the pressure that had been brought to bear upon me.

Both the 1970 Act and the Companies Act Regulations emphasize training, whether for those who become disabled while working for the company in order to permit their continued employment, or for the training and career development of existing disabled employees. Considerable government help can be given in both instances, but it is not always tapped by employers. Through the disablement advisory service attached to job centres, two main schemes operate. The Adaptations to Premises and Equipment scheme (APE) and Special Aids to Employment (SAE) either purchase equipment outright, which is then lent to the disabled employee, or part-fund (up to £6,000) adaptations to buildings.

It is significant that in my own case, although pressured to register by the personnel department in 1980, it is only through my own initiative in finding out these sources that I obtained a special chair, keyboard and footrest in 1990. It is likely that many people are forced to give up work simply because neither they nor their employers know about the advice and funds available.

Many authorities and departments have drawn up codes of practice, not government legislation but morally binding upon the employing authorities. The civil service produced an excellent code of practice for disabled people in 1985 although an earlier statement was in force in 1981. The national museums may be among the smallest government departments but each has its own departmental disabled persons officer. The Arts Council issued its arts and disability plan in 1989 following on from its code of practice on arts and disability which was circulated to all its clients in 1985. The plan is very much a kick in the pants, stating that 'most client organisations have not implemented most aspects of the code of practice. Only one regional arts association had an action plan . . . it was now clear that reliance on the goodwill of clients to implement had resulted in very little progress.' The main thrust in the plan is to make venues accessible, along with encouragement to develop 'employment of disabled people in all areas of the organisations' work'.

In future, clients will have to reach certain access standards in order to qualify for project funding. The Council of Regional Arts Associations has now issued an equal opportunities code of practice in which it is stated that a disabled applicant should not be barred from employment on grounds of 'restricted access and inadequate equipment where both, with reasonable efforts and expenditure, the problems could be resolved'.

Many local government authorities, which run most of the museums in Great Britain, have declared that they are 'equal opportunity employers', yet as the *Local Government Chronicle* admits: 'Disability is the Cinderella of equal opportunities and comprehensive information on what local authorities are doing is virtually non-existent' (Wills 1990). A number have been very active in this area, notably Leeds City, Manchester City, Derbyshire County, Gloucestershire County and the London Boroughs of Lambeth and Hackney. Manchester City Council has pledged £3 million per year to improve access to its buildings and public places and has as its target an employment quota of 9.2 per cent by 1997 – it has currently reached the regulation 3 per cent.

However, according to the *1989–90 Yearbook* Manchester City Art Gallery is noted as having only 'limited access for disabled'. Leeds City Council proudly states in its employment policy that 'inaccessibility of a building is not a reason for refusing a job', (quoted in Wills 1990). However, the entries in the *Yearbook* state for Leeds City Art Gallery 'access for disabled difficult', for Leeds City Museum 'no access for disabled'. Although Leeds Industrial Museum and Lotherton Hall are listed as having disabled access, Temple Newsam House is listed as 'access for disabled difficult'.

In my experience most local authorities, whether county, city or district may well be exemplary equal opportunities employers as regards their civic centre or town hall but not when it comes to their other buildings, particularly their museums. I realize that most of this country's museums are in older buildings, many of historic and architectural interest, which pose problems of access, but that is of little consolation if the much-vaunted equal opportunities statement does not apply to the one council building you want to work in.

There are few disabled curators. This is partly due to intractable buildings that deny access, partly to segregation of the severely disabled into 'special' schooling with less stress on academic attainment, and also to attitudes and prejudice of employers. Regrettably these last two points are commonly encountered and a candidate's disability will be held as an excuse for non-employment, often without legitimate grounds, either through a lack of knowledge or an unwillingness on the part of the interviewer to look at the candidate and recognize ability rather than disability.

Most prospective museum professionals are discouraged even before they reach the interviewing panel. The post-graduate courses at Manchester and Leicester universities rightly demand a serious commitment, which can only usually be demonstrated by volunteer experience. To get a volunteer place is difficult, to get a permanent museum job can be a major battle. Keeping that precious job can also be a battle. Small wonder that many disabled people, whether working in a museum or elsewhere, choose to keep their heads down and not make waves.

Increasingly I am abandoning that attitude and becoming militant, but that is not everyone's choice. It is not surprising that few care to rock the boat, for most are in a catch-22 situation: if you manage to get and keep a museum job at whatever cost or pain, you will not win special facilities if you are seen to be managing, and for many, if you cannot cope you will be quickly retired on ill-health grounds. Consideration of adaptations, government funding and even more flexible attitudes to work and alternative working methods are very rarely considered.

In conclusion I will say that it is not illegal to discriminate against disabled people, however much it may stink morally, but just consider: what would happen to *your* job tomorrow if you became disabled?

This article first appeared in Museums Journal *(Nov. 1990), pp. 28–30.*

REFERENCES

Museums Association Policy Initiatives Drafts, March 1990
The Chronically Sick and Disabled Persons Act, 1970
Arts Council, Arts and Disability Action Plan, October 1989
The Council of Regional Arts Associations, *Equal Opportunities Code of Practice*, 1989
Jackie Wills, 'Cinderella Equality Issue', *Local Government Chronicle*, 9 February 1990
Museums Yearbook 1989/90, Museums Association

13

Money changers in the temple? Museums and the financial mission

Andy Leon Harney

Since the 1980s museums have placed emphasis on generating their own sources of income as never before, yet surprisingly little detailed analysis of this highly significant development has been made. This paper by Andy Harney provides a useful introduction to the broad range of initiatives in this field, and a discussion of the issues and the emphasis on income generation inevitably raises.

The mission has always been simply stated. Regardless of size, a museum's essence is in collecting and preserving our cultural heritage and educating the public. This laudable task has, until late, been the guiding force in the dramatic growth of museums in this country over the past half-century. But for many museums today, the traditional mission has been joined by a more immediate goal: economic survival.

The reality of a deeply recessionary economy has come knocking on the doors of the venerable institutions that enhance cities and towns throughout the country. From science centres and historical sites to zoos and art museums, no institution has been untouched. Tax revenues are down, hence state and local subsidies are cut or done away with altogether. Corporate fat cats who once aggressively sought the prestige of generous gifts to museums now ask the tough questions: 'What's in it for us?' 'Can we afford to be generous in today's economy?' Even philanthropic foundations are complaining that their investments aren't yielding what they used to. Interest rates are low, making available funds for grants smaller. In addition to the bad economy there is a growing sentiment in some quarters, including Capitol Hill, that culture is a frill that can and should be cut in hard times.

All this has left museums to rely on their wits to survive. And as institutions around the country begin to explore territory once reserved for the hardened businessman, there are some surprising and exciting results.

Museums are not new to challenges brought on by changes in the availability of funds. In 1976, the Tax Reform Act dramatically altered patterns of giving for foundations. The new law required them to give away 5 per cent of their earnings every year to maintain their tax-exempt status. As a result of this new pool of money, museums quickly adapted and learned the art of grantsmanship – researching who had money and writing proposals to get it. They also learned how to pursue private donors. Acquisition budgets were structured in part on the assumption that generous donors could do well (with a tax deduction) and do good (by donating expensive works). Happily, in man museums these skills have been carefully refined. Unhappily, there developed a growing universe of groups after the same shrinking pot of gold.

A decade later, the Tax Reform Act of 1986 instituted the Alternative Minimum Tax (AMT) and placed severe limitations on the deductibility of objects that had appreciated in value, sometimes immensely, as the art market went through its boom period of the late 1980s. Owners of fine art simply 'flooded the auction houses with what might have been gifts to museums', says one museum director. 'These people simply couldn't afford to donate objects that had appreciated in value anymore. It made more sense to simply sell them at prices we couldn't afford to pay to acquire them.'

There is further irony in the present economic situation. Museums and other non-profits have watched local, state and federal funding erode along with corporate and private support. But their ability to earn income in the marketplace is severely restricted by the unrelated business income tax law. UBIT, enacted in 1950, was intended to draw the line between what for-profits and nonprofits could legally do to earn money. This line, though, is not always so clear, and interpretation of UBIT remains at best an inexact science.

So far the 1990s have forced museums to begin to restructure themselves not for kinder, gentler times, but for leaner, meaner times.

One result is a virtual revolution in museum administration. Suddenly curators are using the 'm' word – marketing. Directors of development are talking about marketing and demographics. They are looking for ways to bring in more earned income to support the institution. While there is little expectation that museums will ever raise enough funds to become self-sufficient, there is a growing hope that in hard times earned income activities will make sufficient contributions to the bottom line to defray the losses incurred in other areas.

'Museums in the US and Canada are really at a watershed,' says Howard White, head of marketing at the Walters Art Gallery in Baltimore. 'Museums have to adapt to new circumstances. Those who can adapt to a more entrepreneurial, marketing focus, will, I think, survive. Those who won't – well, it reminds me of the neighbourhood where accidents seem to keep happening on the same corner. The neighbours complain to city hall, asking for a stop-light but to no avail. It's human nature to wait for a tragedy – but that tragedy is happening now.'

One worst-case example is the Detroit Institute of Arts. With the city facing severe economic hardship, $7 million was abruptly trimmed from the museum's $26 million budget – a drop that has forced the museum to let go 140 employees and cut operating hours from 48½ hours weekly to 25 hours, during which only half the museum is open to the public at any one moment. DIA is hardly the only museum that has suffered economic trauma over the past few years. Nor is it alone in being forced to turn to new methods of generating earned income.

The options for museums to 'do business' are more than one might imagine at first. They range from admissions – higher 'donation' fees, increased revenues from new members – to increased sales revenues in museum stores. Sales revenues can take other forms: mail order catalogues, licensing of products, publishing of books and videos, theatre or movie revenues, rental of museum facilities, restaurants or cafés, catering and even selling mailing lists. Entertainment activities such as hosting concerts or other performances are another potential source of revenue. So is the education option: formal classes or lectures offered to the public on any variety of museum-related topics. There are other possibilities, too. The point is that when a museum makes the often difficult decision to try to function in the business world, there are at least as many reasons for optimism as for fear of losing sight of the institutional mission – or losing your shirt.

The days of free museum admission have all but disappeared in most cities. The popular approach is a 'suggested' donation ranging from a few dollars to a possibly record-breaking admission fee of $16 – the price for receiving tickets through Ticketmaster for the Museum of Modern Art's blockbuster Matisse show.

'Museums are competing for the entertainment dollar,' says Samuel Sachs, director of the Detroit Institute of Arts. 'We compete with newspapers, magazines, sporting events, etc. The entrepreneurial success story is going to be when museums charge on a per visit basis what they charge for rock concerts or the opera – when, for example, the Museum of Modern Art charges $20 to get into a Matisse exhibit. But I don't see that happening,' says Sachs. Much to the relief, no doubt, of the public.

In looking for earned income options, some museums have gone after the El Dorado of the 'blockbuster' show. On paper this can seem like a great way to improve the bottom line, reach new audiences and increase membership all in one blow. But to even attempt this kind of show requires tremendous resources of people and money. And the net effect is not always what one expects. Museum directors seem in agreement that the blockbuster show presents an unusual set of challenges. One problem is the large numbers of new members who join with the false expectation that the museum is regularly going to sponsor similar events. Retaining those new members has been a problem for many museums.

'I think a blockbuster has to be treated as frosting on the cake,' says Harry S. Parker III, director of the Fine Arts Museums of San Francisco. 'Blockbusters are not predictable. They can't be relied upon. . . . The financial risk is very great. They must be exploited for maximum gain.' Parker cautions that 'renewal rates are much lower on blockbuster membership gains because the commitment by many of those new members is less sincere.'

Some of the highest-profile 'blockbuster' shows to be staged in recent years are the 'Wonders' Cultural Exhibition series sponsored by the city of Memphis. Critics of this unabashedly commercial approach claim that these shows are not 'museum' exhibitions at all, but closer to P.T. Barnum or Walt Disney World. Following on the heels of the highly successful 1986 Ramses exhibition in Memphis's Convention Center, the city fathers decided to sponsor a series on the great wonders of the world as a means of establishing the city as a cultural centre in the South – and as an economic jump-starter for the city. To date, four exhibitions have been mounted using hired curators and a show-biz approach to exhibition design. 'Ramses' drew 675,000 people – nearly half from out of town. The first 'Wonders' exhibition, 'Catherine the Great', drew 603,000 in 1991 and made in excess of $1 million. The city estimates that it brought in over $50 million through hotel room rentals, meals served and other tourist dollars expended. The 'Splendor of the Ottoman Sultans' in 1992 drew 225,000. 'The Etruscans: Legacy of a Lost Civilization', held at the Pink Palace Museum in Memphis, drew about 125,000.

Museum critics say that we're commercializing art,' says 'Wonders' director Jon Thompson, who is also the city's director of cultural affairs. 'I say we're popularizing art – there is a difference. . . . All the museums in town set records for attendance when these exhibitions were held. . . . We are bringing culture to the city. If we can bring ten years of "Wonders" to the city, we have an opportunity to produce a totally different kind of adult. We have the opportunity to bring up children in this area who will have a totally different outlook on life and on culture. After all,' Thompson concludes, 'dynasties are remembered by their cultures – not much else.'

Thompson also believes he is making a long-term contribution to future museum audiences through these exhibitions. 'After they have been to one of our exhibits, they've passed the point of intimidation. They've come to understand that going to a museum or to an exhibition doesn't have to be as passive as looking at pictures on the wall.' Thompson hopes to produce a decade of similar blockbuster shows in Memphis in the 1990s.

In addition to shuddering at some of Thompson's assumptions, some museum professionals are likely to feel threatened by the popular and financial success of the Memphis experience. What will it mean if communities conclude that there is no need for a museum when they can simply hire a curator and mount their own show in the local convention centre, as in Memphis, or even at the Dallas Fairgrounds, where the 'Catherine the Great' show was on view this October at the Texas State Fair?

Despite museums' aesthetic objections to what one Memphis city official calls, with no trace of irony, the 'blood, guts, gold, and sex' of the blockbuster show, elected city officials are likely to look first at the numbers,. both in terms of dollars and people. And the numbers speak for themselves.

Twenty years ago, museums that were able to boast of having a museum shop at all were confined to peddling reproduction jewellery, fine arts postcards and exhibition catalogues. Today, the museum shop has become an essential revenue producer for most larger museums, offering everything from coffee mugs to designer fashions. The Museum Store Association now boasts 1,700 museum members who gather to discuss merchandising and marketing techniques. According to *Money* magazine, of the 8,000 museums in the nation, 3,000 operate shops, as compared to 1,600 five years ago. The magazine estimates that in 1991, the museum retail business brought in revenues of $500 million.

The museum shop has always been an extension of the museum – a way to extend the learning experience, to capture the enthusiasm of young collectors, and to allow visitors to bring home a souvenir of the experience. The shop has also become an important part of the equation in financing the museum's basic mission – so much so that museums have begun to open satellite shops in suburban malls.

'The satellite shops raise the visibility and viability of museums as a community entity,' says Detroit Institute of Arts director Samuel Sachs. 'By keeping our flag in front of the public, we aid our museum, we provide an opportunity for visitors to the shop to become members, to buy a ticket for a film series, or a ticket to an exhibition.

Shops are also a way for some museums to 'suburbanize'. Unlike many inner-city community institutions, museums have not migrated to the suburbs. In post-war America, many churches and temples, for example, have followed their congregations to the suburbs, closing their original downtown locations and opening new suburban houses of worship. Similarly, hospitals have, in some instances, moved to the suburbs or opened satellite clinics there. Many museums, however, have remained in the heart of the city. By establishing shops in the suburbs of New York or Chicago or Detroit, the inner-city museum has found a way to keep its image in front of its traditional audience and, not incidentally, to increase earned income for the 'mothership', as Sachs likes to refer to it.

These moves to the suburbs have not been without controversy – particularly when technically non-profit museum shops go head-to-head with for-profit retailers, raising the question of violations of the unrelated income business tax (UBIT) regulations and charges of unfair business practice. The Metropolitan Museum not only has an extensive mail-order catalogue business, it has a chain of thirteen off-site stores and six boutiques in Japan.

There is also a fear that the merchandising arm may distort the museum's basic mission and that 'crass commercialism' will lead to too much emphasis on the shop. In fact, most museum shops contribute only 2 to 10 per cent of the total earned income for the museum – scarcely enough to sway the museum's overall direction, but enough to encourage museums to continue to rely on the shop's revenue.

Probably the most graphic example of a successful shop is the effort by the Freeport Historical Society in Maine. The society owns two properties, a nineteenth-century National Register for Historic Places home called Harrington House, located in the town, and the pristine, early nineteenth-century Pettengill Farm, located on the water about a mile north-east of the town.

The society had great difficulty raising sufficient funds to maintain the farm and keep it open to the public for educational programmes about nineteenth-century rural life and natural history. The in-town property was in need of a total restoration and there were few funds to support that effort. Taking an entrepreneurial leaf from the pages of its famous neighbour, L.L. Bean, the historical society decided to restore the house and garden in complete period detail and to transform it into a gallery selling only high-quality, period reproduction objects.

The house is now headquarters for the society and serves as an in-town exhibition space. The idea was not only to restore the house but to educate visitors about the way people of the period lived. As it turns out, the society also created a cash cow. Today, four years after it opened, the Harrington House Gallery Store operates in the black with average sales per visitor of about $20. Not only does the shop support other activities of the society in addition to membership fees and a small endowment for the farm, but it pays about 10 per cent of the executive director's salary.

'Out back we have a barn that is still unrestored,' says executive director Ann Ball. 'It's our hope that the money generated by the shop will help to restore the barn and make it into the museum that now only takes a small portion of Harrington House.'

Harrington House's famous neighbour L.L. Bean may have set the trend for mail-order merchandising, but museums are not far behind. Mail-order catalogues have also become a way to bring the museum to those who don't come to the museum. Among the big names in catalogue sales are: the Metropolitan Museum of Art ($81 million on overall merchandising effort in 1991); the Museum of Fine Arts, Boston ($26,650,000 in merchandise operations revenue for 1990–1991); and the Mystic Seaport Museum Stores ($1,615,000 in sales for the fiscal year ending April 1991). Bargain-minded shoppers quickly learn that if they join the museum, they get the special discounts available at the shops or through catalogue sales.

The Smithsonian Institution not only sells products from its catalogue, but even markets its mailing list of 'affluent, well-educated customers' who 'have avidly purchased beautifully crafted gifts and reproductions from the catalogue'. The price is $50 per thousand for buyers of $150-plus items or $60 per thousand if you want to buy the names of those who have purchased specific product types.

Recently museums have become savvy to the profit potential of licensing products reproduced from their collections. The Smithsonian, for example, not only retains strict quality control on the products to be manufactured, but on the manner in which any licensed item is marketed. In addition, the museum generally gets up to a 10 per cent royalty on all net sales by the manufacturer. Industry-wide, depending on the items, royalties can range from a low of 1.5 per cent for bed linens to a high of 10 per cent for some furniture designs.

Even smaller museums can attempt licensing programmes if they are careful about the quality of the manufacturer and the fine print on the contract. Kirk Stieff, a Baltimore silver- and hollow-ware manufacturer, has active licensing agreements with several museums around the country, including the Smithsonian and Monticello. Sue Bates, director of museum shop sales at Monticello, reports that their licensing programme of reproductions from the historic home of Thomas Jefferson has earned about 1 per cent of the institution's entire operating budget.

The advantage of licensing is that not only is the product sold by the museum in whose collection a particular piece is housed, but that people all over the country have an opportunity to appreciate the work and know that it came from that collection. Museums are heavily involved in cross-marketing products licensed from other institutions.

Co-operative ventures are occurring increasingly in the area of video and book publishing as well. It's very difficult for most museums to market a catalogue or book beyond its own walls. With the help of several large commercial publishers, such as Abbeville Press and St. Martin's Press of New York, Prestel-Verlag of Munich, and several university presses, museums have been able to reach a wider, more popular audience. When the Phoenix Art Museum collaborated with Harry N. Abrams publishers of New York, the museum had to guarantee that it would purchase between $20.000 and $30,000 worth of catalogues. The initial budget for a catalogue of nineteenth-century English painting, prior to joining forces with Abrams, was $120,000 for a solo publishing venture. Instead, the museum's initial outlay was a mere $3,000, plus the efforts of its staff.

Says Sherwood Spivey, assistant director of the museum and president of the Western Museums Conference 'It was an everybody-wins situation. We didn't have to publish a book ourselves at greater expense and without the ability to market it. Abrams production quality was superb and they know how to market the book and give it wide distribution.' Spivey also points out that there was a hidden benefit in working with an outside publisher – deadlines tended to be met.

Museums are just beginning to explore the use of videotapes to extend their viewing audiences. For armchair art historians, historic preservation buffs or tourists, videos provide a way to learn about a collection located in distant states or other countries. For the museum, video productions also have the potential to generate earned income. Production costs, though, are extreme, running between $2,000 and $5,000 per finished minute for colour broadcast-quality video. HomeVision, a Chicago based video distribution firm, has made a business of distributing and marketing tapes of museum exhibitions and special single-artist studies.

Museum shops have not yet widely explored the possibility of video rentals, but some museums have mastered facility rentals. The Phoenix Art Museum, for example has just published a brochure, *Special Events*, offering its spaces for lease. The programme is still nascent, but the hope is that in its first year, use of the museum after hours for special events will generate substantial earned income. 'We're meeting with corporations, meeting planners, associations – everyone we can think of who might want to hold an affair here,' says Spivey.

One of the nation's most aggressive proponents of renting museum spaces to defray operating expenses is the Metropolitan Museum of Art. Faced with a monumental deficit in the mid-1980s, the Met agreed that in exchange for becoming a 'sponsor', select corporate entities could hold parties on the premises. Such sponsorship is not cheap. A $40,000 annual contribution entitles the corporation to one event. Corporate sponsors of a specific exhibition – $50,000 and up – can host an opening party. After some initial criticism, the Met now has strict guidelines for on-site events, but still books as many as seven or eight weekly in high season.

The whole idea of 'poaching salmon in propane cookers between galleries' has met with opposition from those concerned about the message given when a museum is 'hired' for the night for parties. The Met has received a great deal of criticism regarding its policies. Is the Temple of Dendur an appropriate setting for a wedding reception? On one occasion it was, but the Met now permits only carefully screened corporate functions throughout the museum.

On the practical level, leasing space can create wear and tear on the museum's collections. Guests dumping champagne in the reflecting pond in the Temple of Dendur might be more comical than dangerous, but if they smoke near rare paintings or brush up against a fine wood sculpture, for instance, real damage might be done. What is the impact of a gallery filled with people who are there primarily to enjoy a party?

Economic necessity may be the driving force in the proliferation of gallery rentals, but precedent is being established. Will rental 'customers' exert undue influence on the use of museum space, or even eventually on their design? And will future exhibition space be planned with rental market in mind?

Many museums in recent years have established restaurants or cafés. Lately some museums are using these facilities to cater affairs, too. 'It's difficult to make money on one meal a day,' says Samuel Sachs of the Detroit Institute of Arts. To help make that part of the museum pay its own way, the museum uses the restaurant to cater some five to ten events a week.

In England, both the Victoria and Albert Museum and the Tate Gallery have made their restaurants competitive, high-quality facilities. The Tate's wine cellar, for example, is known to be exceedingly well stocked, reflecting the kind of customer it wishes to attract. The Guggenheim Museum has contracted with the chic New York caterer Dean and DeLuca to operate its new café. Having lost money for years on its old café, the Guggenheim realized that 'our expertise is not in running a restaurant', says Gail Harrity, deputy director for finance and administration. 'We want the restaurant to become a service first, a destination point for visitors second, and third, we want it to run in the black.' The Dean and DeLuca deal, says Harrity, 'leaves us in the black. We tapped the upside potential and eliminated the downside risk.'

Few cafés or restaurants make much money for a museum, while most barely break even. But there are other benefits to an in-house restaurant. It becomes an additional draw for visitors, a means to extend a visit with a break for coffee or a meal. And it is convenient for staff, too, sometimes even allowing business to be done in-house over lunch.

Renting space may be more of a problem for some museums than renting out collections, an increasing trend. Probably the most significant exhibition of a 'rented' collection is the show at the National Gallery of Art (which opened on 9 May 1993) of the never-before-travelled Barnes Collection of Merion, PA. The rental charges will enable the Barnes to make much-needed multi-million-dollar renovations to its building without having to pay for costly insurance and storage while the work goes on.

In 1983–4, when most museums were thinking about expansion, the Phillips Collection in Washington, DC renovated its main building and took its collection on the road. In 1987–9, during a major renovation of its annexe, the collection went on the road again. Together, both trips netted $2 million for the museum.

The Museum of Fine Arts, Boston, has taken the idea of touring portions of its collection one step further. The museum will open a satellite museum in Nagoya, Japan, within five years. In addition to bringing rotating exhibits from its collection to Japan, the museum will generate income through consulting fees earned by its technical and professional staff.

Education has become the focus for museums in the 1990s, but can such activities be revenue producers? The Smithsonian Institution's Resident Associates programme is probably the most extensive museum education programme in the nation, drawing some 300,000 students a year for everything from classes and workshops for every age group to two-day intensive seminars and trips and tours. One can even go to the 'Campus on the Mall' and earn 'credits' towards a certificate or university degree through co-operative relationships with local universities.

The Resident Associates programme operates with a staff of 67 and an annual budget of $7 million. The programme pays all its own direct and indirect programme costs, from guards to office space rental.

At the opposite end of the spectrum, the 3,000-member Montclair (NJ) Art Museum tracks its barely break-even arts education classes and has been able to demonstrate a net gain of one hundred new members per year, a significant plus to the museum's $1.8 million annual budget.

The fine line museums constantly tread is to do good, in the sense of community service, and to do well, financially. Entertainment activities, from concerts to films and theatre, are used by many institutions to do both. Yet critics of this approach scoff at the pop slant of many of these programmes. Is a singles jazz concert on Friday nights really a part of a museum's mission? Such questions are not new. They are part of the continuing battle of the cultural populists versus the elite.

Financial gain from entertainment activities can have a positive impact on a museum's other programmes. Even when the earned income is modest, the museum can come out ahead on the membership side. But these activities may also have a potentially greater positive impact in building community support, showing that the museum is an active part of the local community's social structure.

Probably the most costly and attractive entertainment activities as a populist 'draw' and an income generator are the IMAX and OMNIMAX theatre systems. Despite the $5-million average price tag for the installation of such theatres, it's an option that some twenty-eight US museums have taken. Raising money for the construction or retro-fit of these theatres via a capital campaign presents its own set of challenges.

The Maryland Science Center in Baltimore had a 52 per cent increase in the record level of attendance after the installation of its IMAX theatre. Other museums provide similarly impressive attendance increases. The Museum Centre at Union Terminal in Cincinnati sold 1.4 million tickets and took $3,056,100 in its first year – $88,000 more than projected. The museum has an OMNIMAX theatre.

To counter those who would say this is museum show-biz, movie producers have augmented their films with additional teaching materials and other activities to ensure that the experience is also educational.

Ironically, the current painful pressures of the recession may contain a hidden benefit. Museums of all kinds across the country are being forced to sharpen their fiscal and entrepreneurial skills. Intelligent economic planning is a smart move, regardless of economic climate. In planning an exhibition, how many institutions do a projected cost/benefit analysis and budget? How many prepare new member retention plans for post-exhibition activities? Clearly, entrepreneurship needs to include administrative planning if museums are not only to survive but thrive.

An example of entreprenerial planning can be seen in the city of San Diego. A single $9.50 'passport' of coupons allows people to visit Balboa Park and select from nine of the museums and other cultural attractions at the park. A similar joint marketing technique is being discussed by the Baltimore Museum of Art, the Maryland Science Center, the National Aquarium in Baltimore, the Walters Art Gallery, the Zoo and the B & O Railroad Museum. At present they are working on details of a single-priced, multi-facility ticket.

As museums begin to experiment further with entrepreneurship, there is a fear that the marketing tail will wag the dog – that museums will neglect the purposes for which they were founded in favour of doing the 'popular' or 'lucrative' thing. And the fear is not entirely unfounded. There are signs of a growing 'creative tension' between marketing people and curatorial staffs. But in many museums, there is a tacit understanding that one cannot operate successfully without the other – that marketing people exist to support the museum's principal mission.

'In a way', says Marion Grzesiak, director of development for the Montclair Art Museum, 'we're just like a store marketing a special book or a baseball. You have to look at what is saleable. It's got to be attractive enough to bring people in – if it's not, they won't come.'

Despite the tension, there is a clear convergence of interests between marketers and curators. 'The role of the curator was as acquisitor for many years,' says Andrew Oliver, director of the Museum Program at the National Endowment for the Arts. 'Today, that person is rare. Most younger curators are presenters.'

As museums continue to confront the challenge of financial survival, they will increasingly have to find ways to both fulfil their principal missions and generate earned income, not necessarily with an eye towards self-sufficiency, but as a means to help in the continuing struggle to defray costs and keep the institution financially solvent in a time of severely reduced funding.

As Samuel Sachs puts it, 'Museums are, after all, money-spending institutions, not money-making institutions.'

The challenge is to find the appropriate way to be both.

This article first appeared in Museum News *(Nov./Dec. 1992), pp. 38–43, 62–3.*

14

Museum planning and museum plans
Alf Hatton

Planning may now be ubiquitous in museums, but managers, as Stuart Davies's survey earlier in this volume suggests, tend to have a rather shallow understanding of strategic management. In this chapter Alf Hatton applies some of the latest thinking in this field to the particular needs of museums.

As management is still a relatively recent member of the museum club, it is perhaps worth reviewing some recent, relevant research in the general management field. in an attempt to provide some thought-provoking pointers.

I am going to apply briefly three pieces of recent research to museums: critical resource; the strategic gap concept; and implementation problems in strategic planning.

In these stringent financial times (when were they not?) museums everywhere are preparing corporate strategies, mission statements, and so on. It could be said that they are indulging in a surfeit of planning.

Perhaps this is as it should be, for it really is not all that long ago when many museums, and certainly the largest among them, would have had great difficulty describing their objectives, let alone showing anyone a plan or formula for achieving their ambitions.

Planning, the first of a four-function definition of the management process – plan, organize, motivate and control – is clearly a key issue in management. It is an important management function to the extent that it is first in many such descriptions of the management process. Another key management issue is resources, to the extent that the term 'resource management' is in common use.

CRITICAL RESOURCES

About resources, Wernerfelt (1989: 4) states: 'Only very few resources are critical in the sense that they can differentiate you from the competition. The resource has to be unique.' There is no doubting that statement. Among many other ways to describe this phenomenon, I would describe it from another management angle as finding your 'market niche'.

So the question museums must ask themselves is: does museum competition come from English Heritage, the National Trust, the members of the Historic Houses Association, zoos, cinema, TV, video? Or all of these?

Does the public (or for that matter, the museum profession itself) fully understand and appreciate the differences between those potential competitors and the unique services museums claim to offer? Maybe the difference, in the eyes of the consumer, is just too subtle. Perhaps museums have failed to inform the public sufficiently for them to see there is a difference? Indeed, is there one, genuinely sufficient to warrant Wernerfelt's 'critical resource' analogy?

What critical resources do museums have? Clearly, one answer is the objects themselves. No two artefacts are the same, and all artefacts are unique, and irreplaceable. Hence, if a museum burns down despite stringent fire precautions, all is lost. Or so one local government treasurer alleged in his opposition to further expenditure on fire security.

The museum's claim was that, though the loss of an entire museum's contents through fire would be an undoubted disaster, the insurance reimbursement – the premiums for which the treasurer was trying to lose from the budget as 'dead money' – would allow over time the assembly of a replacement collection of some sort, which would then create a replacement amenity for the community.

The number of museums that compete with each other, in strict collection terms, is very limited. But perhaps the public does not see the difference between any one museum and another as being all that acute. They are approaching museums as leisure, certainly useful leisure, but they are placing museum visiting in a context of leisure time spent.

They may, of course, differentiate museums on the grounds of satisfaction, of comfort during their visit, of ease of arranging the visit, or of how pleasant the staff were. But it is unlikely that they will differentiate on the grounds of collection quality and range in the way that museum professionals would.

The National Trust, innumerable private and public monuments and historic houses also vie for the public's leisure time. So here, too, museums are in real competition with the National Trust. English Heritage, and the multitude of historic houses the UK has scrupulously decided to preserve. In the public's eye, these competitors may appear to be just more 'homely' museums.

In interpretation terms, they are certainly more tangible than a lot of more traditional museums – everyone recognizes a kitchen or bedroom, regardless of scale, whereas not all visitors will be aware a priori of the subtle difference between an axe and an adze.

Another factor is that there may just be too many museums altogether – especially in the south-east of England: 47.4 per cent of national, government and departmental museums, 27.8 per cent of local authority museums, and 34.2 per cent of others (Prince and Higgins-McLoughlin 1987: 25).

This is the market saturation described by Middleton (1990), but may well be the situation all UK museums are facing. Although for the independents this is a threat to their continued existence, since they have a more precarious financial existence than other museums, there is surely also an implicit threat to all museums?

Or are there simply too many museums with 'uncritical resources'? How does the public choose one undifferentiated product from another? Are museums, using the Wernerfelt analogy, just 'uncompetitive' in the sense that they do not see themselves as competing for anything much, besides objects and government finance?

There is certainly a growing awareness that they are competing for people's time, and – where they charge for admission – much more crucially their disposable income. But only the largest museums can afford an appropriate level of market research to underpin a better understanding of their market.

One might even be more provocative and ask: are English Heritage or the National Trust simply better marketed? They were certainly seen to be marketing rather earlier than many museums. What are their 'critical resources'?

'You cannot expect superior performance in a fair race against equals. Instead, you need to look for races where you have an advantage' (Wernerfelt 1989: 11). Is the size the critical resource here? Do the two national bodies have 'critical mass', whereas the majority of museums are simply analogous to small retailers competing with the supermarket chains? There is certainly a case for more serious joint marketing initiatives, besides distributing leaflets through the tourist boards or partnership in yet another promotional leaflet.

But this also raises the age-old question of which 'race' are museums in: heritage; leisure; tourism; education; conservation; religion; 'edu-tainment'? And when that question is answered, what advantages do museums have over their competitors?

Wernerfelt also poses the question 'Does your business mix sufficiently take advantage of your critical resources?' (1989: 12). Given the newer interpretive methods creeping into museums, are museums being 'uncritical' in terms of their resources? And are they, in fact, competing in an 'unfair race'. Madame Tussauds can de-accession those dummies that no longer appear as the public favourites. They can respond topically in a way museums find difficult. Are museums marketing themselves as a 'place to go' (Mead 1970: 23), in a race against equals?

Clearly, museums need to be in a race where they at least have a genuine and clearly visible 'USP' (unique selling proposition).

Yet, a long and hard look at what appears in print on the subject reveals such generalizations as heritage, leisure, tourism, education, conservation, 'edu-tainment', contributions to the quality of life, and many others, often argued with great conviction, but also susceptible to rapid changes in fashion through either policy or managerial shifts. So are museums trying, by force of financial necessity, to compete in the wrong race(s)?

The fourth function in the management dynamic or process, is control. Often, planning does take place: the myriad new galleries and new schemes that exist is sufficient evidence of that. Museum professional staffs are surely highly creative.

But planning can all too frequently be followed by precious little organizing and motivating. Worse still, it can often be left completely uncontrolled.

Planning, the 'sexy' bit, is a 'turn on'! But plans do not achieve themselves. Staff – probably the most unrecognized critical resource in the museum – need organizing and motivating. But they also need control, to measure progress against the plan.

Otherwise, why bother to plan – except that it may elicit a pat on the back from funding bodies, and the resulting brochure may look glossy and convincing. Then again, this may have been the objective!

As crucial as Wernerfelt's 'critical resources', is the question of the strategic gap (Harrison 1989). Strategic management may be described as the relationship between an organization and its external environment, and the extent to which the organization attempts to steer itself through the turbulent environment in which all organizations now exist. The hypothesis assumes rapid change not just in technology, but also accelerating rates of change – the Toffler thesis (1970) – and it has its proponents in the museums world (Singleton 1979: 11).

THE STRATEGIC GAP CONCEPT

In analysing strategic gap, organizations need to focus on their real capabilities, versus the external countervailing pressures that will defeat their best laid plans.

Harrison argues for two types of strategic gap: positive and negative. A positive strategic gap can be described as the situation where an assessment of the organization shows its capabilities are greater than the countervailing external factors. Negative strategic gap is obviously the opposite, where those external pressures are greater and can conspire to unhinge plans.

Harrison suggests that strategies for dealing with strategic gap fall into four categories: rational; replenishment; reinforcement; and renewal.

A *rational strategy* is where the organization has strengths in excess of external opportunities, but also where its management is effective, its technology advanced, its policies comprehensive, and its resources fully and productively utilized.

A rational strategy situation for museums, in which the museum's strengths are in excess of the opportunities to apply them, is difficult to imagine. Effective management depends, amongst other things, on a receptive board or committee. In many ways also, museum technology is embryonic, rather than advanced; in its basic function of display (let alone in terms of automated stores and inventories), the museum uses a nineteenth-century medium of communication: the written word. But policies are certainly comprehensive these days in most areas.

The rational strategy demands, however, fully utilized resources – and in museums resources are rarely fully utilized in the sense of outputs, as opposed to being fully committed to collection management above all.

A *replenishment strategy* is where organizational strength is, similarly, in excess of external opportunities, but where there are idle resources and under-utilized capability. The way out of this is to diversify (through acquisition or merger), intensify new product development, or 'out-marketing', through licensing, consultancy or leasing.

Replenishment is an easier situation to discern. Museums face an excess of external opportunities for utilization, but there are no idle resources where they commit, on average, up to 70 per cent of all expenditure on direct and indirect collection management costs (Lord and Nicks 1989: 65). The actual figures are 83 per cent for nationals, 70 per cent for local authorities, and 59 per cent for independents. This is staggering in itself, but especially so for the independents, which are often alleged to be leaner in these areas. The museum still functions as a warehouse, and is without its 'retail capability'.

Diversification of the 'museum product' has long been a bugbear of mine. As our markets sophisticate and move, so must museums. If visitors want more entertaining and less didactic history, then we should be creative in finding ways of meeting that need.

But diversification through acquisition or merger presents new possibilities. One could see the development of what is called in the National Health Service an 'internal market', whereby museums sell excess capacity or specialized expertise to each other. Indeed, it already exists to an extent, and has done for a long time through the Area Museum Councils and their various museum services sections. This has to be more cost-effective than all museums simply trying to build up their institutions' expertise-base as widely as possible.

Licensing and leasing arrangements for collections and facilities, which allow a commercial return, also have to begin to make sense, simply as a reasonable use of idle resources (artefacts) which museums are otherwise unable to use for lack of capital. Perhaps this should be seen as a novel way of increasing access to the average 80 per cent of stored collections (Lord and Nicks 1989: 18).

Whilst we have to accept, of course, that much of what is stored is not of display quality, we also have to acknowledge that there is in general little access to it for any use. But this type of methodology might also prove to be a viable income-earning opportunity. Maybe that is what appears so objectionable about it!

Instead of attempting to open yet another museum, a museum conglomerate might decide to lease the resources (objects, space, or both) to a commercial operator. Commercial operators generally do not invest in products without a market. Suitably recompensed, why should museums object?

A *reinforcement strategy* is a situation where the external opportunities are abundant, but where there are weaknesses in the organization. The exit from this situation is to replace top management, combine that with a comprehensive restructuring, replace obsolescent technology, a comprehensive revision of policies, and a reallocation of resources within the organization.

Situations that need a reinforcement strategy are common enough in museums. The replacement of management has been seen in our largest museums over the last couple of years. Although this may have more to do with a generation change at top level than positive Board action. Comprehensive restructuring of staffing and comprehensive revisions of policies, with the consequent reallocation of resources within the organization, is now a fact of museum life. The very public furore over some of the consequences of this process at the Victoria and Albert and the Natural History Museums is evidence enough. Clearly, museum policy makers are aware of, and make use of, reinforcement as a strategy.

Renewal, the 'worst' situation to be in, is where, as in the case of a reinforcement strategy, the external opportunities are in short supply, but are combined with weaknesses in the organization. 'The organisation is usually in the throes of a widespread malaise with deepening symptoms of entropy' (Harrison 1989: 70).

The answer is a complete rebuild of the structure, a retrenchment of all activities that do not contribute directly to viability, and substantial changes in personnel throughout.

In museums, situations requiring renewal strategy seem to be more common still than those requiring reinforcement. The 'widespread malaise' is detectable. Yet there are no signs of attempts at the complete rebuilding of structures, only some fairly substantial tinkering with them. Museum structures continue to grow sideways, although a few brave ones have re-thought the structure completely. Where they have, it has not necessarily been welcomed by staff.

The retrenchment of activities that do not contribute to viability, or instances of complete changes in personnel, have yet to be seen. How many museums yet know the cost of enquiry services to compare with the non-financial benefits of running one?

But before we go too far, we must acknowledge problems in planning, particularly strategic planning. First, the problem in strategic planning is not an inability to use sophisticated management tools, nor an inability necessarily in computerized and numerate techniques. The problem is making things happen.

IMPLEMENTATION PROBLEMS

Genuine problems in attempting the strategic planning approach can be: the separation of planning from management; hopeless optimism; and that implementation and its problems are recognized too late. The barriers to change are not seen, the costs of organizational change consequent on the planned change are not recognized: 'it must be more cost effective'.

There is denial of implementation problems. Plans work by and through the commitment of people at all levels: 'if it doesn't work, its because you wouldn't let it work'. Implementation is bolted on at the end of the plan, instead of being an integral part of the plan itself. Getting the plan achieved is seen as tidying up loose ends for someone else, when the real task – planning – is finished!

Barriers to change, even when seen, are often not analysed. The result can be coercion or its opposite, the dumping of plans altogether. When difficulties are sounded about a plan in the early stages by the people who will have to carry it out, the 'like it or lump it' approach appears – or the plan is dropped – rather than underpinned by an analysis of problems and the barriers to the proposed changes themselves.

The alternative route suggested is not to go for strategic goals or corporate missions, but performance and tactical actions based on what line management says is important. This is concomitant with the flatter organizations much talked about, as a development away from pyramidical and hierarchical organizations: the flatter ones are said to be more responsive.

It may be a while yet before museums can rid themselves of hierarchies, which undoubtedly restrict flexibility and prevent innovation and change.

This particular performance gap is the visionary 'Museum 2000' type of plan that envisages five more museums bolted on to an existing service of two, but fails to see the organization's weaknesses – the local authority (or other funding body) does not see museums as a priority. It fails to assess the external environment – are there enough visitors to justify such expansive growth?

The alternative would be to concentrate on doing what those two museums do well now, even better: greater spreads of visitors from the various sections of the community; a larger proportion of earned income to direct funding; and an improved quality of experience and service to the visitors and users.

However, no museum management contract yet is so specific as to identify performance-related pay with such actual goals. Planning the new scheme, therefore, is still likely to be the performance by which museum managements will be rated for some time to come.

This article first appeared in Museum Development *(Jan. 1992), pp. 32–9.*

REFERENCES

Harrison, E. F. (1989) 'The concept of the strategic gap,' *Journal of General Management* 15(2): 52–72.
Leslie, R. (1987) 'Museums in education: seizing the market opportunities,' in Ambrose, T. (ed.) (1987) *Education in Museums: Museums in Education*, Edinburgh: Scottish Museums Council/HMSO.
Lord, B., Lord, G. D. and Nicks, J. (1989) *The Cost of Collecting, Collection Management in UK Museums – A Report Commissioned by the Office of Arts & Libraries*, London: HMSO.
Mead, M. (1970) 'Museums in a media-saturated world,' *Museums News* 49(1): 23–5.

Middleton, V. (1990) *New Visions for Independent Museums in the UK*, Chichester: Association of Independent Museums.

Piercy, N. (1989) 'Diagnosing and solving implementation problems in strategic planning,' *Journal of General Management* 15(1): 19–38.

Piercy, N. and Morgan, N. (1990) 'Getting planners out of the ivory tower,' *Sunday Times*, Section 6: 6.2.

Prince, D. R. and Higgins-McLoughlin, B. (1987) *Museums UK: The Findings of the Museums Data-Base Project*, London: Museums Association.

Singleton, H. R. (1979) 'Museums in a changing world,' *Museums Journal*, 79(1): 11–12.

Toffler, A. (1970) *Future Shock*, London: Pan.

Wernerfelt, B. (1989) 'From critical resources to corporate strategy,' *Journal of General Management* 14(3): 4–12.

15

Current issues in museum training in the United Kingdom
Alf Hatton

The training of museum staff seems to be a perennial issue of debate and discord in many countries. Six years after the major Hale Report on the question in Britain, training has become more clouded and controversial than ever. Alf Hatton in this chapter, first published in 1989, questions how far new training initiatives in themselves can offer solutions to the lack of equal opportunities in museum employment and provision.

No review of the present position of museum training in the United Kingdom could begin without immediate reference to the Hale Report.[1] Published in August 1987, the report was, in the words of its chairman, Sir John Hale, 'not of an alarmist nature' (Museums and Galleries Commission: 4). Nevertheless, it has provoked a good deal of thinking and rethinking about the nature of not only museum training, of course, but also about the nature of museums – possibly more so than any previous report. This is in part because it tackled a fundamental problem – training – a matter common to all museum professionals, of whatever size or type of museum, and from whatever background, be it curatorship or security. It is in part, also, because for the first time in an officially backed report some of the 'sacred cows' of the profession in the United Kingdom were both questioned and criticized. However, it is true to say that many of the report's conclusions, in terms of the difficulties faced by UK museums in the very late 1980s, were already well known throughout the museums profession, and often discussed, not least by the Museums Association, which was already well into a review of its own training scheme when the Hale Report was published.

It yet remains to be seen just how many of the fundamental changes being considered then, and indeed those produced as a result of the Hale Report, actually come into existence. More important still, how effectively will such changes in training be in eliciting the improvements identified as necessary; 'documentary, administrative, managerial and marketing efficiency . . . the opening up of the watertight compartments . . . a sense of common, planned purpose . . . to maintain and broaden standards of curatorial scholarship' (Museums and Galleries Commission: 3). Should even one of these objectives for change be achieved, the Hale Report will go down as the first-ever governmentally sponsored report (the Museums and Galleries Commission is an agent of the UK Government) on museums in the United Kingdom which has actually been effective. It will deserve its place in history for that alone, for as any student of the museums phenomenon, or any museum worker alert to matters of policy and governance will observe, most of the key reports on British museums since the end of the nineteenth century have been studiously ignored. However, this would be entirely in keeping with the recent history of the Museums and Galleries Commission, which when compared to its predecessor has taken on a very much stronger role in recent years, setting clearly defined targets for the museums movement to achieve, through both its reports and its grant-aiding activities.

Why then should this report on training and a career structure be different? Timing is one answer. Whatever the ills, real or imagined, of the Museums Association's now almost defunct Diploma Training Scheme, there was, it is fair to say, common acceptance that it had become out-of-date and was becoming even more so as the pace of external change affecting museums accelerated, together with changed government policy on public-sector subsidy, economics, technology, leisure, and so on. It is also true that museum management is now beginning to 'grow up' in the sense that it is beginning to leave the 'closed system era', and is moving into the 'open system era', where a more balanced view of the museum, its environment and their inter-relationship will prevail. This is not to be taken lightly, for its represents a watershed in the development of the museum concept away from its original, predominantly preservationist premise.

Despite the grumblings the 'old' Diploma used to generate, two things have to be remembered in its defence; first, that it was heavily subsidized by the profession itself, as the Museums Association's current president, Dr Patrick Boylan, points out:

> Throughout the past 58 years the membership of the Association has subsidised training both directly from subscription income and indirectly through the generous donation of so much voluntary work in teaching, tutoring, administering and examining for the various qualification and training programmes
>
> (Boylan 1989: 194)

Second, it has been responsible for a huge change in standards in museums in the United Kingdom since the 1950s and 1960s, particularly those in the provinces. For those who feel the changes were not sweeping enough, it has also to be borne in mind that museums, as social institutions, tend more to reflect social changes than predict or catalyse them. So, need we worry that museum management is only some twenty-odd years behind the rest?

> In marked contrast to the prevailing wisdom of today, management theory of the first sixty years of this century did not worry about the environment, competition, the market place, or anything else external to the organization. They had a 'closed system' view of the world. That view, myopic as it now seems, centered on what ought to be done to optimize resource application by taking into account only what went on inside the company. It didn't really change much until almost 1960, when theorists began to acknowledge that internal organization dynamics were shaped by external events. Explicitly taking account of the effects of external forces on the organization's internal workings, then, launched the 'open system' era
>
> (Peters and Waterman 1982: 91)

What then, are the problems UK museums were experiencing, at least as hinted at in the Hale Report? Certainly, there is a prevalent view that many, if not most, museums could do with radical updating in their public galleries, in terms of the quality of the display techniques in use, identified by moves towards ever more thematic displays and backed by multi-media communication. Indeed, this is even true in terms of the range of material displayed – as evidenced by the visiting public's taste for variety in what they see in museums – and in the growth of the 'independent' museums in Britain, which tend to specialize in more tangible and discrete social historical themes (Prince and Higgins-McLaughlin 1987: 50).

Finance is also seen as a problem. But surely no professional museum worker in the United Kingdom in the 1980s (or long before?) could seriously have misread the government's intention *not* to 'increase the cake', though there is still a coterie who believe in a change of government as the panacea to all the public sector's financial ills (especially those of museums). But even they are beginning to understand that, were such an event to occur, a speedy return to the public sector museum bonanza (which I and most of my colleagues seem to have missed!) is extremely unlikely. In any case, governments in general do tend to see museums as, if not 'at the bottom of the pile' for consideration in terms of attention and money, certainly very near the bottom, by comparison with other things, particularly economic regeneration. Hence there is a feeling of coming to terms with the reality of museums not perceived as a basic need in society, so much as a desirable extra. Furthermore, it remains a commonly held, but relatively unchallenged, received wisdom that museums do not command economic clout,[2] or indeed electoral clout: no museum issue, not even admissions charges, is likely to either win or lose an election for a government, either local or central.

Then, too, museums are still perceived to be 'elitist'; not in the sense that they close their doors to the poorer socio-economic groups, although the effect of imposing admissions charges, amongst other things, could be said to do precisely this. They are still, however, closing their doors to those who do not have the necessary foreknowledge to make good use of a museum or gallery visit, a sort of intellectual elitism. Their competitors in the historic houses, heritage centres and the media make no such mistakes. Museums are also seen as elitist in that they do not readily respond to specialized needs, be they those of disabled visitors, ethnic minorities, or other user groups: 'Museums should be responsive to all aspects of the community and training should promote an awareness of the needs of the disadvantaged museum user' (Museums and Galleries Commission: 23). Nor do they tend, except, it is alleged, in the independent sector, to go out and win their audiences. In other words, although museums cost money, user/cost ratios merely indicate poor performance in spreading that cost, not, please note, reducing the cost. So, in most public sector museums, even those with an admissions charge, increased visitor activity elicits only a pat on the back, as virtually the only performance indicator in use; conversely, in the 'independents', it acts as a significant financial indicator.

Well, how did Hale intend that new training initiatives should address these problems? First, there is to be training to reflect 'a new emphasis on financial accountability . . . pressure to maximise resources . . . increase earned income and to reach more people' (Museums and Galleries Commission: 20). What this means is that government has stated, quite clearly and loudly, that there will be no significant increase in the state's contribution to the museum service as a whole. It means that the curator/director of the future must become something of an entrepreneur to go out and seek financial support whenever, and wherever, he or she can. Now there are those in the United Kingdom who have been preaching this gospel of self-reliance for at least two decades. They are called the 'independent' museums, i.e. museums that 'rely for their survival on the success of their management and marketing policies in a way which does not yet apply to the publicly maintained museums' (Museums and Galleries Commission: 44).[3] The key word is 'yet'! Those currently working in museums who do not take note of it may find themselves out of a job as their own museum is forced to respond when market forces are allowed to take a role in the business of museums in the next two decades.

Second, what do the users actually want? What exactly are museums to give to 'more people than ever before'?

Accustomed to high standards of display and communication through exposure to television, magazines, commercial exhibitions and shops, the public now demand similar standards in museums. They want to be entertained and informed in a manner to which they have become accustomed, and they expect access to information to be made easy for them.

(Museums and Galleries Commission: 20)

There is a subtle change here, in that entertainment has become the primary objective, and information comes second to it. This, it seems to me, has been the hub of what has been called the 'museum dilemma' since museums began to become a mass phenomenon in the nineteenth century, i.e. the question of whether museums exist to inform or to entertain.

There are those who argue, of course, that these are not mutually exclusive opposites, and that museums can do both. But this is not mere semantics: it is a clear statement of purpose. It also establishes an order of priorities simply because there are limits to the aids even technology can bring to museums to assist them to achieve both objectives. In other words, if they are not mutually exclusive aims, are museums up to the task of achieving both, and will the 'new' training seek to implement such a heady approach? Moreover, it has to be said, few in the United Kingdom really know who is currently visiting their museums, and what their motivation is, let alone have the vitality required to implement the necessary changes in communication, interpretation and exhibition methods. Only recently I visited one national museum whose 'technology' had been out of order for months, apparently due to lack of resources. What price then the implementation of an entirely different, customer-oriented attitude?

The changing needs of society are evoked as a reason for changes in training:

Museums and society are constantly changing and one of the objectives of training should be to equip succeeding generations of museum staff with an awareness of, and responsiveness to, such changes. It will be a major responsibility of the national training body to ensure that training does not fossilise but evolves to meet new situations and opportunities as they arise.

(Museums and Galleries Commission: 51)

Whilst no one would seriously argue the truth of the statement as regards change itself, and though there would be some who might dispute the 'accelerative thrust' (Tofler 1971: 39) so eagerly sought out as a defence by the progressives, there definitely would still be those who argue that this very fact indeed justifies another function of a museum. This is to be somewhere where time is suspended, and in the sense of the original Temples of the Muses, to be a place where people can refresh their spirits, i.e. provide a direct counterbalance to 'change', 'progress' and their classic modern symptom, 'stress'.

On the question of managerial and marketing efficiency, Hale noted a marked difference 'between independent museums and non-independents. . . . One of the most noticeable is the greater percentage of staff employed in independent museums in management, administration, administrative support, sales, marketing and fund raising' (Museums and Galleries Commission: 44). And the stranglehold over management posts in museums maintained by the curatorial ranks is also under scrutiny:

Until now, this managerial role has been almost exclusively the preserve of the curatorial staff. There is now an increasing demand from other categories of museum staff for equal opportunity to train for top management, and in some instances of the recruitment of senior management staff from outside museums altogether

(Museums and Galleries Commission: 20)

Why have curators gained a monopoly on management posts? It has to do with this whole question of role. If a museum exists to collect, then clearly those who have the necessary skills in this field will in time become the persons with overall responsibility for museums. This might not seem unreasonable, and indeed is not unique to museums; generally, it is teachers who become head teachers, and so on.

Why then is it a problem? Because it has led to the absolute dominance in museum thinking in the United Kingdom of collecting, as a single function of museums, where all else is subordinated to that function. The consequences have been over-collecting, unsystematic collection, duplication between museums, poorly thought-out display policies relatively non-existent visitor services, and precious few attempts at sustained genuine outreach. This has reinforced the time-honoured image of museums as 'fusty and dusty'; and still it continues. Hale did not address, indeed could not address, the whole question of why museums collect, what they should be collecting, and how much rational planning of collections there ought to be across the country as a whole.

One can be pragmatic and take the view that to be forewarned is to be forearmed, but I have yet to detect a wholesale recognition of the need for better management training amongst the profession as a whole, though both the Museums Association and the Museums and Galleries Commission have recognized this, and openly said so. How many museum managers, quite happy to spend the equivalent of a year in full-time training for professional curatorship, have had the energy and courage to do the same as a way of preparing themselves for professional museum management? As evidence, there would appear to be less than a dozen holding a postgraduate diploma in management studies, and none so far holding an MBA. Indeed, why have we waited until now yet again to react to external pressure, rather than being prescient and, identifying a trend for which we could have forearmed ourselves, been 'one step ahead'?

The whole question of the museums 'culture' comes up. Museum curators tend to see themselves still to a very great extent as specialists: they are either art historians, or archaeologists, or natural scientists – only rarely museums specialists, as it were. Nor is this new, it was pointed out over twenty years ago (Parr 1960, 1964). Hence Hale opines: 'We are particularly concerned that museum staff should be trained to see themselves as part of a team and not just a collection of specialists who happen to work in the same building' (Museums and Galleries Commission: 50).

Despite Hale's recognition of 'a growing body of opinion within museums which realises that museums must take the initiative in providing a more relevant service for the public', clear notice still had to be given to reluctant curatorial brides, of their impending enforced betrothal: 'This realisation has not yet permeated all coteries within the museum service, and is not always welcomed when it has, because to satisfy these expectations calls for different priorities and additional skills to those of a "traditional" museum curator' (Museums and Galleries Commission: 20). For the nearest thing to a statement of museum purpose yet, Hale suggests:

> Few would dispute the importance of museums as tourist attractions. Over 68 million people 'visited the country's museums and galleries in 1985 . . .'. More people visit museums than go to the performing arts, football matches or the cinema. However, the Government department responsible for tourism policy (the Department of Employment) and the British Tourist Authority believe that the majority of museums have by no means reached their full potential within the tourism and leisure industry.
>
> (Museums and Galleries Commission: 22)

So this question of purpose is not of minor importance. Even Hale noted a certain variation in the differing types of museums: 'These variations in the pattern of employment in the three main museum categories reflect to some extent the different emphases in the respective functions of these museums' (Museums and Galleries Commission: 44).

What other problems are there which were not identified by Hale, either as a limitation of the brief, or by omission, apart from the lack of a clear, distinct and authoritative statement of *raison d'être*, acceptable to the profession? First, perhaps, there are simply far too many museums? It has to be said that there is some cause for alarm in a society that is establishing museums at the rate at which they are currently being opened in the United Kingdom. Whilst one may not accept Hewison's (1987) basic premise that this is stifling initiative in creating other more firmly based (meaning manufacturing) industries, it has to be said that there is a limit to the number of museums that can be created which will add something tangibly new to the existing tapestry of UK museums.

Why are there not more women in management positions? (Prince and Higgins-McLoughlin 1987: 87) and, more tellingly, why are there not more ethnic minorities represented in the work-forces, other than as attendants?[5] Is there some quasi-shamanistic role at work here which eliminates from participation some, and not others, from the cultural hierarchy? Or is it just a case of bad management?

Has anyone addressed the fact that museums are currently riding on the back of a cresting leisure and recreation wave rather than creating specific new markets for themselves, or being more socially conscious and getting out and reaching all sections of society, and with new types of museum experience beyond the visual/quasi-intellectual?[6] In other words, when the present leisure/tourism trend fades, or is replaced by some other, will museums still be receiving visitors by the million, because even silent participation in the museum experience means more than just a 'day out'? Why has nobody in the United Kingdom yet taken up the challenge laid down and questioned this role of museums as nothing but an alternative form of leisure?

But if they are to be leisure/tourist vehicles – Mead's 'a place to go' (1970) – why is the government not investing in them? Years of under-capitalization, and poor resourcing can neither be rectified by changes in training, at least not quickly, nor even by the implementation of sound cash limits and good management. For such wholesale changes require changes in attitude above all, as Hale did point out: 'Training to meet these requirements involves attitudes as well as skills, which has implications for the initial selection process of candidates entering the museum service' (Museums and Galleries Commission: 20). Indeed, why do we have no national policy at all? Such a policy should set out a national structure for museums as leisure, tourist, educational and cultural agencies, which should co-operate with each other and other bodies with similar aims, such as English Heritage, the National Trust, the Historic Houses Association and others. Museums have no monopoly in any of the fields above.

Is training really the answer to all this? The Museums Association has responded with a unanimous decision to back an independent training consortium which, though working closely with the Association, will maintain the 'arm's length principle', and so be able to be critical of the providers of training, and the standards set for training:

> After care and consideration, the Council has decided unanimously to support
> in principle and put forward for full consideration by the whole of the museum

movement, plans for the establishment of the 'industry-wide' training consortium sought by both the Minister for the Arts and the Training Agency, under the name 'Museum Training Institute'.

(Boylan 1989: 194)

Being semi-independent, it is to be hoped that the new institute may find a way to address itself to fundamental issues. No doubt it will not be briefed, nor even will it be equipped, to consider problems created by the 'museum culture', such as questions of inter-museum rationalization and even sensible de-accessioning of the basement stock-piles of 'reserves'. But it must address problems such as training for skills, as opposed to 'knowledge', and qualifications. It must also address the question of selection into the profession in all its various guises, from warders to directors, although quite how it will tackle that question is also difficult to envisage.

Also, if we are seeking future museum entrepreneurs, it is perhaps ironical that a recent study has suggested that Britain's top entrepreneurs today reveal an inverse proportion of qualifications to success (as defined). In other words, the majority left school at 16 years of age with few formal qualifications, let alone postgraduate ones (Bown 1988). Can the new Training Institute, then, implement a system for recognition of management, if not entrepreneurial, talent, simply by validating or not validating courses? And if it can, will the profession accept it? Will personal bibliographies on job applications be replaced by copies of the last five years' balance sheets from one's present post? Will the profession accept a change-over to entrepreneurial, customer-orientated activity, after so many decades addicted to academic, educational and object-orientated service?

For as Peter Gathercole said recently to a meeting of museum archaeologists, but I think it bears scrutiny for all curatorial and collection-based museum workers, we have become 'institutionalized within power structures'.[7] How will a new institute tackle those structures? If the key question is changing attitudes, and hence the generation of change in museums (if change is what we want), the selection of who enters the profession at the bottom of the ladder is the prime area for action. Will we, the people making that selection into university courses, and in junior, nay even senior, posts in museums be so very different from our peers in other 'professions' and rise to the challenge of selecting people so radically different from ourselves?

This article first appeared in the International Journal of Museum Management and Curatorship 8 *(1989), pp. 149–56.*

NOTES

1 'The Hale Report'. Museums and Galleries Commission 1987.
2 See Bloom and Powell (1984: 20) on economic impact in the USA, and Myerscough (1988: 13) for a recent UK study; 132 million admissions during 1984–5 to museums, galleries and heritage attractions, with museums and galleries taking 73 million of the total, and together exceeding theatre, concert and cinema visiting. This equates to an estimated consumer spending of £52 million during 1985–6 (Myerscough 1988: 19), i.e. just 12 per cent of the total £433 million, with museums and galleries representing just over 6 per cent of that sector's total. Will the purpose of museums become, then, economic regeneration? Will we be establishing museums in the future purely to create jobs, and act as catalysts to fading economies?
3 But these independents also receive a significant, one might even suggest the most significant, portion of their revenue income from the public purse by various routes (Prince and Higgins-McLoughlin 1987: 155), i.e. 41 per cent.
4 The original source of the figure was Prince and Higgins-McLoughlin (1987: 135).

5 Dr P. Green, comment in paper on 'A Future for Museums – The Vision' (1988).
6 I. Robertson, comment in paper on 'A Future for Museums – The Vision' (1988).
7 P. Gathercole, comment in paper on 'Theoretical Approaches in Museums' (1988).

REFERENCES

Bloom, J. N. and Powell, E.A. (eds) (1984) *Museums for a New Century: A Report of the Commission on Museums for a New Century*, Washington: American Association of Museums.

Bown, W. (1988) 'Britain's entrepreneurs: shopkeepers not scholars', *Independent*, Thursday 29 December: 18.

Boylan, P. J. (1989)'President's view', *Museums Association Bulletin*, 28(10): 194–5.

'A future for museums – the vision', The First Annual Christmas Lecture in Museum Studies, 15 December 1988, University of Leicester Department of Museum Studies.

Hewison, R. (1987) *The Heritage Industry: Britain in a Climate of Decline*, London: Methuen.

Mead, M. (1970) 'Museums in a media-saturated world', *Museum News*, 49(1): 23–5.

Museums and Galleries Commission (1987) *Museum Professional Training and Career Structure: Report by a Working Party, 1987*, London: HMSO.

Myerscough, J. (1988) *The Economic Importance of the Arts in Britain*, London: Policy Studies Institute.

Parr, A. E. (1960) 'Is there a museum profession?', *Curator* 3(2) 101–6.

Parr, A. E. (1964) 'A plurality of professions', *Curator* 7(4): 287–95.

Peters, T. J. and Waterman, R. H. (1982) *In Search of Excellence*, New York: Harper & Row/Warner Books.

Prince, D. R. and Higgins-McLoughlin, B. E. (1987) *Museums UK: The Findings of the Museum Database Project*, London: Museums Association and Butterworths.

'Theoretical Approaches in Museums', session at *TAG '88: Tenth Annual Conference*, 13–15 December 1988, University of Sheffield.

Tofler, A. (1971) *Future Shock*, London: Pan.

Young, A. (1988) *The British Entrepreneur 1988*, Cranfield: Cranfield School of Management, as reported in Bown (1988).

16

Performance indicators: promises and pitfalls

Peter M. Jackson

It is a welcome sign when museum management issues begin to receive serious attention from academics in the management field. In this chapter, Peter Jackson, Professor at the Management Centre, University of Leicester, England, makes a convincing case for the development of performance measurement in museums, drawing on and applying approaches already adopted in the public sector.

INTRODUCTION

In 1989 about £300 million of public expenditure was allocated to national and local museums in the UK. A basic question is, did the taxpayer receive value for money from this expenditure? How well are museums managed?

To answer questions of this kind it is now customary to measure the performance of museums by means of performance indicators. This is not, however, a straightforward technical procedure: it is full of problems and pitfalls for the unwary. The apparent technical sophistication of performance measurement is a mask that can hide conflicting values and deep-rooted conceptual issues such as what is performance, and what is meant by value for money?

This chapter reviews a number of the conceptual, measurement and behavioural problems that those who engage in performance measurement and performance review should be aware of. Without an appreciation of these issues a blind application of managerialist prescriptions could have the unintended effect of depreciating the performance of museums.

WHY PERFORMANCE MEASUREMENT?

The financial climate within which public-sector museums in the UK have to operate has become more hostile in recent years. From the mid-1970s the objective of successive governments has been to contain public expenditure increases. This has resulted in reductions in budgets (in real terms) and a greater emphasis placed upon the marketplace as an alternative source of income. Museums have not escaped these general changes in public expenditure policy. Local authority museums rely heavily upon grants from local government: about 16 per cent of their incomes comes from the 'marketplace' through earned sources. Independent museums have not escaped these financial pressures. A survey carried out by the Museums Association found that 42 per cent of the income of independent museums came from public grants in 1985 (Myerscough 1986, 1988).

Irrespective of whether museums are located in the public or the private sector of an economy, the financial environment which they face is extremely uncertain. In the future the operating grants for UK museums are likely to remain constant. Any developments will, therefore, need to be resourced either from cost savings within existing budgets or from the generation of additional incomes earned from the marketplace. This will not be an easy task. Labour costs account for over 50 per cent of museums' operating budgets. There is, however, little scope for productivity increases in labour-intensive organizations such as museums. The managers of museums, given this general background, now need to pay closer attention to the performance of their budgets. Are existing museum activities and services providing value for money? Are current resources being allocated efficiently and effectively? To answer these questions managers need measures and indicators of their performance.

For many organizations, such as museums, the bottom line of profit, which is frequently used as the ultimate test of performance, does not exist. This is true for public-sector museums and for those private museums that are organized on a 'not-for-profit' basis. In these cases both financial performance and the impact of services are difficult to measure. Nevertheless, it is important to know if museums' resources are being allocated efficiently and if they are being employed in such a way that will have maximum effect. Managers of museums require information on efficiency and effectiveness if they are to evaluate the performance of their organizations. This information is provided through performance indicators. Without the information provided by performance indicators, managers are in danger of allocating resources 'in the dark'. The management of one museum will not know how their performance compares with that of other similar museums, or how their own performance has changed over time. Without such information they will not know when diagnostic investigations of their current management practices will be necessary.

Performance measurement contributes to a number of management's activities:

1   It assists in the formation and implementation for policy.
2   It assists in the planning and budgeting of service provision and in the monitoring of the implementation of planned change.
3   It helps to improve the standards of service content and of organizational effectiveness.
4   It helps in the review of the efficient use of resources.
5   It is used to increase control and influence over decision-making.

Performance measurement improves management practice. It provides essential information to management by enabling activities to be monitored on a regular basis at several levels within the organization. Performance measurement also provides information for strategy post-mortems when policies, management practices and methods are evaluated.

A survey of the current use of performance measures in UK local authorities, carried out by the Public Sector Economics Research Centre at Leicester University, found that managers regarded the best features of performance measures to be:

(a)   the ability to make comparisons of actual performance against targets; against performance in a previous period; or against the performance of similar departments or programmes;
(b)   the ability to highlight areas of interest and the relevant questions to ask;

(c) the ability to provide a broad ranging picture of a service;
(d) the identification of trends over time;
(e) the development of local bench marks, norms or targets.

(Jackson and Palmer 1989)

The use of performance measures is, therefore, an essential management tool. Performance measures provide the information that managers require to enhance the performance of their organization. Some, however, see performance measures exclusively in the context of improving managerial control. Information is a means of exercising control and strengthening accountability. It cannot be denied that performance measures can and should be used in this way but to focus on the control aspects is to run the danger of performance measurement being regarded with suspicion and to invoke undesirable responses to its introduction. There is a more positive aspect to the use of performance measurement; it enables organizational learning. If actual performance falls short of a pre-set target then management can ask the question, 'Why was there a short-fall?' and learn from the answer provided.

Performance measurement is, therefore, necessary for accountability and control but it is also essential for organizational learning which is, in turn, necessary for improving the performance of the organization. The measurement of performance must take place within a framework and it is to such a framework that attention is now given.

CONCEPTS AND FRAMEWORK FOR PERFORMANCE MEASUREMENT

An organization such as a museum can be thought of as a system which is dependent for its resources upon its relationships with the external environment. Public-sector museums are heavily dependent upon their relationships with sponsoring central and local government departments. Private and 'not-for-profit' museums depend upon the marketplace, private sponsors and benefactors. Clearly, the system of mixed public and private finance that now characterizes UK public-sector museums involves a complex web of resource dependency relationships. This means that there are a number of different constituencies whose interests museum managers seek to satisfy. It is not inconceivable that these interests will at times come into conflict with one another. Management is faced with the task of choosing which interests to serve at the expense of others or to seek a reconciliation of interests. All constituencies will wish to be satisfied that they are receiving value for money. Performance is, therefore, evaluated within a value-for-money framework (VFM).

Museums, like any other organization, use their resources to purchase inputs (labour and capital, e.g. buildings, materials) in order to provide an output or a service which clients/customers demand. The value-for-money framework essentially examines the performance of a museum in terms of the relationship between its resources inputs and its service outputs while at the same time seeking to establish whether or not the service outputs that are being provided are those which are valued by the museum's various constituencies.

There are three fundamental elements to the value-for-money framework that are commonly referred to as the 'Three Es'. These are economy, efficiency and effectiveness:

Economy is concerned with minimizing the cost of resources acquired or used, having regard to the quality of the inputs. In short, economy is about spending less.

Efficiency is concerned with the relationship between the output of goods, services or other results and the resources used to produce them. How far is maximum output achieved for a given input, or minimum input used for a given output? In short, efficiency is about spending well.

Effectiveness is concerned with the relationship between the intended results and the actual results of the projects programmes and services. How successfully do the outputs of goods, services or other results achieve policy objectives, operational goals and other intended effects? In short, effectiveness is about spending wisely.

The value-for-money framework as set out above, has been developed in the UK by the National Audit Office, which is responsible for ensuring that central government funds are being spent in a way that maximizes performance as measured by the 'Three Es'. The Audit Commission for England and Wales and the Accounts Commission for Scotland serve a similar function for local government public expenditures.

In reality, the boundaries between economy, efficiency and effectiveness are seldom clear-cut. Nevertheless, this troika does provide the basis for a VFM examination. For example, a VFM examination of museums might cover any or all of the following aspects:

1   The tendering, contract, project control procedures, used for capital construction work; the purchasing procedures used for acquisitions and the purchase of materials. This will give management information about whether or not purchasing is being carried out at the best possible set of prices consistent with the desired quality of inputs (economy).

2   Utilization of facilities; staff allocations and mix, integration of services; maintenance; management and resource allocation systems (efficiency).

3   Results in terms of consumer satisfaction; improved educational value; improved awareness of a nation's cultural heritage, etc. (effectiveness).

Managers of museums should have as their objective the maximization of value added. The VFM framework enables them to demonstrate whether or not they are achieving this objective.

Clearly, some of those who come from a non-managerialist culture will challenge the values contained in the above normative statement that the managerial objective is to maximize value added. Some might even feel that their professional values are threatened by such an approach. A moment's reflection should, however, reveal that the values of museum professionals can be consonant with the managerialist values. This is not to deny that the approach is not without its own problems, which will be explored at greater length later in this paper.

Value added is simply the difference between the value of a museum's inputs and its outputs. Problems arise with the notion of value added because it is very difficult to obtain information about the value placed upon the outputs of museum services – especially when there is no market test, such as how much individuals are willing to pay to obtain these services, as in the case of private-sector museums.

Minimization of the value of inputs is a relatively straightforward task for managers seeking to maximize value added. It is an exercise in cost minimization and budget restraint. However, both sides of the equation are not independent. An over-zealous attempt to contain costs can spill over into a reduction in the quality of the output (services) with the result that the valuation of that output falls also. Cost containment is, therefore, not necessarily consistent with the maximization of value added. Attention has to be given to the valuation of the service provided. Not only are there measurement problems such as how to place a monetary value on an intangible service that is not traded in the marketplace but there are conceptual problems to be addressed also. Whose values are to count? This is another way of asking the questions, who are the consumers of museums' services; who are the custodians of their values?

Asking questions of this kind, within a VFM framework, throws into relief those issues which some museum workers might regard to be threatening to their set of professional values. For some time now throughout the public sector (and indeed the independent sector) there has been a growing view that it has been the interests of professional monopoly suppliers that have dominated the design of service levels, quality and mix rather than those of the consumer or taxpayer. Service providers have failed to take sufficiently into account the views of their customers or when those views are sought they have tended to override them.

There are two distinct dimensions to the VFM framework. One focuses upon minimizing the cost of inputs; whatever service is produced should be produced at minimum cost consistent with quality constraints. The other dimension, which is usually forgotten, requires that the service which is produced is, in fact, valued by those who use it. There is no rationality in producing something at minimum cost if no one wants it. The VFM framework places the values of consumers back into the managerial decision about determining service levels, mixes and qualities. Obtaining information about consumers' preferences and their evaluations of services is no mean task. Indeed, many professional groups would question the worth that should be placed upon such information. These are valid responses but what should be recognized is that by paying attention to consumers' wishes, these problems are brought into the open.

In the case of museum services many – perhaps most – consumers do not know what they want and having experienced the service they do not know what valuation to place upon it. A customer-centred management will, however, seek to find out what its customers think of the services that it is providing. Rather than simply taking the attitude 'we are the professionals and know best', a customer-centred service will approach the problem in a variety of ways, paying attention to the need to educate the public to value aspects of their cultural heritage; to find out what consumers find appealing; to learn about why some consumers visit museums whilst others do not. This in turn requires performance indicators on service usage and it is an example of how performance indicators can be used as a means of organizational learning. If, as a result of changing the type of services provided by a museum, attendance figures increase significantly, then this is an indication that consumer interests are being served and that value has been added.

There can be a tendency to make use of elaborate customer surveys using questionnaires or to seek information about consumer complaints. While these approaches can be useful means of obtaining information about customer evaluations of the service they are not without problems that museum managers should be aware of. First, they can be expensive to organize. To obtain value for money from such information means that the value of the information obtained should outweigh the cost of obtaining it. This requires attention and care to be given to the design of questions. Second, many consumers' complaints arise not from the fact that there is anything wrong with the level or quality of the service but because consumers hold a misguided set of expectations. The fault lies with the consumer and not with the producer. In that case there is a strong case for the producer to educate the consumer and, thereby, to change consumer expectations. Third, relying only on 'complaints' information can give a biased view of consumer satisfaction. It is found from market surveys of consumers generally that only 20 per cent (on average) of those who are dissatisfied with a service will complain. This means that complaints data need to be multiplied up by a factor of 5 to give a realistic picture of consumer attitudes.

BEYOND THE 'THREE ES'

The basic VFM framework established above argues for judging the performance of organizations in terms of whether or not they are achieving economy, efficiency, or effectiveness. This also requires the collection of data on consumer evaluations of services. Some, however, argue that this approach focuses upon a very narrow concept of performance. There are other equally important dimensions to performance which also need to be evaluated.

Here are other categories of performance which have been suggested for inclusion in the VFM framework.

Equity

This concept raises a number of interesting problems which are not adequately captured in the narrow VFM framework. Some services might have as one of their objectives the targeting of the service to specific user groups. If such groups have a lower average valuation for the service then, by definition, achieving the equity objective means that some potential value added has been given up. A trade-off exists between managerial objectives. This means that when evaluating overall performance managers will be required to justify their choice of trade-offs.

Equity considerations also force a further consideration of whose values are to count when calculating value added. Are the views of all customers to be treated equally? Should more weight be given to some groups compared to others? It is useful at this point to raise a question which it is easy to lose sight of in the managerialism of VFM: who are the consumers of museum services and can they be easily identified? One important group who cannot be left out of the answer to that question is future generations. Museum services are not just provided for today's consumers. Decisions taken today, however, will have significant implications for the provision of services for future generations. How are their values to be expressed and who looks after their interests?

Excellence

This brings the service quality dimension into relief. Quality has been touched upon already but following the work of Peters and Waterman (1982) customer-centred management needs to pay particular attention to the quality of service that is being provided. Total quality management and systems of quality assurance are now becoming popular managerial functions.

Crude budget cutting exercises that result in reductions in quality to levels below those regarded as acceptable by consumers add nothing to value. Again this highlights another of the trade-offs that managers face. Improved budgetary performance in terms of economy and efficiency at the expense of a reduction in quality has to be justified. A reduction in quality will only add to value if the previous level of quality was in excess of that which customers were prepared to pay. To know this, however, again requires obtaining information from consumers.

161

Entrepreneurship

As museum managements are increasingly being forced to seek alternative sources of finance they are having to be more imaginative and enterprising in their approaches to service provision. Entrepreneurship has been usefully defined by the economist Joseph Schumpeter as 'creative destruction'. Old, outmoded values and beliefs are discarded and replaced by new ways of thinking.

Entrepreneurship involves cultural change. For the museum professional it requires a reassessment of traditional professional values based upon a system of purely public finance to incorporate the values required for a mixed system of public and private finance. Again, incorporation of entrepreneurship will introduce another set of trade-offs. How much effort should go into seeking private market-led finance is that is at the expense of the equity objective?

Expertise

Adoption of the VFM framework as the basis of managing in a high-performance environment requires new managerial skills. A significant constraint upon the achievement of improved performance will be a lack of expertise among museum managers to deal with the complexities of value-for-money auditing. To overcome this, changes need to be made to the *education* programme for museum professionals.

Electabilily

This final dimension raises an important series of issues for public-sector museums. There is a political dimension and a series of political accountabilities to be considered. These are left out of the narrow VFM framework. What is the political value placed upon museum services? What role is played by national and local politicians in ensuring the performance of museums? These questions are not confined to public-sector museums. Private-sector museums are also dependent upon political patronage in a variety of ways, e.g. the way in which the fiscal system treats private collections in terms of wealth taxation: the donation of works of art in lieu of taxes, etc.

The extended VFM framework, which incorporates equity, excellence, entrepreneurship, expertise and electability by adding them to economy, efficiency and effectiveness, brings the issues of performance measurement much closer to the reality of the management problem. There are many different dimensions to performance and the problem that faces management is to choose the appropriate trade-offs between each of the elements. In defining what is appropriate, management needs to pay attention to the views and values of a number of different constituencies, each of whom judge the performance of museums according to different criteria. These constituencies will include: the users of museums; sponsors; politicians; and museum professional associations. The assessment of performance is not a purely technical matter. It is value-laden. The question that remains is whose values should drive the system?

WHAT IS TO BE MEASURED?

The above discussion has been general. It has attempted to sort out the different elements of performance. This is necessary before proceeding to consider measurement. While the phrase 'performance measurement' is frequently used, it is useful to distinguish between performance measures and performance indicators. Where economy, efficiency and effectiveness, and the other Es set out above, can be measured precisely and unambiguously, it is usual to talk about performance measures. However, when, as is most often the case, it is not possible to obtain a precise measure it is usual to refer to performance indicators.

Performance indicators are statistics, ratios, costs and other forms of information that illuminate or measure progress in achieving the aims and objectives of an organization as set out in its corporate plan. The use of performance indicators is an aid to good judgement and not a substitute for it. Performance indicators are provocative and suggestive. They alert managers to the need to examine the issue further. Thus, for example, the unit costs of museums as measured by the cost per employee, the cost per person admitted, or whatever, is not a performance measure – it does not suggest that one museum is more efficient than another because its unit costs are lower. It is, instead, a performance indicator, since it signals to management the need to examine why the difference exists.

What form do performance measures and performance indicators take? What is, in fact, measured? In an interesting paper Ames (1991; chapter 2 in this volume) points out that performance measurement and the use of performance indicators is an underdeveloped area among museologists. He then proceeds to suggest a number of indicators that might be used. In the UK, the Audit Commission has also made an attempt to define basic performance indicators for local authority museums (1986). Some of the indicators proposed in these two publications are now presented within the context of the VFM framework along with additional suggested indicators.

Cost indicators (economy)

- Gross costs of service;
- Gross costs per visitor;
- Ratio of revenue to gross costs;
- Conservation/curatorial expenditure;
- Operating costs per visitor

Level of resourcing indicators

These indicators will include index of revenue resources, capital resources, equipment and buildings. Examples of indicators of resources will include:

- The number of staff on the pay roll;
- The ratio of administrative staff to operative staff;
- The square footage of building space;
- The ratio of the square footage of space devoted to specific activities to the total available space

Source of funds indicators

- The ratio of public to total income;
- The ratio of market generated income to total income;
- The ratio of income from various sources to total income

Volume of service

These indicators are a crude signal of the demand for the service:

- Number of attendances;
- Attendances per day open;
- Attendance trend – this year's total attendance divided by the average attendance for the last three years;
- Days open per year;
- Hours open per day;
- Collection use, i.e. ratio of total number of objects exhibited over the number of objects in the collection

Productivity indicators (efficiency)

Productivity indicators are available for the museum as a whole or for specific departments or activities within the museum:

- Energy efficiency – the ratio of energy costs to total square footage;
- Per visitor gross sales income (i.e. sales income from admissions, shops, food, parking, etc.);
- Marketing efficiency – the ratio of the change in the marketing budget to the change in total admissions or total admissions income;
- Shop efficiency – ratio of sales per square foot or per buyer or per visitor;
- Fund-raising efficiency – ratio of the change in fund-raising costs to fund-raising income;
- Proportion of collection documented;
- Proportion of budget allocated to conservation activity

Availability of service (equity)

- Low income accessibility – ratio of hours per week available free to total hours per week accessible during minimum three-month period of maximum public accessibility;
- Minority attendance – ratio of annual minority attendance to total attendance;
- General accessibility – average number of hours open: per week or per week other than 9.00 a.m. to 5.00 p.m. on Monday to Friday;
- Number of concessionary users;
- Number of concessionary users as a proportion of total users;
- Number of users in target groups as a proportion of the total number in the target group

Quality

- Exhibit maintenance – ratio of number of exhibits out of order to the total number of moving part exhibits;
- Number of complaints from users;
- Expertise of staff – ratio of staff training expenses to total number of staff (in full-time equivalents)

Outcome indicators (effectiveness)

- Results of surveys of customer's perceptions of the displays etc.

This list of performance indicators is nothing other than suggestive. It is not prescriptive, nor is it exhaustive. Given the state of the art of performance measurement in the museums service any indicator of performance needs to be tested with a view to establishing whether or not the data exist for it to be calculated; the utility of the information that it provides for management purposes; and the costs of acquiring that information relative to its utility. After a few years of testing a stock of reliable indicators should emerge.

Performance indicators are themselves of little interest or value. The information content of indicators is only realized if the latter are compared with something. This could be a set of indicators from different museums offering a similar range of services or it could be values of a single museum's own indicators taken from previous years. Variations in the indicators as between similar museums or between different years might invoke management to enquire as to the reasons for the variation.

Another way in which indicators are used is to set target values for them. If actual outturn is below the target then a diagnostic enquiry may be set up to find out why – did some unexpected event that lay outside of the control of management cause the deviation? Were the targets set unrealistic, or was the shortfall due to poor performance on the part of the management?

It should be clear from this discussion that variances between a performance indicator and its comparators does not automatically imply poor performance. They simply give signals suggesting that further investigation is necessary. There are many different reasons for such variances and poor performance is only one.

Jackson (1988) has set out a number of criteria that can be used to judge the usefulness of performance indicators.

Consistency. The definitions used to produce the indicators should be consistent over time and between units.

Comparability. Following from the requirement of consistency it is only reasonable to compare like with like.

Clarity. Performance indicators should be simple, well defined and easily understood.

Controllability. The manager's performance should only be judged (measured) for those areas that he or she has control over.

Contingency. Performance is not independent of the environment within which decisions are made: this includes the organizational structure and the management style adopted, as well as the complexity and uncertainty of the external environment.

Comprehensive. Do the indicators reflect those aspects of behaviour that are important to management decision-making?

Bounded. Concentrate upon a limited number of key indexes of performance – those that are most likely to give the biggest pay-off in terms of valuable management information.

Relevance. Many applications require specific performance indicators relevant to their needs and conditions. Do the indicators service these needs?

Feasibility. Are the targets based upon unrealistic expectations? Can the targets be reached through reasonable actions?

TAKING THE FIRST STEPS

The point has already been made that performance measurement is a relatively new managerial innovation within the museum service. Lessons can be learned from the experiences of other services which have embarked down this road. Initiation of a performance review exercise requires strong leadership from the top of the organization. It requires a partnership between the various constituencies within the organization between senior management, middle management, operatives, and in the case of public sector museums, between management and elected members. Without this unity of purpose, which is ground out of establishing a partnership, effort will be diverted to debates about the utility of performance review rather than getting down to the business of carrying out the review.

Strong leadership is required to bring about *cultural change* within the organization. This is essential if performance reviews are to have their desired effects. What is meant by cultural change in this context? It has already been touched upon when the notion of entrepreneurship was introduced and when the point was made that the new managerial ethos, which is implied by performance measurement, challenges certain cherished professional values. Cultural change means changing the system of beliefs and values that guide the top management team of an organization like a museum. This usually involves a change from an ethos of reactive administration (e.g. administering a museum's collection) to a more dynamic proactive management of the organization, which places the needs and interests of the consumer at the centre of decision-making and which judges success and performance in terms of serving consumer interests within a VFM framework. Indeed, part of the cultural change required is to accept the new language of VFM auditing and the idea of consumers who have preferences rather than passive service users.

The message of cultural change has to be transmitted throughout the whole organization, from top to bottom. It requires the establishment of total organizational commitment. Individuals, it has been found, time and time again, perform better in terms of contributing to the operations of the organizations if they know how their activities relate to the workings of the total organization. One means of achieving this is to ensure that service objectives are clarified and that these are communicated and translated into specific results and performance expectations at all levels in the organization.

Bringing about cultural change within an organization is most readily achieved through an organizational development programme in which training plays a central role. This will impart the ethos of a high-performance organization while at the same time providing staff with the skills and expertise that are required to achieve improvements. Enhancement of performance requires, in most instances, a reorientation of existing practices which, in turn, demands a new set of expertise. Performance review, then, not only involves an information audit – i.e. are the appropriate performance indicators available as part of the management information system? – it also requires a skills audit. What new skills in the areas of communication, customer–client relations, financial management, human resource management, informatics, and so on, do operational staff require before improvements in performance can be secured? Senior and middle management in the organization will also require training in the development of managerial styles that emphasize the building of teams and the motivation of staff.

In most instances the new information and VFM auditing systems, which will generate the performance indicator data, will need to be negotiated into place. For some managers this will require the acquisition of negotiating skills. A top-down approach, in which the new systems are imposed from above, is doomed to failure. To operate successfully the VFM approach requires data to construct performance indicators and those further down the organization will only release data of the quality required if they feel comfortable with the organizational climate within which the new systems are to be implemented. If they are introduced in a threatening fashion, which emphasizes their use as a tool of managerial control, then it is unlikely that co-operation will be forthcoming. On the other hand, if they are presented as a means of organizational learning, then co-operation and success is more likely.

Unless sufficient resources are allocated to the acquisition of new skills at all levels in the organization then improvements in performance will be put at risk. The new management information systems implied by the VFM framework are necessary but not sufficient for enhanced performance. These information systems are only beneficial if service managers know how to use them effectively.

CLARITY OF OBJECTIVES

The first stage in any performance review exercise is to clarify the strategic or corporate objectives of the organization. It is these objectives which, in part, define the effectiveness dimension – indicators of effectiveness demonstrate the degree to which the organization has managed to achieve its strategic objectives. Unless the corporate objectives are clearly stated there is a high risk that the organization will sub-optimize. That is, although the constituent elements of the organization might meet their operational objectives, if they are not clear about how their actions contribute to the corporate objectives, then there is no guarantee that these strategic objectives will be achieved.

While at the most general level the strategic objective of any organization is the maximization of value added, subject to the constraint that the quality of the process through which value is added is acceptable, such a statement is too abstract to be of practical use. Moreover, some of the problems of defining value added have already been rehearsed. Strategic objectives need to be more concrete if they are to be translated into operational objectives.

Examples of the corporate objectives of a museum will include the following list:

- To meet satisfactorily the demand for its services;
- To provide services of quality;
- To develop services in line with demand;
- To carry out all statutory duties;
- To maintain charges at tolerable levels;
- To seek new sources of finance;
- To assist individuals and specified groups to develop their potential;
- To be a good and caring employer;
- To develop a performance-oriented management style;
- To encourage an awareness in the general public of the visual arts and crafts, and of national and local matters of historical, cultural or scientific note;

167

- To ensure that there are clear policies for collection management and for targeting users;
- To ensure that special events and exhibitions relate to the stated policies;
- To ensure that the layout and quality of displays is visually attractive and of a high standard;
- To ensure that facilities are fully utilized within policy guidelines;
- To foster the protection of primary evidence of national and local history and natural history, and improving awareness of it

PITFALLS AND PROBLEMS FOR PERFORMANCE MEASUREMENT

While performance measurement undoubtedly has many benefits to offer there are a number of pitfalls that those who use performance indicators need to be aware of. Some of the problems of implementing performance indicators have been dealt with in previous sections.

Unless performance indicators are sufficiently robust then those who supply the raw data for their compilation will tend to distort information in order to present themselves in the best light. This is especially true if the emphasis is placed upon performance review for control purposes rather than for organizational learning. These distorting tendencies will, therefore, reduce the value of performance review unless they are recognized in advance. There is also a tendency to fall into the trap of 'if it cannot be counted then it doesn't count'. This overemphasis upon quantification can drive out qualitative performance indicators and the unquantifiable dimensions of performance that are often more important when making decisions.

Performance indicators are a means to an end. They are an aid to improved decision-making and hence a means to enhanced performance. A situation can arise, however, where the generation of performance indicators becomes an end in itself. So many indicators are produced that managers suffer from information overloads: analysis paralysis. The question is often asked, how many indicators are required? Obviously, there is no hard and fast answer to this question. Managers must judge how many indicators are manageable, what is the value of the information that indicators provide, and how much does it cost to produce the indicators. Experience suggests that most managers use a limited set of key indicators. As one travels up the organization, the number of indicators is reduced and they become more general in their application and in the picture that they reveal.

Some performance indicators over-emphasize the short-term dimensions of performance. There can be a tendency to go for the 'quick fox' and thus to ignore the longer-term and more enduring aspects of performance. This can be a problem if performance indicators are used for career development purposes. Not only is there the danger of distorting information as discussed above, there is also a bias for thrusting career-minded managers to concentrate upon those activities which will give them the maximum pay-offs in as short a time as possible. This can often result in an unbalanced mix of services; dissatisfied groups of consumers whose interests are not being served; and a lack of investment of resources in developing the service over the longer run.

At a more general level, managers should be aware that if performance indicators are used exclusively for control or appraisal purposes then this is likely to set up a series of behavioural responses that will have both unintended and undesirable consequences. Not only will there be an incentive to distort and to withhold information, but also attention will be given to the measurable dimensions of performance at the exclusion of those aspects that are more difficult to quantify. Again, this is likely to result in an unbalanced mix of activities and consumer dissatisfaction. A crude example can be used to illustrate this general point. If performance is judged purely in terms of maximizing the number of attendances then the incentive thereby created will be to mount popular exhibitions only. This will result in a reduction in the average quality of exhibitions and will also leave dissatisfied those groups of consumers who have minority interests. Managing the use of performance indicators requires that managers are aware of these behavioural dysfunctions, and that a broad range of indicators is employed that covers different dimensions of performance, both over the long run and the short run.

Finally, there are severe problems involved with the interpretation of the statistics that are used to form performance indicators. At a basic level, a choice has to be made when using cost data between gross cost and net cost. Since net cost is a function of a museum's charging policy then variations in net cost will probably reflect differences in charging policy rather than differences in performance. Gross costs should, therefore, be used whenever possible, especially when making comparisons between museums. Per capita cost measures also present a number of problems. What is the relevant population variable that should be used to deflate the cost data? Is it the total population in a local area if it is a local authority museum that is being reviewed? Or should it be the numbers who visit the museum? Or the potential target population of museum users? Obviously, the choice of indicator will depend upon the question being asked; however, some perverse results can emerge for the unwary. For example, if the total population of one local authority is falling while that of another local authority is rising, and if each spends an identical amount on museum services, then in the first local authority per capita museum expenditure will be rising while in the second it will be falling. Does this mean that the first is less efficient than the second? Clearly not. If, however, expenditures were deflated by the number of visitors then the number of visitors to museums in local authority one is rising while in local authority two it is falling. The ranking would then be reversed.

This serves to illustrate some general problems of using ratio analysis. First, a ratio is sensitive to the choice made regarding the denominator – in this case, population. Second, a ratio will change if the numerator changes or if the denominator changes (or both change). Examining trends in ratios over time or comparing the ratio for one museum relative to that for another is an exercise full of pitfalls. Ratios hide a great deal of useful information. To interrogate a ratio it is necessary to hold on file the absolute values for the numerator and denominator. Often this is not done, which limits the usefulness of ratio analysis.

The previous example also helps to illustrate the difficulties of drawing up 'league tables' that compare the relative performances of similar museums. The rankings tend to be very unstable and are sensitive to the choice of indicators used to construct the ranking. Moreover, rankings are a snapshot of performance at a single moment in time. They wash out of the picture the dynamic aspects of performance. Different museums will be at different stages in their development cycle. One museum's expenditure in a single year might be relatively high because it is has recently invested resources in developing new services while other comparable museums incurred such expenditures many years previously.

Another problem involved with the interpretation of league tables is that it is usually the arithmetic mean that is used as a bench-mark. Choice of the mean has to be justified since there are other measures of central tendency that would be more appropriate in most cases. The median, for example, takes into account the extent to which the distribution of performance indicators is skewed. Moreover, those who are below the mean or the median are not necessarily museums that are superior in performance terms. As has been demonstrated, there are many dimensions to performance, including quality. The unit costs of one museum might be below average simply because it produces services of an inferior quality to those museums whose unit costs are above average.

This observation does not justify arguments for those museums whose unit costs are below average to spend more in order to raise their quality of service, nor for those whose unit costs are above average to cut spending and reduce quality. These might be sensible policies, but are not necessarily so. It depends upon consumers' preferences. If consumers in the high-spending authority are perfectly satisfied with the quality of the service and are prepared to pay for it through higher local taxes or user charges then so be it – there is no inefficiency. Equally, if consumers in the low-spending authority are satisfied with the quality of service that they are provided with and are not prepared to spend more then again there is no inefficiency. League table rankings do nothing other than signal differences. It is up to management to enquire further about the reasons for these differences.

SOME UNRESOLVED ISSUES

The approach adopted in this chapter has been unashamedly manageralist in its emphasis. This has, however, in the case of public-sector museums, to be balanced against the reality that there is a public-service element to be taken into account and that political account- ability is different in essence to the market notion of accountability to the consumer. Few would disagree that public-sector organizations generally and museums in particular require a new culture: one which is open, democratic, and self-critical; one which encour- ages risk-taking, learning and performance evaluation to replace the heavy-laden, closed bureaucratic organizations populated by self-interested professional monopoly groups. Local voters and taxpayers are now more critical in their expectations of the services that are supplied to them. The management literature has introduced the concept of 'listening organization', which pays attention to consumers, which opens up channels of communication between producers and consumers, and which is willing to learn about consumers' needs. These values have already been highlighted within the context of the VFM framework.

It is, however, necessary to look behind the rhetoric of managerialism and to enquire about what changes have, in fact, been made. The culture and the ethos may have changed superficially, the language used might now be different, but has anything of real substance changed? How is power in practice shifted from suppliers to consumers? What are the processes through which listening to consumers takes place? Which consumer groups are listened to? Are the disadvantaged consumers of museum services, for example, better off now than they were ten years ago? Do museum managers know who these disadvantaged groups are? Is customer care nothing other than an expensive public-relations exercise? Is an appearance of listening and caring given while the customer–producer power relationship doesn't change?

A managerialism that emphasizes customer care tends to ignore that many public services, including museums, involve collective consumption rather than individual consumption. Although the consumerist movement is dominated by individualist think- ing, political processes attempt to reconcile conflicting individual preferences for differ- ent types of museum services and services of differing qualities. Also, consumerism, by focusing purely on the individual consumer, ignores the external benefits of museums, that is, the benefits of living in a society that places a value on its cultural heritage. Because public-sector museums are part of the political decision-making process, it is reasonable to ask if local citizens are drawn into the making of local decisions that will influence local museum services. The managers of public-sector museums are accountable to their citizens as well as being responsible to consumers.

In Britain local areas are becoming more diverse in terms of religious and ethnic group-ings and income groupings. This diversity of preferences has to be managed (governed) and presents the managers of public services such as local museums with the problem of having to respond to the demands of a diverse set of organized interest groups. The management model often portrays the efficient high-performance organization as one that responds smoothly to consumer demands in a least-cost way. But in reality democracy is messy. Consumerism washes out the diversity of preferences and the conflicts of democracy (Hambleton and Hogget 1987).

What is being argued here is that managerialist models have much insight to offer but they must be set in context to be of real value. It is not possible to transport without modification the performance framework that has been employed in the private sector and use it in public-sector organizations.

Lest it be thought that these problems are exclusive to public-sector museums, a moment's reflection reveals that the managers of independent and 'not-for-profit' museums face similar problems, if to a lesser degree. They often have to reconcile the conflicting prefer-ences of sponsors, trustees and different customer groups.

Finally, consideration has to be given to the role that is played by locally elected council-lors in the performance review of local museums. In some local authorities it has been elected members who have initiated the performance review process. If elected members are to play an active role in setting strategic objectives, in reading and commenting upon departmental reports on performance and then acting upon them, then the cycle of committees needs, in most local authorities, to be critically reviewed. Space has to be carved out of an already overloaded timetable if members' involvement in perfor-mance review is to be anything other than token. Members, like officers and staff, also need training in the expertise required to make a contribution to performance review (Stewart 1990).

CONCLUSIONS

Performance measurement and review is a relatively new set of activities within the world of museums management. In this chapter, the value-for-money framework has been presented in an enhanced form that takes into account that performance is a multi-faceted phenomenon and that those who manage the performance of museums must make judgements about the trade-offs between the different dimensions of performance.

A number of performance indicators have been presented in a speculative way which it is hoped will stimulate further debate. The problems and pitfalls involved in imple-menting performance indicators have also been examined along with the limitations and unresolved issues of applying a managerialist approach to public-sector organizations.

Despite these problems, pitfalls and limitations, the culture of public-sector management has now changed. The challenge that faces museums management is to implement the VFM framework in a thoughtful and critical way.

This paper first appeared in S. Pearce (ed.) (1991) Museum Economics and the Community, *London: Athlone, pp. 41–64.*

REFERENCES

Ames, P. (1991) 'Breaking new ground: measuring museums' merits', in G. Kavanagh (ed.), *Museum Management*, Leicester: Leicester University Press.

Audit Commission (1986) *Performance Review Supplement: Implementation Guide*, London: HMSO.

Hambleton, R. and Hogget, P. (1987) *Decentralisation and Democracy: Localising Public Services*, Bristol: University of Bristol, School for Advanced Urban Studies.

Jackson, P. M. (1988) 'The Management of performance in the public sector', *Public Money and Management* 8: 11–16.

Jackson, P. M. and Palmer, D. R. (1989) *First Steps in Measuring Performance in the Public Sector*, London: Public Finance Foundation.

Myerscough, J. *Facts about the Arts 2*, London: Policy Studies Institute 656.

—— (1988) *The Economic Importance of the Arts in Britain*, London: Policy Studies Institute 672.

Peters, T. J. and Waterman, R. H. (1982) *In Search of Excellence* New York: Harper & Row.

Stewart, J. (1990) 'The role of councillors in the management of the authority', Mimeo.

17

The development of Beamish: an assessment[1]

Peter Johnson and Barry Thomas

Any strategic review of a museum and its management should involve an element of historical analysis. As part of a major research project on the economic impact of Beamish, the North of England Open Air Museum, in this paper Peter Johnson and Barry Thomas have produced what could serve as a model for future studies of this kind.

It is the purpose of this chapter to trace and assess the development of Beamish from its beginnings to the late 1980s. The first section provides a brief outline of the museum's history. The second gives a preliminary assessment of the museum; it identifies factors that have played a key role in the development of the museum and assesses the latter's success on various criteria. The third section concludes the study, and suggests some tentative generalizations that might be made from the museum's development.

THE HISTORICAL BACKGROUND

Developing the concept, November 1958 to September 1966

The first formal proposal for an open-air museum in their region was put to Durham County Council's Bowes Museum Sub-Committee on 27 November 1958.[2] The proposal was prepared by Frank Atkinson the (then) newly appointed curator of the Bowes Museum, whose ideas originated from a visit to an open-air museum in Scandinavia in 1952.[3] His initial proposal envisaged a museum that was primarily rural in character.[4] In February 1959,[5] the Sub-Committee agreed that the existing collection at Barnard Castle should be enlarged and that the appropriate officers should investigate the suitability of a site for the museum. The next few years saw the Bowes Museum build up its collections in readiness for the new museum. The collection policy adopted by Atkinson was wide ranging, a policy which he was later vigorously to defend: '"unselective" collecting "applied both to the general content of the material – 'you offer it to us and we'll collect it!' – and also to its physical size".'[6] Such an open-ended policy inevitably led to resource pressures. These early years also saw a change in emphasis on the nature of the museum. A wider vision of the museum was articulated by Atkinson in a report in 1961.[7]

> the museum *should attempt to record* and wherever possible *portray* all aspects of rural life from the Pennines to the harbours of the North East of England. It should also attempt to record and portray the historical background of the industries of coal mining, coking, iron and steel, leadmining, quarrying, railways, textiles, etc., in relation to the North East of England [original emphasis].

The Museums Sub-Committee took the view that this much more comprehensive museum concept could not be developed by Durham alone. It therefore proposed that the County Council should convene a meeting of local authorities with a view to establishing a *regional* industrial museum. Such a recommendation should be seen in the context of the growing emphasis by government on regional economic development and planning that occurred in the mid-1960s.[8] This conference eventually took place in May 1966, attended by representatives of thirteen councils and other organizations. The local authority representatives supported the establishment of the museum in principle, although a number raised questions of location and finance, two issues which were to reappear frequently in discussions. The conference decided to set up a working party to look into the possibilities. Durham County Council subsequently agreed[9] to defer consideration of the development of its own rural museum until the working party reported.

Towards a regional open-air museum, October 1966 to February 1970

The first meeting of the working party was held on 4 October 1966, and eleven local authorities were represented. The working party agreed that the museum should show 'every aspect of life in the past of the region, i.e. Industrial, Agricultural, Urban life and village life'.[10] It also resolved to call the museum the *Regional* Open Air Museum of the North of England, and to apportion the costs of the Museum among the participating local authorities on the basis of population. At the second meeting of the working party in December 1966,[11] a shortlist of possible sites was considered. Following subsequent site inspections the working party unanimously recommended Beamish Hall as the most suitable location.

Difficulties over securing agreement between the authorities surfaced from the beginning.[12] Cumberland County Council, for example, thought that its financial contribution should reflect its relatively distant location. (It did in fact later withdraw, along with the North Riding of Yorkshire.) Darlington raised the possibility of disagreement over the museum's location, and several authorities expressed reservations about the method by which expenses were to be shared. The financial pressures faced by the authorities were illustrated by their response to Atkinson's request that each authority should be asked to provide in their estimates for 1967/68 a *pro rata* contribution of £5,000 to permit the acquisition of exhibits which might become available before the museum's establishment and whose purchase might be a matter of urgency.[13] However, of the eleven authorities involved in the working party, only five were willing to provide a contribution at that time,[14] and the idea was therefore dropped.

Over a year later – in January 1968 – and after extensive negotiations between the local authorities, the working party recommended that Beamish be purchased and the museum developed on a long-term basis. Durham County Council would acquire the Hall and then lease part of it back to the local authority consortium. It was also recommended that a joint committee representing all the participating authorities should be set up. Atkinson's own enthusiasm and vision for the proposed museum, and the publicity he stimulated, was a major factor in generating support for the project.

In January 1968, while negotiations between the local authorities were taking place, the 'Friends' of the museum – a voluntary organization strongly encouraged by Atkinson – was formed to give moral and practical support for the museum. The organization grew rapidly and played an important role in generating interest in and momentum for the Museum. It also offered practical help by raising finance, assisting in public displays, and dismantling, transporting, reassembling and restoring specimens. Support for the museum came even from the Bishop of Durham, who urged readers of his Diocesan *Newsletter* to become Friends.[15]

The joint committee met for the first time on 16 October 1968 – Beamish had been purchased by Durham in the meantime – and recommended acceptance, with minor amendments, of a draft joint agreement. It also recommended starting the museum on a 'care and maintenance' basis with annual expenditure limited to £12,800 (a sum considerably lower than that proposed by Atkinson) and initial staff to three.

The next year was occupied with preliminary planning and with negotiations between the local authorities, many of whom continued to express their concern over the apparently open-ended nature of their commitment.[16] This opposition was largely overcome by provision for a five-year 'rolling' programme of development and expenditure under which each year the constituent authorities would approve the programme for the following five years. Thus the authorities would be committed up to the agreed planned level of expenditure – thereby giving the joint committee some certainty – but would play a crucial part in determining that level of expenditure. The agreement was finally signed by eight authorities in February 1970,[17] the month in which the first staff were employed (Atkinson was appointed first director of the museum).

Preparations for opening, March 1970 to March 1972

It had originally been intended to open the museum in July 1970, but it soon became clear that this target was not attainable. In September 1970 it was proposed that a preliminary exhibition should be opened just before Whitsuntide, 1971.[18] The financial sensitivity of the local authorities remained clearly visible. For example, Northumberland County Council asked, in October 1970, for the estimate for net expenditure in 1971/72 to be reduced from £45,500 to £35,000 on account of economic pressures.[19] The director and treasurer had initially proposed an *increase* (to £52,600) for this year to reflect *inter alia* the fact that the museum would be opened in that year and the urgent need for new storage facilities.[20] The joint committee eventually agreed to reduce the 1971/72 figure to £35,200.

The museum's first development plan, written by Atkinson and the Chief Planning Officer for County Durham, was adopted in December 1970.[21] This plan confirmed that the objectives of the museum were 'to study, collect, preserve and exhibit buildings, machinery, objects and information, illustrating the historical development of industry and the way of life of the North of England . . . [to] endeavour to deal comprehensively with the social, industrial and agricultural history of the region, and to bring together the buildings and artefacts of recent centuries'. The resource implications of pursuing such an all-embracing objective were huge, and in the light of the constraints on local authority financing which had already surfaced, rather unrealistic. However, Atkinson and his supporters had little to lose in pitching the initial bid at a high level.

The first few months of 1971 saw continued intense activity in preparation for the opening of the preliminary exhibition. This exhibition, entitled 'Museum in the Making', stayed open for twenty-one weekends, attracting in all about 50,000 visitors. Atkinson was quick to contrast the success of the exhibition with the very small resource base on which he was operating. He pointed out that voluntary labour could not be relied on indefinitely.[22] He also reminded the committee that much essential museum work – for example conservation, cataloguing and research – had not been undertaken. In addition, the exhibition itself had experienced substantial overcrowding in peak periods. Against this background Atkinson argued for more resources, a request that the joint committee approved,[23] but he was later turned down by the constituent authorities.[24] At the end of 1971,[25] Atkinson suggested that the idea of setting up a trust for the museum should be explored, a proposal that many years later reached fruition.

The official opening of the museum, based round the theme of 'Beamish coming to life', took place in May 1972. Again, the museum experienced lengthy queues at peak times and severe overcrowding.[26] In all, 80,000 visitors were attracted in 1972/73, most of them coming in the summer of 1972 (see Fig. 17.1).

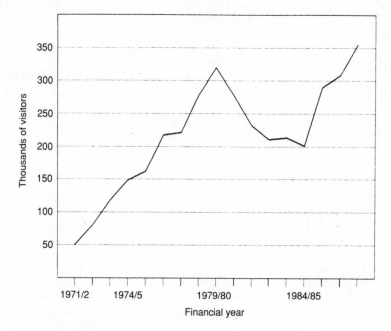

Fig. 17.1 Visitors to Beamish

One way in which these pressures could have been alleviated would have been through higher prices. Given the novelty value of the museum and its very wide support among the general public, it is likely that revenue could have been increased by such a policy. However, a policy of charging what the market would bear was not one that was appealing to the joint committee. It was particularly alien to the concept of Beamish, whose collections (in the words of Atkinson) were 'of the people, by the people, for the people'.[27] To an extent of course the pressures experienced at the museum were self-imposed, resulting from the comprehensive vision and approach adopted by Atkinson. These pressures would have remained even with a 'market' approach to pricing.

Establishing the museum, April 1972 to March 1977

The period April 1972 to March 1977 was marked by a constant struggle to place the museum on a firm financial footing within a framework in which the local authorities continued to be the main source of funds. On the basis of the pressures faced by the museum in 1972, Atkinson and the Treasurer submitted revenue expenditure estimates for 1973/74 that were more than double (at £98,500) the likely outturn for 1972/73 and the 1973/74 figures previously agreed as part of the 'rolling' plan.[28] The main increase in costs concerned staffing: nineteen new staff were proposed. The proposed departure from the agreed rolling programme evoked a strong negative response from some constituent authorities. However, the joint committee finally agreed at its meeting in October 1972 to recommend revision of the 1973/74 estimate to approximately £80,000. This figure was later reduced to £60,800,[29] although it was also agreed that, should Sunderland and Tynemouth become members, the committee should be allowed to spend any additional funds forthcoming from these authorities. The problems over the 1973/4 budget clearly illustrated the difficulties of getting agreement between so many authorities, each of which was reluctant to commit itself without commitment from the others.

In January 1973 the chairman of the Friends again raised the possibility that local authority financing might be linked with industrial money, with the museum being run on a commercial basis. It was agreed that such a proposition should be 'borne in mind', a formula for deferring action. Although this option came to assume increasing importance in later discussions, practical steps in this direction were a long way off. Two months later the joint committee was informed that the proposed *capital* programme for 1973/74 of £80,000 was also under threat. Four of the nine constituent authorities, which together contributed 53 per cent of the total capital budget, indicated that they would be unable to provide funds for that year.[30] (A fifth authority was willing to make an allocation only if all the other authorities did likewise.) Eventually, three of the four authorities that had withdrawn from capital financing relented, enabling £75,000 – much less in real terms than the 1972/73 figure – to be spent in 1973/74.

One outcome of the wrangling over capital finance was the reinstitution of a rolling programme for capital development, which was seen as enabling local authorities to plan more effectively and to be aware of their commitment. When the rolling programme appeared in mid-1973 it offered two options: a five-year programme (1974/5–1978/9) involving a total capital spend of £926,000 (requiring £183,000 in 1974/5) and a 'stretched' version of this extending over ten years.[31] The joint committee recommended that the five-year plan be adopted.[32] Despite these positive moves, the director's report to the joint committee in March 1974 recorded that the amount of capital available for 1974/75 had still not been agreed. It also added that 'the inability to maintain a steady forward planning operation makes for inefficient operation and unsatisfactory arrangements for our visitors'.[33]

The 1974 reorganization of local government decreased the number of constituent authorities on the joint committee, a development that was favoured by the chairman and director on the grounds that it reduced the likely problems of obtaining agreement for revenue and capital financing.[34] This reorganization did not, however, provide a guarantee against financial problems for the museum. Indeed, at a meeting of the joint committee in July 1974,[35] the Treasurer advised that 'the financial situation of local authorities was unlikely in the foreseeable future to improve but rather the contrary'. Because of the uncertainties about economic prospects, no capital expenditure for 1974/75 had yet been made.[36] Once again, it was suggested that other avenues of financial support be explored.

In this environment, the director, at the request of the joint committee, submitted (in July 1974) a development programme for the years 1974/75–1979/80. The director took the opportunity to reiterate the crucial importance of increased revenue and capital spending if the museum was to achieve its original aims, and proposed a very substantial increase in capital spending and in the local authority contribution. The suggested increase was too great for the joint committee,[37] who were clearly unable to match the director's enthusiasm for development. The committee proposed acceptance of a modified capital programme,[38] but a month later it reported that given the general economic crisis the constituent authorities were able only to maintain their present commitment, possibly supplemented by support from individual authorities for particular projects. Indeed, the initial budget for 1975/76 made no provision for capital development.

The capital position eased somewhat in the summer of 1975 as a result of an allocation by Tyne and Wear of £30,218.[39] This contribution was followed by one of £5,000 from Northumberland[40] and an offer from the English Tourist Board of £15,000 (conditional on a matching amount from the local authorities) for a 'Visitor Interpretative Centre'. Durham, however, was not prepared to offer anything. In the event, real capital expenditure in 1975/76 was marginally higher than that for 1974/75.

Further optimism on capital development was generated by the English Tourist Board, which had indicated that it regarded Beamish as having substantial development potential.[41] The museum also continued to obtain substantial help from volunteers and local companies. Another source of assistance was the Manpower Services Commission Job Creation Scheme. This additional source of labour enabled a range of extra activities to be undertaken, including the improvement of storage facilities, cataloguing and the provision of information leaflets.

The 1976 summer season saw attendances up by 35 per cent over the previous year, although inevitably this success placed pressure on visitor facilities. The increased visitor numbers had the effect of raising income to a level significantly higher than that estimated. This in turn generated an unexpected surplus which the joint committee suggested should be retained for the museum – rather than be used to reduce the contribution of the constituent authorities – a proposal accepted by the authorities and later converted into a more general 'rule' of financial operation.[42]

Early in 1977, the joint committee received the consultants' report which it had commissioned to consider the possibility of an appeal. This report was the first *outside* assessment of the museum and thus carried particular weight. It reiterated the financial and planning limitations that derived from local authority financing, while at the same time taking the view that the museum was at a critical 'take off' stage. It concluded that the museum was in some danger of outgrowing its strength with the growth in visitor numbers placing heavy strains on facilities and management structure. As the museum's subsequent history showed, this warning had considerable substance. The report also came out against wholesale reliance in the future on local authority financing, but added that Beamish was not yet geared up to alternative sources of income on the scale required.

Following consideration of the report, the joint committee accepted the principle of an appeal.[43] It also reached agreement – short-lived as it turned out – that the constituent authorities should maintain at least their present revenue contributions to Beamish, increasing them in line with inflation, with the joint committee seeking additional support only in exceptional circumstances. On the capital front, the joint committee decided to ask the constituent authorities whether they could commit themselves to a capital contribution over a period of years. In the event none was able to do so.

Greater independence, April 1977 to March 1980

The last few years of the 1970s were marked by considerable 'bullishness' over the museum's prospects – despite some setbacks over financing – and by a move towards less reliance on local authority financing. On the basis of the consultants' report referred to earlier, the preparation of yet another five-year programme was authorized. However, the director's ambitions for the museum were clearly still ahead of those held by the local authorities. His five-year programme, eventually submitted in September 1977, was criticized for being substantially greater than that envisaged by the consultants and likely to place strains on the management structure of the museum.[44] It was rejected in favour of the more modest plans proposed by the consultants. At the same time a significant move towards greater reliance on external funding occurred early in 1978, when the joint committee finally agreed to set up a trust to run the appeal.[45] An appeals director was appointed on 15 May 1978.

The year 1977/78 was regarded by the museum as 'a most successful year' in all three areas – collections, visitor services and development.[46] In July 1978 a four-year rolling capital programme for 1978/79–1981/2 was submitted and accepted.[47] It was the first programme to place any reliance – for over 30 per cent of funds – on appeal finance. It also envisaged a further 37 per cent coming from the English Tourist Board. In November 1978 the latter offered £200,000 towards several specified projects. The offer of the grant was conditional on a number of requirements that were later to present major problems for the museum. However, it marked a further important stage in the museum's financial development. Earlier grants had been obtained from a variety of sources – including the English Tourist Board – but none had been on such a substantial scale and none had been of a 'programme' nature.

In January 1979 the appeal was formally launched. Like the English Tourist Board grant, the appeal provided a source of funds that was independent of the constituent authorities, and complemented the greater freedom provided by those authorities when they agreed the principle of allowing the joint committee to keep any revenue surpluses. Another source of independence was the continuing assistance 'in kind' from the Manpower Services Commission schemes which at their peak had led to 120 extra employees at Beamish.

Despite the museum's outward signs of success – visitor growth was strongly positive (see Fig. 17.1) and 1978/79 was the fourth year in which the accounts showed a revenue surplus – a number of major problems were building up. The first of these surfaced in late 1979 when an internal audit of the museum revealed a number of shortcomings in internal procedures relating to contracts.[48] Personnel had been appointed to posts for which there was no budgetary provision and for which there had been no committee approval. As a result of this over-commitment the museum was facing its first revenue deficit for four years. The problems over the deficit were compounded by the pressures local authorities were facing from central government to cut back on expenditure and by the constituent authorities' decision to charge the museum for the administrative and other services they provided.[49]

The downward slide, April 1980 to March 1985

Towards the middle of 1980 the treasurer produced a detailed document on the financial state of the museum.[50] It made depressing reading. A number of capital projects started in previous years were either overspent or uncompleted, or both. This was due to 'inadequate planning and control of capital projects'. The slippage on the capital programme meant that some of the conditions attached to the English Tourist Board's £200,000 grant had not been met. As a result, new terms involving a much smaller grant were eventually imposed.[51]

A further report by the treasurer highlighted the lack of skilled manpower to design, implement and monitor the capital programme.[52] It also drew attention to the problems faced by the museum in the short term in reacting quickly to a shortfall in its capital resources, when the joint committee was dependent on sources of finance over which it exercised no real control – those from the constituent authorities. The difficulties were compounded in that the English Tourist Board had set current price limits on its grant, a fact not realized by the museum, and by the assumption – incorrect as it turned out – that the local authorities would maintain their contributions constant in real terms.

In January 1981, an additional problem emerged: although a revenue surplus was expected for 1980/81, income from visitors was likely to be down because of a fall in visitor numbers, the first since the museum's formation.[53] This decline evoked a response from the museum management whose analysis focused on the relative market position of Beamish. The director's report for March 1981[54] stressed that Beamish was operating in a competitive environment and that any marketing effort should find 'what the visitor needs, satisfying the need with the right product at the right price in the right price, properly presented'. The correctness of this analysis is supported by Fig. 17.2, which shows that the museum was suffering a loss of market *share*.

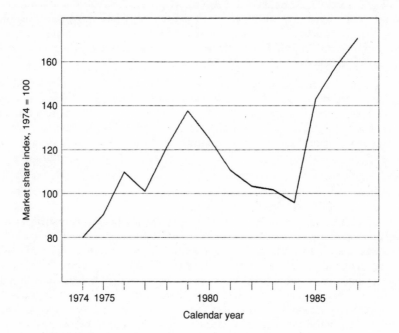

Fig. 17.2 Market share index

This relative decline reflected *inter alia* a decline in the museum's innovatory appeal and image; significant new product developments were now necessary to maintain the museum's market position. The museum responded to this challenge by seeking specialist advice from a tourism marketing consultant. Undoubtedly the first ever decline in visitor numbers stimulated this relatively intense interest in marketing. Up to 1980/81, it is probably fair to say that the orientation of the museum was largely towards 'production'. Certainly, the original aims were production orientated and did not refer to visitor needs or markets.

By May 1981,[55] the treasurer was already predicting a substantial deficit for 1981/82, pointing out that, with 62 per cent of the budget being spent on staff, the room for manoeuvre was limited. However, the local authorities eased the situation somewhat by providing a further contribution of £40,000 to wipe out the deficit (and the accumulated deficits of previous years).

Not all was gloom, however. In May 1981, the Manpower Services Commission approved a new set of schemes. The Trust Fund was also meeting further success: by June 1981 it reported that it had reached four-fifths of its £½ million target. Funds were forthcoming from other external sources. For example, in March 1981 the European Regional Development Fund (ERDF) offered £200,000 for the development of the town area.[56]

The 1982/83 budget prepared in early 1982 was based on the assumption that the possibility of any significant increases in visitor numbers was 'remote in the extreme'.[57] To limit the financial problems that could arise, vacant posts remained frozen. This initial pessimism on the 1982/83 financial year continued through the summer.[58] However, by January 1983 the Treasurer was able to report that a number of measures designed to avoid a deficit were likely to be successful.[59] By the end of the financial year, the expected deficit for the year had turned into a small surplus. Indeed it is interesting to note that, after 1979/80, the published revenue account remained in surplus throughout the period of declining visitor numbers. One important reason for this was the introduction of tighter financial controls and of cost reduction measures (for example, changes to the contracts of temporary workers virtually eliminated premium overtime rates). Without the intense economic pressures placed on the museum it is unlikely that these changes would have come about so soon, or even at all.

For 1983/84 visitor numbers were expected to remain virtually static.[60] The prospects for the revenue budget were, however, improved by the decision of two authorities to cease charging the museum for services rendered and by a substantial increase – objected to by several councillors – in admission charges. Despite the obvious difficulties, the 1983/84 budget allowed for a £10,000 increase in marketing. On the capital side there were some grounds for optimism. Substantial funds were becoming available from external sources. For 1983/84, £197,600 of the £324,700 planned capital expenditure was scheduled to come from outside bodies, including the Trust.[61]

The Friends continued to maintain an active role in supporting the museum, although the nature of that role was changing. In the early days they had provided vital support for the concept of the museum and its initial development. They had also been a crucial source of voluntary labour and capital. In the 1980s their activities were centring much more on the organization of special events at the museum and on providing general 'moral' support.

The revenue budget for 1985/86 produced in December 1984 assumed a small rise in visitor numbers although still below that estimated for 1984/85.[62] The capital budget for the same year assumed that nearly 80 per cent would be found from non-local authority sources, a development made all the more necessary by Cleveland's announcement that it would probably not be able to provide any capital contribution in 1985/6.[63]

The director proposed yet further strengthening of the marketing side of the museum in January 1985, a proposal that reflected the conviction that Beamish should be seen as operating in a market in which competitors could not be ignored. This perspective was reinforced by the growth of alternative leisure facilities in the region. The joint committee accepted the director's proposal for some expansion of the staff in this area.

Although the Trust had been given a new 'independent' look in January 1983, with trustees being drawn from leading figures in industrial, commercial and financial companies, it had effectively remained 'in limbo' because of resignations and illness between August 1983 and September 1986. The delay meant that the Beamish Appeal had acquired 'an understandable but unwarranted degree of suspicion in charity circles'.[64]

Recovery, April 1985 to March 1988

The 1985/86 season got off to a good start. For the first time for several years, the museum recorded an increase in visitors. The April–June figures for 1985 were up 31 per cent on those of the previous year. One factor behind this increase was the opening of the Town in the July.[65] As Fig. 17.2 shows, the recovery also expressed itself in a sharp rise in market share. In September 1985, the museum received a welcome boost from Tyne and Wear County Council, which was being abolished under local government reorganization. The Council offered £680,000 towards a new visitor centre, which was also supported by £300,000 from the European Regional Development Fund.[66]

A few months later the most optimistic rolling programme yet (four years: 1986/87–1990/91) was approved by the Joint Committee.[67] The programme allowed for a total capital spend of £2,910,500 with less than a third coming from the local authority. The revenue budget for 1985/86 and 1986/87 was also highly optimistic, with the 1985/86 revenue estimated at December 1985 as exceeding the original budget by £150,000.[68] After taking increased expenditure – much of it stimulated by increased visitor flows – into account, a surplus of £71,000 was projected, compared with the original forecast of break-even. The out-turn surplus was in fact £97,499. The success of the previous year was continued in 1986/87. In the six months from April to September numbers were up 6 per cent.[69] The museum also received the Museum of the Year Award. The reported deficit for that year is more than accounted for by a very substantial jump in revenue expenditure on 'maintenance' – a category that may not be significantly different from capital expenditure.

An event of some significance in the history of the museum occurred early in 1987, when Atkinson announced his retirement. Fittingly, one of his last duties was the opening of a new visitor centre. The new director, Peter Lewis, from Wigan Pier, took up his duties in June 1987, but during 1987 there were a number of other key events. The Trust, which had appointed a new director in September 1986, launched its Plan of Action early in 1987. Then in June the museum received the European Museum of the Year award, a fitting conclusion to Atkinson's time as director, and in September the revised development plan was issued.[70] The main thrust of the plan was on consolidation.

At the end of 1987, the museum published a six-year (1989–94) capital programme, with an estimated total expenditure of £3,820,000.[71] The Trust agreed to raise £1 million towards this total. Other external contributors envisaged in the plan were the European Regional Development Fund (£1,750,000) and Durham County Council (for road improvements: £50,000). The plan anticipated a contribution from the local authorities of £700,000. The main purposes of the plan were four-fold:

1   To provide 'all-weather' displays of European quality, thereby attracting more visitors to the region and to Beamish.
2   To market a two-day Beamish ticket, thereby increasing the propensity of visitors to stay in the region.
3   To provide regional displays, thereby encouraging tourists to stay longer in the region.
4   To provide, directly or indirectly, increased employment and spending power in the region.

It is interesting to note the emphasis on consumer needs and on the wider economic implications of the museum's activities in this plan.

When the year 1987/88 ended visitor numbers had increased by over 20 per cent, and had at last exceeded the previous peak of 1979/80 (see Fig. 17.1). Significantly, visitors from outside the North East exceeded those from within its boundaries for the first time.

AN ASSESSMENT

In this section two main questions are addressed. First, what were the key factors that led to the museum's being established and developed in the way that it was? And second, how successful has the museum been? Of crucial importance to this second question is of course the criteria of 'success' that are employed.

The museum's development: key factors in its establishment and development

The role of Atkinson and his staff

There can be little doubt that without Atkinson's initial vision and his energy and enthusiasm for the museum, and what it stood for in terms of museum development generally, the project would never have got off the ground in the way it did.[72] He was not put off in the early days by the difficulties of securing financial support. Once the museum was established he constantly pushed the local authorities to the limits of their financial commitment, a pressure which sometimes led him into conflict with councillors and officers. He mobilized widespread support for, and commitment to, his ideas. As a result the proposed museum achieved a public profile which provided crucial backing for the initial negotiations with the local authorities. He showed considerable skill for seeking out additional sources of funds and motivating staff. He was able to adapt to changing circumstances and opportunities while retaining his underlying commitment to the fundamental concept of a museum designed to provide a 'living' portrayal of the region's heritage. For example, he saw and exploited the increasing potential for fund-raising that lay in the promotion of Beamish as a tourist attraction even though he himself would have rejected the latter term as not accurately reflecting the concept underlying the formation and development of the museum.

Atkinson's passion for the museum did, however, bring its difficulties. His commitment to collect everything and anything that came his way inevitably created resource pressures on both labour and physical capacity. Atkinson's support for such an open-ended collecting policy was understandable: once a unique item is lost, it is lost for ever. Such a loss seemed all the more acute at a time of rapid social change such as that experienced in the late 1960s. It is also the case that *ex ante* it is not always possible to identify those items that will prove to be particularly valuable reminders of an industrial or social heritage. Yet, in a context where resources are under particularly heavy strain, some selectivity becomes all the more pressing.

As the first section of this chapter showed, Atkinson also found himself in some conflict with the local authorities. Part of this conflict may have been due to his impatience with local authority procedures, some of which may have seemed an unnecessary bureaucratic impediment to the realization of an ideal. (As early as 1968 he had warned about possible adverse effects of local authority control on museum operations.)[73] Although these tensions with the local authorities were at times considerable, at the same time

183

Atkinson and these authorities shared an underlying commitment to the non-commercial nature and purpose of the museum. Indeed it was this common perspective that was a key factor in the museum's establishment and subsequent development.

Under Atkinson, a committed team was built up. In the early days, particularly, working conditions and the scale of voluntary activities demanded a high level of loyalty to the underlying notion of a museum (a loyalty which is still evident today and which is in part reflected in the very low level of staff turnover). It is unlikely that the initial vision for the museum could have reached fruition without that commitment.

The local authorities

Atkinson would not have been given the chance to put his ideas into practice without financial assistance; and it is most unlikely that at the time the museum was founded such assistance would have been forthcoming in sufficient quantities from any source other than the local authorities. The role of the local authorities in launching the museum was therefore critical. They also provided important technical expertise. However, there were also a number of important limitations associated with their role. First – and particularly in the early days – decision-making was constrained by each local authority's desire to ensure that none of the other local authorities had a 'free ride'. Decision-taking also involved an iterative process that made progress difficult. The consortium type of arrangement underlying the joint committee was certainly imaginative but it inevitably brought drawbacks with it. Although the committee was the formal vehicle for managing Beamish, it was the parent local authorities who ultimately made the resource decisions. Second, the financial pressures faced by the local authorities, and their vulnerability to central government economic policy, made financial planning and management very difficult. For example, as the previous section has shown, local authorities were sometimes unable to make a firm commitment to capital financing until immediately before or after the start of the relevant year. This difficulty was particularly injurious to the planning of longer-term projects. The *relative* financial role of the local authorities on both capital and revenue account has been reduced over the years. This fact should not, however, detract from the important primary role that they played in the early days. It must be remembered too that their contribution is still substantial, accounting (on the revenue account) for just below 20 per cent of total income.

The local authorities also sought to keep prices low in the early years, a restriction that played an important part in the rapid growth of visitor numbers up to 1979. Apart from any political disposition against commercial types of operation that some of them had, they saw the museum as 'belonging' to the region's people, who in turn were entitled to easy access. In this particular respect their views dovetailed with those of Atkinson.

Outside sources of assistance and funds

At the inception of the museum, the Friends were a particularly important form of financial, practical and moral assistance. Without the labour supplied by the Friends, the museum would have been in great difficulty running the early exhibitions. The first chairman provided important backing for the museum's case for better funding and for a move away from relying on voluntary labour for routine tasks. The formation of the Friends was in part a reflection of the very widespread support that existed among the general public for the museum, support which Atkinson had played no small part in generating. As the narrative shows, outside funding for capital development has played an increasingly important role in the museum's development. It is unlikely that such external funding has crowded out local authority funding.

External factors

It is important that the influence of Atkinson and his staff, and of the local authorities, should be placed firmly within context. At the time the museum was first proposed and the working party undertook its work, social and industrial change seemed particularly rapid. In such an environment any plan to preserve something of the past was therefore likely to receive attention and backing. The imaginative idea of an open-air museum was thus even more welcome. The greater emphasis on regional issues and policy in the mid-1960s also provided a sympathetic environment for the launching of what in effect was a regional museum. Furthermore, in the late 1960s central government interest in the development of museums was supportive. In the early 1970s it was tending to favour widening public appreciation rather than catering for the needs of specialized interests,[74] an emphasis that particularly favoured Beamish. On the other hand, central government restrictions placed some part in holding back the subsequent development of the museum, particularly in the late 1970s. At a more general level Atkinson has also made the point that the stronger community spirit in the North East provided a much better base for a museum of the Beamish type.

The museum's success

Any evaluation of the museum's success must be against explicit criteria. The choice of criteria depends on the purpose of the exercise. Several possibilities are outlined below. It seems appropriate in the first instance, however, to examine whether the museum's *own* objectives were sufficiently explicit to provide an operational yardstick against which to assess the museum's 'internal' success.

Success in terms of the museum's own objectives

There can be little doubt that the basic objective underlying the formation of the museum has been met. Beamish now provides in broad terms the kind of museum experience and service initially envisaged by Atkinson and the joint committee. It might be argued, however, that the museum has not yet reached the comprehensiveness envisaged in the first development plan; indeed, the intention to provide coverage extending over several centuries has been replaced by a much more closely focused emphasis on the years immediately preceding the First World War. Some aspects of past northern life are not illustrated at all: some have been abandoned, while others await resources.[76] Thus against the narrow criterion of the development plan's objective, the museum has been only partially successful; attention has already been drawn, however, to the lack of realism in this objective. Indeed, this 'lack of realism' may have been a deliberate strategy to achieve a greater allocation of resources.

The initial objective for the museum made no reference to the basis on which financial resources might be allocated to it. Although implicit in the 1977 change of policy in respect of the local authorities' contribution was the notion that the museum would have to survive on the basis of that contribution remaining constant in real terms, this simply defined the *minimum* requirement, rather than the specification of objectives. In any case, as indicated earlier, the local authorities' intention was never fulfilled.

A variety of *external* criteria may be applied to the museum's success. Some of these are examined below.

Innovativeness

Beamish is included in Hudson's review of 'museums which have broken new ground in such an original and striking way that other museums have felt disposed or compelled to follow their example'.[77] Beamish was not, however, the first open-air museum. In 1891, Skansen in Stockholm was started and was the forerunner of all open-air museums. It was followed in 1912 by the Netherlands Open Air Museum at Arnhem. In the United Kingdom, the Welsh Folk Museum at St Fagans, near Cardiff, was established in 1949 and the Ulster Folk Museum in 1958.

Yet Beamish has some claim to be innovative at least as far as the United Kingdom is concerned. Its strong commitment to industrial as well as rural history provided a new emphasis: in Hudson's words, the Museum 'brought industrial society uncompromisingly within the definition of a folk museum'.[78] The sheer scale of the Beamish site also gave a new flexibility and potential to open-air operations. On the organizational side it was the first open-air museum to be developed by a consortium of local authorities. And within the confines of the North East, Beamish represented a museum and tourism development that was unquestionably innovative. Despite the Museum's initial innovatory appeal, the decline in market share in the late 1970s suggests that at least some of this appeal was lost as a result of the lack of new developments, a deficiency that was rectified in the 1980s.

Market share

One success criterion commonly applied by business managers is the behaviour of market share. There are considerable problems associated with calculating the market share of Beamish.[79] However, it is probably fair to say that Fig. 17.2 gives a reasonable indication of the position of Beamish, relative to its direct regional competitors. That figure shows that between 1979 and 1984 there was a steady fall in market share as the 'innovative' character of Beamish wore off. However, the trend over the whole period has been upwards. Such a trend may be expected for a new museum which is in the process of establishing itself; inevitably some levelling off will occur. The fact, however, that it has not yet done so does provide some indication of the strength of Beamish's drawing power.

There is of course no reason why market shares and economic viability – no matter how the latter is defined – should be positively related. Indeed increases in market share may sometimes be obtained by *reducing* economic viability. Such may have been the case in the second half of the 1970s. It is important, therefore, that the viability yardstick should also be considered.

Economic viability

The underlying question behind economic viability is a simple one: do benefits outweigh costs? However, benefits and costs may be defined at either the private or the social level.[80]

1 *Private costs and benefits.* Such costs and benefits accrue to the decision-taking unit, in this case the museum. One way of looking at the issue is to pose the question: If the museum were a private-sector firm, would it survive? In its present form, and without the financial support of the local authorities, the answer is almost certainly negative. The revenue deficit, excluding the local authorities' contribution, has mostly varied between £100,000 and £300,000 (in 1988 prices) since 1971/72.[81] Even with a more 'market-oriented' pricing system, which would probably lead to an overall rise in museum prices and some discrimination – with peak period

visitors being charged more – it is unlikely that the deficit would be covered. It should also be noted that the deficit makes no allowance for capital financing. However, the museum probably could survive in a much reduced form as a private-sector initiative without public finance. Much of the curatorial work – which is not directly revenue-earning – would probably disappear, and other revenue-earning activities would be introduced and existing ones developed. Of course, many private-sector firms (for example in the defence industry) rely heavily on public funds. Definitionally it is true that with the same level of public support for the museum, which may be seen as 'purchasing' various services, including preservation of the heritage, putting the region on the tourist 'map', and regenerating local economies, a private-sector firm could survive. Such an arrangement would probably require the full level of public assistance to be made explicit and translated into a financial payment. Thus, apart from the present revenue funding from the local authorities, any implicit subsidy in the museum's operations, e.g. in relation to rental and to the provision of ancillary services, would have to be estimated.

2 *Social costs and benefits.* Social cost and benefits are those which accrue to society as a whole. They may sometimes diverge from their private counterparts. For example, where the museum pays a wage to someone who would otherwise be unemployed, it incurs a private cost, the wage paid; but the 'real' social cost, in terms of the output forgone elsewhere by employing the individual concerned, may be very small or zero. Sometimes the private cost may be lower than the social cost where a subsidy is involved. Adjustment of the revenue expenditure figures to a social cost basis suggests a deficit, excluding the local authority contribution, in 1986/7 of just under £200,000.[82]

It is on the benefits side that measurement problems at the social level are particularly difficult. Some of the more important possibilities are considered below. It is not possible to undertake a full analysis here; only the broad thrust of the different approaches can be illustrated.

(a) The measurement of consumers' surplus: one important analytical tool in economics is the demand curve, which shows the relationship between the prices charged and the 'quantities' demanded at those prices. All other factors, e.g. incomes and tastes, are assumed constant when this price–quantity relationship is examined. In the case of Beamish, the demand curve shows the relationship between the admission charge (price) and the number of visitors (quantity). Fig. 17.3 illustrates the position. A linear demand curve AEB is assumed. The admission charge is p and the number of visitors is q. Total revenue is OpEq. Now it is clear that for all but the 'marginal' visitor, visitors are willing to pay more than the amount they actually do pay. (The amount they are willing to pay is OAEq; the amount they actually do pay is OpEq.) The difference between these two is 'consumers' surplus' which is measured by area AEp in Fig. 17.3 (theoretical problems of aggregating over consumers are ignored).

The estimation of consumers' surplus presents major theoretical and empirical problems that cannot be examined here. However, preliminary estimates, based on reasonable assumptions, indicate that the consumers' surplus of Beamish visitors comfortably covers the deficit for 1986/87 mentioned earlier, even though there is no corresponding financial flow to the museum.[83]

(b) Externalities: the private demand curve (AEB in Fig. 17.3) may not capture all the demand for the museum. For example, some individuals may not themselves actually visit the museum but may wish to have the *option* of doing so, or at least may wish to see (and be willing to pay something towards) the preservation of the region's heritage in a museum. They may derive satisfaction from the enjoyment of others from preservation. Such preservation may have widespread benefits beyond those provided by the narrow curatorial function. For example, it may generate pride in the region's past, giving a sense of regional identity. In this way the museum may raise the general quality of life in the region.[84] It may also be seen as putting the region 'on the map'. The museum also provides an important educational function to local schools. If these various 'spillover' benefits are significant then the social benefits as measured in the previous section will be understated.

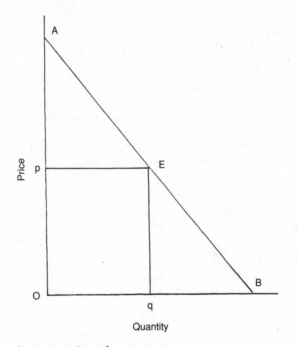

Fig. 17.3 Demand and consumers' surplus

Further benefits which should be included in the list of social benefits are the jobs which are generated by the museum. (In August 1988, 203 individuals were employed at the museum.) This is the subject of another paper and is not considered here.[85] It is enough to note, however, that employment itself may be perceived as bringing important social benefits to the community, thereby in effect moving the demand curve for the museum to the right. The problem with these social benefits is that they are difficult to measure and that consequently they could be used, in effect, to justify virtually any level of activity. However, if it is the case, as suggested earlier, that the revenue deficit is outweighed by consumers' surplus, any positive externalities represent a net gain.

CONCLUSIONS

Despite the problems that it has faced over the years, Beamish is now well established as a major museum and as one of the main tourist attractions in the North East. On the evidence available, its growth in visitor numbers in recent years is better than that in many other major attractions in the region. While the museum in its present form would probably not be commercially successful *overall*, the calculations in the previous section do suggest that, on rather broader criteria, it currently generates a satisfactory return. So far the museum has successfully managed to combine the need to have tourism 'appeal' with the maintenance of historical authenticity.

As the previous sections have shown, Beamish as it exists today is the product of an extensive range of complex and interacting factors. Some of these factors may rightly be regarded as more important than others. For example, the availability of the Beamish site, the commitment of Atkinson and (later) his staff, and the willingness of the local authorities to provide financial support, were all key elements in the formation of the museum. However, the interdependence of these factors should also be recognized: no one element would have led to the development of the museum without the contribution of the others.

The particular constellation of personal, institutional and environmental factors which led to the formation of Beamish and its subsequent development is unique and cannot of course be replicated. There can be little doubt that, if the museum were being launched today, the project would be tackled and developed in a different way, at a different pace and with a different outcome. The uniqueness of the museum's development process means that any attempt to reach generally applicable conclusions must be regarded with some scepticism. However, there are some elements in that process which suggest that certain tentative generalizations may be made.

First, the museum's history demonstrates the limitations of using local authority finance where anything other than a very short-term planning horizon is used. As the first section in this chapter showed, the museum sometimes did not know its capital allocation until just before or even after the start of the financial year. Such an arrangement became a more serious deficiency in later years, where the sums and development times involved were much greater. Any assessment of the limitations of local authority finance must however be balanced by the high probability that in the case of Beamish – at least in its early years – no other source of finance would have been available.

Second, it is clear from experience at Beamish that a wide range of professional skills is necessary for the management function of a museum, whatever its objectives. This requirement becomes all the more pressing as the scale of operations increases. These skills do of course extend far beyond the curatorial function, although many curators may possess them. Well-developed financial information systems and controls are also important.

Third, museums operate in a market, whatever their objectives may be. Awareness of market trends and their determinants is crucial wherever visitor numbers and revenue have any relevance to museum management and the achievement of its objectives. Experience at Beamish has shown that even where the product offered is innovatory, the appeal of such a product does not last forever: a stream of new developments is required if visitor numbers are to be maintained and increased.

Finally, a museum like Beamish faces considerable difficulties in reconciling a multiplicity of objectives. Beamish has served a wide variety of purposes: the preservation and display of 'heritage'; conservation and scholarship; education; the encouragement of a regional 'identity' and pride in the past; the provision of an enjoyable experience for local people and others from outside the region; and the generation of economic activity and employment. It is not difficult to see possible conflicts between these objectives. The

189

resource trade-off between these objectives is a major task of management. One factor that might reduce the difficulties in this area would be the provision of a clear financial objective which management would then be given freedom to pursue (within certain broad guidelines). Such an objective need not necessarily imply profit maximization in a narrow commercial sense. It might also help to clarify the resource issues if the scale of local authority funding were determined on a clearer economic basis, rather than on historical precedent. Thus such funding might be provided for specific activities which are not (or only partially) capable of revenue funding, but which are nevertheless regarded as socially worthwhile. Local authority subsidy would also be necessary if marginal cost pricing were to be employed, or if certain groups of visitors were to be offered discounted admission charges. There may, however, be some cases where this kind of approach cannot be followed because the relevant 'output' produced by the museum is not quantifiable. The encouragement of a regional 'identity', for example, would be difficult, perhaps impossible, to measure. An even clearer view of the true resource costs of running the museum would be provided by ensuring that all services to the museum by the local authority are fully costed. This kind of approach, involving a movement away from general subsidy to payment for specific services and functions, would effectively 'privatize' the museum while at the same time maintaining an appropriate public services element in its activities.

At the present time, there are grounds for some optimism over the museum's future. Growth and development in the last few years, together with the public recognition received, has gone some way towards restoring the confidence lost in the downturn of the early 1980s. Prospects for expansion look good. However, as indicated earlier, Beamish is in a market, competing with other claims on consumer expenditure. It is also vulnerable to changes in general economic conditions. Both of these factors make constant adaptation and improvement of the 'experience' offered essential.

This article first appeared in Museum Management and Curatorship 9 (1990), pp. 5–24.

ACKNOWLEDGEMENTS

Thanks are due to the Joseph Rowntree Memorial Trust at York for financial assistance for this study, and to the many staff at Beamish, and particularly to its present director, Peter Lewis, who so willingly co-operated in the research. Rosemary Allan, Peter Blagden and John Gall provided helpful comments on the first draft of this paper. Thanks are also due to the staff at Durham and Cleveland County Councils who kindly made records available to us and to Frank Atkinson, first director of the museum, who spent some time discussing the development of Beamish with us. However, any errors or omissions, and the conclusions drawn, remain the sole responsibility of the authors.

NOTES AND REFERENCES

(*Note:* The following abbreviations are used: WPM = Working Party Minutes; JCM = Joint Committee Minutes; JCF(GP)SCM Joint Committee's Finance (and General Purposes) Subcommittee Minutes.)

1 This paper draws heavily on Johnson, P. S. and Thomas, R. B. (1989) *The Development of Beamish: An Assessment*, Durham: Department of Economics, University of Durham. Tourism Working Paper No. 3.
2 Minutes of the Further Education Sub-Committee, 10 December 1958: 411 (The Bowes Museum Sub-Committee reported to this Sub-Committee).
3 *The Times*, 18 June 1986.
4 See the report of the chief officers to the Museums Sub-Committee, 7 September 1965.

5 Minutes of the Further Education Sub-Committee, 18 March 1959: 530.
6 Atkinson, F. (1985) 'The unselective collector', *Museums Journal 85*: 9–11.
7 *Open Air Folk Museum; Report 1961*. This report is unsigned but originated from Atkinson.
8 The authors are grateful to Frank Atkinson for making this point. See McCrone G. (1969) *Regional Policy in Britain*, London: Allen & Unwin.
9 Minutes of the Museums Sub-Committee, 16 September 1966: 331.
10 Minutes of Working Party set up to consider the establishment of a regional open-air museum, 4 October 1966.
11 WPM, 14 December 1966.
12 See the report of the secretary on the draft agreement: 26 January 1967.
13 WPM: 14 December 1966.
14 WPM: 31 January 1967.
15 *Northern Echo*: 27 June 1968.
16 See, for example, JCM: 6 February 1969.
17 County Councils of Durham and Northumberland, County Boroughs of Darlington, Gateshead, Hartlepool, Newcastle, South Shields and Teesside.
18 JCM: 18 September 1970.
19 JCM: 23 October 1970.
20 Report by the treasurer and museum director, October 1970.
21 JCM: 11 December 1970.
22 Report by the treasurer and the museum director: August 1971.
23 JCM: 10 September 1971.
24 JCM: 11 February 1972.
25 JCM: 10 December 1971.
26 Report of the director: 8 September 1972.
27 See Atkinson, F. (1985) 'The unselective collector', *Museums Journal 85*: 9–11.
28 JCM: 8 September 1972.
29 JCM: 8 December 1972.
30 JCM: 9 March 1973.
31 *Rolling Programme 1975–79*: document submitted by the museum director and treasurer to the joint committee's Finance Sub-Committee: 29 August 1973.
32 JCM: 28 September 1973.
33 JCM: 8 March 1974.
34 *Administration of the Museum in 1974*, document for submission to the Special Sub-Committee: May 1973.
35 Minutes of the (Interim) Joint Committee: 10 July 1974.
36 JCM: 10 July 1974.
37 Minutes of the (Interim) Joint Committee: 10 July 1974.
38 JCM: 6 September 1974.
39 JCFSCM: 2 July 1975.
40 JCM: 11 July 1975.
41 JCFSCM: 21 August 1975.
42 JCM: 26 November 1976.
43 JCM: 4 April 1977.
44 JCFGPSCM: 16 September 1977.
45 JCM: 13 January 1978.
46 Report of the museum director to the joint committee: 14 April 1978.
47 JCM: 3 July 1978.
48 Internal Audit Report – Contract Procedures. Report to the joint committee: 11 January 1980.
49 JCM: 11 April 1980.
50 Financial Situation 1980/81: 22 May 1980.
51 JCM: 18 September 1980.
52 Revenue and Capital Programmes, 1980/81–1984/85: 19 August 1980.
53 Estimated Outturn 1980/81: 14 January 1981.
54 Report of the museum director to the joint committee: 6 March 1981.
55 *The Budgetary Implications of Falling Visitor Numbers*. Report presented by the treasurer to the joint committee: 26 June 1981.
56 JCM: 6 March 1981.
57 JCM: 8 January 1982.
58 JCFGPSCM: 24 September 1982.
59 JCM: 14 January 1983.
60 *Revenue Budget 1983/84*. Report of the treasurer to the Finance and General Purposes Sub-Committee: 27 January 1983.

61 JCFGPSCM: 3 March 1983.

62 JCFGPSCM: 11 December 1984.

63 JCM: 8 March 1985.

64 Meeting of the development funding group: 12 March 1985.

65 See Darnell, A. C., Johnson, P. S. and Thomas, R. B. (1990) 'Modelling museum visitor flows: a case study of Beamish Museum', *Tourism Management* no (2): 251–7.

66 JCM: 13 September 1985.

67 JCM: 10 January 1986.

68 JCFGPSCM: 9 December 1985.

69 JCM: 14 November 1986.

70 JCM: 11 September 1987.

71 JCFGPSCM: 11 December 1987.

72 See Atkinson, F. (1968) 'Regional museums', *Museums Journal* 68: 74–7; and Atkinson, F. (1975) 'Presidential address', *Museums Journal* 75: 103–5.

73 Ibid.

74 See Peacock, A. and Godfrey, C. (1974) 'Economics of museums and galleries', *Museums Journal* 74: 55–8.

75 Atkinson, F. (1985) 'The unselective collector', *Museums Journal* 85: 9–11.

76 From the outset it was agreed that some aspects of North East industry – notably shipbuilding – would lie outside the remit of the museum.

77 See Hudson, K. (1987) *Museums of Influence*, Cambridge: Cambridge University Press.

78 Ibid.

79 For a fuller discussion of the problems involved see Johnson, P. S. and Thomas R. B. (1989) *The Development of Beamish: An Assessment*, Durham: University of Durham. Tourism Working Paper No. 3: 75–6.

80 There appears to be a lack of clarity amongst commentators on the nature of, and relationship between, costs and benefits. For example, Hudson argues that museums must 'be financially viable' and must 'make sense within the economy . . .'. He goes on: 'this may involve methods of funding and organisation which the purists could find distasteful' (Hudson, K. (1987) *Museums of Influence*, Cambridge: Cambridge University Press: 194). It is difficult to place any exact meaning on such statements.

81 Johnson, P. S. and Thomas, R. B. (1989) *The Development of Beamish: An Assessment*, Durham: University of Durham. Tourism Working Paper No. 3: 53.

82 Ibid: 52–6.

83 Ibid: 56.

84 This kind of benefit was behind Atkinson's original vision for the museum. In 1968 he argued that a regional museum like Beamish could cause a region to 'undergo some kind of rejuvenation, a discovery of pride in its regional character' (Atkinson, F. (1968) 'Regional museums', *Museums Journal* 68: 74–7).

85 See Johnson, R. and Thomas, B. (1990) 'Measuring the local employment impact of a tourist attraction: an empirical study', *Regional Studies*, 24(5): 395–403.

18

Job attitudes and occupational stress in the United Kingdom museum sector: a pilot study

Howard Kahn and Sally Garden

Human relations issues in museum management have been relatively ignored. Howard Kahn and Sally Garden's exemplary study of job attitudes and occupational stress in British museums is all the more welcome for this reason. Their findings have profound implications for museum managers, particularly in terms of management styles, job definition and organizational culture and structure.

BACKGROUND

Traditionally, the key functions of museums have been seen to be 'the management of, and research into the collections they maintain, and the presentation of the collections to, and their use by, the visiting public' (Thompson and Prince 1984), and the public perception of museum staff has been that of a relatively low stressed and comparatively static occupation. Indeed, a rating of various jobs placed that of museum staff in the 'very low stress' category: only librarians came lower in a league table of 104 occupations (Wilby 1985). However, changes in the United Kingdom national economic climate since the 1980s, and in public and government attitudes to museums and their management, have meant that museum managers and curators are now required to be more resourceful: (1) in arguing their case for support to central and local government; (2) in securing private sector support through sponsorship and partnership agreements; and (3) in generating income from their services activities (Ambrose 1991).

At the local government level, financial pressures have contributed to museum closures, and the future budget policy plans of local government show that in some areas there are real possibilities of further staff and service cuts to cope with under-provision for inflation (Boylan 1991). Continuous cuts in grants for funding have resulted in grants remaining static for some museums, and being withdrawn completely from others. Many museums are now required to obtain funds through the government-run Business Sponsorship Incentive Scheme, and many have established separate trading companies to improve the management of their trading activities. As traditional forms of sponsorship have become more difficult to find, so some museums have turned to schemes aimed at corporate patrons, via Corporate Partnership Programmes and Patrons Schemes, and to support from Business in the Arts.

Many of these recent developments have been criticized as turning museums into 'marketing showrooms', but it is probably inevitable that the United States model of museum management will be increasingly developed in the United Kingdom. In these cases, gallery directors cultivate a wide circle of interested local supporters, and curators cultivate potential donors by advising local private collectors. In addition, United States museum boards of trustees now place emphasis on specific personal qualities, such as the abilities to assess critically, reason, communicate, persuade, listen, facilitate, challenge, inspire and exercise vision, as well as providing learned and practical experience in such areas as long-term planning, human resource development, finance, marketing, the law, computers, professional standards, research methodology, collections care and management, presentation and interpretation, facilities and securities management and personnel management (Tolles 1991).

As a further pressure, the coming of the Single European Market means that if United Kingdom museums are to obtain European Community funding they will be required to make radical changes, e.g. selection techniques will need to be improved for those intending to make museum work their career, and there must be better in-service training, with adequate and attractive financial rewards for those who improve their qualifications, particularly in developing a high proficiency in foreign languages, etc. (Hudson 1990).

It is clear, therefore, that staff working within the museums and galleries sector now face major changes and challenges to their traditional methods of working, and indeed to their possible preconceptions and beliefs about the purposes for which museums and galleries exist. One question which follows from these changes, and from the prospect of further changes, concerns the effects that these have had and may yet have in terms of the stress they cause to museum and galleries staff at all levels.

Much work has been carried out on the nature of occupational stress. The basic premise of stress is that of a mismatch between the individual and his or her job. Early research assumed that stress was related to and/or caused by high levels of responsibility and accountability, but more recent studies have shown that it is not power but more often *powerlessness* that causes stress. Research evidence indicates that the sources of stress in a particular job, together with certain individual characteristics, are predictive of stress manifestation in the form of job dissatisfaction, mental ill-health, drug and alcohol abuse, and social or family problems. Stress appears to be related to other psychosomatic ailments including hypertension and heart and circulatory diseases, cancer, intestinal disorders and chronic headaches (Cooper and Marshall 1976). The 'work symptoms' of stress include increased absenteeism, higher accident rates, inferior quality control and high staff turnover, and these are expensive at the individual, organizational and national level (Cooper *et al.* 1988).

Once the sources of stress in a job and the stress-prone individuals in these jobs have been accurately identified, deficiencies in staff training, lack of standards, poor job design, etc., can be tackled. Among the causes of stress which may be particularly relevant to managers, curators and other staff in museums due to the recent changes in the museum environment noted above are: (1) occupational locking-in; (2) job insecurity; (3) the need to change the organizational structure and corporate culture of museums in order to improve efficiency and reduce costs; and (4) changes in training for museum staff. These four sources of stress are now discussed in further detail.

Occupational locking-in

This occurs when an individual has minimal opportunity to move from his or her present job. This may be due to lack of suitable employment alternatives in the marketplace, or to the inability to obtain a different job within the current organization. The feeling of being trapped in a job leads to job dissatisfaction and reduced mental well-being (Sutherland and Cooper 1986). Professionals who report being 'locked into' their job endure extreme costs. They have lower feelings of self-worth, more negative encounters in their marriages and less marital satisfaction, and report more depression, poorer physical health and less life satisfaction (Wolpin and Burke 1986).

Job insecurity

The threat of job loss or unemployment is associated with health problems including ulcers, colitis and alopecia (Cobb and Kasl 1977), and with increased muscular and emotional complaints (Smith *et al.* 1981). These outcomes may be aggravated when no suitable employment alternatives appear to be available, or when retraining is necessary to obtain a new position. Where an individual who is concerned about job loss is middle-aged, the outcomes may be increased by the recognition that learning seems to take longer, energy is more scarce and opportunities are less, and by the threat of a keen, younger work-force competing for jobs (Sutherland and Cooper 1988). It has been noted above that many museums and galleries face the prospect of closure or a reduction in staffing.

Change of structure

Typically, where organizations have restructured or attempted to change their corporate culture in order to improve efficiency, each department or section within the organization has become a 'cost centre' and is required to obtain a 'balanced budget'. This is often achieved by budget cuts, changes in organizational goals, reduction in organizational slack, etc. Individuals in such organizations may be subject to a number of sources of stress including role confusion, job insecurity, work overload, career plateauing, poor incentives, organizational politics, lack of participation in decision-making, tense organizational climate, ideological disagreement and job and personal life conflicts (Jick 1983). Museums and galleries are now faced with the requirement to improve efficiency, increase revenue, reduce costs and meet many other new demands.

Changes in training

Museum staff are now expected to undertake various training and learning schedules. However, many museum managers and their staffs may prefer to deal with objects rather than with people, suggesting difficulties in achieving the organizational development and personnel management aims of the newer forms of training and learning, and of the consequent existence of human resource management problems in museums.

OBJECTIVES OF THE STUDY

The objectives of the study were: (1) to examine job attitudes; and (2) to identify sources of job dissatisfaction and stress, among staff in the UK museum sector.

METHODOLOGY

Table 18.1 shows the sample frame of the study. A total of seven United Kingdom museums participated in the study and 28 structured interviews were carried out with museum staff (13 male, 15 female). Museums fell into one of three categories – local authority, independent, or national, and a minimum period of 30 minutes was scheduled for each interview session (45 minutes for directors), although in practice the average length of time for interviews was approximately 70 minutes. Interviewees were encouraged to comment, at any time, on points raised in the interview.

The overall aim behind the design of the structured interviews was to gather background data about individual interviewees, as well as job-specific and site-specific data. A number of questions were designed to enable cross-reference to be carried out. For instance, interviewees are asked in more than one part of the interview about their attitudes to promotion, where they would like to be professionally in five years' time, etc. Anonymity of all interviewees was a feature of the project.

Table 18.1 Sample frame of study

Museum type	*Job function of interviewee*						*Location of museum*			
	1	2	3	4	5	(Totals)	Scot.	Eng.	Lon.	(Totals)
Local authority	4	2	5	2	4	(17)	3	1	0	(4)
Independent	2	0	1	1	2	(6)	1	1	0	(2)
National	1	0	3	0	1	(5)	0	0	1	(1)
Totals	7	2	9	3	7	(28)	4	2	1	(7)

Key: Job function of interviewee (and generic term used): 1 = curator/director etc. (directors); 2 = deputy curator etc. (middle managers); 3 = specialized management, keepers etc. (middle managers); 4 = marketing/information officer etc. (middle managers); 5 = attendant/warder etc. (attendants). Location of museum: Scot. = Scotland; Eng. = England outside London; Lon. = London.

RESULTS

The major results of the study are presented within eight sections, namely work experience, job functions, reporting structure, education, training and career, job dissatisfaction, work planning and scheduling, likes and dislikes, and data arising from discussions with museum directors. Where convenient, generic terms are used to refer to museum staff (see key to Table 18.1).

Work experience

Fig. 18.1 shows that the majority of interviewees had spent more than half their working lives in the museum sector. Indeed, all seven museum directors had spent more than half their working lives in the museum sector. Only two-fifths of the interviewees had spent a greater proportion of their working lives in non-museum jobs. Three directors had no experience outside the museum sector, and of the remaining directors, three had teaching backgrounds (school or university). Only one director had come from a managerial position within industry. This represents a heavy bias towards academic skills at the expense of commercial experience. Fig. 18.2 shows that more than half the interviewees had been promoted within the previous five years. Three interviewees had not been promoted within the last fifteen years, and two of these were museum directors. Turnover of museum directors appears to be virtually static. The only interviewee who had been promoted within the last twelve months was an attendant who had been promoted to superintendent. Over half the interviewees had been promoted to their current job from within their current museum.

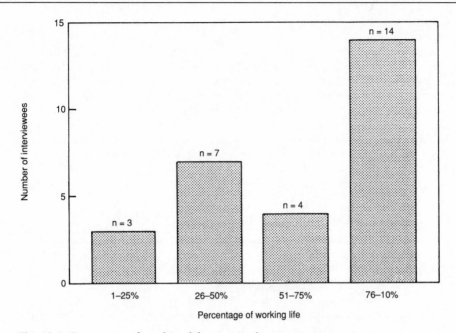

Fig. 18.1 Percentage of working life spent in the museum sector

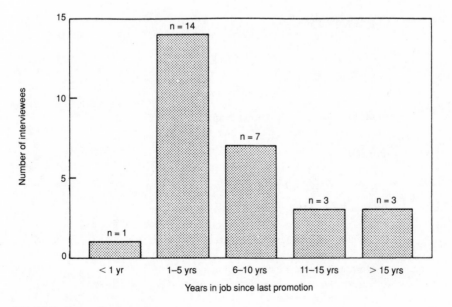

Fig 18.2 Rate of promotion

Job functions

Interviewees were asked of the extent to which there was a variance between their work activities and their job description. Table 18.2 shows the variance between actual and described job functions which was found over the whole sample of twenty-eight interviewees, grouped into six work categories. The job function exhibiting the most variance was 'enter and update catalogue records' with 25 per cent of interviewees claiming some difference between their actual job and their job description. All interviewees believed that they were carrying out this function when, according to their job descriptions, they should not. Some expressed the need for the appointment of a documentation assistant. In one local authority museum, middle managers were struggling to cope with a documentation backlog of some years. In this instance, the local authority continued to refuse

Table 18.2 Variance in job functions

	Job function	*Variance (%)*
(i)	Manage the collection(s):	
	Set and monitor budgets	11
	Set long-term plans and objectives for museum	4
	Oversee acquisitions	4
(ii)	Help generate revenue:	
	Oversee sales and/or marketing	21
	Generate new ideas for sales and/or marketing	18
	Work in museum shop or café	14
	Oversee public relations exercises	11
	Liaise with sponsors and/or seek potential sponsors	7
(iii)	Document and record the collection(s):	
	Enter and update catalogue records	25
	Plan and oversee archiving/cataloguing operations	14
(iv)	Care for the items in the collection(s):	
	Carry out treatment on items in the collection(s)	14
	Manage the storage of items	14
	Oversee conservation and restoration programmes	11
	Move items around the museum	11
	Maintain the good condition of displays	7
(v)	Security:	
	Plan or assist in the securing of items and/or the site	14
	Plan or assist in stocktaking (i.e., non-retail)	7
(vi)	Communicate about items in the collection(s):	
	Guide and inform visitor(s) about items in the collection(s)	21
	Develop and undertake research	14
	Provide learning resources for schools and colleges	14
	Manage loan services	11
	Respond to visitors' queries about items in collection(s)	11
	Devise exhibitions	4

permission for museum staff to use computer systems to alleviate the situation. The middle managers and director at this museum felt that the local authority plan to offer the museum its own version of professional documentation software, at some date in the future, was 'ludicrous' and likely to worsen the pressures on staff.

Two job functions, viz. 'oversee sales and/or marketing' and 'guide and inform visitor(s) about items in the collection(s)' were noted as presenting a 21 per cent variance between the actual and described job. For the latter function, all interviewees reporting this variance said that they were guiding visitors when they believed that they should not. For the function 'oversee sales and/or marketing', two-thirds of the interviewees said they were carrying out this function when they believed they should not. The job function 'generate new ideas for sales and/or marketing' indicated an 18 per cent variance. Just over half of those interviewed stated that they were carrying out this function when they believed it was not part of their job description. The remaining interviewees, however, felt that they should be contributing towards sales and marketing in some way.

The job function 'liaise with sponsors and/or seek potential sponsors' was found to have a relatively low variance (7 per cent). This low figure probably reflects the fact that few of the museums in the sample were heavily involved in seeking sponsorship. However, comments received in conjunction with the question of sponsorship indicated a major organizational flaw in two museums at least. The director of one museum admitted that he did not know which of his staff, including himself, was technically responsible for managing sponsorship activities within the museum. This director went on to argue that if responsibility for sponsorship management was to be devolved downwards, then staff involved should be given special training. Similarly, the director of a second museum admitted that he found sponsorship management very time-consuming relative to the benefits accrued, and his policy was to leave this task to other staff in the museum. One middle manager found it difficult to answer the questions about job functions since he felt that the 'catch all' phrase in his contract, i.e. '. . . and anything else not covered in the above . . .', meant that his job had no definite boundaries. This represents a clear case of job ambiguity and lack of job clarity.

Reporting structure

We examined the reporting structure of museum staff, in terms of numbers of the external bodies, individuals within their employing museum and internal committees reported to. All the directors in the sample reported to external bodies (e.g. local authorities, heritage organizations, funding bodies). The director of one local authority museum was an extreme case, reporting to some twenty-five external bodies. There was a wide degree of variation in the total amount of reporting carried out by individual directors, but this was not reflected in the size of the museum, as might be expected. Three of the fourteen middle managers in the sample reported to external bodies, but this was also unrelated to the size of the museum worked in. It was noted that in one museum, the middle manager interviewed reported to more external bodies than did the director. Surprisingly, it was found that one attendant supervisor reported to an external body.

We also examined, for each participant in the study, the number of people from whom work was received, and the number of people to whom work could be delegated. The director of one independent museum had an unusual delegation pattern, receiving work from five others, and delegating work directly to twenty-two others. This is explained by the fact that the five members of the museum's board of management are technically all permitted to delegate work to the director. This museum was found to have a very flat organizational design, in terms of (a) the number of staff to whom work could be delegated, and (b) the number of persons from whom work could be received, and was missing a layer of management (there were only two middle managers). Because of this, the director personally delegated work to some twenty volunteers. This director was not satisfied with the situation, claiming that time spent on volunteer management was excessive and detracted from more important management tasks, including seeking sponsorship. A second museum also indicated a lack of middle management. The director of this museum had personally to manage a large element of casual labour. This situation was largely a reflection of his lack of status with and lack of adequate resourcing received from the relevant local authority museum service. On the other hand, two directors had complete autonomy and did not receive work from any one individual.

Although the director of the national museum in our sample delegated, on paper, to one individual only, the case was very different in practice. He felt that it was his 'privilege' to delegate to all members of staff and to 'interfere' with their work as a way of 'keeping in touch' (the director's words). Though probably well intentioned, this 'interfering' was not welcomed by others in the museum, e.g. one of his middle managers felt that work could too easily be disrupted by informal lines of delegation (involving 'old boy networks') and that the lack of 'clear rules' made it difficult to retain control of her job and of the objectives she is expected to meet. This suggests that the autonomy of middle managers in that museum may have been compromised.

Apart from one exception, the attendants in the sample were found to have a well-defined pattern of work delegation, with work received from one individual only. All four attendants who delegated work had supervisory positions. Among middle managers, three interviewees delegated to twenty or more others. This was explained by the fact that two of the middle managers in one museum delegated both to attendants and to other middle managers. This indicates informal lines of delegation in operation, since other middle managers of equivalent status did not delegate to attendants. Whether or not this constitutes a possible source of stress for attendants is uncertain, but it does point to the fact that there are ambiguities in the organizational structure of at least one museum.

Education, training and career

Of the seven museum directors interviewed, one possessed a formal United Kingdom museum-oriented academic qualification (and one other had yet to complete). None of the museum directors had a dedicated management or business qualification. The director of one independent museum had no degree, but had management/supervisory experience in the manufacturing sector.

Fig. 18.3 shows that nearly three-quarters of the interviewees had taken part in in-service training during their current museum employment. (Though this does indicate a high incidence of training, it was not within the scope of the present study to ascertain the type or quality of this training.) A majority of the interviewees (twenty-five interviewees, 89 per cent) stated that they would be prepared to take further training for their job. Of these, all but two said they would be prepared to study in their own time. The methods of training preferred by interviewees are shown in Fig. 18.4. Day-release courses (whether on-site or outside the museum premises) are the method of training preferred by nearly three-quarters of the interviewees. Many commented on the lack of time available for training and added that training in short sessions, and at frequent intervals, would make the least impact on workflow in their jobs.

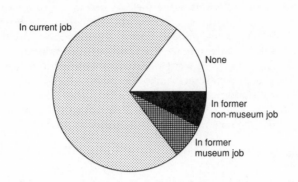

Fig. 18.3 In-service training experience

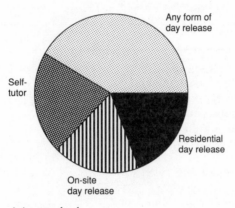

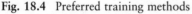

Fig. 18.4 Preferred training methods

Interviewees were asked whether or not they thought they would have the opportunity of gaining promotion from their current job. Nine interviewees thought that they had a chance of gaining promotion at some future stage. Eight interviewees, mostly directors and those who particularly wished to remain in their current job, said that promotion was not relevant in their case. Only one interviewee was not at all interested in promotion, and one (working in an independent museum) noted that promoted posts were rarely available. However, nine interviewees said that they would seek career change or advancement outside the museum service, for reasons including: a dislike of new career options following local authority restructuring; no route to move across the non-professional/professional barriers; quality of life more important than promotion; discouraged (for 'practical reasons') from obtaining further qualifications by his museum director.

Interviewees were also asked whether they had any personal ambitions regarding their current jobs. All but one interviewee (an attendant) indicated some ambitions, and most expressed these in terms of development of their organization rather than in terms of personal career moves. Many interviewees expressed frustration due to the unlikelihood of their achieving these ambitions. Nevertheless, there was found to be a high incidence of in-service training across the sample, but there was little consistency in the type of training people were receiving. Though further investigation is needed to ascertain the level, quality and value of this training, it was observed that during the interviews, interviewees used specifically management terms at random and out of context. This suggests that training has been superficial. The relationship between the high cost of training and the fact that the museum sector does not tend to recruit people from outside the sector must be addressed, since it indicates an unwillingness to recognize generic skills and to profit from experience gained outside museums.

Job dissatisfaction

We asked interviewees about their satisfaction or otherwise with various aspects of their work. Table 18.3 shows the percentage of museum staff that found each of these items of their work to be a source of dissatisfaction. Thirteen issues caused dissatisfaction to at least 50 per cent of staff, and thus the greatest potential to result in stress. The factors underlying these issues are now discussed.

Table 18.3 Dissatisfaction in museum staff

Source of dissatisfaction	% finding source dissatisfying
Lack of consultation and feedback	76
Conflicting tasks and demands in my job	75
Having far too much work to do	67
Insufficient finances/resources to work with	61
Inadequate guidance and backup from superiors	61
Ambiguity in the nature of the job role	58
Rate of pay or salary	57
Mundane administrative tasks or 'paperwork'	57
Coping with politics in the museum	54
Keeping up with new issues in museum world	54
Threat of impending redundancy/early retirement	53
Lack of power and influence	50
Feeling isolated	50
Managing or supervising other people	43
Inadequate or poor training for my job	43
Not fully understanding the work	43
Inability to delegate	42
Coping with large amounts of information	39
Changes in the way I am asked to do my job	39
An absence of any potential career advancement	36
Underpromotion – working below your ability	36
Attending meetings	36
The degree of my financial responsibility	32
Covert discrimination and favouritism	29
Dealing with the general public	29
Personality clashes with others at work	18
Competing with colleagues	15
Not having enough work to do	11

Management style

'Lack of consultation and feedback' was a problem at all levels, including some directors who felt that communication with local authorities or boards of management was less than satisfactory. Some middle managers also felt that staff to whom they delegated work did not always communicate well with them, or that decisions affecting them were made in isolation. 'Inadequate guidance and backup from superiors' was a major problem. Management style would thus appear to be a major source of stress for many of the interviewees.

Finance

'Insufficient finances and resources to work with' was found, as might be expected, to represent a source of dissatisfaction. Due to local authority restructuring and the possibility of Compulsory Competitive Tendering (CCT), many felt that the 'threat of impending redundancy or early retirement' was sufficient to cause them dissatisfaction. Lack of finance and resources combined with the threat of redundancy or early retirement not only creates a feeling of insecurity, but ultimately wears down motivation. This fact is reflected in the range of comments received to questions about personal ambitions. Some interviewees felt that there was no point in having ambitions in their current job when there were no resources with which to facilitate the plan or projects for which they had ambitions. One interviewee had become aware over time of the futility of trying to build for the future of his museum and admitted that he had begun to 'switch off' and lose motivation. 'Lack of power and influence' was seen as a source of dissatisfaction by 50 per cent of interviewees and this was a particular problem when negotiating budgets with local authorities or boards of management.

Job definition

'Conflicting tasks and demands in my job' coupled with 'ambiguity in the nature of the job role' combined to cause a great deal of dissatisfaction. This suggests a lack of adequate job definition among museum staff, and indeed three interviewees had no job description whatsoever and over half the interviewees had no objectives set for them.

Time management

Time management was a problem for many interviewees since 'mundane administrative tasks or "paperwork"' and 'having far too much work to do' caused dissatisfaction. Many museum directors and middle managers felt unduly distracted by administration and 'interruptions'. The fact that these tasks, including the need to maintain a high workflow under the pressures of change and interruption, are central to the role of a manager was not, on the whole, appreciated by interviewees. Many preferred to focus on the creative and research aspects of their jobs (see Table 18.4). This indicates that there is a need to change fundamental attitudes to the nature of management, and to equip staff with skills in, for example, time and project management. One director felt very strongly that staff within the museum sector generally did not take full advantage of the range of management training which was now widely available.

Pay or salary

Though there was some dissatisfaction with pay (57 per cent of interviewees), the level was not as high as might have been expected. This suggests that job dissatisfaction in the museum sector cannot be ascribed to pay alone. Two-thirds of interviewees said that they knew the basis on which their own salary was set, and a larger proportion (over three-quarters) said that they were aware of other people's salaries within their museum. One-third of interviewees said that those salary differentials of which they were aware did cause them some concern. Of this latter group, half were directors, and half middle managers or attendants. Only two interviewees had salaries based upon performance-related pay. One was director of the sole national museum in the sample, the other was a middle manager from a local authority museum. Some two-thirds of the interviewees felt that performance-related pay would not be appropriate for their jobs. Several interviewees commented on their belief in the unworkability of performance-related pay, and the difficulty of applying quantitative measures to their jobs. The fact that interviewees believed that quantitative measures or indicators are necessary in order to implement performance-related pay indicates a misunderstanding of the issue. The director of an independent museum regarded performance-related pay as pointless, since there was no likelihood of finance being available to support such a scheme in the museum. Other interviewees commented on the potential political problems likely to arise amongst staff if performance-related pay was introduced to their museum.

Isolation

Half the interviewees said that 'feeling isolated' was a source of dissatisfaction. This feeling of isolation related not only to individuals within their own organization, but to museum departments as a whole. The 'Cinderella' effect was commented on by more than one interviewee in this context. One of the main attractions of museum work for many interviewees was the opportunity to make contact with other people in the same or related fields to themselves within the sector (see Table 18.4). Feeling isolated, therefore, is a likely source of stress for museum staff.

Unsocial hours

All but one of the interviewees worked unsocial hours (e.g., evenings and weekends), and over half this group said that they worked unsocial hours 'often'. Just over one-quarter of the group received additional payment for the unsocial hours which they worked. Over half the group stated that the unsocial hours affected their social life, and six interviewees said that they wanted to change their job because of the unsocial hours.

Interaction with colleagues

Interviewees were asked to say how well they got on with their colleagues at work. The distribution of responses was heavily biased towards a positive view, and 89 per cent said they either got on 'quite well' or 'very well' with their colleagues. This suggests a good work atmosphere, with a team spirit and lack of competitiveness. Table 18.4 shows that working with other people in the same or a related field is a strong attraction to museum staff. However, this lack of competitiveness (only 15 per cent of interviewees cited competition with colleagues as a source of dissatisfaction) suggests that organizational structures, while stable, may be stagnant, and that external pressures in a period of rapid change are not being acutely felt. Museum directors may be shielding staff from market realities, or there may be an element of 'bunker mentality' amongst staff. This lack of competitiveness may be viewed as a feature to be dealt with by training in team building. Some two-thirds of interviewees socialized with their colleagues outside work. This also implies a degree of team spirit. Three of the seven directors did not socialize with their colleagues, and one cited the problem of perceived favouritism as a reason. Some directors appear to fear losing a measure of their authority by mixing socially with their colleagues.

Recognition

Over half of the interviewees said that they received recognition for performance in a form other than pay. Most cited the local press as the most frequent vehicle for such recognition. Only one interviewee had achieved recognition through academic research. This interviewee also commented, however, on the increasing lack of time in which to carry out research and to write papers for publication, so that this source of non-remunerative recognition for performance was diminishing. Some interviewees felt strongly that there was a negative aspect to recognition of performance via public credits. One director stated that his privacy was threatened through receiving unsolicited phone calls from the general public at his home. One interviewee was particularly upset by the attitude of the public towards the types of exhibitions his particular museum was constituted to hold. This interviewee felt trapped between an unsupportive board of management and a hostile public.

Work planning and scheduling

Fig. 18.5 demonstrates the way in which directors' and middle managers' jobs are polarized between two extremes of work planning: never knowing what work to expect from one day to the next, and knowing of work plans several months ahead. The majority

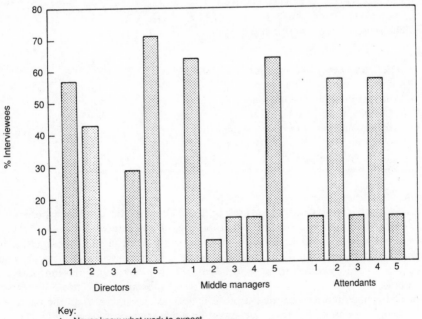

Key:
1 = Never know what work to expect
2 = Know what work to expect one day ahead
3 = Know what work to expect one week ahead
4 = Know what work to expect one month ahead
5 = Know what work to expect months ahead

Fig. 18.5 Work planning

of attendants in the sample knew their job tasks about one day in advance. Over half the interviewees were happy with the level of work planning which they experienced, though a contradiction was found in the responses to this question from one museum. Whereas the relevant director stated that day-to-day tasks disrupted forward planning, but that no major project had yet been stopped as a result, his two middle managers complained of the difficulty of working on planned projects which had to be dropped for periods of time.

Likes and dislikes

Interviewees were asked to comment on any aspects of their jobs which they particularly liked or disliked. Comments were grouped into themes or work issues and are shown in Table 18.4.

Table 18.4 Job likes and dislikes of museum staff

Issue	*Number of comments*
Likes:	
Creative aspects of job	12
Working with peoples in same/related field	7
Variety of the work	5
Contact with the public	4
The museum as workplace	4
Educational work	2
The sense of opportunities	1
Dislikes:	
Issues concerning organizational structure	5
Administration and meetings	5
Work planning and work load	5
Accommodation issues	3
Carrying out non-core tasks in job	2
Dealing with human resources issues	1
Contact with the public	1

Almost half the interviewees commented on their liking for the creative aspects of their jobs. Several also made the comment that meeting or working with other people in the same or related fields was a feature they particularly liked in their jobs. These likes, together with the preference for job variety, suggest that the interviewees may have preferences for an academic culture at work. Also, any hypothesis that museum staff might find contact with the public a source of stress is not substantiated, since it appears high on the list of likes and low on the list of dislikes. Museum staff are, on the basis of this study, 'people oriented', a feature that might be made more of in developing service sector skills. Two female attendants commented on their lack of confidence in technical matters, and this suggests that training in relevant technical subjects might be beneficial to women in the museum sector as a whole. The findings indicate that women in the museum sector can experience difficulty in crossing the (cultural) threshold into areas of work traditionally dominated by male staff.

When asked where they would like to be in approximately five years (excluding four who wished to be retired), eighteen interviewees wanted to be still working in the museum sector. Of these, nine wished to remain in the same job and nine wished to be promoted. Only three interviewees wanted to leave the sector, and three had no clear idea of where they wanted to be. Two of the interviewees who wanted to leave the museum sector said that they would prefer to be 'in any other job' rather than their present job.

Data arising from discussions with museum directors

Four of the seven museums had low staff turnover levels, though there did not seem to be any discernible pattern across the various types of museum in the sample. Only two museum directors considered their level of staff turnover to be a problem, and reasons for difficulties included the high turnover of volunteers, and recruiting and retaining professional staff in a relatively remote location. There was some confusion of priorities apparent in directors' replies to questions about staff turnover. One director felt that normal to high staff turnover exacerbated the training demands placed on his organization, while others were content to maintain static organization. These comments indicate a degree of short-termism and lack of exploitation of pre-trained and experienced staff from other, non-museum, sectors. Few directors had thought about the issues of fresh input of skills, and the trade-off between the cost of training staff and of recruiting trained staff.

Of the seven museums, six had had a dismissal or industrial tribunal hearing within the previous five years. One disciplinary hearing was due to the unpopularity among staff of a 'duty officer' scheme that had been implemented, despite staff objections, by a director. Given the relatively low levels of staff turnover in the museums sampled, this level of dismissals and industrial tribunals/hearings appears exceptionally high, and indicates an inability to deal with human resources issues in a constructive manner.

When asked about finance, six of the seven museum directors had experienced major changes or constraints within the previous twelve months. When asked whether further changes were anticipated in the future, six out of the seven directors did anticipate major changes or constraints. Three directors referred to local authority restructuring and the possibility of CCT as an anticipated change. One director felt that market pressures would continue to cause most constraint on finances. Six of the seven museums had formal organizational objectives. Three museums had objectives set internally and three had their objectives set by negotiation with their local authority, board of trustees, etc. All museum directors felt that they had sufficient day-to-day freedom of financial management. However, only four directors felt they had sufficient freedom of financial management on a strategic basis (e.g. capital expenditure, acquisitions). Three of the museum directors also had defined spending authorities, and two of these felt that the level defined in the spending authority did not give them sufficient freedom of financial management. It would appear, therefore, that though strategies are set (via formal organizational objectives), the means or resources by which to achieve these strategic objectives are not readily available. This contradiction can be considered as a likely source of stress amongst directors.

Towards the end of the structured interview, directors were given the opportunity to expand on any issues they felt had not been discussed, or to which they wished to draw attention. These comments represented directors' further concerns and worries, and fell into the four main managerial issues, as shown in Table 18.5. When asked for their views concerning the future of their respective museums, three directors were optimistic, three pessimistic and one had no definite views. Two of the optimistic directors were embarked upon or about to enter a 'honeymoon' period in the evolution of their museum: one

Table 18.5 Managerial issues raised by museum directors

Issue	No. of directors raising issue
Human Resources Development (HRD)	5
Organizational, strategic and financial	4
Marketing and public relations	2
Accommodation	1

director had come to his job after a period of renaissance in the organization which had resulted in a new building; the other director was looking forward to entry into a new building. Both of these directors, nevertheless, headed museums with current and anticipated financial constraints. The director whose optimism was probably best founded was the director of an independent museum who anticipated improving the status of his museum by gaining recognition of his collection as one of national importance.

SUMMARY AND CONCLUSIONS

This study has examined the job attitudes of a sample of staff working in the UK museum sector, and has determined that they face a number of potential sources of job dissatisfaction and stress. These may result in the operational inefficiencies and negative personal outcomes noted earlier. Sources of potential stress are summarized in Table 18.6 under six headings which are now discussed.

Management style

A lack of senior management skills was indicated by the incidence of human resources issues that arose in the study. Directors exhibited a range of management styles, with varying types of top-down communication. In general, directors did not set their staff personal work objectives and did not leave individuals with sufficient autonomy in their work. An unexpectedly high incidence of dismissals and industrial tribunals/hearings provided further evidence that senior management skills were weak. Inappropriate management style, caused by an emphasis on academic as opposed to business skills, was found to be a source of stress not only to middle managers and attendants, but also to directors themselves, particularly in relation to human resources issues. One of the major causes of dissatisfaction is connected with the process of management – whether on the receiving or transmitting end. Many of those managed feel that their managers do not know how to manage, and many managers resent having to manage. The need for museum managers to answer to many masters causes stress and frustration because of conflicting agenda, bureaucracy, etc., which slows down and/or affects decision-making. Many of those to whom museum managers report may know nothing of museums. Similarly, museum staff coming primarily from the academic or museum sector may know and appreciate little of the pressures and constraints operating on their governing bodies. Better management skills and training would be valuable in overcoming these problems.

Volunteer turnover was identified as a problem, and indicates that many museums rely on volunteers without knowing how to use them effectively, or understanding the particular motivation of volunteer staff. If managers have difficulty managing their full-time staff they will probably be even less able to manage volunteers. The relationships are

Table 18.6 Summary table of results: potential sources of stress in museum staff

Management style:
 Lack of human resource development skills amongst directors and middle managers
 Lack of objective setting and autonomy for middle managers
 Emphasis on academic skills versus business skills
 Lack of guidance and backup from superiors
 Lack of consultation and feedback

Job definition/extension:
 Poor documentation resources
 Carrying out sales and marketing tasks in addition to core work
 Sponsorship management devolved to inadequately trained staff
 Conflicting tasks and demands in job

Organizational structure:
 Local authority restructuring and compulsory competitive tendering
 Sales and marketing not recognized as a primary function
 Informal lines of delegation
 Insufficient finances and resources to work with
 Managing volunteers and casual labour at expense of other work
 Exposure of individuals to negative feedback from the public

Narrow skill base:
 Lack of pre-museum work experience and training
 Lack of traning in technical subjects for women

Accommodation:
 Inability to deliver full service due to poor standard of premises

Other issues:
 Poor time management skills and inadequate understanding of managerial role
 Demotivation caused by perceived low status of museum

different and managers will have to modify their management style. Museums have a potentially valuable resource which is not being exploited fully, indicating a clear management training need. However, many managers appear to enjoy the creative aspects of their work, and feel that their management responsibilities intrude on the 'real' nature of their job. As a director, *management* is also their real job, and this is as much an attitude problem as a training issue. Development and implementation of the requisite skills is an important issue. This will require an acceptance by museum managers of their new role as a museum *manager*, and commitment to the role of management. So long as the emphasis in recruiting museum managers remains on museum skills to the almost total exclusion of business skills and experience, these problems will continue to exist.

Job definition and extension

Variance between the actual tasks an individual carried out and those defined in their job description was used as a measure of job drift, job ambiguity and job extension. Job ambiguity was explained by poor, or in some cases non-existent, formal job descriptions. Job extension was found in cases where individuals were carrying out sales and marketing tasks when, according to job descriptions, they should not. Whereas sales and marketing would normally be represented as a primary function within a market-oriented organization, this was not the case within the museums examined. Several staff were compensating for the lack of documentation resources (e.g., assistants and/or computer systems) by attempting to meet documentation backlog clearance requirements themselves. Carrying out the tasks of sales and marketing, or of documentation, or of sponsorship management, in addition to the core tasks of their job, is a source of stress to individuals, caused by added workload, lack of appropriate training, etc.

Organizational structure

Local authority restructuring and the prospect of Compulsory Competitive Tendering was recognized as a major source of stress within all the local authority museums sampled. These issues affected the performance of staff at all levels by increasing uncertainty and reducing job security. Also, a layer of middle management was found to be lacking in many museums, and directors had personally to carry the burden of volunteer management or management of casual labour. This was done at the cost of undertaking sponsorship activities and other strategic tasks crucial to the museum.

Narrow skill base

Museums were found to be bearing the costs of staff training because of insufficient recruitment of staff with skills in finance, marketing, computing, etc. Staff were keen to undertake further training for their jobs, partly because they enjoyed the sense of personal development, and partly because they felt inadequately trained for the tasks they were expected to carry out. Directors were found to lack financial and business skills, and middle managers were found to lack skills in human resources development. It was also found that there was a demand for training in technical subjects from women who felt insecure in tackling traditionally male-oriented tasks. The rate of promotion in the sample was also found to be slow, with the problem exacerbated by the slow turnover at director level. This represents a source of stress to staff, not necessarily in terms of career blockage, but in terms of static organizational culture. Through their personal ambitions, staff displayed loyalty towards their museums, but were frustrated by the lack of organizational development in fulfilling these ambitions. There are obvious skills gaps and training needs in the whole area of management, supervision, job descriptions, etc. Women who have chosen the role of 'pioneer' in the museum sector will be subject to particular problems, but assertiveness and communications training, knowledge of how to set up and use networks, etc., can be of benefit to them. Customer care training also appears to be required.

Accommodation

Lack of suitable accommodation or changes in the structure of premises was found not only to lower the likelihood of museum staff being able to deliver a quality service to the public, but was found to demotivate staff, especially where staff perceived the status of their museum to be low.

Other issues

Other sources of job dissatisfaction and potential sources of stress included a lack of time management and other managerial skills. Some of the effects of work volume, lack of resources, etc., could be reduced by better planning and organization, and by reducing the bias against appointing to directorial posts individuals with business and administration skills.

Overall, this study has shown that a number of potential sources of stress exist in United Kingdom museums. However, the results of the study should be regarded as indicative only. The number of staff interviewed was small, and the amount of time devoted to each participant limited. The number of topics covered was also limited. Further detailed investigation of the job attitudes of a larger sample of staff working in the United Kingdom museum sector is nevertheless indicated. Objective stress data concerning the effects of museum work upon individual staff members should be obtained. Such an investigation would provide valuable information which would help improve the efficiency and effectiveness of museums and of the people who work in them.

This article first appeared in Museum Management and Curatorship *12 (1993), pp. 285–302.*

ACKNOWLEDGEMENTS

The authors wish to acknowledge the support of the Museum Training Institute, Bradford, in funding the research upon which this paper is based.

REFERENCES

Ambrose, T. (1991) *Money, Money, Money and Museums*, Edinburgh: Scottish Museums Council.

Boylan, P. (1991) 'End of an era', *Leisure Management* 11 (8): 38–40.

Cobb, S. and Kasl, S. V. (1977) 'Termination – the consequences of job loss', *USA: HEW Publications* 77–224, NIOSH.

Cooper, C. L. and Marshall, J. (1976) 'Occupational sources of stress', *Journal of Occupational Psychology* 49: 11–28.

Cooper, C. L., Sloan, S. J. and Williams, S. (1988) *Occupational Stress Indicator*, Windsor: NFER-Nelson.

Hudson, K. (1990) *1992. Prayer or Promise*. London: HMSO.

Jick, T. D. (1983) 'The stressful effects of budget cutbacks in organisations', in Rosen, L. A. (ed.) *Topics in Managerial Accounting*, New York: McGraw-Hill.

Smith, M. J., Cohen, B. G., Stammerjohn, L. W. and Happ, A. (1981) 'An investigation of health complaints and job stress in video display operations', *Human Factors* 23: 289–400.

Sutherland, V. J. and Cooper, C. L. (1986) *Man and Accidents Offshore: The Costs of Stress Among Workers on Oil and Gas Rigs*, London: Lloyds List/Dietsmann (International) NV.

—— (1988) 'Sources of work stress', in Hurrell, J. J. Jun., Murphy, L. R., Sauter, S. L. and Cooper, C. L. (eds.) *Occupational Stress: Issues and Developments in Research*, London: Taylor & Francis.

Thompson, J. M. A. and Prince, D. R. (1984) 'Introduction', in Thompson, J. M. A. (ed.) *Manual of Curatorship*, London: Butterworth.

Tolles, B. F. Jun. (1991) 'Looking for leaders', *Museum News* 70 (4): 43–4.

Wilby, J. (1985) *Good Career Guide*, London: Sunday Times.

Wolpin, J. and Burke, R. J. (1986) 'Occupational locking-in: some correlates and consequences', *International Review of Applied Psychology* 35: 327–346.

Postscript

Shortly after the completion of this study, serious breaches of security occurred within a number of major United Kingdom museums. It should be noted that interviewees, all questioned before these incidents occurred, held differing views about security. In the small museums (< 10–50 staff) directors, by necessity, took an active role in security. In the medium-sized museums (51–l00 staff) there was some disparity. Whereas one director felt that security should be managed as a specialist function with trained staff, two other directors had no formal policy and no strong feelings on the matter. As would be expected, the largest museum in the sample had an established security function in which the director was not involved.

19

Image and self-image
Marista Leishman

The role of the museum attendant is being radically reappraised in British museums at present. In this chapter Marista Leishman reviews the very welcome major developments in terms of job enrichment, job rotation and customer care that are taking place.

'In England, where ignorance, vulgarity, or something worse are the characteristics of the lower orders, and where frivolity, affectation, and insolence are the leading traits of a class of lounging persons who haunt most public places, it would be the excess of folly for gentlemen who possess valuable museums to give unlimited access to the public.' In 1806, when this was written for the catalogue of the gallery at Cleveland House it was also requested that in wet or dirty weather visitors would arrive in carriages. Some fifty years earlier the British Museum opened in Montagu House and one of the trustees noted: 'If public days should be allowed, then it will be necessary for the trustees to have the presence of a committee of themselves attending, with at least two justices of the peace and the constables of the division of Bloomsbury.' The need to guard valuable collections has as long a history as the admittance of visitors, so spare a thought for today's warders and attendants working within a tradition which once allowed ticketed entrance only to 'studious and curious persons'.

All dressed up with nowhere to go, most attendants have about as much to look forward to as an underemployed sub-policeperson. After all, rarely do thieves remove paintings in broad daylight, or vandals spoil precious objects. And it is not that often either that curious hands fondle exhibits, umbrellas jab enthusiastically at canvases or children stick chewing gum on to the noses of statues. But these are the few moments in which the traditional attendant comes into his or her negative own, fulfilling the message of the stern uniform, and mingling assumed authority with the sheer relief of having something to do. Intervention becomes the high point of the day.

Most of the time the job is unspeakably boring and even staying awake becomes a problem. One attendant described his patch as 'a beautiful prison, into which not many people come, not even troublemakers'. Not surprisingly, visitors are put off by this band of melancholy minders who communicate their dejection, subtly suggesting that museums perhaps aren't very interesting after all.

Most larger museums grew up in the nineteenth century often as assertions of civic triumphalism; the demeanour of the warding staff was consistent with the grand manner of such institutions. But, since the 1960s many new places have opened. As well as the steady acquisition of properties by the National Trust and the National Trust for Scotland, historic house in private ownership, heritage centres, visitor centres attached to open-air sites and theme parks began to compete for the public attention. Independently run specialist museums appeared: for the first time there were specific collections for cycles, pencils, lace and lawnmowers. In 1984 English Heritage began work to present some 400 historic properties with push and profile and their Scottish counterpart followed. The royal palaces continued to absorb millions of visitors, the cathedrals even more.

These new 'visitor attractions' (the phrase itself is significant) use new kinds of staff. Historic houses may be staffed by volunteers who take pride in knowing about the history of the house and its inhabitants. At mining or maritime museums staff may be ex-miners or seamen – proud of their pits and their ships, and more concerned with the safety of the visitors than the exhibits. The farmstead at Aden Country Park in Grampian is staffed by farmworkers who explain what they are doing. At Blists Hill Open Air Museum, part of Ironbridge Gorge Museum, demonstrators dressed in character work as locksmiths, iron-workers, candlemakers and so on while at the same time chatting with the visitors. At hands-on science centres like those at Catalyst, Snibston Discovery Park and the Museum of Science and Industry in Manchester, staff are there to explain how things work, to see they don't go wrong and, occasionally, as at Eureka!, to engage the interest of younger visitors. At Amberley Chalk Pits Open Air Museum volunteer staff drive the traction engine and work in the sandwich bar.

In most of these places the staff that visitors meet have responsibilities and objectives different to those of traditional museum attendants. They are there to welcome and to answer questions rather than to exercise a watching brief. This puts pressure on museums with displays of valuable and vulnerable objects to provide the same service to their visitors, and to encourage them to feel at home, but without putting collections at risk. There was no place for traditional warders (*'les gardiens-robots'*) at the Pompidou Centre in Paris when it opened in 1977. Instead, *'hostesses d'accueil'* combine the tasks of welcoming and interpreting with responsibility for security. At the 1991 Japan exhibition at the Victoria and Albert Museum separate staff responded to visitors' enquiries in addition to normal warding staff – a solution out of the reach of smaller museums.

Other museums and galleries are reassessing the role and image of the traditional warder. At the Royal Naval Museum in Portsmouth, Melanie McKeown, customer services manager, seeks to relate customer care to security. One of the warders, Ken Shergold, tells how he 'thinks customer' by asking himself how would he like to be treated if he were a visitor. Susan Bourne, curator of Burnley's Towneley Hall Art Gallery and Museum believes that appearance and personal pride are important and that police-style uniforms are now redundant. At the National Museum of Scotland, Alan Young, head of administrative services, looks forward to a service which is rewarding for staff and more welcoming for the public. This calls not for a reduced security role, but for a more discreet one which replaces an aloof presence (with matching uniform and persona) with a more outgoing image (without a peaked cap) but with authority still intact. Windsor Castle, despite, or perhaps because of the blaze, will continue to be near the top of the league table of visitor numbers. In the view of the management the formal dress of the warders makes ever more important their need to relate well to the thousands of visitors.

In spite of these changes traces of the old culture persist in some museums. There is still the unmistakable feeling that makes the visitor ill at ease, that forces him or her to experience the museum as solemn and the staff as grim. Too often, visitors keenly seeking information are met with attendants who neither know nor care. For a visitor fresh from a historic house where questions are likely to be encouraged such treatment is unlikely to prompt a return visit.

Recently, in reply to a visitor's very ordinary question, an attendant in a national museum quickly said he had no idea. 'I'm only a menial here,' he explained. Museums may be working on the external image of their attendants but are they looking to improve the self-image of the individual? Christopher Amey, head of security at the National Portrait Gallery, feels that warders must be conversant with the subject of the gallery's exhibitions. To work well and to project a positive image, attendants need support and training. Attendant staff need to be fully integrated. This means keeping them informed of what is happening in the museum, why and when. If attendants are not told about a new development, given an explanation of a new exhibition or the chance to ask questions, they receive the unequivocal message that they are unimportant and that the important matters are going on elsewhere. It also means more than team briefing, feeding information from the top down. Managers must listen to the experience and advice of attendants who regularly witness the reactions of the public. As Sir John Harvey-Jones says: 'We make pathetically inadequate use of the capabilities of our people.'

At Stoke-on-Trent Museum there is a regular exchange of information between front-of-house staff and curators. At Tullie House Museum in Carlisle, director Nick Winterbotham, like management at Marks & Spencer, regularly arranges temporary closures for in-house training. Duties are rotated hourly because boredom is inimical to a happily operating institution and curators as well as front-line staff meet the public. Staff at the National Museum of Wales are considered the public face of the museum, and their training programme involves everybody, at all levels. Training programmes at Iron-bridge Gorge Museum include site maintenance workers, curators and telephonists. At the National Maritime Museum the view is that 'we are here for the customers'. Regular team briefing and training are embodied in the museum's corporate plan, according to Stephen Deuchar, development manager.

But training is not so simple. Disappointingly, the Hale Report on museum professional training and career structure (Museums and Galleries Commission 1987) does not recommend career structures for attendants. Failing to notice the ways in which the role of the attendant has changed, the report offers little in anticipation of continuing development. Instead it proposes a core syllabus – an inadequate response to an important need.

In addition, training alone is not enough. In the *Industrial Society Magazine* (March 1989), David Turner regrets that training is becoming 'hung up on standards, qualifications, status and accreditation. The real issue is how to move away from standardisation in favour of individuality and from conformity to creativity.' He goes on to note that the concept of accumulated competences for training at all levels is sound, 'blending the skills, knowledge, aptitudes, temperament and personal qualities' that are needed by all members of the work-force. But when these competences 'are required to conform to a set of standards defining a performance requirement' and leading to an award, something is missing. A single national set of standardized competences, however diligently prepared, should be understood as a menu and not as a diet. Museums, people and circumstances all vary; museum managers and attendants need to be able to choose from a broad spectrum of training material and approaches.

When training becomes a prescription for action, it shows. The telephonist, lifelessly delivering a formula response ('Good morning, Jones and Baker here, Brian speaking, how can I help you?') voices a contradiction between style and content. At one gallery the double doors are importantly flung open by an attendant on either side at the approach of every visitor. Flattered, a visitor enters, only to catch part of an uninterrupted dialogue on pay and conditions from the other side of the gallery. The mechanics of training are there but the central matter is lost. Managers should encourage human rather than mechanical responses, and give attendant staff the confidence to relate easily to visitors. This will help them to remain interested, alert and welcoming and to convey through their attitude the message that all questions will be dealt with politely, that information or assistance is there if needed and that complaints will be taken seriously.

Museums have come a long way from those early days when they worked to keep the public at bay. Those museums who through their staff are 'engaged in a dialogue with the public', as Val Bott, curator of the Passmore Edwards Museum, put it (*Museums Journal*, February 1990: 28) are now getting the results they deserve. By investing in front-of-house staff, museum managers can move attendant staff out of the category of 'the menial' to their proper place at the forefront of the museum experience.

This article first appeared in Museums Journal *(June 1993), pp. 30–2.*

20

Museums and marketing

Peter Lewis

What is marketing and why do museums need it? In this chapter Peter Lewis, by addressing these fundamental questions, opens up a timely debate, and also valuably considers the nature of a range of marketing activities in museums.

Most museum people react to the word 'marketing' with the same predictable distaste that Pavlov's dogs showed to water. The feeling that marketing equals crass commercialism equals a threat to professional standards needs to be refuted as the palpable nonsense that it is.

For many years, however, there was no reaction at all. Museums and marketing ignored each other. In the last edition of the *Manual of Curatorship* there was one reference to marketing, but one can also search academic marketing books for any theoretical or practical comments on museums. In recent years there has been a meeting, albeit an uneasy one, between marketing practitioners and museum professionals. Most of the energy and enquiry has come from the world of marketing. The museum world has remained distrustful. At the 1988 Museums Association Conference in Belfast,[1] itself devoted to marketing, a fellow delegate explained the problem to me. Imagine, he suggested, marketing as a kind of H. M. Stanley who, after lengthy travels, approaches a museological Dr Livingstone. The outstretched hand and that famous greeting is met by damnation of his presumption and chastisement for transatlantic impertinence. The simile is a seductive one. Livingstone was a venerated explorer whose journeys, inadequately funded by the state, were supported by private zeal and funding. He was a man with a strong sense of mission, possessed of the quality described by African Arabs as *baraka*, an ability to convey blessings, a capacity to explain and enhance life. Stanley was younger and brasher. He was hard, quick, egocentric and American, driven by *kudos*, the love of fame and prestige.

Historically, of course, the meeting between Livingstone and Stanley was not like this. It was marked by amiability rather than abrasion. 'When my spirits were at their lowest ebb', Livingstone recorded in his diary, 'the Good Samaritan was close at hand . . . the flag at the head of the caravan told of the nationality of the stranger. Bales of goods, baths of tin, huge kettles, cooking pots, tents, etc., made me think this must be a luxurious traveller, and not one at his wit's end like me!' Stanley's description is equally vivid. He approached the missionary with caution and reported, 'We both grasped hands, and then I said aloud "I thank God, Doctor, I have been permitted to see you!" He answered, "I feel thankful that I am here to welcome you!"'.

I do not wish to push this parable too far. The salvation of museums does not lie solely in marketing initiatives. It is valid, however, to point out the parallels. Livingstone's mission, though worthy, was poorly equipped and had lost a sense of direction. Nor did the government make any moves to go to his assistance. Missionaries are always an embarrassment to the establishment unless there is a direct trading profit associated with the mission. Sir Richard Burton, when approached to assist Livingstone, remarked with the semi-sardonic, semi-laconic air of a modern-day Minister of the Arts, that it was 'infra-dig to rescue a mish' (Moorehead 1960).

The intended moral of this sermon is simple. A museum needs to combine *baraka* and *kudos*. It needs to declare and demonstrate both its integrity and its ability to confer blessings. *The Scottish Museums Council* has expressed this clearly and concisely in an important policy statement:

> A museum does five main things: it preserves, documents, exhibits and interprets material evidence and associated information for the benefit of the public, and it is normally concerned to add to its collections. . . . The revolutionary re-thinking in recent years . . . by professionals and public alike, imposes an obligation on existing museums, however long they have been established, to re-examine their functions, in order to determine the contributions they are making to the society that is being asked to support them. To achieve this, each museum needs to identify for itself its distinctive purpose or 'mission' and to prepare a master plan which maps out its future programme in five key areas: conservation, research, interpretation, marketing and financial planning.
>
> (Scottish Museums Council 1988: 7)

The final words are important. They emphasize the need to strengthen the continuing traditional priorities of conservation, research and interpretation with the new skills of marketing and sound financial management. The five key areas have to be given equal weight. The mark of a real 'museum professional' is not to cling to claims of curatorial primacy but to recognize the professionalism of other professionals – to 'feel thankful' that we are 'still here to welcome you'.

WHY DO MUSEUMS NEED MARKETING?

One reason, often given, for an alliance with marketing is that museums are in crisis and must do something to survive. Faced with falling attendances, towering budgets, crumbling buildings or any combination of all three, there is perceived to be a need to achieve extra visitors and additional sources of finance. One route is for the director, or his curatorial colleagues, to adopt selling or publicity roles; to do aggressively and officially what they have before done subconsciously. This is often performed with great energy and enthusiasm in the sure knowledge that a degree in archaeology and a diploma in museum studies fit one to do anybody else's job with total confidence. Alternatively, the museum may bring on to its staff, usually at a low level, someone to deal with publicity and advertising Sometimes, given fair fortune and good people, these strategies can work. Usually they do not, because the theory itself is wrong. The assumption made is that the role and status of the museum is perfect and that the public and the establishment only need to be educated, cajoled or bludgeoned into recognizing this self-evident truth. This is not marketing but selling. Selling is sometimes a respectable activity, but it bears the same relationship to marketing as the banana skin does to wit. It is also self-deceptive. Success is ascribed to curatorial brilliance; failure to the fault of inefficient marketing. As in the theatre, so in museums. Success is credited to the brilliance of the director and cast, failure to poor publicity and incompetent critics.

The second argument is more subtle and one advocated by museum professionals who have attended the occasional seminar. This argument is akin to the one recognized by parents as the 'everybody else in my class is allowed to wear high heels' syndrome. Simply because the world has changed, so, it is argued, ought the museum. This theory is lucidly expressed in the Association of Independent Museums' *The Principles of Marketing, a Guide for Museums*:

> It is acknowledged that museums are in competition for a share of the public's time, interest, energy and support. . . . Consumer goods now offer their purchasers not only function but added value 'experience' in terms of image and lifestyle. . . . The pure 'experience industry', which includes sport, package holidays, theme parks, heritage centres, theatres, museums and kissograms is expanding rapidly. It has essentially only one thing to offer its customers – quality of experience. . . . Added experiential value . . . is already, and will progressively become, more important.
>
> (Bryant 1988)

The argument is a seductive one. The theory that 'we must adjust the way we sell ourselves in the market place' is at least one stage up the evolutionary scale from 'we should tell people about ourselves'. Bryant, the author of the Guidelines quoted above, makes the important point that marketing 'has much to do with change'. The rate of change, itself, he suggests, is speeding up at an extraordinary rate. 'If museums resist change, and do not respond to new demands, they will be left behind – out of touch with the realities, needs and demands of the day'. That is a dangerous double-ended argument. I can think of many within our profession who would argue that their precise function is to 'afford themselves the luxury of being in the past, closeted away . . . from time'! I would, intellectually, support this fundamentalist stance, if I was convinced that the decision was one that had been carefully weighed and considered. Often, however, the proclamation of allegiance to 'old values' is the noisy articulation of an inner timidity, a mindless resistance to change.

The real reason why museums need to incorporate marketing into their central core of management is a simple one – it is a sensible thing to do. Museums have become a valuable, if not always valued, part of the nation's cultural life. They are *so* important that they must be managed well if the central spiritual, educational reason for their existence is not to wither. Service institutions like charities, hospitals, theatres, orchestras and political parties have all recognized the need for such professional services as personnel recruitment, training, purchasing, accountancy and audit. So have museums. The other service institutions have also incorporated marketing and so must museums. Otherwise they will wither away.

At a critical stage of growth in any institution there comes a need to change managerial methods. In the museum world this occurs when the original collector/entrepreneur or his successor is unable to continue running the institution with the aid of helpers. A new style is required. Management change is needed. That change is possible only if 'basic concepts, basic principles and individual vision are changed radically' (Drucker 1974: 8). The American writer on management matters Peter Drucker has compared these two kinds of institution to two distinct forms of organisms: 'the insect, which is held together by a tough hard skin, and the vertebrate animal, which has a skeleton'. He goes on to explain that land animals, supported only by a hardened skin or carapace, cannot grow beyond a few inches in size. To be larger, animals need a skeleton. The skeleton does not grow, does not evolve out of the hard skin 'for it is a different organ with different antecedents' (Drucker 1974: 13). When an institution reaches a size of some complexity it needs a different form of management. That form replaces the hard-skin structure of the original entrepreneur. It is not its successor, but something new. When does a museum reach the stage when it has to shift from 'hard skin' to 'skeleton'? I would suggest that the line needs to be drawn at a level just above the smallest of museums. Peter Drucker draws an exemplary illustration of a small research laboratory employing twenty to twenty-five people from a variety of disciplines. Museum people will recognize the picture:

> Without management things go out of control. Plans fail to turn into action, or worse, different parts of the plans going at different speeds, different times, and with different objectives and goals. The favour of the 'boss' becomes more important than performance. At this point the product may be excellent, the people able and dedicated . . . but the enterprise will begin to founder, stagnate and soon go downhill unless it shifts to the 'skeleton' of all managers and management structure.
>
> (Drucker 1974: 13, 14)

That same guru, talking of marketing within the management of an institution, has much to offer museums. He starts from the premise that marketing is 'the distinguishing, unique function' of any enterprise and that any institution which relies on support from people should 'have two – and only these two basic functions: marketing and innovation. Marketing and innovation produce results; all the rest are "costs"' (Drucker 1974: 56, 57).

In museums we claim to know a great deal about innovation. What do we make of marketing?

WHAT IS MARKETING?

Like 'heritage' or 'history' there is no simple definition of 'marketing'. Reading through the works of the academic marketing community, especially those textbooks used in a wide variety of university courses, is a dispiriting process. Definitions offered by academics can be mindbendingly difficult to analyse:

> Marketing is the process whereby society, to satisfy its consumption needs, evolves distributive systems composed of participants, who, interacting under constraints – technical (economic) and ethical (social) – create transactions or flows which resolve market separations and result in exchanges and consumption.
>
> (Bartels 1968)

They can also possess a deceptive simplicity that leaves a student little wiser than before:

> Marketing is the creation of time, place and possession utilities.
>
> (Converse *et al.*, 1965)

> Marketing is the set of human activities directed at facilitating and consummating exchanges.
>
> (Kotler 1977, 2nd edn)

> The generic concept of marketing . . . is specifically concerned with how transactions are created, stimulated, facilitated and valued.
>
> (Kotler 1977, 2nd edn)

It is easy to be cynical about the inability of the marketing profession to provide a simple explicable definition of the word 'marketing'. We should remember that our own profession is still embròiled in an attempt to provide a comprehensive and overall definition of 'museum'.[2]

The British Institute of Marketing definition can provide us perhaps with a starting point in approaching a simple definition. Marketing is, the Institute suggests, 'the management process responsible for identifying, anticipating and satisfying customer requirements profitably' (Wilmshurst 1984). At first reading this concept would appear to be light-years away from museums. Most marketing textbooks are geared to the selling of a *product* rather than the supply of a *service*. Concepts like *customers* and *profit* are guaranteed to raise curatorial hackles. Few of our institutions make a profit unless it be at the expense of their integrity. What indeed would happen to museums and galleries if they acceded totally to customer demands? Do we in fact even know what these demands might be? We are, I would suggest, in the business (and I use the word deliberately) of giving our users what they need rather than what they demand. If we see ourselves as missionaries then we have a right to hang on to the eternal verities and not allow our congregations to fall into the modern-day heresies of heritage centres and theme parks.

My advice is that we should take a deep breath and stand back from the marketing of handbooks. We need to look 'through a glass darkly' at the terms we distrust – business, profit, product, consumer, etc. – and see what is of value to us. If we do we shall see that *marketing* has two levels of meaning. It is first what the textbooks refer to as a *concept* and what I would prefer to call a *philosophy*. Second it is a generic term that lumps together a series of practicalities, advertising, market research, public relations, publicity, etc. These latter activities are only part of the process of marketing. They are the ways by which we do things but are not in themselves the *why* of our existence. Philosophy comes first. We have to see what we do through the eyes of the people we do it for, the people who use museums and those who, directly or indirectly, fund and support our activities. Since no practical marketing manual exists for our profession I would suggest, as a starting point, a reworking of The British Institute of Marketing's definition to read as follows:

> Marketing is the management process which confirms the mission of a museum or gallery and is then responsible for the efficient identification, anticipation and satisfaction of the needs of its users.

I have chosen words like *needs* and *users* with some care. I recall the words of John Cotton Dana, the founder of Newark Museum, who opined in 1909 that 'a museum can help people only if they use it; they will use it only if they know about it'.[3] I would add to that remark 'and if they understand its purpose'. I applaud and endorse John Cotton Dana's insistence that museums exist to *help* people and that people should be encouraged to *use* museums. I would rather welcome *consumers* than *punters*, rather have *tourists* than *consumers*, *visitors* rather than *tourists*, *users* rather than *visitors*. To invite people to consume, visit or tour what we offer in museums is to behave in an arrogant way. To invite them to participate and to use the museum is properly to behave as professionals. It forces us to rethink our philosophy.

I doubt whether any institution, including and, especially, that museum that I direct, has seriously looked at its purpose, at its articles of faith. One of the side-effects of the ongoing museum registration scheme was to force us to dust down our foundation documents. There were many museums who were forced to recognize that they had never possessed statements of purpose or that much was now irrelevant. Trustees and boards of management found themselves endorsing hastily rewritten statements of policy to satisfy the basic and, as yet, far from stringent requirements of the Museums and Galleries Commission. We have no cause then to stand on our dignities. The acceptance of a marketing philosophy must start with a managerial audit. We would do well to adopt and adapt the planning cycle advocated by J. Walter Thompson. It asks a series of deceptively simple questions:

Where were we when we started?
Where are we now?
Where could we be?
How could we get there?
Are we getting there?

The cycle then begins again with the 'Where are we now?' question and the process continues. It is, as Patricia Mann has said, 'a valuable discipline for thinking . . . it can be used at a variety of levels of sophistication . . . it demands the creation and testing of hypotheses' (Mann 1988). When the hypotheses have been tested and the mission clarified that philosophy needs to be accepted throughout the whole organization. Within the museum, from volunteers and Friends, to curators and cleaners, to technicians and teaching staff, indeed everybody from the director upwards, have to understand and endorse the way we do things and the fundamental reasons why we do them. It is easier to understand this process if we look outside the museum world to retailing or other leisure industries. The reputation of Marks & Spencer or Sainsburys has little to do with price but everything to do with value. They have achieved customer loyalty by close attention to customer service and care. We see little if nothing of the higher management, but their company style comes through the behaviour of their visible staff. The same is true of museums. The success of some fast-food chains owes more to the courtesy of the staff and the rigidity of standards than it does to the delights of the burger. We may not wish to ape the exhibits of theme parks like Alton Towers or to send our senior staff on long trips to Disneyland but we *should* seek to emulate their day-to-day professionalism and staff training. This is not a descent into commercialism but a recognition that, if museums are as vital to the nation as we believe, they should be run to the highest standards.

This thinking process and the planning that follows does not challenge the integrity of the artefact nor the sanctity of scholarship. It strengthens them. What it does do is remind all of us that museums are not about objects but the understanding and appreciation of objects. Museums are for people not about things. A collection of objects is not a museum until staff accept professional responsibility for collections and their users.

Kenneth Hudson (1987), in his book *Museums of Influence*, neatly and with typical wit summarizes 'the recipe for survival and growth in the museums field' as:

First the museum must be financially viable. . . . Second, it must find ways of linking itself closely and actively with the local community and of satisfying real, rather than imagined tastes and needs. And third, it must never lose sight of the essential truth contained in the apparent paradox that successful popularization can only be achieved on a basis of sound scholarship. We are going to see a good many fly-by-night museums fail as a result of ignoring this maxim, and it is going to be a sad process to watch, *as sad as contemplating out-of-date museums fade away and eventually possibly die from a surfeit of learning, dullness, obstinacy and arrogance.*

(Hudson 1987: 194)

THE PRACTICALITIES OF MARKETING

Once the painful process of defining the mission of a museum is complete, it needs to be reconsidered at least once a year and a total redefinition done every five years. The mission may not change but the recognition of the *status quo* is an important judgement.

Having identified and anticipated needs, the process of satisfying those needs can proceed with the supply of services. Business economists, concerned with *product*, generally distinguish four areas of need:

1   Analysis and forecasting, i.e. market research and post-marketing audit.
2   Product development and design.
3   Influencing of demand – design, advertising, media relations, etc.; and
4   Service, staff training, distribution, after-sales service, etc.

Economists would further suggest that successful marketing depends upon a selection of these separate ingredients to achieve a suitable mix, a recipe relevant to a particular institution. The areas listed above are those appropriate to the manufacture of a product. They can be easily adapted to the needs of a museum, in which case the ingredients would include corporate identity, market research and visitor surveys, design and interpretation, publicity, advertising, public and media relations, staff training, etc. One common system of analysis lists the variables as the 'Six Ps': product, place, presentation, promotion, price and people. The Association of Independent Museums (AIM) Guidelines, quoted above, take this form of segmentation and give a useful breakdown of a typical museum mix. I have strong doubts about mnemonics of this kind, which generally reinforce the image that marketing is a form of mumbo-jumbo based on slogans rather than science. It is perhaps more appropriate briefly to discuss each of the elements identified before coming to a discussion of marketing mix and the implementation of a marketing plan.

CORPORATE IDENTITY

I came to the museum world after time spent in teaching, retailing and the professional theatre. I was surprised and shocked to see how poorly museums identify themselves and their purpose. This reticence may be inbred or may be instilled by those self-appointed cultural historians who make judgements on us all. Despite the eminence of Robert Hewison (1987), he is wrong to suggest that museums and galleries should be 'neutral facilities for the presentation of individual acts of creation'. Neutrality or blandness is not what we are about. For good or ill, all museums have their own personalities. If they are positive they should be promoted. If they are negative they should be changed. Until the individual characteristics of the museum are understood it cannot be decided whether its image should be preserved, modified or radically altered. I have throughout this paragraph been referring to the museum as a single unit. There is a problem when an area, perhaps that served by a local authority, promotes all its museums together under one procrustean policy which makes them all seem the same. This is a waste of time, money and energy. Such authorities need to free each individual unit to express its own personality. The National Museums and Galleries on Merseyside campaign is an excellent example of such confident promotion.

Names and titles are important. They are frequently longer and more pompous than they need to be. It is better to be 'The Science Museum' than 'The National Museum of Science and Industry', better to be the 'Natural History Museum' than the 'British Museum (Natural History)' and better still to be 'Wigan Pier' than 'The South Lancashire Heritage and Field Study Centre'. There is little point in insisting on the primacy of 'The North of England Open Air Museum' if your friends and users refer to you always as 'Beamish'.

Whatever the name, however, it is important, once chosen, to test its efficiency. Play devil's advocate games and look for potential comment or jokes. Remember that fish fingers were first going to be called cod pieces by an agency with no sense of the ridiculous. The name should be incorporated into a logo and a house style that reflects the tone of the museum. You should then stick tenaciously to it, remembering the reported words of St Francis, 'Do always what you believe to be right, Brother, and if it proves to be wrong, repent later!' (Houseman 1922). The logo and a designated typeface should appear on everything to do with the museum, stationery and signposts, posters and pamphlets, paper bags and lavatory doors. Have photographic bromides of the logo available for printers and the media; insist on your own typeface at all times. This face need not be exclusive to you but you should use no other. It takes a long time to build up a corporate identity. Do not change because it might be fun to do so this year – and ignore the bizarre or the over-fashionable (e.g. antique, medieval, gothic, playbill or computer graphics). The one factor common to all these faces is illegibility in 72 point viewed from 20 feet away.

The design of a corporate identity by a competent designer is expensive but should be afforded. The quality of the design will only be as good as the briefing you give to the designer. Museums with a minuscule budget or no budget at all should approach local colleges of further education with print or design departments. The creation of a corporate logo is a suitable project for a competent student, as is the artwork for promotional leaflets and brochures. The gain for the student is a piece of real rather than theoretical work in her or his portfolio.

LEAFLETS, BROCHURES AND POSTERS

All museums need leaflets or brochures. These can be simply designed, but never use single-sided sheets giving details of opening hours and of the range of exhibitions and services. Ideally, they should be coloured brochures using a range of photographs. Do not, however, illustrate, discuss or tell all you do. Convey the quality of the experience but surprise your visitors with the excellence of the real thing. It is wise to show photographs in short shot or from angles other than those which the visitor usually gets. Brochures should be finished and folded to A5 or smaller. Other sizes are distinctive and different but will not fit standard display stands in tourist information centres, libraries or elsewhere. Distribution within your area can usually be done cheaply or free on exchange days organized at a single site by your local tourist authority. Distribution outside your area will cost you more. Few museums in my experience need posters. A sensible idea is to design an A5 brochure which unfolds to incorporate an A3 poster. Do not print posters larger than A3 size. Schools, libraries and information centre notice boards are too small to incorporate large posters. It is sometimes worthwhile to involve yourself in a poster campaign on bus or railway station sites. Then you need to go really large to four-sheet size.

Carefully designed, a leaflet or brochure can be made to stretch to two years, but this requires a forward discipline of well planned and agreed hours of opening, admission prices (if appropriate) and discounts. Small museums should discuss with their local museums service whether there are any joint marketing promotions planned. For example, in Museums Year, the North East Museums Service recently successfully designed and printed a large map which listed free of charge the address and telephone number of each museum in the area. The cost was covered by grant and paid advertising on the rear. Your local authority, be it county, district, or borough, will also be promoting the area which includes your museum, as will your local tourist board. Ensure that these institutions have bromides of your logo, coloured slides and black-and-white prints of your best features, and know your address, telephone number and opening hours. Remind them every two months or so. People change and departments are shifted and reorganized. Nothing is worse than free publicity which is inaccurate or does not reflect the reality of your museum.

ADVERTISING

Advertising is costly and is best done with the advice of an agency. Do not automatically dismiss the use of an agency as expensive because a part of their income is derived from discounts not available to you. The agency needs from you a tight brief, a clear statement of what you want to achieve, i.e. more local visitors, more organized parties, more tourists, etc., and a stated budget beyond which they may not go. They will recommend a package of suggestions for you to approve and will themselves commission artwork and copy. Be critical if you do not feel that it represents the museum fairly. Avoid the temptation, however, to put in more and more information. Most readers or viewers can only take in three pieces of information in any message – a place, an event, a time. If you can afford it advertise on local television, which is particularly advantageous at the start and midway through the season – do not advertise at peak times.

General 'puff' advertisements, statements of your excellence and worthiness are a waste of your budgets. Keep local advertising to an absolute minimum and promote events, special days, new exhibitions. Do not forget local radio advertising but keep your time slots to the important drive-in and drive-home times. Remember that local radio and newspapers, as well as national papers like the *Guardian* and the *Independent* and others run free listings for special events. Do not be afraid to use them and be brave enough always to resist cold telephone calling from publications and gazetteers. Remember that even if these agencies are honest, and many are not, the cost will not marry with any advantages to you. If your budgets are small, advertise first in some tourist board publications, specialist coach and driver magazines, educational heritage groups, etc. If you take advantage of your local education authority's distribution system to schools, send two brochures to each school, one for the headmaster and one for the staff room. Should you have no advertising budget at all, rely on your ingenuity and charm to persuade the media to give you free editorial coverage.

PUBLICITY AND EDITORIAL COVERAGE

Contrary to common belief, all publicity is *not* good publicity. Avoid stunts, especially those suggested by professional publicists. Good publicity is often bad marketing. Consider, for example, the coverage given in recent years to the problems of the Victoria and Albert Museum and the Natural History Museum. Rarely turn down a request from radio or television but, if the image they are going to project is not positive, refuse pleasantly but firmly. From the factual basis of any story construct a scenario to suit the narrative needs of radio or the visual requirements of television or the press. The television news and current-affairs magazines need stories each day. Museum tales are often the statutory happy story to balance the bad news. Do not be afraid, however, to court regular national programmes like *Blue Peter*, *Any Questions*, *Today*, *Around Midnight*, *Down Your Way*, the Sunday religious slots, etc. They are all seeking venues and topics. They provide you with a coverage that would cost a fortune to pay for. With your local press maintain a steady stream of stories and picture opportunities. Do not overdo it or they will become bored; once a fortnight is a reasonable timespan. Although it takes time, do not give everybody the same press release. Is it a local story, a possible *Guardian* feature or a television news item? It may be all three and, if so, angle the story differently. If you are asked for a spokesman or spokeswomen make sure that they have character. Serious political problems must be handled by the Chairman of Trustees or the Director. Otherwise, let your staff do the interviews. The greater the number of voices and faces, the more real the stories, the more coverage to the museum.

MARKETING RESEARCH

'Marketing research' is not the same as 'market research'. The first involves an enquiry into the response of the users of a museum, the second into the size, status, composition of potential markets. Both should be done but the first is more fundamental to museum work. Marketing research is 'the gathering, recording, analysing and reporting of facts relating to the transfer . . . of goods and services . . . based on statistical probability theory and always uses the scientific method' (Adler 1969). Most museums do not know accurately how many people use their services; even more know nothing of why they are used or how people value those services. They should. Some museums, by simple observation or by intermittent visitor surveys, find out some facts. They are diligent in the gathering, recording and reporting of findings. They are still poor, and I include the institutions with which I have been associated, in the objective rather than subjective analysis of these findings. 'Research', the dictionary tells us, means 'a careful search . . . endeavour to discover new facts . . . by critical investigations'. 'Scientific' means 'according to rules laid down . . . for testing soundness of conclusions, systematic, accurate'. There is no point in specifying time or money on research if you are not prepared to be surprised by the results and to react to them.

Some research will already have been done for you. The government, via HMSO, produces a mass of statistical data, though with a considerable time lapse. Similar, though more specific, information is available from national and regional tourist authorities, though these statistics appear to me to be often 'optimistic' in tone and should be treated with caution. Visitor surveys by other museums can also be valuable, as long as users clearly understand that this information is based on small samples of those people already using existing museums. There is some information on the wider public view of museums. The Scottish Museums Council in 1985 commissioned a survey into 'Public Attitudes to Scottish Museums'. This showed a higher level of response to museums in the A, B and C socio-economic groupings, appearing to confirm the widely held view that museums and galleries attract the well-educated middle and upper classes. A survey of an individual museum may well show otherwise. Beamish has been interviewing users for over fifteen years and our statistics show a different result to that of Scotland with a higher proportion of people at the extreme end of these groups, with more A and E visitors than usual. Both Beamish and Scotland's survey highlighted, as do surveys in the performing arts, a greater interest among men than women and a higher degree of criticism in respondents between 20 and 30 years of age.

Commercial companies presented with such statistics would be inclined to narrow their selling activities into receptive areas of the market. Museums need to do the opposite. Some specialized museums will obviously cater for their own adherents, but most museums, given their missionary zeal, exist to serve all of their local, regional or international congregations. They should, therefore, use facts to correct failings and not merely to reinforce existing situations.

It is likely, given the funds available to museums, that they will give priority to question-naires and interviews with their present users. Museums can design their own question-naires and do their own surveys, though the process is littered with stumbling blocks and pitfalls. The questions need to be carefully chosen, to be unambiguous and be capable of statistical analysis. The list must include control questions to ensure consistency and the survey should be done on a controlled random basis to ensure that all sexes, ages, days of the week, months of the year, etc., are covered. Questioners can be members of your staff, staff specially recruited or staff from outside agencies. The first is the most difficult, but there is an emotional appeal in using curatorial staff at times. If nothing else it exposes them, in exhibitions they have themselves planned, to the views of people they rarely see or listen to.

Any survey that does not include at least 1,000 interviews is probably useless. For this reason, if no other, it is sensible to allow your own surveys to be done. Resist the attempts of schools, colleges and individuals to do their own surveys. This can lead to friction with the users of museums.

Jonathan Bryant (1988) in the AIMS Guidelines gives a long and very valuable section on visitor surveys which is worth study. He advises that competent professional advice is preferable and recommends institutions like MUSEUMSCAN or university or college departments. I have a more open mind on the subject, particularly when museums, large or small, have difficulty in raising finance. Some area museum councils, independent trusts and local authorities have been known to part-fund surveys. Ask them for help. If the museum has no money at all then use existing staff.

The museum director should read all letters and reply to them personally within three days of receipt. She or he should not only glory in the bouquets but take seriously the brickbats. Staff at all levels should be encouraged to report comments both favourable and unfavourable. We have formal systems to report accidents or incidents. A formal reporting system of opinions is just as valuable.

PUBLIC RELATIONS

Museums are about people: the people who work in them and the people who finance and use them. Curators, and especially directors, rarely meet the public. Attendants, sales staff and demonstrators do so. It is important then that all staff should understand the mission of the museum and are given positive leadership.

Each year museums should do a customer audit and this should be followed up each and every day. The museum should open on time and all its services (the lavatories, cafe-terias and retailing areas as well as the galleries) should be cleaned and ready and should be monitored throughout the day. I have mentioned institutions like Marks & Spencer before and make no apology for doing so again. Their staff, from management to shop floor, are excellent marketeers. Their commitment to what they are doing works rather like osmosis but does not come about by accident. All staff are trained to be pleasant and helpful. They worry about the quality of the service they offer. This does not mean that museums need to develop an obsequious 'the customer is always right' attitude, nor adapt the mindless 'have a nice day' kind of transatlantic jargon. Firmness and control are an important element of customer-care. Attendants are there not only to 'help the visitor' but also to deter the visitor from 'helping themselves'. It must be realized, however, that junior staff when faced with complaints should be able to refer those comments upwards, either immediately or by noting the details, and to promise a telephoned or written response from someone in greater authority. Junior staff must also be trained to be neutral in their response. A tacit agreement that all is not well, that 'I've been telling the high-ups this for months but they never listen' does irreparable harm to the museum.

Attitudes of positive help can only be achieved by thorough induction and regular systematic training. It is every bit as important that staff with public contacts receive training in customer-care as, for example, that a conservator should receive professional training in paper conservation.

One anecdote may serve to illustrate this precept. I am fond of one large museum outside London which has superb collections, imaginatively and professionally exhibited. Its building is formidable. The frontage, a classical temple-like structure, is accessible by a high flight of steps. The large notice board proclaims only its title, gives no information, verbal or pictorial, as to its contents or opening hours. A temporary notice tells those with disabilities to go to the rear of the building and to ring at a numbered door where wheelchair access can be arranged. The entrance for able-bodied visitors is via one of a number of enormous doors, one of which is open each day. Users enter via a lobby full of quasi-military uniformed attendants and a collection of negative notices. The lobby itself is poorly lit, so it is with some trepidation that potential users even manage to penetrate the museum. Lavatories are at the rear of the building as are the catering facilities which open an hour later than the museum itself, which itself often opens late and chases away early those brave enough to attend. The staff entrance is on one side of the building so curators are probably unaware of the experience of the museum users.

A simple user audit of this museum could bring its standard of service up to the undoubted excellence of its collection and scholarship. But the marketing will is not there.

Museums of any size need to consider the messages they transmit. Never use negative notices. Thank people for *not* smoking, welcome guide dogs and, if objects must not be touched, design the exhibition to avoid that. If the museum is popular do not indulge in the intellectual arrogance that numbers must somehow be limited. Devise systems to cope with popularity. Unless a museum adopts a positive marketing approach to its users they will not come back to use the museum again.

SPECIALIST GROUPS AND MAILING LISTS

I have been talking throughout this brief article as if all users were individuals. Whilst museums and galleries wish to stress and hold on to their very specific roles they do have to recognize also that they are 'visitor attractions' or 'tourist spots' and that party bookings, whether educational or social, are essential elements of a museum's 'congregation'. They have to be given equal value.

Changes in educational philosophy and the management of schools have impacted on museums. In some regions there are less school visits or there has been a change in the numbers coming from junior schools as compared with secondary schools or colleges.

Any museum where schoolchildren are less than 20 per cent of its total is failing in its essential mission. The days of the school pleasure trip are numbered. Teachers are now required to justify the educational value of activities outside the classroom and need detailed advice not only on specific educational gains but also the level of the project as it applies to the National Curriculum and GCSEs. Museums have to provide this and, via the distribution schemes available through educational activities, to ensure the information reaches teachers. The work of pupils, which is now predominantly project-based, has forced changes even in how children move around museums. Small groups attached to teachers and minders are becoming rarer. A freedom of access with teachers in fixed locations to welcome the children is becoming common. Museum staff need to be aware of these new systems and to react positively.

The museum also needs a policy for adults in specialized groups. Contact with local organizers, coach and tour operators, and coach-drivers clubs can all be furthered by up-to-date mailing lists, attendance at travel fairs, special seminars, etc. There needs to be a person or department within the museum that copes with these special needs and serves as an efficient point of contact. Mailing lists are difficult to build up. They can be bought or borrowed. Equally importantly they need to be kept up to date. Old information should be deleted. The records should be cross-referenced. Numbers are not everything in museums but they are some indication of success. Analysis of those museums with sophisticated party booking organizations suggests that it is this sector of the market which is growing faster than individual visits. A professional approach to these kinds of users is not a sell-out to sordid commercialism but a necessary part of a museum's mission.

THE MARKETING PLAN

Museums articulate the past; they offer explanations or expositions of history. Unfortunately, management techniques often have the same obsession. The average administrator or director spends too much time reviewing the past or struggling with the present. Management and marketing are dynamic situations. They have been defined in a rather 'cookie fortune cracker' way as 'making the future happen'. Though, as museum folk, we are suspicious of slick slogans, this one merits attention:

> To make the future happen one has to be willing to do something new. . . . One has to be willing to say: 'This is the right thing to happen . . . we will work on making it happen . . . it is rational activity'. And it is less risky than coasting along on the comfortable assumption that nothing is going to change, less risky than following a prediction that what is likely to happen is the most desirable.
>
> (Drucker 1967)

The dictionary definition of the word 'plan' is 'to arrange beforehand'. Forward arrangement of priorities is the essential aspect of marketing and the prime function of management whether in museums or elsewhere. Having established the 'mission' of the museum, the consequences of that judgement have to be understood and a strategy implemented.

Plans, whether corporate or marketing, are not immutable, but it is just as well to behave, at least for the first year, as if they were. Changing needs, priorities, costs, external events will lead to adaptations, but resist the temptation to tinker with the basic precepts. Do not, however, take an unreasonably long-term view. 'Mission', to the Catholic church, may have a time-span of eternity, but in business practice 'mission' is defined more succinctly 'the paramount objective of any organization for the intermediate future'. A *Forward Planning Manual* for museums and other arts institutions, published by the Museums & Galleries Commission and HMSO in 1991, seeks to provide principles and practical guidelines. Realistically it is envisaged as a volume with a life-span of five years. That is a cool but competent professional judgement. It highlights the apparent paradox that forward planning, though the most important task, is itself transitory. It has to be done all over again, every year, every five years, every decade.

I do not propose to offer a detailed schematic marketing plan for a typical museum. A useful and intelligent one can be found in AIM'S Guideline 16 (Bryant 1988), referred to above. This will need adaptation by each institution. I would wish, however, to highlight some important points.

Evidence of comprehensive forward planning is now expected by grant-making bodies and government departments. Area museum councils, who have themselves been through this process, can show you their scars and offer advice. Planning is as essential for small museums, even voluntary organizations. The proclamation that small is beautiful may be seductive, but the assumption that everybody in a small organization knows its plans for the future is false.

Any marketing plan should, therefore, include the following:

1   A *definition*, i.e. a proclamation of purpose. What are the missionary aims of the museum?

2   *An assessment*, through some sort of sound research into who is presently using the museum, how they are using it and whether their needs are being met.

3   A *judgement*, realistically made, of the operational opportunities and constraints from outside the museum. Are there policies of local or national government which determine or inhibit the museum's operation? Should the museum stay within its present organizational framework, seek charitable status, go 'independent', or reinforce its local links?

4   A *forecast* of the quantity and quality of visits by users. What numbers can we expect? How will we cope? If the museum charges for admission, what should those charges be and how can those who might not be able to afford those charges be accommodated?

5   A *policy* of what publications, retail and catering services are appropriate. These should only be planned if they marry with the museum's image, do credit to its reputation and provide a sensible and achievable net profit, which should itself be used to improve the museum's central functions of collection, conservation and education.

6   A *promotion* of the museum's services. This will involve a mandatory programme of all staff training and a regular update of all internal communications. It may, if affordable, involve a programme of media advertising, exhibitions, mailings, posters, pamphlets and trade shows. This should never be less than 10 per cent, including staff costs, of the museum's revenue income. If the museum, laudably, has a policy of free admission, it should calculate what its income might be if charges were made and include that same percentage in its forward plans.

7   A *timetable* with a rational time-scale. Museums tend to take over-long views of time needed to plan exhibitions and implement schemes. 'Slippage' is an ugly word but an even uglier practice. Take shorter-term views than are currently fashionable. Long-term plans with no end-date are examples of museological lethargy.

8   *A budget* which forecasts both income and expenditure. Set a realistic figure and keep to it. If good fortune occurs, if a sudden unexpected donation or course of finance happens, then adapt the plan. If money is short, if there is a sudden inflationary surge, keep within the budget and cut accordingly.

9   *A dream* is always necessary. Most great museums were founded by eccentrics or entrepreneurs who defied convention. The idea that God, government or a 'generalized good' will provide is not totally out of date. But remember, as the New Testament reminds us, that rewards go to those who use and multiply their talents, not to those who bury them in the ground in order to preserve them.

MARKETING: A FINAL THOUGHT

I made, in the preamble to these notes, a distinction between marketing as a philosophy and marketing as a set of practices. In museums we tend to be pompous about the philosophy and cynical about the practices. 'Business' is still a dirty word with us. Marketing departments like 'planning departments, personnel departments, and management development departments' can be, as Robert Townsend reminds us in his tongue-in-cheek book *Up the Organization* (1970), 'camouflages designed to cover up for lazy or outworn chief executives'. But, marketing, as he goes on to stress, is 'in the fullest sense of the word, the name of the game. So it had better be handled by the boss of his line, not by staff hecklers!'. The museum profession sometimes seems to be a highly structured form of institutionalized heckling. It must not remain so.

Marketing is an attitude of mind, transmitted into actions, that permeates an institution from bottom to top. It starts from the premise that management is not just common sense or a collection of codified experiences but is an organized body of knowledge. The knowledge that it seeks to organize is the good of society. Each institution exists to contribute to the satisfaction of those who use it or ought to be using it. It does not exist to supply employment for staff, kudos for politicians or dividends to shareholders. Jobs, kudos and dividends are necessary means but not ends. A hospital should not exist for the sake of consultants, nurses or orderlies but for the benefit of patients. A school does not exist for the sake of teachers and administrators but for students. A museum does not exist for curators, business managers, attendants or academics but for its users.

Museum people are rightly proud of their care of objects and learning. As managers they have to be stewards of what exists. Whether they like it or not they have to be administrators. They also have to be innovators, risk-takers and entrepreneurs so that the services they offer and the artefacts they preserve survive beyond the lifespan of this generation. Future users will only be able to give thanks that they, like Stanley, 'have been permitted to see you', if museums ensure, like Livingstone, that they are still 'here to welcome you'.

This paper first appeared in J. M. A. Thompson, et al. (eds) (1992) Manual of Curatorship: A Guide to Museum Practice, *London: Museums Association/Butterworth, pp. 148–58.*

NOTES

1   Most of the papers presented at the 1988 Museums Association Conference in Belfast are published in *Museums Journal* 88(3), (Dec. 1988). Intriguingly, the keynote address, given by the then director general of the Institute of Marketing, was omitted. Another useful collection of articles dealing with marketing and museums can be found in *Museums Journal* 88(2), (Sep. 1988).

2 At the time of writing the Museums Association is considering the differences between its own definition of a museum or gallery and that of the International Council of Museums (ICOM).

3 John Cotton Dana (1909), quoted in Thompson (1984): 75.

REFERENCES

Adler, M. (1969) *Lectures in Market Research*, Crosby Lockwood.

Bartels, R. (1968) 'The general theory of marketing', *Journal of Marketing*, 32, London.

Bryant, J. (1988) *The Principles of Marketing, A Guide for Museums*, Chichester: Association of Independent Museums Guideline 16.

Converse, H. and Converse, M. (1965) *Elements of Marketing* 7th edn, London: Prentice Hall.

Drucker, P. (1967) *Managing for Results*, London: Pan.

—— (1974) *Management: Tasks, Responsibilities, Practices*, London: Heinemann.

Houseman, L. (1922) *Collected Plays of St Francis*, London.

Hewison, R. (1987) *The Heritage Industry*, London: Methuen.

Hudson, K. (1987) *Museums of Influence*, 194, Cambridge: Cambridge University Press.

Kotler, P. (1977) *Marketing Management*, 1st and 2nd edns, London: Prentice Hall.

Mann, P. (1988) 'Delivering the right product to the right people', *Museums Journal*, Dec.: 139–42.

Moorehead, A. (1960) *The White Nile*, London: Penguin.

Scottish Museums Council (1988) *A Framework for Museums in Scotland*, Edinburgh: SMC.

Thompson, J. (1984) *The Manual of Curatorship*, London: Butterworth.

Townsend, R. (1970) *Up the Organization*, London: Hodder Fawcett.

Wilmhurst, J. (1984) *The Fundamentals of Practice of Marketing*, London: Heinemann.

21

Marketing in museums: a contextual analysis
Fiona Combe McLean

In this chapter Fiona McLean picks up the debate initiated by Hugh Bradford and Peter Lewis on the applicability of commercial marketing approaches to museums. In arguing that marketing in museums is even more context-specific than has previously been suggested, McLean has pushed forward a debate that is likely to be the subject of interest for some time to come.

INTRODUCTION

For museums in the United Kingdom, the 1980s can now be seen as a period of transition, and the upsurge of interest in marketing has reflected one response to this transition. The principles of marketing have, to varying degrees, been adopted within the general operations of many museums. However, little attention has been paid to marketing in the museums literature. By contrast, much has been written on the distinguishing features of museums, although no attempt has been made to relate these to the marketing of museums. Where marketing in museums has been examined, the emphasis is on transferral of marketing theories and practices to the museum. These theories have themselves been transferred, by means of a deductive process, from the concept of goods marketing to non-goods related situations such as service and not-for-profit organizations. The deduced theory is then slotted into a specific situation, further stretching concepts that are already fully stretched.

This chapter re-evaluates the marketing process in museums by taking the museum, as opposed to the theory, as the starting point. The marketing of museums is then treated in terms of the context of the museum, and is not imposed from external practices. The aim of this study, therefore, is to examine the nature of marketing in the museum context.

The first section is a critical appraisal of current marketing thought in the museum literature. The next section considers marketing in the museum context, drawing on the findings of research initially conducted in the North East of England, and subsequently reinforced by an examination of museums throughout the United Kingdom. The findings are outlined as categories of relevance to the marketing process within museums, namely: the collection; the museum building; the staff; what has been termed the organizational mechanisms; and the public. A discussion evaluating these findings ensues, which concludes that marketing in museums needs to be reassessed in the light of the context-specific issues that are raised.

REVIEW OF MUSEUM MARKETING LITERATURE

There is no comprehensive publication on museums marketing, the literature being confined mainly to journal articles. These articles are inclined to be anecdotal and to draw on the experiences of adopting marketing techniques in a museum situation. Where marketing guidelines are developed, they supplant those derived from goods marketing, no acknowledgement being made of the context of the museum in the marketing process. As a result, the practice of marketing theories in museums has been criticized for its lack of relevance and the specialized language, which reflects a commercial process, has been mocked for its impracticality. Peter Lewis, for example, refers to marketing as 'mumbo jumbo', and declares that, 'reference to the seven Cs the four Ms and the three Ps of marketing do nothing but reinforce our doubts' (Lewis 1988: 147). Articles on museum marketing have consequently tended to be polarized towards either accepting or denouncing marketing principles.

The only guidelines currently available for museum marketing were compiled by Jonathan Bryant (1988) on behalf of the Association of Independent Museums. Bryant ascribes the fundamental requirement for marketing in museums to competition:

> The earliest public museums operated in a supply led market. There were few alternatives open to the average man (*sic*) seeking to 'improve' himself, or looking for a respectable, and cheap, outing for the family. The goods on offer in the first public museums effectively sold themselves. Today the circumstances are somewhat different. It is now acknowledged that museums are in competition for a share of the public's time, interest, energy and support.
>
> (Bryant 1988: 1)

What 'competition' means in this context is neither tangible, nor quantifiable. With what are museums competing? Do museums regard their public in terms of popularity? Is the notion of 'competition' valid here? In describing the marketing process, Bryant replaces the notion of 'profit' with the museum's principal objectives (1988: 9), but how can 'profit' be equated with 'objectives'? The museum context, then, is slotted into the goods marketing mechanism. Is Bryant suggesting that 'not-for-profit' therefore means that 'profit' no longer exists? In goods marketing, 'profit' is money accrued, whereas here it has come to mean 'benefit'. Is it appropriate to change the meaning of the term to suit the context?

Similarly, when writing about marketing the visual arts, Leslie W. Rodger (1987) assumed that art gallery marketing is not different from marketing in the commercial context, and proceeded to adapt the gallery context. When discussing 'price' as part of the marketing mix, for example, Rodger defines public subsidies which reduce or eliminate admission charges, as 'the price the public is paying, albeit indirectly' (Rodger 1987: 30). When paying for a ticket, is the 'value' inherent in the cost of the ticket, or in the experience of the visit? According to Marxists, 'value' in the capitalist mode of production is 'surplus value' in terms of money accrued over and above production costs. Can 'value' in museums be equated with financial worth? Equally, can 'value' be detached from public recognition and response to the way a museum is displayed and moderated?

Otherwise, the emphasis in the museum marketing literature has been on learning from practice. The museum adopts the principles of marketing theory, implements them and then, through trial and error, defines examples of good practice. Lessons are then outlined to be learned by other museums, which, in turn, can adopt these 'good practice'

233

methods. Hugh Bradford (1991) has assumed this method in his recent research at Strathclyde University (chapter 4 in this volume). His study involved a detailed on-site investigation into the activities of selected 'successful' museums in Scotland. The aim of the study is to consider the marketing activities of these museums in the context of other management activities and to take account of the operational and financial constraints, under the terms of the marketing process.

Through this process, Bradford has isolated three areas of concern for the museum curator: the management of the museum itself, that is the collections, objectives, staff and exhibition programme; the management of the relationship with patrons, whom he defines as the museum's funders, encompassing the local authorities, trustees, sponsors and grant awarding bodies; and the management of the museum's reputation, through the media, the Tourist Board, visitors and the local community (Bradford 1991: 93). This is a useful guiding tool for curators since it makes a distinction, lacking in other museum marketing literature, between marketing externally to prospective visitors and internally to its patrons. He also takes the external marketing mechanism a step further by including organizations such as the Tourist Board, where reputation needs to be fostered.

Bradford refers to 'patrons' merely as 'funders', although their influence may be considerably more all-encompassing than through funding alone. The grant awarding bodies may not in fact have made any awards to a museum, but they could influence it through other means, such as the Museums and Galleries Commission's registration scheme. Trustees also may not necessarily be funders. They may guide museum policy, but not necessarily by funding the museum. Are 'Friends' organizations included under the patrons banner, even though their support may not be financial? Are the traditional 'patrons' of museums, the benefactors of collections, necessarily funders? This concept of 'patrons' appears to be inadequate.

Bradford does not address the issue of competition raised by Bryant. Does 'management of the museum's reputation' include the notion of competition? If so, this is not explicit and if not, does Bradford reject the notion of competition in museums? Bradford's category for 'the management of the museum itself' does not specify the museum building. Surely management of the building is arguably more salient than an exhibitions programme? In addition, Bradford claims that he intends to show curators how to target activities, rather than simply respond to the blanket encouragement to do more marketing. However, if the functions of the paradigm are ambiguous, and the emphases within the functions are debatable, can this model be a practical tool? Bradford does not develop the concept of *what* is being marketed. There is an inadequate emphasis on the context of the museum, in which the curatorial management process operates. Bradford has placed the curator in the central position in his framework. However, as this chapter will illustrate, it is the museum that is central, with the curatorial orientations developing from the context of the museum.

Although Bradford's curatorial management framework has its limitations, it is nevertheless the most helpful model that has been devised for museum marketing. He opens up the marketing debate from its present narrow confines of the commercial benefits of marketing. The influence of institutional politics on museums is taken into account, the marketing framework being fitted round the political structure. He also recognizes the key position of the curator in the management framework.

Museums, however, are still tending to adopt a trial and error approach to their marketing. Agencies such as the Museums and Galleries Commission (MGC) have advised them literally to adopt a few marketing initiatives that are achievable, and likely to be successful, and in this way build a marketing framework into the museum. Such initiatives include the MGC's one-day marketing consultancy scheme set up in 1989. This may heighten the profile of certain initiatives, but it does not enable the museum to adopt a marketing orientation. Bradford discovered in his studies that the successful museums under investigation did not regard marketing as a separate activity, but rather as integral to their operations. This confirms what has already been recognized in the best firms. Therefore, he concluded that, 'Grants given to encourage museums to "do a bit of marketing" are unlikely to result in sustained improvement' (Bradford 1991: 96).

Although it is increasingly being recognized in the museum marketing literature that the museum context regulates the form marketing can take, the analysis is still one step removed from actually enabling that context to shape the marketing principles. Peter J. Ames (1988) entitled an article on museum marketing, 'A challenge to modern museum management: meshing mission and market' (chapter 1 in this volume), while Peter Lewis (1991: 26) has defined museum marketing specifically in its own context as: 'Marketing is the management process which confirms the mission of a museum or gallery and is then responsible for the efficient identification, anticipation and satisfaction of the needs of its users.' Both Ames and Lewis recognize that the mission or purpose of a museum is inextricably linked with the marketing process. Marketing serves to achieve that mission. However, neither commentator expands on the notion of the museum's purpose. Without contextualizing the purpose, the devolved process of goods marketing is still pursued.

When transferred to services, the key issues of marketing become intangibility, inseparability, heterogeneity, perishability and lack of ownership (see, for example, Cowell 1984). Most museums are heterogeneous and offer both tangibles and intangibles: tangibles in the form of shops, cafes, publishing and so on; intangibles in the form of such 'experiences' as the visit, the lecture series and the identification and enquiry services. Most museums marketing literature focuses on the intangibles and tangibles separately, considering shops to be a commercial aspect of the museum, and offer advice on a separate marketing strategy to be developed for the commercial function. Does this mean that there are two types of marketing to be adopted by museums? The intangible that is focused on is the 'experience', and this is regarded as the product of the museum. Having 'experience' as a product may not necessarily be valid to every visitor to the museum. The 'product' could be many things: a particular item in the collection; the café or even social acceptance. The product is defined by the visitor, and may not simply be the 'experience'. The inseparability of services is valid in museums, although the visitor is in a position to define this inseparability rather than the museum. The museum 'experience', similar to other services, is also perishable. However, the experience is not necessarily irrevocably perishable. It may be possible to return again and again to view a museum object, and recreate the same experience. These concerns are crucial. It implies an admission that we do not really know why people go to museums at all. Nor do we know how they qualify and quantify the experience. What is the value of experience? It cannot be equated with ownership of a product. As regards the lack of ownership of services, could sponsors not be regarded as temporary owners? Local authority museums, in particular, may counter that their local public owns the museum, not directly, but through their local taxation.

In not-for-profit marketing, it is recognized that there are two constituencies in the marketing process (see, for example, Kotler and Andreasen 1987). Thus, in museums, the visitors would be one constituency and the museum's funders the other. The museum would need to market itself to both of these parties. There has been little recognition of this concept in museum marketing literature, the approach focusing on the visitor not the funder. This could partly be attributed to the complexities of the museum situation, and partly to the increased need for money in the 1980s. However, the funder is perhaps too narrow a focus for museums. They rely on both funding bodies and, in paying museums, the visitors for funding. Further, the museum is not solely dependent on resource attraction, but also on recognition and on moral and professional support, as well as financial support. Thus, trustees may not fund the museum, but they may have a very important role in ensuring its survival. Similarly, a local authority may not fund a museum, but its encouragement and professional support could be essential to a museum's existence. It is too simplistic to define resource attraction in museums as merely financial. The situation is considerably more complex.

Where these marketing theories are flawed is in their transferral from one context, where the concepts are already being stretched and are often contradictory, to another context where they are so far removed from their original meaning that they become meaningless. However, as is already being recognized by the museum marketing literature, if the marketing of museums is central to the museum mission, then the context of the museum is also central. Bradford (1991) discovered that the museums marketing literature had failed to take account of the institutional politics of museums. It has, in fact, failed to take into account the whole context of museums. It is this context which should shape the form taken by marketing.

MARKETING IN THE MUSEUM CONTEXT: AN ANALYSIS

The theory of marketing needs to be set aside while an assessment of the marketing function in museums is made. Substantiating evidence, therefore, is drawn from the practice of marketing in museums, from examples taken from research conducted in the North East of England and from throughout the United Kingdom (Matheson 1992). The method pursued was to derive marketing strategies for a number of museums, representing a cross-section of museum types, in the North East of England. The strategies were implemented with grant-aid assistance from the Museums and Galleries Commission and the North of England Museums Service, and subsequently monitored and evaluated. A survey was also conducted of the general population of the North East, to ascertain the profile and opinions of non-museum visitors. The findings revealed a number of issues which were then assessed and substantiated in relation to a selection of museums throughout the United Kingdom. These issues are now selectively examined. They are not mutually exclusive, but, on the contrary, appear to be linked in a structural framework relating specifically to the museum context or culture. They are, nevertheless, discernible as distinct factors, and so are treated separately for ease of evaluation. It is acknowledged that differences between museum types and individual museums will exist within the classifications examined. However, the differences occur within the category, and do not diminish its legitimacy as a predominating aspect of the marketing function. The issues that emerged from studying the practice of marketing in museums are the collection, the museum building, the museum staff, the organizational mechanisms – a term coined by the author to encompass the internal organizational structure of the museum and the external agencies which in some way influence the museum organization – and the public. A model to illustrate this contextual framework is shown in Fig. 21.1.

Fig. 21.1 A contextual museum marketing framework

The collection

An examination of the historical development of museums establishes that collections were not put together by the public, but by single individuals, in most instances for their own purposes and not for the gratification of the masses. The intrinsic character of museums, even today, still portrays the individuals who produced them. To the extent that a collection might have been developed without reference to society, its relevance needs to be assessed. How is potential value measured? More significantly, why is this sense of value not necessarily translated into visitors to museums?

A museum would not exist without a collection. A variety of collections have been amassed for a number of reasons by various people, and have ultimately been stored and displayed in different ways in a museum. Any other aspect of a museum is peripheral: it is the collection which ultimately defines its character and determines its context. If the collection is removed, the peripheral aspects of the museum would become meaningless. The collection gives a museum meaning. Museum marketing theorists have failed to recognize the significance of the museum collection. While defining the 'product' of the museum as the 'experience' the museum creates, no attempt is made to reconcile 'experience' and the collection. However, the collection, its interpretation and its presentation are crucial factors for the public and for marketing.

The collections in museums vary according to, first, their nature, and second, their display. The nature of the collection is shaped by its subject type, its scope, its size and its financial and cultural value. It is the nature of the collection which is the overriding factor inducing the museum visit. For example, the value of national collections, by implication, far exceeds the value of local collections. A criterion for qualifying as a national museum is a collection of national and, perhaps, international significance. The nature of collections in national museums is therefore wider in scope, greater in size and of considerably more financial and cultural value. The importance of the collections is borne out by the value placed on them by the general public, who visit the national museums in far greater numbers than the small local museums. The collection and the reputation with which it endows the museum are the main determinants for visiting the museum.

Museums, to varying degrees, reflect the attitude of the curatorial staff and the museums' organizational mechanisms in their collection presentation and interpretation. Decisions on which artefacts should be displayed, on de-accessioning, on acquisition and on choice of temporary exhibitions, each demonstrate the dialogue between the public and the museum (both its staff and its organizational mechanisms), and their specific sense of the collection. The tension between the collection and its value to the public, and the attitude of the museum's staff and organizational mechanisms, both to the collection and to the public, should not be under-estimated. Each of the museums investigated for this study, whatever the nature or display of the collection, revealed that the collection was the essential determining feature of their marketing thrust. The relationship between the museum and the public depended on the perception of the collection.

However, it would be inane to suggest that the performing arts' criterion for marketing, a 'bums on seats' approach (Wright 1990), or numbers through the turnstile, is the criterion for successful marketing in museums. This is not the reason why the collections were originally formed. Nor is it an aim that has evolved in the general development of museums. Museums operate 'for the public benefit' (Museums Association 1984), not for increasing their annual turnover. It is a fundamental weakness of much museum marketing thought to measure success in terms of turnover, when it is not a fundamental concern of museums. What is fundamental, however, is the value placed on the collection by the public, which in turn reflects the quality of experience. Success in marketing terms can only be measured in terms of the quality of that experience. Increased visitor numbers can be the resulting outcome, but the prerequisite is that the visitors experience something worthwhile. If the role of the museum and the collection are to be fulfilled, then the response of the visitor, both during and after the visit, should be ascertained to assess their sense of experience. But is it possible to approach this problem so simply? How can experience be measured? Can experience be generalized? Experience is not solely to do with the quality of the communication of the contents.

Attempts have been made in the museums profession to address the issue of visitor experience, and various suggestions have been mooted. Mark O'Neill (1991) considers that accepting responsibility for the quality of experience 'does not mean determining what people experience, but stimulating, enabling and supporting people in choosing what they want for displays and events' (O'Neill 1991: 34). Neil Cossons (1991) admits that the curator is not infallible in terms of stimulating a relationship between the collection and the public: 'Good popularisation needs high-grade scholarship, for people who not only know their collections but can interpret them to the public. But scholars do sometimes need extra help in the process of interpretation and they should not be ashamed of that' (Cossons 1991: 187).

Acceptance of the public consciousness has led to a review of the methods of presentation and interpretation of the collections. In the past, most museums were arranged historically, or in subject categories. Increasingly, they are being arranged in terms of social categories. Thus, the new Chinese gallery at the Victoria and Albert Museum attempts to humanize the display of artefacts by using them to shed light upon simple questions about the life and time of the culture. There is a similar aim with living history re-enactments, which are an obvious attempt to bring the objects to life.

Another response is to endow the collection with a positive image in tune with the attitudes of the general public. Through research, the Science Museum in London had discerned that a negative perception of science in a large proportion of the public was translated into a lack of interest in visiting a science museum. The response was to challenge these perceptions and to create a more positive attitude to the collection. In an advertising campaign, therefore, the focus was on particular objects in the collection, attempting to arouse interest in the artefact.

The National Gallery in London has addressed the issue of the relationship between the collection and the public yet further. Curators regularly lecture to the public, explaining, for instance, why pictures are hung in a particular way, and the reasoning which prompts their restoration. This reflects an attempt to reconcile what Tony Bennett (1988) has criticized as seriously lacking in museums:

> Few museums draw attention to the assumptions which have informed their choice of what to preserve or the principles which govern the organization of their exhibits. Few visitors have the time or inclination to look beyond what museums show them to ponder the significance of *how* they show what they show. Yet, this question of *how* is a critical one, sometimes bearing more consequentially on the visitor's experience than the actual objects displayed.
>
> (Bennett 1988: 83)

The problem for the museum profession is not so much how to enhance the experience of the public, but how to ascertain what that experience is. The public visits museums for various different reasons: from curiosity; to be improved; to get out of the rain; to visit the café. . . . Whatever their motives, though, they are all treated exactly alike. The museum offers various activities, such as lectures, to those who are motivated, but they represent only a minority. For the rest, all that is available to them is an exposure to the artefacts. Visitors expect different things from museums. Is it possible to cater for all? Equally, how often do people think about visiting museums? A marketing response is to target particular sectors of the public, and to cater specifically to them. Their needs and wants may be determined to a certain extent, and reflected in the display and interpretation of the collection. However, in stressing a relationship between the collection and the public, the museum is prey to raising expectations and to disappointing in reality. This can only be avoided if the museum has a sense of the visitor's and the potential visitor's expectations and what would meet them.

The museum building

The collection endows the museum with an identity. In marketing, it is this identity which is perceived by the public, in terms of the visitor's experience. Experience, though, is not confined to the artefact. The museum building's structure and facilities contribute to the museum's image, and accordingly to the public's impression and response. Museum buildings vary in terms of, first, their physical structure and, second, the facilities they offer. The fabric, design and age of the structure of museum buildings varies. These variations affect the expectations and demands of the public and are often a central concern of the museum's staff and organizational mechanisms.

Historically, museum buildings were not constructed with the public in mind, but to display artefacts in a manner befitting them – in buildings resembling the stately homes wherein they were originally collected. The national museums in London are vast, imposing buildings, mainly erected in the nineteenth century. Their appearance is awesome, but perhaps because of their national status, they can project a palatial regality. Nevertheless, the Victoria and Albert Museum has erected large banners and advertising hoardings on its frontage in an attempt to brighten it and make it more accessible. The national museums' size and age pose various problems for presentation of the collection. Through various initiatives attempts have been made to overcome these difficulties. Thus maps are distributed free of charge at the Victoria and Albert Museum, while some temporary exhibitions are sited on the second floor to attract visitors upstairs. The museum is also continuously refurbishing its galleries to incorporate new design and conservation techniques. The appearance of a building can, on the other hand, offer advantages to a marketing strategy. The Lady Lever Art Gallery in Port Sunlight has an uncanny resemblance to the Taj Mahal. An advertising campaign capitalized on this, promoting the museum as the 'Taj Mahal of Merseyside'.

These are modern responses to older building structures. They attempt to make the building more accessible to the public, while at the same time ensuring the continued preservation of their contents. Often these two issues are polarized in museum terms. Increased access can detract from, or even harm, preservation. Without a well-preserved collection there would be no point in inviting access. Raised expectations would be disappointed and the quality of the experience would be reduced. Preservation can only contribute to the experience. Marketing therefore needs to recognize the role of preservation, and not focus solely on access or on increasing visitor figures.

Marketing techniques may in fact capitalize on ameliorating the access versus preservation debate. The museum can increase the value of the artefact to the public by making its preservation more accessible to them. Thus, the Natural History Centre in Liverpool is devoted to linking preservation and access, by making the museum's research collections available to the public. Further, as Neil Cossons (1985) has indicated:

> There is also a real and growing demand for the specialist and scholarly services which a museum provides. The need for market awareness is no less relevant in these areas and museums must increasingly examine the way in which they handle enquiries, the quality of their documentation systems, in short, all those aspects of their work which provide access to their collections.
>
> (Cossons 1985: 47)

The contemporary demands made on museum buildings for improved display, conservation and so on have resulted in increasingly sophisticated design demands. New modern purpose-built museums, such as the new museum housing the Burrell Collection in Glasgow, are in a better position to incorporate such techniques. Often, the outcome has been museums which differ quite markedly in outward and internal appearance from the older Victorian buildings. The image of the museum has shifted, but has the public image of the museum also moved on? How do the public see museums? Are these new modern buildings any more accessible than the original Victorian buildings, or are they equally awesome, with their somewhat clinical, clean-cut appearance? A public consciousness of the museum building needs to be ascertained both in museum and marketing terms.

The location of the building can also present opportunities or hinder a museum. Its collection is often dictated to by its location in a particular area. For example, Beamish Museum regards itself as the regional museum, identifying itself as the North of England Open Air Museum. A sense of place is often an important ingredient in the image of the museum projected to the public, contributing to the total experience. Although the National Museums and Galleries on Merseyside are national in status, their distance from London creates difficulties in attracting national media attention. Consequently, considerable effort is expended to convince the media that they are not parochial. These are both marketing responses to a museum's location, either by ensuring that place does not detract from experience, or by enhancing place to contribute to the overall image.

Modern architectural responses to museums are also increasingly reflecting public expectations. Experience is therefore considered as a response not only to the collection, but to services and facilities. Services are offered anywhere, although in a different order of priority from museums. Thus, there are some theme park activities which might legitimately be excluded from the museum activity. The museum is no longer an institution which merely preserves artefacts. Many museums have shops and cafés, and attempt to create an ambience. Often, though, these facilities are seen in terms of the benefits that can accrue to the museum, as opposed to the public, through income generation. Increasingly, for political as well as financial reasons, museums are being exhorted to increase their self-generated sources of income. The focus of marketing has therefore been directed to a greater degree to income generation, and is not so much market-led as profit-led. Visitor experience is marginalized, with increased emphasis being placed on amount of spend per head during a visit.

The staff

The museum's resources are its collection and building. It is also its staff. Bradford (1991) has affirmed the curator as the pivot round which the rest of the museum operates. Although the curator is a key factor, it is apparent that the staff as a whole are central to the museum's operations. This is particularly the case in a non-hierarchically structured museum which is run solely by volunteers, and also in a slightly autocratic staffing structure. The degree to which the museum's collection is owned by its trustees can be instrumental in dictating the extent to which they participate in the everyday operations of the museum. Thus, supremacy may lie not so much with one individual, but with a number of individuals who have a personal interest in the museum.

The curators' interpretation of the significance of the museum's collection, on collecting, conservation, documentation, acquisition, display and de-accessioning, their attitude to the scope of the museum building, their relationship with the museum's organizational mechanisms and their attitude to the public are critical determinants of the museum's nature and of the public's perception of the museum. The other members of the staff, both professional and non-professional, are crucial in forming a relationship between the museum and the public, while they may also contribute to the decision-making process. Although the degree of influence on the museum of the curator, voluntary staff and ancillary staff, varies according to the organizational structure of the museum, their actions are predominant in shaping the culture of the museum.

The staffing of museums has developed this century into a professional workforce, although there are exceptions in smaller, independent museums. Alongside the curators are educationalists, conservators and even marketing officers. The level of sophistication in the national museums is even greater, being structured into departments, including a marketing department. It is the attitude of the staff to the collection, and to the public, which often determines the tenor of the experience for the visitor.

Many museums still link public needs to education. Here, the expectations and experience of the visitors may contrast sharply with the professional's view of the relationship between the objects and the public, i.e. that there should be an overt educational message. Some museums are tilted in favour of curatorial control at the expense of other areas of expertise, and the result then can be a lack of educational and recreational inputs for the public. The museums staffs' response to these distinctions can reflect on the ultimate public representation amongst the visitors.

241

The variety of types of staff engaged in museum work reflects the variety, and possibly divergences, in the functions of museums. The national museums have made a concerted effort to attempt to balance these various functions, bringing them closer together and developing a public consciousness throughout. Increasingly therefore the influence of the marketing function has extended to decisions on such areas as exhibition programming, and collections management and presentation, as well as on the commercial and promotional functions. There is also an appreciation in the national museums that internal marketing is an essential prerequisite if other museum staff are to accept this influence: considerable hostility has to be overcome. The separation of the marketing department from other departments does not necessarily facilitate good working relations between the different functions. Where marketing assumes a significant role in the museum's staffing structure, with a marketing department and marketing officers, it does not necessarily tally that its influence is more pervasive than in a museum which does not employ marketing officers. On the contrary, these marketing personnel have other, considerably greater, difficulties in overcoming hostile attitudes from some staff members to the extending influence of marketing. In a smaller museum where few people are employed, it may be easier to negotiate the integration of marketing techniques, when opposition is encountered to a lesser degree or on a smaller scale. Thus, although the marketing may be more sophisticated in terms of the type of techniques adopted, a museum with a marketing department or officer may not necessarily reflect more of a marketing orientation. Co-operation needs to be facilitated from the other members of the staff. To overcome the attitude that marketing is a threat to the other functions, a sense of trust and a validation of the other functions needs to be forged. Thus, at the National Museums and Galleries on Merseyside, the marketing department arranges for articles on conservation in the museum to be included in press releases. This creates good public relations internally, as well as satisfying a visitor demand for making the reserve collections and their management more directly available.

More fundamentally, a greater understanding and awareness of the purpose of marketing needs to be fostered. As John Everett (1988: 157) has stated: 'A museum's staff, its human resources, are the most valuable asset in the successful implementation of a marketing plan.' Everett perhaps overestimates the value of the staff. They could be offering a very superficial experience, taking the museum down the theme-park road. The contents of museums, by virtue of being there, should to a large degree speak for themselves. The value of the *Mona Lisa* is inherent. In a heritage centre the actual value of the artefacts may be negligible, it is artifice rather than reality. The experience is different. The museum, on the other hand, offers more than immediate gratification. What it offers cannot be quantified, but it is capable of a longer lifespan than the heritage centre experience. The marketing is dependent on the collection which is available to it. It cannot create fantasy.

The role of the ancillary staff has also been heightened in marketing terms. The relationship which attendants develop with the public is increasingly being recognized as a crucial element in the experience created. The concept of 'customer care' has precipitated training courses, with the Museum Training Institute taking the lead in encouraging such training initiatives. The cleaning staff have also come under the jurisdiction of the marketing role, where the experience of the visitor may depend more on a clean loo than on the glories inside the museum! The sales staff also have a part to play in stocking the shop to meet demand. Again, a public consciousness needs to be inculcated along with a sense of the museum's purpose in terms of the public. All members of staff need to know why the public is important to the museum, and how to aid them in achieving the intended experience.

However, as Bradford (1991) emphasized, it is the personality and attitude of the director that so often shapes the response and attitude of the staff. It could be suggested that, as a consequence of directorial support for marketing in the national museums, they are at the forefront of marketing techniques. The director is often the impetus who generates ideas and developments or enables their staff to take initiatives. As witnessed throughout the history of museums, from Sir Henry Cole to Elizabeth Estève-Coll, the director can be the overriding facilitator, shaping the museum's policies and determining the direction it should take.

Organizational mechanisms

The staff, the museum building and the collection are subject to further pressures which influence, both directly and indirectly, the museum culture. These are what could be termed the museum's 'organizational mechanisms'. This umbrella term incorporates the internal organizational structure of the museum and the external agencies which impact on the museum, either through funding, through example, through persuasion, or through coercion. The organizational framework of museums consists of: national museums; university museums; local authority museums; independent museums; or a mixture of independent and local authority museums. The control of the organizational structure over the museum usually lies in its funding mechanisms, while it may also have a political or social influence.

The generation of income in larger museums has reached a level of sophistication far removed from the world of the smaller museum. To facilitate this a number of innovations have occurred. Philanthropic and corporate giving, and sponsorship are high on the agenda for all of the national museums, reflecting the direct encouragement of central government. The Science Museum offers corporate membership, where, in return for financial support, the companies receive a portfolio of benefits. Admission policies may also be subject to influence from the organizational mechanisms. Thus central government pressure has contributed to committing the Science Museum to charging an admission fee.

The relationship between the museum and its funding body is central to the determination of policy. Museums are treading a wary path where their funding bodies have the power of withdrawal of funding. Building up a relationship with funding and influencing bodies is a fundamental aspect of a museum's operations. This can be achieved not only by attempting to increase visitor figures and generating income, so often demanded by the funders, but by being seen to be active – by raising the museum's profile. Thus, lecture series, recitals, open days and favourable publicity are all examples used to convince the funding bodies of the value of the museum. Some museums have adopted performance indicators to measure success, such as the number of educational and other groups visiting the museum and the amount of media coverage attracted. Often, though, value to funders is seen in terms of 'value for money'. Museums were not originally established to make money, nor is their current *raison d'être* income generation. That can be left to commercial leisure organizations, or until the spectre of privatization becomes a reality. 'Value' in museums is the value of the collection, manifested in its value to the public in terms of their experience. Value is not financially driven in museums but experience-driven.

There is a fatal flaw in commercialization of museums. Unlike some other leisure organizations, museums are not self-supporting. They are charitable institutions, and as such are not profit-making. Except in rare circumstances, they are incapable of making a profit. However, unlike many other business organizations, museums are survivors.

They are less likely to go bankrupt and be closed. Their permanence enables their policies to retain a sense of stability. But there are also coinciding problems. Alan Morton (1988), or example, has stated that:

> If there is no intention that public museums should compete directly with commercial organizations (and there are certainly not the resources to do that effectively) then an important problem for museum staff is to fashion and maintain a clear identity for museums as different kinds of institutions from those in the commercial arena.
>
> (Morton 1988: 137)

The answer is already implicit in museums. They are not commercial organizations. They exist 'for the public benefit' (Museums Association 1984), not to profit from them. Such a motive is an indictment of their commercialization.

Most museums are conscious that to attract sufficient visitors they have to offer something more attractive than other museums and leisure attractions. Beamish Museum is also increasingly aware of competition and has attempted to counter this by working with its perceived competitors, such as the Metro Centre shopping centre at Gateshead, promoting joint short breaks inclusive of a visit to each location. The sense of competition, it could be argued, though, even in the larger museums, is not overriding. Museums are not operating on equal terms with commercial organizations. It is this which differentiates them.

Museums are also subject to the impact of other external agencies. Bradford's (1991) research is useful in appreciating the influence of external organizations, where he emphasizes the importance of building up a relationship with such bodies when managing the museum's reputation. These influencers may also be opinion-formers, setting the debate in museums. The influence of the Museums and Galleries Commission's policies have already been recognized through its funding capacity and its ability to confirm or deny museum status through the registration scheme. Thus, although the nationals may lead the way in innovatory practice, they are equally subject to external factors in defining their parameters.

The public

The response of the museum to its internal and external organizational influences has obvious ramifications for the collection, the museum building and the staff. It also has implications in terms of the public. The relationship between museums and the public has altered appreciably in recent years, from a situation where the public had little say in museum affairs to one where the sense of the public is an overriding factor. The meaning of the collection has also altered accordingly, from objects collected for their own sake by an individual, to one where the choice and display of the objects is shaped by public concerns. The public are the focus of museums, as they are the focus of marketing. The objects in a collection are given meaning when they are seen by the public. The museum is attempting to attract members of the public, and in order to do so needs to establish a relationship with them. There are various issues involved in making the public a visiting public, such as access, through physical access, positive discrimination and target marketing.

Market-awareness parallels a public awareness in museums. But why have the public become important in the museum's policies? Is it because of the demands of the funding bodies or because of the supremacy of the public in independent museums, which depend on visitors for their survival? Is it because of an increased public consciousness in society or a recognition that the objects in a museum are given meaning when experienced by the public? Whatever it, is, it is indisputable that today museums operate 'for the public benefit' (Museums Association 1984). But the degree to which this philosophy is adhered to varies between museums. What do the public mean to museums? They can be visitors, 'Friends', or income generators, and they can even produce the magic number of visits required by funders. But there is no general understanding of what the relationship between the museum and the public actually signifies. It is to educate, to entertain, to stimulate. It is each of these things and more. The relationship is often seen in terms of communication. But what is being communicated? There are limitations to this notion, as recognized by Stephen E. Weil (1990), who questions the concept of communication: 'By equating the visitor's experience of museum-going with the successful receipt of a message, this notion both over-estimates the role of the museum's intentions and underestimates the wealth and emotional range of visitor responses' (Weil 1990: 63).

For a museum to operate successfully it needs to have more refined notions of the general public. To what end is a museum communicating? To what extent can experience be embodied in communication? How can experience be determined? To whom is the museum communicating? Evaluation of what is provided needs to be very specifically tailored. This involves a conscious policy decision on whether the museum is operating for less than the whole public's benefit. Why does a museum confine its communication to targeted visitors? When is a decision made that the museum is operating for a chosen public? Does the nature of the collection determine this? Access is also a critical factor in this debate. The degree of access reflects the museum's attitude to the public by determining the profile of the visiting public. Thus, by introducing voluntary admission charges at the Victoria and Albert Museum, the visitor figures have accordingly been reduced. In some instances, because of the profile and attractiveness of the museum's subject area, a particular target market does not need to be encouraged to visit. Accordingly, the Science Museum does not actively publicize itself to schools, since the museum is already inundated with school parties. The attitude towards the museums may also have affected the visitor profile. Some of the London national museums, for example, regret that they do not attract more participation from their local public. This was considered to be difficult to counter because of the perceptions of these museums as national rather than local, and therefore not embracing their local constituency. Beamish Museum, depicting regional life, by direct contrast attracts considerable local interest and also participation in its Friends organization.

However, if a public is to be targeted, the museum needs to know why they visit or what would make them visit. What do they expect to gain from a visit? Museums are responding to the public in terms of their consciousness of their worth through display and facilities. The degree of sophistication and the innovative additions to facilities and displays, particularly at the national museums, is markedly higher than at the smaller museums. The degree of participation, however, is perhaps less active in the nationals compared to small, locally run museums, where the public can have a significant say in the museum's operations. In larger museums, participation is confined, at the most, to voluntary work, to joining Friends organizations and to being involved in activities.

There is a distinction between a museum visiting public and a non-visiting public. The marketing framework outlined here has dealt with the museum context, how the museum relates to the public that is visiting it. A relationship can be built, and attempts made to persuade these visitors inside the building of the value of returning again. However, the museum context does not actually persuade the general member of the public to visit. It can only act as an incentive, as an enticement. The marketing strategy needs to persuade the targeted public to visit by using the context as an inducement. To do otherwise would raise expectations only to disappoint. Therefore, the persuading techniques of marketing, the promotion of the museum, still require the optimization of the total experience of the museum.

There is no specific reason why the museum should in any way relate to the public. In fact, some museums choose not to do so, by closing their doors to them. Strictly, restricted access is more common in some major American collections than in the United Kingdom. The question of why museums want or ought to communicate with a public in some way is legitimate. Part, at least, of the museum's *raison d'être* would be 'for the public benefit' (Museums Association 1984). The central questions here are to do with identifying the 'public', establishing the 'benefit' contained and, in governmental terms, the cost of the 'benefit'. Marketing has been in the centre of this dispute. Its business-oriented approach to 'turnover' in visitor figures and 'profit', whilst alienating many museum professionals, has generated an instructive debate about the role, purpose and self-presentation of museums. They offer a seemingly intangible range of experience. In order to establish a consciousness of the public in the museum, the marketing agent requires a more than superficial understanding of the museum.

DISCUSSION

This assessment of the museum context has raised a number of issues which, although treated in isolation, are interdependent. It has concluded that the focus of marketing is the sense of experience stimulated in the visitor, that experience initially having been determined by the museum's context. A public consciousness is developed within the museum context, a consciousness that delineates the public who could be stimulated into an experience. The museum's purpose is not to increase visitor figures, to generate income or to offer value for money. These may be outcomes. The ultimate purpose is the museum philosophy as developed since its inception. Recognition of these influences increases the possibilities of attaining the museum's goal. Marketing is no more, nor less, than maximizing the sense of public consciousness in the museum's purpose, and by implication maximizing the experience of the appropriate visiting public in terms of the museum context. Marketing is the appropriation of 'the public benefit' (Museums Association 1984) within the total museum environment.

A museum is not a large conglomerate; nor is it a McDonald's hamburger restaurant; it is not a hospital nor an educational institution; nor is it a theatre. A museum is different things to different people; it is not one entity, but enshrines a multiplicity of values and images and attitudes. It cannot be compartmentalized merely as a service or a not-for-profit organization. It has these characteristics, but is more complex than such definitions would suggest. It does not have a defined 'product', a consistent 'customer' profile, or a defined communication system between a 'product' and a 'customer' (Kotler and Levy 1969). It is not necessarily communicating with a 'customer' in order to make a 'profit', or 'the best possible financial outcome' (Diggle 1984). It may have various motives of 'identifying, anticipating and satisfying the needs of its users' (Lewis 1991), which may have little to do with 'public benefit'.

Nevertheless, a museum does have a purpose, however unclearly stated, which depends on: its collection, however disparate; its building or site, whatever location or structure; its staffing structure, however inadequate; its organizational mechanisms, both internal and external, whatever their function; and its public, whether visiting or non-visiting. From these ingredients a singleness of purpose is somehow conveyed to the public. Herein lies the basis of the marketing problem. As the American Association of Museums (1984) envisaged:

> Marketing as a consistent effort builds a foundation of public understanding and appreciation. Over time, the public learns about the values on which museums are founded, the heritage they collect, the knowledge they embody and the services they perform. In turn, with greater understanding, the public will use and support museums more fully.
>
> (American Association of Museums 1984: 100)

It is not only the public that supports a museum, but also its organizational mechanisms, both internal and external. Sustaining a museum, ensuring its stability, depends on sources beyond a general public, on organizations which have the capacity to shape the character of a museum and its contents. Such agencies are integral to the marketing framework. The task of marketing is not solely public-focused. Organizational support is engendered by reputation. Reputation evolves from the collection, the building, the staff and, significantly, the attitude of the public. Public support ultimately sustains the museum. That support is won through bringing the museum alive, evoking a sense of value of the collection, imparting this to the visitors and disseminating it to a specific public. The museum may even make a significant difference to the lives of its chosen public. But to what extent could marketing convey the possibility of the enrichment of an individual's experience? This cannot be answered by the scope of this research alone. The marketing framework evolved here has underwritten the importance of visitor experience. Further research needs to put a value on the experience that museums give, and accept that it may be unquantifiable in depth and kind. Museums have the capacity to fulfil the individual. The collection, the building, the staff, the organizational mechanisms, the public – all act as catalysts at the moment of encounter. In this the marketing and organizational machinery falls away and the individual takes possession of aspects of the collection in a manner which transcends literal ownership.

CONCLUSION

It is increasingly being recognized in the marketing literature that the transferral of goods marketing techniques to service and not-for-profit organizations may not be appropriate. Nevertheless, current museum marketing literature has adopted this marketing approach and adapted it. This chapter has shown that the practice of marketing in museums is more museum-specific than the theory would suggest. A number of issues are highlighted which receive inadequate coverage in the museum marketing literature. The marketing of museums needs to be reassessed in terms of the museum context. This study has identified that context as the museum's collection, the museum building, the staff, the organizational mechanisms and the public. The emergence of context specific marketing is one step towards developing an applicable and, ultimately, appropriate orientation to marketing in museums.

This article first appeared in Museum Management and Curatorship *12 (1993), pp. 11–27.*

REFERENCES

American Association of Museums (1984) *Museums for a New Century*, a report of the Commission on Museums for a New Century, Washington DC: American Association of Museums.

Ames, P. J. (1988) 'A challenge to modern museum management: meshing mission and market', *International Journal of Museum Management and Curatorship* 7(2): 151–7.

Bennett, T. (1988) 'Museums and "the people"', in Lumley, R. (ed.) *The Museum Time-Machine: Putting Culture's on Display*, London: Routledge.

Bradford, H. (1991) 'A new framework for museum marketing', in Kavanagh, G. (ed.) *The Museums Profession: Internal and External Relations*, Leicester: Leicester University Press.

Bryant, J. (1988) *The Principles of Marketing: A Guide for Museums*, Association of Independent Museums Guideline No. 16.

Cossons, N. (1985) 'Making museums market orientated', in Scottish Museums Council, *Museums are for People*, London: HMSO.

—— (1991) 'Scholarship or self-indulgence?', *RSA Journal* 89(5415): 184–91.

Cowell, D. (1984) *The Marketing of Services*, The Institute of Marketing Series, Oxford: Heinemann.

Diggle, K. (1984) *Guide to Arts Marketing*, London: Rhinegold.

Everett, J. (1988) 'Taking your staff with you', *Museums Journal* 88(3): 157–8.

Kotler, P. and Andreasen, A. R. (1987) *Strategic Marketing for Nonprofit Organizations*, 3rd edn, Englewood Cliffs, NJ: Prentice-Hall.

Kotler, P and Levy, S. J. (1969) 'Broadening the concept of marketing', *Journal of Marketing*, January: 10–15.

Lewis, P (1988) 'Marketing to the local community', *Museums Journal*, 88(3): 147–9.

—— (1991) 'The role of marketing: its fundamental planning function; devising a strategy', in Ambrose, T. and Runyard, S. (eds) *Forward Planning: A Handbook of Business, Corporate and Development Planning for Museums and Galleries*, London: Museums and Galleries Commission and Routledge.

Matheson, F. C. (1992) *Museum Policy and Marketing Strategies*, unpublished thesis submitted in June 1992 for examination for the award of Ph.D. University of Northumbria at Newcastle.

Morton, A. (1988) 'Tomorrow's yesterdays: science museums and the future', in Lumley, R. (ed.) *The Museum Time-Machine: Putting Cultures on Display*, London: Routledge.

Museums Association (1984) Definition of a 'Museum', agreed at the Annual General Meeting, see *Museums Association Code of Practice for Museums Authorities*, London: Museums Association.

O'Neill, M. (1991) 'After the artefact: internal and external relations in museums', in Kavanagh, G. (ed.) *The Museums Profession: Internal and External Relations*, Leicester: Leicester University Press.

Rodger, L. W. (1987) *Marketing the Visual Arts: Challenge and Response*, Edinburgh: Scottish Arts Council.

Weil, S. E. (1990) *Rethinking the Museum: and Other Meditations*, Washington DC: Smithsonian Institution Press.

Wright, P. (1990) 'Eyes on stalks', *Arts Management* 9: 13.

22

Irresistible demand forces
Victor Middleton

Victor Middleton is a British management consultant of long standing, with particular experience in museums, heritage and the leisure industry. This chapter, first published in 1990, offered what has turned out to be a prescient analysis of developments in the decade so far, and makes a powerful case for museums to become much more market-oriented.

Two striking contradictions relevant to museums were revealed at the centenary conference. The first is the placing of 'public service' ideals on a pedestal because they lie at the heart of the museums service. It has been claimed that the provision of public enlightenment and education were, and must remain, the guiding philosophy for museums, and the principal justification for public sector financial support. Yet after a century of claimed devotion to public service ideals, we know that nine museums out of ten do not serve the general public in any overall sense at all; they serve the better-educated middle class and have little or no appeal to the lower socio-economic groups in their present form. The point is not that public service ideals are wrong, only that they are clearly not being achieved.

While the concept of 'public' service has gained its own mystique as something that is automatically good and honourable, serving tourists is said to involve trivializing museums and to undermine the proper goals of research, scholarship and academic contributions. Yet in London more than four out of ten museum visitors are foreign tourists. At least another three out of ten are domestic tourists or day visitors drawn from considerable distances. Outside London the tourist figures are less but, making allowance for day visitors travelling to and from their homes, more than two out of three museum visitors are not local residents. In other words, in the 1990s, 'public service' actually means serving visitors, many of whom are tourists. The public service ideal is, in practice therefore, a tourism service ideal. For most museums, the notion of serving the community appears to be more a convenient myth than a current reality.

A second myth is that museums and galleries have much to teach and little to learn from management practice in commercial organizations and that attempts to apply commercial management methods can be a recipe for disaster in museums. As a consultant with some years' experience of museums, I have to say that such belief in the general management capability of museums is completely outside my experience. The recent Hale Report and the papers supporting the Museums Training Initiative appear to be a better guide to the current state of management practice within museums.

Interpreting the words of the Museums Association's own definition, management must involve a balance between the needs of collecting and preserving objects for their own sake and exhibiting and interpreting them for the public benefit.

Traditionally, of course, museums devoted the bulk of their energies to collection-related objectives, which focus on: guardianship of assets; zealous curatorial care; research and scholarship; and requirement for funding. The problem is that the internal pressures created by collections tend to focus management attention inwards on: the insatiable demands of caring for and interpreting the objects; staffing needs and organization based on the collection; capital programme requirements, for purchases, buildings and display needs; and coping with the annual crisis of budget shortfalls in the 1980s.

At best, with adequate public funding, the inwards focus on the objects has led to curatorial excellence, creative research and scholarship, and some exhibitions of the highest international quality. At worst, however, an inward focus may degenerate into the self-indulgent pursuit of personal, intellectual interests and hobbies and a totally distorted balance between the fascination of scholarship and the demands of improved public access. It is also associated with an annual begging bowl mentality that demands public funds as of right, but fails to deliver accountability. The greater the squeeze on public sector funding the less tenable the traditional objects-oriented ethos of museums management becomes.

On the other side of the museums management equation, visitor-related aims focus on: providing enjoyment and satisfaction for the public; display and interpretation; management and marketing skills; and generating capital and revenue. In practice it is not possible to create more or better access for more visitors without looking outwards to the external influences affecting museums. 'Market forces' are one of the influences and clearly a pejorative term for curators. It means only that members of the visiting public have choices and will not visit museums unless they are persuaded that it is a worthwhile and enjoyable use of their time in competition with the many other options open to them. Since museums cannot force the public through their doors, even when they make no admission charge, they have no choice but to attract visitors by appealing to their interests if they are to achieve their object of providing public access.

At best, a visitor-oriented approach may lead to exciting, stimulating displays in which the stories of objects are communicated most effectively to the general public in a welcoming atmosphere. Museological objectives may be facilitated by the revenue which the majority of visitors are now clearly willing and able to provide. At worst, of course, it may lead to trivialization of the displays and cynical commercial exploitation of heritage for money. It is not difficult to find examples where short-sighted tactics for survival belittle the long-term mission, but such examples do not constitute a rule.

Obviously all museums are responding to some aspects of change, although the evidence suggests that the majority has not yet come to terms with the scale and the speed of change, and the impact of pressures upon them. The first pressure to change comes from the growing volume of visitor attractions competing for visitors in the 1980s. Whatever the exact figures are for the number of museums opened every few days over the last decade, and there are many more heritage attractions in the pipeline at the present time, the factor of increasing supply is a matter of concern for all established museums.

Fig. 22.1 shows the pattern of demand for museums growing slowly at nothing like the rate of increasing capacity. The obvious implication is that more and more attractions are under growing pressure to compete for the same visitors and, unless demand can be stimulated, the less successful attractions will suffer a decline in their visitor numbers over the next decade.

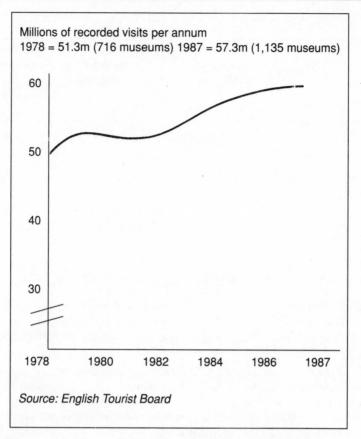

Millions of recorded visits per annum
1978 = 51.3m (716 museums) 1987 = 57.3m (1,135 museums)

Source: English Tourist Board

Fig. 22.1 Volume of visits to museums and galleries in England 1978–87

The third pressure, and the most significant aspect of change in demand in recent years, is the extent to which the public generally has become more sophisticated in its expectations and demands. It is in the high street that such changes are most evident. Large service organizations such as banks deal with all sections of the public from the most to the least affluent. Sustaining product quality, providing value for money and a wholly new approach to attracting and serving customers are the characteristics of successful businesses, and these are not organizations whose market is confined, as is the case for museums, largely to the middle class.

The fourth of the irresistible pressures reflects the financial structure of museums. Table 22.1, drawing on the most recently available figures, demonstrates that the museum world is still highly dependent on the public sector. Turnover from merchandising in the national institutions increased from £8 million per annum in 1985/86 to £28 million in 1989/90. Many who recognize the potential for merchandising in museums believe this figure could easily treble again in the next three years or so. With potential revenue gains of that order in mind, and noting the achievements of non-public sector funding in North America, it is not surprising that the government is exerting pressure on museums to find alternative, supplementary sources of funding.

Exacerbating the overall financial dependency on the public sector and the current squeeze on annual grants is the fact that many museums now need massive capital injections

Table 22.1   Museums and galleries: income sources 1983–5

	National museums and galleries (OAL funded)	Local authority (England & Wales	Other museums and galleries
	%	%	%
Public funding	93	91	54
Admissions & sales	7	5	37
Private sources	–	4	9
	100	100	100

Source: Policy-Studies Institute

for refurbishment. Funds are needed not only to maintain buildings and other structures in a sound condition but also to carry out essential rebuilding in some cases as well as to provide for heating, lighting and enhanced displays. It is widely recognized that, whereas sponsorship appeals may be launched successfully to support the capital costs of creating new museums and new displays, there is much less interest in contributing to the basic requirements of maintenance and refurbishment.

Although 'management' is a word in constant use, it is clear that it means different things to different people. Here I use 'management' to mean the process of organizing human and capital resources in more efficient and cost-effective ways in order to achieve stated objectives. Adapted as necessary, management principles are applicable to the public sector and to most types of organization, for which profit or return on assets is not the major criterion.

Drawing on experience of current management practice in commercial attractions, five implications for the management of museums in the 1990s are discussed below. First, as part of the response to increasing consumer sophistication, there has been a revolution in the management of service businesses in the commercial sector throughout the 1980s. Rather slower in its impact, but a revolution none the less, has been the impact of changing management attitudes in public sector services such as higher education, public utilities and many leisure services. It is a revolution in the corporate style of commercial organizations, which puts the customer at the centre of decisions and concentrates on delivering improved product quality. Among visitor attractions, the management style and 'guest' orientation of the Disney Corporation is internationally acknowledged to be the leader.

It is a revolution that must have its first and major impact on senior managers if it is to succeed in changing and sustaining attitudes throughout an organization.

It is a revolution that is taking effect at a time when traditional, bureaucratic, public sector-funded organizations are being seen around the world to be inefficient and costly in the management of their operations. Above all it is a revolution driven by awareness of irresistible external market and other forces, within which any organization operates. This revolution changes the way that organizations make and implement their decisions. It produces proactive and innovative responses and encourages the finding and exploiting of opportunities. Such responses are quite different from traditional bureaucratic management responses, which are typically reactive – reluctant and often too late – to pressures that will not go away.

The international management revolution described above has not yet had much impact on the majority of curators and trustees of museums. There are a few standard-bearers but little sign yet of widespread recognition of the changes to come. The implications noted below cannot take full effect until the change in attitudes occurs.

Second, among the first fruits of the management revolution, is a corporate or business plan. Most museums will claim that they already have such plans. In practice, however, many so-called plans are buried in the minds of curators or directors and are not written down or communicated this means they can be amended to suit whatever an occasion demands. Many more 'plans' are written as broad aspirational assertions that cannot be measured, such as 'providing better quality of displays'.

To make any organization accountable and to measure its progress and achievements, it is first necessary to define, agree and communicate goals and objectives towards which the organization will work over a period of years. Defining objectives is the essential preliminary to developing strategies to achieve them. Typically, this process will involve dividing the total corporate entity into its component parts and defining achievable objectives for each of those parts within a framework of the overall goal or mission. Examples are separate objectives for visitor admission revenue (for each type of visitor targeted), or objectives for merchandising, for sponsorship, or for events and exhibitions. The corporate plan co-ordinates the subsidiary objectives.

It is only in the last five years or so that museums and their trustees have begun to evolve realistic corporate plans of the type common in much of the commercial world for the last quarter of a century. Museum plans have mostly been reactive because they were demanded by a government suspicious of public sector profligacy, or incompetence, or both. With longer experience it is widely recognized in successful commercial visitor attractions that systematic business plans based on regular market research surveys are the only basis for efficient, cost-effective management.

Third, the word 'product' is still anathema to many in museums. It is often erroneously characterized as commercializing museums and selling them like soap powder in a supermarket. It is used here to describe the remarkably complex experience that visitors undergo having made the effort to visit a museum and paid (if there is a charge) for admission.

To the general public, a visit to a museum is an experience. The experience has many aspects which, combined, add up to what may conveniently be termed a product. It comprises everything from the initial process of awareness, which may involve publicity, and motivation as one steps inside the doors and receives the first impression of what is available – sight, sound, smell, and the appearance and attitudes of staff. The experience develops as the visitor moves around any displays and responds to the interpretation provided. It may include interaction with the staff who provide guidance and information, and it includes the use of shops, cafeterias, and perceptions of litter (or cleanliness) and toilets.

For many curators, improving displays and interpretation of the objects in their care is seen to be their main responsibility and they allocate their time and resources accordingly. However, the positive effects of a good display may be completely negated by other parts of the experience, so that overall satisfaction is low. The only way to find out what visitors experience is to ask a sample of them, for their views. Effective management means intervening at each stage of the product to create a better experience overall and improved value for money.

Fourth, successful commercial attractions are distinguished by their management information systems. These are typically based on a detailed computerized analysis of the revenue-flows from all the subsectors of the operation, with comparison against budget estimates. This analysis is supported by a systematic market research programme designed to establish the public's changing awareness of promotions, details of the experiences they receive, and their satisfaction.

Commercially successful visitor attractions in the private sector tend to be much larger than most museums; they seldom achieve less than 200,000 visits per annum. Even at this level the tendency for attractions to have management links appears to be a significant pointer to the future. Linkages may involve common ownership, for example Madame Tussauds or the National Trust, or voluntary collaboration such as the (eight) 'Treasure Houses of Great Britain'. It is widely recognized that the majority of museums receive fewer than 30,000 visits per annum. Although individually they can do much to manage their operations more effectively, it is obvious that the staff and budgets of most museums are just too small to engage effectively in the 1990s in the forms of management discussed here.

One may speculate that many smaller collections will not survive into the next century on an independent basis but be taken over by larger neighbours with compatible collections or the organizational ability to diversify and absorb the smaller collection. But many smaller museums would be better able to survive, in the face of fiercer competition for visitor numbers, through co-operation and linkages with other institutions. Links may be formed to share costs or secure the economies of scale, which exist for example in: management education and training (e.g. in corporate planning); print production and advertising and other forms of promotion, for example joint stands at exhibitions; market research in which the administrative costs of running a survey may be shared between sites; computerization for catalogues or to maintain records; exchange of market information; conservation skills and purchasing of stock for sale in shops.

Museums will have no choice but to engage in more professional management in order to surive and remain 'open for business', in the more competitive conditions of the next decade.

With hindsight, over a century of museum development, it is possible to discern a pattern of organization in which most museums pursued self-professed public service ideals within the structures of public sector organizations. Management procedures were similar, in principle, to those adopted for the provision of public education, libraries, housing and, more recently, leisure facilities.

My prediction, for the next two decades at least, is that public service ideals will be redefined to reflect management accountability and the modern reality that public access is increasingly by tourists or day visitors rather than local communities. The relevant organizational models are unlikely to be public welfare models but professional management models in which goals are precisely defined and achievement measured.

NOTE

The views expressed in this paper draw on the author's wide experience in analysing the confidential management and marketing operations of many museums and other attractions in the UK and abroad, gained primarily through the work of Ventures Consultancy Ltd (VCL). The views of K. G. Robinson, managing director of VCL, who read and commented on the draft of this article, are also acknowledged. *The article first appeared in* Museums Journal *(Feb. 1990), pp. 31–4.*

REFERENCES

Of the many published sources consulted, including MGC annual reports, *Museums Journal*, and the English Tourist Board's annual reviews of visitors to museums and other attractions, the following are noted:

Cossons, N. (1984) 'When is a museum not a museum?', *The Listener*, August.

Myerscough, J. (1988) *The Economic Importance of the Arts in Britain*, London: PSI.

Middleton, V.T.C. (1988) *Marketing in Travel and Tourism*, London: Heinemann.

Museums and Galleries Commission (1987) *Museum Professional Training and Career Structure: Report by a Working Party 1987*, the 'Hale Report', London: HMSO.

Prince, D.R. and Higgins-McGloughlin, B.E. (1987), *Museums UK: The Findings of the Museum Database Project*, London: Museums Association and Butterworths.

23

Exhibitions: management, for a change
Roger Miles

How can projects such as exhibitions be managed to produce the most creative and effective end results? Roger Miles, in an article first published in 1985, reviews the traditional management structure, and outlines the team approach developed at the Natural History Museum in London. This important issue needs to be debated much more fully.

CASTING AGAINST THE PART

Museums are disabling systems, at least when it comes to the design and production of educational exhibits. By this I mean that, despite the best efforts of all involved, the end result is often a failure because the system is set up in such a way that failure is almost guaranteed. A look at the usual system for mounting exhibitions will show where the problems lie. In this system:

1 People are working in separate, unco-ordinated departments with no one person responsible for the mediation of the creative process, so that important matters go unconsidered and important things remain undone, and mutual suspicion gets in the way of team work.

2 Curators are the power brokers, able to decree what objects are selected for display, how they are shown and what is said about them, and by virtue of their calling they care about objects rather than people (who they may actively dislike in their museums); they tend to be concerned with looking good in the eyes of their fellow specialists rather than with the public's needs, and they act as though the public visits their exhibitions to pass judgement on their scholarship.

3 Designers, having no role in the selection and organization of the information to be communicated, attend to the 'packaging' without thought to the purpose their work could be serving.

4 Educationalists are brought in too late to contribute to the planning of the exhibits, and are often left to make the best of a bad job *after* the exhibition has opened.

5 The referring upwards of work for approval by people outside the creative team, that typically takes place at each stage, leads to a playing for safety, self-censorship and a fear of error, and rules out innovation.

6 The absence of feedback makes improvement by trial and error impossible, either in the functioning of the system or in the quality of the exhibits; self-examination and self-renewal are discouraged.

The underlying truth is that exhibitions 'model' (in the cybernetics sense) the teams that put them together. Thus if we wish to produce a new sort of exhibition – new not just in superficial appearance but in some more profound way, say in educational effectiveness – we shall need a new sort of team to produce it. Or, to put it another way, if we wish to produce significantly better exhibitions than in the past, we shall need a team that is much improved in its organization and function. The general lesson is one of having the right team for the job. This may be understood by successful commercial organizations, but it seems to be almost unheard of in the museum world. Thus it is not uncommon to come across museums that have initiated new exhibition programmes but, using the same methods and organization as before, have finished up with exhibits having all the faults of those they were designed to supersede (see Fig. 23.1).

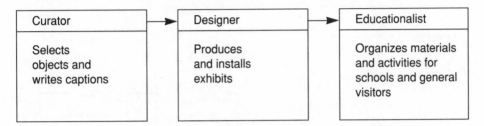

Fig. 23.1 The traditional system for mounting exhibitions

The Natural History Museum's Department of Public Services was formed in 1975 – from the former independent Exhibition and Education Sections – to carry out a new programme of exhibition work. Careful attention was paid to the structure and composition of the department in the light of the problems outlined above. The old system had produced exhibitions that were dull and too technical for the visitors, being arranged mostly along taxonomic lines to reflect the administrative structure of the museum (determined by Victorian museum politics and curatorial convenience) rather than to meet the needs of the public. With hindsight it is also clear that some of these exhibitions had taken an unconscionable time to produce.

BETTER PUBLIC SERVICE

The Department of Public Services is responsible, among other things, for the conceptualization, planning and development of the exhibitions, related publications and educational service in the Natural History Museum. Working from a long-term plan for permanent exhibitions, it prepares proposals and then a brief for each phase of work, which, after approval by the director ('Authorization'), it develops into detailed specifications from which the exhibits can be built (see Fig. 23.2).

Procedures exist for consultation and co-operation with the museum's scientific staff, who advise on the current state of the science, points of interest, possible lines to pursue, people to get in touch with, and so on. The important point is that curators are here operating as subject-matter experts, a role that their experience and training properly fits them for. They do not have responsibility for the effectiveness of the communication, an area which is generally outside their experience and expertise. Another important point is that authorization for the work to go ahead is given on the basis of the brief – this is the last stage at which the project will be referred up to the director and heads of the scientific departments, though subject-matter experts will continue to be consulted all the way through – so leaving some 'creative space' for the design team.

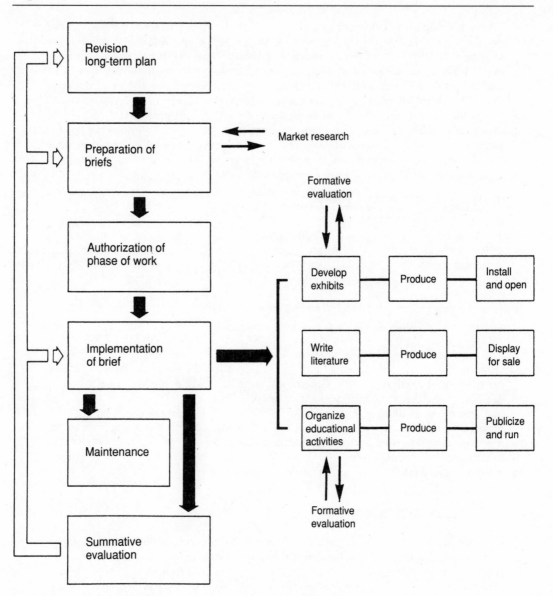

Fig. 23.2 Activities involved in planning, designing and producing exhibitions and related publications and educational services in the Natural History Museum

The brief is a crucial document; it guides the whole undertaking and frequent reference is made to it during the development stage. It must set out the constraints (money, time, space, etc.) and give a clear idea of what is proposed, but not suppress the design team's creativity. Responsibility for writing the brief rests with a senior member of Public Services, though a number of other people make contributions. These include an educational technologist who advises on matters such as the formulation of teaching points and the structure and pacing of the proposed piece of communication, and an evaluator who carries out 'market research' to determine the potential audience's prior knowledge, misunderstandings, interest, expectations and so on. It is perhaps worth stressing that the brief is concerned with the message to be communicated and rarely lists objects to be exhibited. It *never* takes the form of a list of objects with accompanying captions or text, the selection of objects and writing of text being part of the creative work that takes place during the development of the exhibition from the brief.

The creative nuclei of the development team comprise partnerships of a three-dimensional designer and 'exhibit developer' (ideally someone with a degree in a biological science, a passion for communication and some understanding of the educational technology approach to the design of educational materials). The work of these partnerships, who transform the subject-matter from a text-book form that suits the expert into a form suited to the museum visitor, is also the basis of publications and educational materials related to the exhibitions. The work is carried out in co-operation with a number of people including the educational technologist, editors, subject-matter experts (from both within and outside the museum) and co-ordinators responsible for the content, design and production of the exhibitions. The output from the development process is drawings and written specifications from which the exhibits can be built and installed. The work of the various members of the team is integrated by a project control system which sets deadlines and includes meetings to monitor progress. These meetings are important management checks. They are attended by Public Services' senior staff and function as a quality, as well as a quantity, control system.

When the proposed exhibits lend themselves to formative evaluation and resources allow it, rough mock-ups are produced and tried out on volunteer members of the public. Such evaluation is done by the designer–exhibit developer partnership in conjunction with the evaluator. Lay members of the public can reveal where the proposed communication is likely to fail, but they can tell us nothing about the accuracy of the scientific content. It makes sense then to try out the mock-ups on subject-matter experts as well. The two groups are complementary because the subject-matter experts can say little or nothing about the difficulties faced by lay visitors in approaching the subject for the first time. In going to the public in this way to check on the worth of proposals, one is in effect seeking the approval of the public before going on to the next stage, rather than that of someone higher up in the organization. This is likely to cause problems in rigidly hierarchical management systems because the views of the visitors are quite likely to be in conflict with those of the management. Hence few museums have adopted formative evaluation in developing their exhibits, even though all experience (in a variety of institutions) testifies to the immense value of evaluation in improving the quality of the work.

MANAGEMENT IMPLICATIONS

The traditional system for mounting exhibitions, as described at the start, can sometimes give good results. Just now and again museums are in the fortunate position of being able to follow Thomas Beecham's dictum – employ the best people available and leave them to get on with it. But there can be no doubt that most museums, most of the time, are not in this position, and for them to act as though they are leads inevitably to disappointment and to failure. A better method for most of us, then, is to adopt an old Prussian approach to the practical arts and systematize things as much as possible, hoping to achieve by organization what genius fails to provide. There are drawbacks, of course. Some aspects of the work are more easily systematized than others, and those that depend on trained perception and subtle discrimination are not easily brought within the fold. The point about diagrams like Fig. 23.2 is that it is not the activities *per se* that determine success, though a systematic approach is an essential first step, but the details of what is done. In other words, attending to the system to the exclusion of the art can also be fatal.

Shifting from one system to the other, as we have done at the Natural History Museum, has a number of predictable consequences. No matter how much people agree that change is necessary, bringing it about is a different matter. Change brings with it the need for new attitudes and new practices, it means adapting to new and unfamiliar circumstances, and it may be uncomfortable or even painful to live with. People are therefore liable to resist change, and they find reasons against new proposals, even thought they may have agreed earlier that change is essential.

On the whole, curators are used to taking all the big decisions and see exhibitions as primarily a showcase for their learning, so have the most to lose. They tend to resist almost any change in the system. Not all curators are like this. But just one or two disaffected individuals can give rise to enormous problems. It is no secret that such squabbles are widespread in the museum world (even the *Encyclopaedia Britannica* has a section on conflict of interest in museum operations). They call for courage, a clear sense of purpose and firm management at the head of the museum if efforts to serve the public are not to be distorted.

Other consequences of changing the system along the lines indicated involve designers and educationalists. Like curators, both groups are called upon to play new roles for which they may be ill-equipped by inclination, training and experience. Take, for example, the museum educationalist who is trained in face-to-face teaching (and may even be a refugee from the stressful school environment), and is suddenly faced with the problem of advising the exhibition team on techniques of distance teaching. In such circumstances a lack of ability to cope is likely to make itself felt in a lack of sympathy for the whole enterprise. Sympathetic management, training and, as opportunities arise, careful recruitment are of vital importance. But the real answer to resistance to change is, in our experience, non-stop propaganda – perhaps concentrating this on one or two key individuals who can act as agents of change – with the aim of developing a new ethos within the organization.

Another major problem concerns schedules and working to deadlines, which are essential in any system like that outlined above. Most designers who work in museums appear to start off with only vague notions of the need to complete work on time and within budget. The concept of doing the best job possible within the time (and money) available seems often to be alien, the only sense of purpose being that of doing a vaguely defined, infinitely good job in an indefinite, if not infinite, length of time. Unhappily, matters tend to be worse with curators, for, unlike designers, deadlines are rarely part of the broader practice in their profession, and traditionally they have been encouraged to spend a lifetime exploring their chosen field of scholarship, often with no very definite end in sight. We have of course had to work to strict deadlines in mounting new exhibitions in the Natural History Museum, but constant vigilance is needed to maintain a tight project control system when one is working in the somewhat unsympathetic environment of museums. Problems can arise with key people who are employed in various curatorial and service departments but are outside the exhibition team, and therefore not covered by the project control system. For, unless these people are managed with equal rigour, there is a danger of the whole system winding down to run at the pace of its slowest contributors.

Providing good creative environments is something that the large departmental museums seem to find hard to do, and indeed may be almost prevented from doing by their history, organization and self-image. Much of what has been said above can be summarized as a plea for appropriate organization, effective management and a clear sense of purpose. Our way of doing things at the Natural History Museum is certainly not the only way. But I believe it is a reasonable response to the environment in which we have to work.

The article first appeared in N. Cossons (ed.) (1985) The Management of Change in Museums, *London: National Maritime Museum, pp. 31–4.*

NOTE

I am indebted to my colleagues Giles Clarke, Anita Morris and John Peake for the comments on an earlier draft of this paper.

24

Museums as organizations
William M. Sukel

In this chapter first published in 1974, William Sukel then Assistant Professor of Management at the University of Illinois, USA, sketched out possible approaches to the study of museums as organizations. Only in the 1990s, as museum management has become both a key issue and a valued topic of study, has this challenge finally been taken up.

Students of organization have given much attention to the study of business firms, but museums and other culture-related institutions are often ignored. There are many reasons for this.

First, museums are not perceived as important economically, even though they are similar to small corporations. All museums manage considerable assets, large payrolls and many employees. Some have budgets over several million dollars.

Second, museums are but a small fraction of the total number of organizations in the country, and they have therefore been passed over. Most communities have more schools, hospitals and even fire stations than they have museums, but there are thousands of museums in the United States.

Third, museums and similar organizations such as symphony orchestras and ballet companies remain quiet organizations that go about their functions unobtrusively.

In many ways, museums possess striking similarities to business organizations. First, like all organizations, museums are goal-oriented. They are entrusted with one of society's most important goals: the preservation and presentation to the public of contemporary as well as historical developments in the arts and sciences, and the generation of new knowledge to their audiences.

Second, museums accomplish their goals with an organizational structure. All this means, of course, is that most goal-directed activity requires others working in a co-operative spirit to accomplish the goal. Work is divided among departments and people, and the evolving patterns of co-ordination form the structure. The museum director (the counterpart to the corporation president) performs the planning, control, and other functions.

Third, the familiar functional type of structure is usually found. In business the work of the organization is to produce something, sell it, and finance the operation. This generates functional specialists – people involved in sales, production and finance. The museum also has functional specialists – curators, conservators, etc.

At the same time, museums possess striking differences from business firms. First, while museums are goal-directed, the goal is not to make a profit. Business firms may have vague objectives beyond profit, such as 'being a meaningful part of community life', 'providing good service to consumers', and 'being socially responsible', but the museum's primary objective is unique: to collect, conserve and interpret objects of art, science and history.

The goals of museums may seem intangible, but they are very real. They are socio-cultural rather than economic, and therefore evaluations of museums should be tempered with an understanding of the correct goals, correctly defined.

Many non-economic factors should be considered in such evaluations, including: the number of visitors to the museum; the number of exhibitions; the number of students and researchers using the facilities; the number of new members; member retention; volunteer retention; staff selection; recognition by professional societies; and recognition by the community. These are valid criteria by which to judge museums, and the administration should keep records on these aspects just as closely as it keeps records of dollars, setting standards of performance and continually re-evaluating them.

Obviously, economic factors are very important in operating a museum. Budgets have increased enormously. Operating and maintenance costs have risen, as they have in every business. Repairing and insuring works of art is more expensive. Scientific equipment is more expensive. The museum is expected to have more exhibits and longer opening hours. Services to maintain the same physical plant increase, and the salaries of secretarial, custodial and security personnel rise every year. Staff salaries are also increasing, although there is still too much dependence on volunteers and dedicated but underpaid employees. Most museums pay less than can be had elsewhere, and directors, curators and secretaries can all command more handsome salaries in business organizations. Consequently museums experience a continual and serious drain of their human resources.

There are additional financial questions. Is the museum spending its money wisely? Where can it cut costs? Where can it increase revenues? Is there inefficient use of funds? Are maintenance, security, electric, and other costs in line with those of other museums? How can loss and theft be diminished? Museums may not be businesses, but they can be run efficiently, just as police departments, hospitals, universities and other organizations must be operated efficiently, even though they have other criteria than making a profit.

Resolving the questions of goals and finances involves all the people who work at the museum. While the organizational structure has similarities to business, it also has unique aspects. Professionals – more than in business firms – are on the staff, as are volunteers and para-professionals. While the director must perform essentially the same managerial role as a corporation president, he is often not a trained manager but a scientist or art historian; this is akin to the surgeon becoming the hospital administrator. Some directors have no desire to become involved in the mundane task of administering the museum – they prefer to seek out specimens or works of art, to balance the collection, to steer the organization towards artistic perfection or scientific excellence. The role of the director – whether art expert, scientist, administrator, functionary, whipping boy for the board, fund-raiser, babysitter for the wealthy, or any combination of these – should be carefully defined by the board of trustees, the staff and the director himself.

Boards of trustees oversee the functioning of the museum, and when they misunderstand the goals of the museum and expect that it will be run like a business instead of a socio-

263

cultural institution, there can be significant conflict between the board and the staff. While the director is expected to watch costs, somehow generate additional revenue and operate on a balanced budget, most directors and staff worth their salt want to do more. They want the museum to grow in acquisitions and events, in personnel and in contributions to the community. But this requires a commensurate growth in funds, and deficit spending is now a common museum practice. Every penny must be begged. The few generous, magnanimous donors who contribute with few or no strings attached are little compensation for those who give, it seems, grudgingly.

Museum attendance is accelerating faster than population growth, and museums find their services in increasing demand, both in the exhibition halls and in the community. If museums are to survive and prosper, more attention must be paid to their organizational functions. The problems of boards, directors and staffs all must be defined and then dealt with in a systematic way. A study of museums as organizations is a worthy and important task.

This article first appeared in Curator *17(4) (1974), pp. 299–301.*

25

Risking it: women as museum leaders

Kendall Taylor and Tracey Linton Craig

Why are there so few women museum directors? There has been some improvement since this article by Kendall Taylor first appeared in 1985, but this issue remains a vital one. Taylor introduces the key arguments and Tracey Craig's profiles offer some valuable insights.

Five years ago, there was no woman on the United States Supreme Court. No American woman had ever been an astronaut. And no woman had ever shared the presidential ticket of a major political party. Today we have Sandra Day O'Connor, Sally Ride, Geraldine Ferraro. Things are changing – albeit slowly. Young women choosing a career today have many more options open to them. Everything seems possible to these women and, in fact, maybe it is.

Today's young women aiming for museum careers are not, as previously, only heading in the direction of staff positions: curatorial work, registrarial activity or educational interpretation. Now, an increasing number of them want to be directors – of historical societies, of museums, city and municipal museums, science centres, the whole range of cultural institutions. And they are planning their careers carefully, career-pathing at 21 for directorships at 30.

Today, the general attitude toward women as leaders is rapidly changing, and women in all fields are moving up in the leadership ranks, dropping accommodative behaviour for success-oriented behaviour. They are learning to take career-related risks and meeting them with excitement instead of fear.

Part of the process has necessitated putting aside the notion that they need to do a job absolutely perfectly before accepting a leadership position. Women are coming to realize that growing into the position while on the job is normal, is what men have always done and what women have either not realized or been afraid to do. Seldom does one ever have the exact skills necessary when beginning a new position. Up until recently, women have considered such professional moves too 'risky'. Now, they are beginning to view them as challenging. Men have always viewed them that way. They have generally felt entitled to make mistakes – to once in awhile fall flat on their faces. They know occasional defeats are all part of the game. Women, on the other hand, as a minority in the power structure, have not felt entitled to error, and the fear of falling short has held them back. What many women are coming to realize is that the constant worry over how good one is saps the very same energy necessary for further growth and expansion. To combat these fears, women are now learning to perfect a specific area of expertise and to build on that expertise. They are becoming recognized as experts at something, choosing only certain areas to be expert in, other areas to be just good in and still others to lay aside or drop.

Female role models in the museum world as well as in all the other professions have aided women in this process. Within the past five years, women have come to prominence as leaders in all fields – law, medicine, politics, sports – the whole range of human endeavour. If a woman can become president of a university, a mayor, a jet pilot, an industrial engineer or an architect, becoming a museum director seems almost tame by comparison.

Young women completing undergraduate fine arts, history or science degrees and coupling these degrees in a pure discipline with an MBA or museum studies degree readily consider the top positions in the museum world to be open and attainable to them. They are planning their careers with more care and precision than did women of earlier generations. While in the university, they begin to look for mentors and sponsors to help guide them in their career paths, and they have taken to charting these paths in organized and creative ways. My own female students appear before me with graphs setting out the next ten years, structured into categories with short- and long-term goals blocked in according to section: where they wish to be in 1995 in terms of profession, personal relationship, finances, geographic location and so forth, with the yearly steps the intend to follow in order to get there. They choose internships with the same predetermination of medical students, looking carefully at what skills these internships will afford them. Except for occasional and unfortunate exceptions, gone are the days of interns and standing at copying machines doing mindless work.

Today's future professional uses her apprenticeship period to develop capabilities, decide on the focus of her career and begin to build a network of professional alliances. These women form an early coterie of mentors, guides, sponsors and peers, all of whom play an important role in their professional life. Men have frequently had this 'old boys' network' of informal advisers and advocates, but women have just begun to develop their own professional support systems, choosing to align themselves with female as well as male leaders.

The current generation has found inspiration in people like Katherine Coffey, Adelyn Breeskin and Jean Boggs, as well as women who have risen through the ranks more recently – Anne D'Harnoncourt, director of Philadelphia Museum of Art, Lisa Taylor, director of the Smithsonian's Cooper-Hewitt Museum in New York City, and Jan Muhlert, director of the Amon Carter Museum in Fort Worth. They have shown women that a leadership role in the museum world is attainable. These role models, along with the literally hundreds of other women professionals in the field, have helped women view themselves as potential leaders rather than as supporters of leaders.

Only a few years ago, women looked for assistant to the director and assistant director positions, thinking they could safely try out their skills before deciding to aim higher. Today they are more often than not applying for the top position. That is not to say they are always getting it. As Linda Sweet has pointed out, while women in the museum field have made impressive progress, they still face difficulties breaking into senior positions in the largest museums. Speaking at the 1984 AAM annual meeting session, 'Room at the Top', Sweet observed that women are still often not perceived by boards of trustees as being capable of or prepared for holding these top positions. Boards still question whether a woman director can be as effective as a man at garnering the necessary respect from business leaders, politicians and other influential people in the community. Most women who have broken into directorships have been hired to head small museums or museums that have had a troubled history. Or they have been on the spot when the directorship opened – perhaps in an acting director capacity or as an administrator or curator. A few were connected with a particular institution through family wealth, previous family association or perceived professional influence before becoming a director.

Stereotypes about women as candidates for leadership positions are changing. Notions that women lack business acumen, that they are too temperamental, overly manipulative, that they are specialists rather than generalists and too threateningly competitive to female as well as male board members, are being rethought. The way in which women have started to view themselves – as strong, independent, savvy about business and the politics of power – has precipitated a change in the way others view them. And the overall change in the general climate surrounding women as potential leaders had had an extraordinary positive effect on people's thinking. In addition, the prevailing attitudes of museum trustees are changing as board structures themselves change. In the past, the average board was predominantly male, with females represented by women from wealthy families, or wives of influential or wealthy men. More and more, however, as board members retire, women professionals are taking their place: lawyers, bankers, doctors, stockbrokers, professors, designers, media people – women from all professions who are financially and professionally successful in their own right.

What remains to be seen is how soon these women will be able to support other women for potential directorships. My guess is it won't take long. Women who seek a leadership role in the museum world are no longer assuming that competence and confidence alone will suffice. Instead, early on they are putting their professional alliances into place and making themselves visible as potential leaders. Young women are making their way up through the professional ranks today are far more aware of how important alliances are in hearing about, and being considered for, leadership positions. Engaged in careful and rigorous career planning, mapping out strategies to achieve their goals, they make their decisions with their larger career picture in mind, rather than viewing each job in isolation. They are learning the rules of professional advancement.

To prepare themselves for managerial positions, and with the awareness that they are generally perceived as less experienced in management skills than men, women are entering management training programmes *en masse*. Ten years ago, when Harvard's museum management training programme was still running, the typical class was predominantly male. Nowadays, the ratio for similar programmes is 50–50, with women applying yearly in increasing numbers. The Museum Management Institute at Berkeley, Museums Collaborative in New York, the Metropolitan Museum's workshop programmes, the American Management Association's seminars and university MBA programmes all report increased female participation.

Women entering leadership positions in the museum world are also acknowledging and dealing with the concept of 'paying dues'. It's a fact that you can't use your influence until you've got it, and organizations frequently will not allow the new leader to implement her ideas until these dues are paid. While the concept has been around a long time, it is a notion frequently outside the experience of women. Only now, with women becoming increasingly aware of power tactics in the workplace, has it become a major issue for them.

Dues-paying, women have found out, usually splits into two categories. Part of the payment is personal, assessing one's own style relative to the style the organization needs. The other half is structural – learning the unwritten rules of the organization, such as where the power in the board really rests, what past alliances and obligations must be taken into consideration, who the key people with regard to the institution are and what decisions can be effectively made at what time. All this takes time, but women are noticing that the payment process can be shortened if they have full access to vital information. As Lois Hart and Karen Stoltz have written, there are other methods to speed up the process: quickly discerning the formal and informal game rules and being willing to accept them until the initial payment period is over, not waiting for an opportunity to excel but making that opportunity occur, developing a personal style of leadership that is intelligent, professional and confident, yet not asexual, stressing the positive instead of the cynical or bitter, being assertive yet patient, having a network of outside professional associates who can give honest feedback and encouragement, and keeping one's personal life completely separate from business activities.[1] That may seem to be a heavy order, but one women have come to understand is crucial to achieving success in a previously male-dominated museum-managerial world.

Being a leader is like being a coach. As head of that team, the woman manager needs to understand what the team expects from her and what she expects from them. She needs to make all this clear – sharing goals, planning well, implementing, then evaluating. Good delegating is critical to the process, and is one of the toughest skills women have had to learn. It is hard to break away from the notion that 'nobody can do it better than I'. Increasingly, however, women are learning the steps of effective delegation and incorporating them into their managerial behaviour. Developing a climate for delegation, becoming familiar with the strengths and weaknesses of each staff person, determining objectives and developing a plan, women leaders are becoming more comfortable in letting go of certain tasks, in communicating their expectations, monitoring progress and then evaluating – and in some cases reassigning – work. Knowing when to delegate and when not to is the key: if someone likes doing a specific job better than you do, is faster than you, or can do it less expensively than you. Delegating is teaching and trusting. It's like showing someone how to ride a bike; eventually they take off on their own and do just fine.

It would be nice to be able to say that women are doing just fine, for in many ways they are. But in other ways their advancement into the management ranks has brought to the surface a different set of problems. In April and May of this year, the *Wall Street Journal*, in conjunction with an American Institute of Public Opinion Gallup poll, surveyed more than 700 female executives from a variety of fields, questioning them on how their careers had taken shape and how they felt about their positions as leaders. What were the rewards and the sacrifices? Their honest answers describe the unique and often difficult role women professionals play in today's world, for with the euphoria of landing the top job often come conflicts not fully anticipated. Frequently, even when they reach a high level, many women still find themselves patronized by men in leadership positions. More than 25 per cent of those women polled by Gallup said that, on the whole, their life and work experience was still largely undervalued, and that men all too frequently did not take them seriously. Younger women, in particular, complained that men often exhibited resentment and had difficulty taking orders from them. They described compromises with personal life as tremendously taxing, to the point that many women executives frequently chose to stay single or become separated or divorced. Less than half, 48 per cent, of the female executives Gallup polled had ever had children. One young woman told the interviewer, 'You have to be very asexual in your image and . . . hide your personal life.' Another went further, saying, 'My job has definitely stood in the way of marriage. I feel that if I were to marry there'd be a new set of expectations and I would be unable to fulfil them at the same time as doing my job.'[2] The married woman museum director, returning home late from her institution, may still feel she has to put something together for dinner. And if she has children, the responsibilities are manifold. In contrast, male counterparts frequently have a spouse at home who can provide that support base. It makes a difference.

Women who make it to the top also frequently experience a special type of power failure in that they are often unable to translate their own professional credibility into an organizational power base. Even though a woman may be doing an outstanding job, neither men nor women have traditionally viewed women managers as being capable of empowering and sponsoring peers and subordinates. Because women are viewed as recipients of power sponsorship, rather than as sponsors of power themselves, they are not seen as being able to pass on favours or make use of their own resources to benefit those who work with them. Herein lies the basic reason that both males and females alike, in 1985, still generally prefer working for men rather than women.[3]

All this, however, is gradually changing, and as the overall structure in America alters, the constructs of power in particular professions will change. What will quicken the pace in the museum world is women forming power bases with and for other women, so that women occupying leadership positions in the museum world increasingly become more powerful by virtue of who they know and what influence they personally wield.

Fortunately, women are finally coming to believe that they have the expertise, experience and intelligence to be leaders in the museum world. No longer are they willing to passively accept a back seat; they will not be wished away. In the past twenty years, women have actively transformed society. Sixty per cent of all women now work outside the home, earning $500 billion a year and taking home nearly one-third of the nation's pay. These earnings, however, average out to only three-fifths of men's earnings, and women's jobs are almost always at the bottom end of the power line. But this too is changing. Women now form a majority of college graduates, and more women vote than men. The gender gap is rapidly going the way of the generation gap. Within the framework of the museum world, women may not succeed in all cases. But within this century the male-dominated leadership of America's museums will become a phenomenon of the past. The result will be exhilarating: a rejuvenated profession in which the leadership will be shared by men and women working together.

We have much to learn from one another.

NOTES

1 Hart, L. and Stoltz, K. (1980) 'Paying your dues: how and for how long?', *Management Review* October: 19–24.
2 Rogan, H. (1984) 'The trials and successes of women executives', *Wall Street Journal National Business Employment Weekly*, 18 November: 23–4.
3 Kanter, R. M. (1979) 'Power failure in management circuits', *Harvard Business Review*, July–August: 69.

FROM DREAM TO REALITY: LISA TAYLOR

Director, Cooper-Hewitt Museum, the Smithsonian Institution's National Museum of Design, New York City

'I felt I couldn't make even one mistake,' remembers Lisa Taylor, who in 1969 was the first woman hired to direct a Smithsonian museum. 'If I did poorly, it might be another 150 years before they hired another woman museum director!'

An artist by training, Taylor didn't initially plan on a career in museums, though she'd been involved indirectly from the beginning – her father was an architect, her mother painted. She graduated from the Corcoran School of Art to discover 'there were only three galleries at that time in Washington – and I didn't paint stripes'. So she took a job with the President's Fine Arts Committee, working at the Corcoran in the late 1950s and early 1960s. The Smithsonian first hired her to develop their courses for members, now called the Resident Associate Program. She laughs about those days: 'The Smithsonian hired me while I was still a hippie – I cut my pigtail when I went to work.'

The programme was a tremendous success from the start. She believes the visibility it enjoyed made a difference. 'What I did *happened*,' she explains. 'There are so many wonderful women in museums whose work is unrecognized. I am where I am because I was publicly visible.' She thinks visibility is an important factor for women. 'Don't get buried in the stacks,' she advises those just entering the profession. 'You must have confidence in your abilities – and be willing to be judged.'

When the Smithsonian asked her to take on the directorship of the old Cooper Union in New York and develop the concept for a public museum of decorative arts, she was thrilled with the opportunity. She knew she had 'good eyes, as far as the work itself', and thought that with common sense, she'd get along. She was 35 at the time and 'looked 17 – that was a real handicap!'.

An important part of the job was raising money, something she hadn't had a great deal of experience with and still doesn't especially like, though she's currently in the midst of a $20 million campaign to expand the museum. 'So much of running a museum is the need to raise money. You're forever giving and going to parties; your job never really ends.'

Taylor says that as a woman it's hard to make a complete separation between work and family. From the start, she has had household help, but she has also found ways to spend time with her two children and three stepchildren. Until her youngest boy turned 12, she went home daily to have lunch with him. She still goes home – two blocks from the museum – for lunch, sometimes entertaining there.

For Taylor, the distinction between work and family is blurred. At home, she finds she still needs to put in extra hours. 'When everyone is fast asleep, I get up,' Taylor says. 'I do some of my best thinking sitting on the bathroom floor at two and three o'clock in the morning.'

She didn't plan it this way. In fact, she thought she would work for a couple of years, 'and then go back to painting and making babies. But it became so much a part of my life. There is a great sense of personal fulfilment in creating programmes,' she says. 'Taking my dream or someone else's and making it a reality – I never thought I had it in me.'

She's not ready to stop yet: 'Every time I think I've done it all I discover there is a whole new challenge, an area that we haven't touched yet. The day that doesn't happen, I'll leave.'

Taylor has some additional advice for women entering the profession. 'Learn as much about as many different things as possible. Learn a special area in addition to art history', she says, pointing as an example to video, which she feels will soon play a substantial role in museums. In addition to doing work that is publicly visible, she reminds women, 'Don't be too proud. Younger people are afraid they will be stuck doing something they don't like. When the chips are down, I'm not above stuffing envelopes, though I don't have to do it too often!'

Finally, Taylor says, there is 'nothing more lovely than being able to rely on good staff. Delegating is hard to learn, but important to strive for, because it frees you to do creative things. I never tell someone *how* to do anything, but *what* I want done. You need to be able to hand someone something and say "This is yours".' Admitting your mistakes and rectifying them is important, too: 'If you discover a better way to do something, you should be able to say, "I goofed", rather than running it into the ground.'

A CRASH COURSE IN MUSEUM POLITICS: SUSAN BERTRAM

Executive Director, Museums Collaborative, Inc., New York City

'When you're looking at it from a snowdrift in Minnesota, MOMA takes on mythic proportions,' reminisces Susan Bertram, explaining how she came out of Carleton College with a BA to be dazzled by New York City's cultural milieu. She began her career as a cataloguer in the film department at the Museum of Modern Art, before moving on to international programme assistant. 'It never occurred to me to negotiate salary. I considered myself fortunate to get the job.'

Things were to change soon, and change dramatically. The year was 1969, and Bertram agreed to substitute for a vacationing friend who worked in the museum library duplicating announcements and such. The museum workers went on strike. And Bertram found herself the only one in the communications office. She ran off sheets announcing strike meetings, and ended up as a spokesperson to the media. She later became head of the union. 'It was a crash course in the more painful aspects of museum finances and management,' says Bertram. 'It gave me a broader perspective on problems. And I became more interested in museums as institutions and in the role they play.'

Five years later, she was recruited to work for Museums Collaborative as director of the Cultural Voucher Program, which brought museums together with community-based organizations. In 1977, she became executive director, and was charged with general management, programme development and fund-raising among other responsibilities. The collaborative, a non-profit organization, provides mid-career training for senior museum personnel, undertakes research and demonstrates projects on issues of concern to the field and offers consulting services to museums and other cultural organizations.

For Bertram, taking risks has been a theme: 'I have always taken on jobs that I thought were a little beyond my reach – for example, the union at MOMA. And the collaborative – before coming here, I had no management experience. You rise to meet the demands and you learn in the process.'

In some ways, she says, her career would have benefited from more conscious planning: 'I could have been more aggressive.' She will consider future job opportunities more cautiously because she would like to have a role in shaping the future of museums, in helping people to understand museums. She's not yet sure what that next step will be. At present, she is on maternity leave, having worked until the day before the baby was born. 'At this point in my career', says Bertram, who is in her mid-thirties, 'it was a pleasure to take off the five months.'

One of the problems for women in museum work, believes Bertram, is that as a group, they do not receive the amount of encouragement men do. Though she acknowledges the importance of mentors, she says, 'It didn't happen that way for me. Some people need to find their own way.' Paraphrasing Benjamin Franklin, she added, '"Experience may be the best teacher, but it takes longer".'

YOU'VE GOT TO SAY NO: BETTYE COLLIER-THOMAS

Director, National Archives for Black Women's History and the Mary McLeod Bethune Museum, Washington DC

'You've got to say no. You can't be all things to all people.' For Bettye Collier-Thomas, director of the Bethune Museum and National Archives for Black Women's History in Washington DC, those words of wisdom were learned the hard way. 'Last February', she explains, 'the doctor sent me home with chronic fatigue. I had 43 invitations to speak that month. I had to turn almost all of them down.'

Thomas had been, as is her style, working nearly non-stop. An administrator, she also has her hand in planning exhibits, research projects, outreach and other programmes for the museum and archives, a young institution that she developed at the invitation of the National Council of Negro Women in the late 1970s. Within two years, with the assistance of a small but dedicated staff, she had opened the museum to the public and designed, directed and produced the first national scholarly research conference on black women.

To do that, she says, she worked literally seven days a week. In addition, she has served as a special consultant to the National Endowment for the Humanities, travelling and providing technical assistance to minority museums and historical organizations throughout the country. She co-ordinated the first national black museum conference in 1980. She has published a number of articles and speaks at professional conferences of the AAM, the Organization of American Historians, American Historical Association and the Association for the Study of Afro-American Life and History, to name a few. And she is working on two books, one on Baltimore's black community, the other a history of black women's organizations. Prior to the doctor's diagnosis of fatigue she had been working full-time and going to the Library of Congress every Saturday and Sunday, as well as two or three nights a week.

'Like many professional women,' Thomas says, 'I'd sleep three hours, and then get up and work. I thought I would run on that agenda forever', she says ruefully.

It was Thomas who created the museum and archives, providing a structure where there was none and developing the physical facility: 'If you're wedded to your work, to the creation of an institution, you feel obligations others may not feel.' She notes with pride that few institutions in five years can match the growth of Bethune, 'but it has been at a personal cost to me and the staff.'

'I'm an enthusiastic person. I believe in going for the top. I thrive on challenge, on the impossible', says Thomas. A supportive husband made a difference, she believes, as did the fact she has no children: 'In many cases, my family does not impinge on my professional designs.'

Thomas, who earned her MA in 1966 from Atlanta University and her Ph.D. in American history from George Washington University in 1974, points out that there are not many Afro-Americans with similar credentials in the museum world: 'We need more academicians in the museum world. We need people with that expertise who can take on difficult research projects and interpret within the context of a museum.'

There is a need for more minorities in the profession, at many levels, she says. 'Until recently, many did not even think of it as an option. I would like to see more Afro-American women seriously consider art history and museum studies. There are more jobs than they know.'

Thomas feels that it is difficult to separate obstacles on the basis of race or sex. There are really two levels of discrimination that come into play she notes, and they are brought home by the comment of a black male historian, who asked her, 'When will you move back to the mainstream of Afro-American history? Don't you think women's history is a fad?'

A self-defined workaholic, Thomas doesn't even hesitate when asked if she'd do it over again: 'Definitely. But I'd go back, build in more time for things beyond the museum.' Now she is spending more time on her books, which are important as she moves towards recognition as a major professional historian.

She's worked hard to get where she is, and her advice reflects that: 'Do not expect people to give you anything. You have to go out and get it.'

This article first appeared in Museum News *(Feb. 1985), pp. 20–6.*

26

The more effective director: specialist or generalist?

Stephen E. Weil

Stephen Weil's chapter, in spite of its title, is as much about who should determine the mission or vision of a museum as the nature and skills of its leader. In making a forceful case for directors to be given the power to direct, Weil has opened up a discussion around one of the most controversial issues in museums in the 1990s – leadership.

Discipline specialist or management generalist? The immediate question posed is which of them might be more effective as the director of a museum, a horticultural garden, or a similar interpretive/preservative organization – an individual solidly grounded in the organization's particular discipline (or at least a kindred discipline) or somebody whose training has been in management generally and whose experience has been in some other field.

Rather than attempt to answer this directly, I will digress to consider three other questions. The answers to those should, in turn, help us to address the original query. Throughout this digression, the word 'museum' should be understood to include the entire range of interpretive/preservative organizations (including horticultural gardens), and 'he' and 'his' are, of course, intended also to include 'she' and 'hers'.

The three other questions are:

1   Can museum presentations be value neutral, or do they inescapably reflect a point of view?
2   If such presentations do inescapably reflect a point of view, is it necessary or desirable that this point of view be consistent throughout a museum?
3   If it is necessary or desirable that a consistent point of view be reflected throughout a museum, then whose point of view should it be?

CAN MUSEUM PRESENTATIONS BE VALUE NEUTRAL?

René d'Harnoncourt – the late director of New York City's Museum of Modern Art – is supposed to have said, 'Simply to place an object is to interpret it'. This seems correct. To select a particular object for exhibit, to put that object into juxtaposition with other objects and to dispose of those juxtapositions in a three-dimensional gallery space – these are all interpretative acts. As such, they must necessarily to a degree be coloured by our values, our beliefs, our interests and our taste. Each of us has a truth, but all of our truths are not the same.

Journalists try to distinguish between what is reportage and what is editorial (albeit that there are some who doubt that any such distinction is even possible). Museum presentations, however, are almost invariably editorial. They do more than simply report. For the most part, they also argue, they urge, they seek to convince. What makes a great museum exhibition memorable to us is not its dispassionate quality or the objective skill with which it describes or documents some particular phenomenon. To the contrary, what makes such an exhibition memorable is its capacity to move us, to provide us with a fresh outlook, to induce in us a sense of revelation. Describing the new Holocaust Museum soon to be built in Washington, its director has said the effect it will strive for is 'emotive'.

Even if objectivity were to be our goal, the very physicality of the museum enterprise might well limit our ability to achieve it. The *New York Times* may have enough space to carry 'All the News that's Fit to Print'. Those who deal in objects have no comparable luxury. They must of necessity be selective. This at once means that judgement and connoisseurship – neither of them value neutral – must come into play. Invariably, these will be functions of our values, beliefs, interests and taste. Inescapably, they will reflect some point of view.

IS IT NECESSARY OR DESIRABLE THAT THIS POINT OF VIEW BE CONSISTENT THROUGHOUT A MUSEUM?

Those who argue against such consistency generally do so from one of two assumptions – either, first, that the museum has a basic obligation to be 'fair' and to present all legitimate points of view or else, second, that the members of the museum's curatorial staff enjoy some equivalent of academic freedom that thereby entitles them to present a variety of differing views.

A dramatic effort to establish the 'fairness' argument occurred in the late 1970s when several creationist groups brought a lawsuit against the Smithsonian Institution's National Museum of Natural History. Their claim was that the museum was – through its exhibits – both implicitly and explicitly endorsing a Darwinian theory of evolution. Among the remedies they asked was that the court direct the museum to give equal exposure to their own creationist point of view.

While this lawsuit was dismissed for reasons not germane here, the 'equal treatment' question it raised must be considered. Are museums required to be 'fair'? Should museums be treated like radio and television stations, which must, by law, give 'equal time' to rival political candidates and observe a 'fairness doctrine' with respect to controversial public issues? Or should museums be treated like newspapers and periodicals, which are constitutionally protected against any such public interference and retain the unbridled right to espouse their own views and to exclude the views of those with whom they disagree?

In a free society, it is the restraint imposed on broadcasters – and not the privilege extended to a free press – that is the anomaly. 'Equal time' and the 'fairness doctrine' were not established as being in themselves desiderata. They were simply the by-products of a licensing system mandated by the scarcity of available broadcasting frequencies and the perceived public need to allot these on some orderly basis. Our broadcasting laws were intended to assure that the monopoly granted to operate a particular frequency did not permit the operator also to monopolize the points of view that could be broadcast over that frequency.

There is no parallel here for museums. While the resources available to museums may sometimes seem scarce, the fact remains that the public is entitled to have all of the museums – and all of the points of view – that it wants and is prepared to support. To require that museums be licensed would be no more tolerable in a free society than to require licenses of newspapers or magazines. In the same vein, to require that a museum fairly represent every point of view would be as intolerable as prohibiting a newspaper from endorsing a political candidate or a magazine from taking an editorial position on a controversial issue. If creationists do not like what they find in an existing natural history museum, then the proper solution is for them to start a museum of their own in which they will be free to adopt and disseminate whatever point of view they want. The fairness argument has no application to such an open-ended situation.

What, then, of the argument that members of the curatorial staff have, or should have, some equivalent of academic freedom? Are not museums, as educational institutions, somewhat akin to colleges and universities? If so, does not a curator occupy a position that parallels that of a faculty member? If so, may he not then be entitled to employ the museum's programmes and facilities as vehicles through which to express his own personal convictions and preferences on matters that fall within the scope of the museum's subject matter?

The difficulty with this argument is its assumption that academic freedom has evolved primarily as a right or benefit conferred upon those by whom it might be exercised. What this argument fails to recognize is that the evolution of academic freedom must be seen as inseparable from the development of the medieval university in which faculty and students conjoined to form an academic community. Neither the history nor structure of the museum parallels that of the university. The differences between them might well be symbolized by the titles generally conferred upon their highest executive officers. The museum has a director who directs. The college has a president who presides.

Beyond this, moreover, the relationship of museum curators to museum visitors is in no sense anything like the relationship between faculty members and students. In contrast to the faculty member's obligation to his students, the curator's basic responsibilities are to the administration by which he has been hired and to the collections entrusted to his care. While that administration may invite his participation in formulating an institutional viewpoint – he might for example serve on a curatorial committee that reviews the museum's programmes – the argument that he is independently entitled to use the museum's facilities to present his own point of view in opposition to the administration's does not seem to carry weight. Curators are not tenured, and notwithstanding that their scholarly concerns may be similar to those of university faculty members, they are not teachers and do not function as part of an academic community.

What about the other side? If these arguments *against* consistency fail, is the argument *for* consistency any better? I would argue that it is. Museums must rely on continuing support from outside patrons. Those most likely to be supportive are those who share an institution's values. Unless such values are projected in some consistent and coherent way, such support may be difficult to obtain.

Imagine, for example, the situation of a natural history museum in which the departments of entomology and botany both took an actively positive view towards a Darwinian theory of evolution while the department of invertebrate zoology opposed such a theory with equal vigour. Or imagine an art museum in which the curator of prints was collecting the work of Leroy Neiman with the same avidity that another curator was concurrently de-accessioning and disposing of that same artist's paintings. At best this would be confusing; at worst, self-defeating.

In a great university, the expression of a multiplicity of views may be a sign of open and healthy inquiry. At their current level of development, the same may not be true for museums. It might be taken instead as a sign of managerial disarray. While consistency need not be carried to every last detail, the successful operation of a museum today would still seem to require that it project some basic point of view, some over-arching set of values. A history museum that at one and the same time treated the American labour movement as a vital force for progress *and* as a quasi-criminal intrusion upon the rights of capital might forfeit any claim to be taken seriously. A contemporary art museum that accorded equal importance to the paintings of Jackson Pollock and of Norman Rockwell would be open to general ridicule.

IF A CONSISTENT POINT OF VIEW IS TO BE REFLECTED, WHOSE POINT OF VIEW SHOULD IT BE?

For many of the world's museums, this is a simple question. These museums operate under ministries of culture or ministries of education. The point of view to be reflected is that of the government. In those instances where the government and a political party are virtually coextensive, then the line of that political party becomes the museum's mandatory point of view. In the German Democratic Republic, for example, the line that was dictated in 1972 by the ruling Socialist Unity Party provided that historical scholarship

> takes as its point of departure that the socialist world system gathered around the Soviet Union is the inevitable result of the entire course of world history and that the GDR is the legitimate heir to all the revolutionary, progressive and humanistic traditions of German history and, above all, of the German workers movement.

To this day, the history museums of the GDR reflect just that point of view.[1] Here, for example, is how East Berlin's Museum für Deutsche Geshichte – the Museum of German History – describes its overall programme:

> As a socialist centre of education, [the Museum] acquaints visitors with the revolutionary, democratic and humanist traditions of the German people. It emphasizes the role of the masses as the real makers of history.

In the United States, by contrast, we have no centralized source of ideology for museums. Our thousands upon thousands of museums are independently governed. Even if we did have some inclination to make them all march in ideological lockstep, we lack any effective means to do it. Each museum will have its own point of view.

The question remains, though, as to who it is, within each museum, that is to establish this point of view – the board, the director or the staff? We can, I think, rather quickly dispose of the possibility that it might be the staff. A museum is not a democracy. One of the director's principal roles is to direct the staff, not to represent it. His authority is delegated to him downwards by the board, not conferred upon him upward by his staff acting in the manner of an electorate.

What of the board then? Beyond question, a museum's board of trustees has the *authority* to establish the institution's point of view. The more pertinent question is whether it has the *competence* to do so – and to do so at any useful level of detail. Most often, board members will have been selected for their competence in some other field (law, finance, communications) or their access to desired resources (money, collections, local government) rather than for any detailed knowledge of the museum's subject matter. Moreover, the very size of many boards (as well as the procedures by which they operate) would render them highly ineffectual in formulating the reformulating a museum's point of view on any detailed and ongoing basis. At best, the board's role in the formulation of an institutional viewpoint is an indirect one. It is manifested through the board's designation and retention of a director.

This is not to diminish such a role. It may even be the single most important function that a board performs. It is not, though, the same as formulating ongoing substantive points of view on the wide variety of instances that may fall within the scope of the museum's subject matter. To paraphrase one commentator, the board's job is not to run a museum but, rather, to see that it *is* run.

In the end, then it is to the director that we must look to establish a museum's particular truth, its point of view, even – if you will – its taste. While the conclusion may seem startling – and not at all a happy one for those who would prefer to see museums organized on some more collegial basis – it may well be that a museum operates best on that same hierarchical model as does the army, the church and the traditional industrial corporation. This is a model in which decisions on matters of grave institutional importance – on matters, if you will, of faith and morals – are made at the top and disseminated downwards. It is the director's great privilege – and his awesome responsibility as well – to determine the truths that a museum will tell and the beliefs that it will transmit.

But here of course, is the catch. For the director to be effective, it is not sufficient that the points of view he brings to the museum be consistent. They must also be persuasive. The director, after all, does more than simply direct the staff and formulate the museum's various points of view. He also acts as its principal public spokesman. When he expresses a museum's point of view, he must do so in terms that can be broadly accepted as informed and authoritative by all of the museum's various constituencies. He must speak in terms that can command the respect of its board, its staff, its patrons, its visitors, its community, its commentators and even its critics.

We return then to our initial question: which of them might be more effective as the director of a museum – a disciplinary specialist or a managerial generalist? While many arguments can be adduced on either side, it seems to me that a consideration of two of the roles that a director must play – those of formulating the museum's ideological stance and of acting as spokesman to disseminate that stance to the museum's several publics – tilt the balance conclusively in favour of the disciplinary specialist.

The managerial generalist cannot be expected to have the education or experience that would enable him successfully to formulate a consistent, persuasive, informed and authoritative point of view with respect to the museum's subject matter. This task – as important, perhaps, as any in the museum – would of necessity have to be delegated to subordinate staff members. Neither could such a generalist necessarily be expected to act effectively as a spokesman with respect to the museum's subject matter. Again, his only choice – absent some talent in the use of cue cards – might be to delegate this duty to subordinates.

In the absence of a candidate who presents an ideal balance of disciplinary knowledge and managerial skills, those who select a museum director must choose between a disciplinary specialist prepared and able to learn the rudiments of management or a managerial generalist who either can quickly absorb the methods, ethics, literature and value of a disciplinary field or who is otherwise prepared to delegate several key elements of his directorship to his subordinates. Considering this very alternative with respect to art museums, the Association of Art Museum Directors concluded in its 1978 report on training needs that 'It makes more sense to train art historians to be managers than to train administrators – who are not naturally inclined toward the visual arts – to understand and be sympathetic to art or to comprehend the role of the museum.'

A decade later, that conclusion still seems right.

This paper first appeared in S. Weil (1985) Rethinking the Museum and other Meditations, *Washington, D.C.: Smithsonian Institution, pp. 95–103.*

NOTE

1   This chapter was first published in 1985, before the collapse of the communist regimes in Eastern Europe.

27

MGR: a conspectus of museum management

Stephen E. Weil

*There have been few attempts to date to develop a body of museum-specific manage-
ment theory, despite the apparent need to adapt general theories and practices to take
account of the particularities of the museum context. In this ground-breaking paper
Stephen Weil proposes an integrated approach to the management process in museums,
if not a system to be rigidly adhered to.*

In a 1975 *Harvard Business Review* article, Henry Mintzberg observed that the tasks
a typical manager performs on a daily basis are characterized chiefly by their 'brevity,
variety and discontinuity'.[1] His observation appears valid for museums. To those in senior
management positions nothing could be more evident (and sometimes more frustrating)
than their constant diversion from what they may suppose to be the classic tasks of management – planning organizing co-ordinating and controlling – in order to deal with a
kaleidoscopic array of seemingly unrelated matters in need of urgent attention. What
about a curator's request for additional travel funds? Should Gallery 302 be shut to the
public so that the floor can be fixed? Will the museum honour its agreement to send an
exhibition to an East European country with which diplomatic relations may momentarily
be severed? Would the funding application for a forthcoming exhibition be better
addressed to the National Endowment for the Arts or the National Endowment for the
Humanities?

A corresponding situation prevails in the study of museum management. The complaint
most frequently heard from management students concerns the apparent lack of connection among the topics that typically constitute their course of study. What sense they
ask is to be made of a day spent jumping quickly from the mysteries of accrual-basis
accounting to the implications of McGregor's assumptions X and Y to the intricacies of
by-laws and governance? What has long-range planning to do with situational leadership? How do either of these relate to professional standards?

MGR was originally developed for the Museum Management Institute in order to show
more clearly the underlying continuity among the varied tasks that together constitute
the museum manager's daily work. It is *not* a system of management. It is, rather, a
provisional effort to describe how the concerns with which every manager must regularly
deal relate to one another and to the overall purposes of the museum. While it is based
primarily on the governance structure of the private voluntary museum – the organizational form of more than half of American museums – it can be adapted as well to state,
county and municipal museums, and to museums that are subunits of some larger entity
such as a university or cultural complex.

'MGR' is an acronym: 'M' for 'Methods', 'G' for 'Goals', and 'R' for 'Resources'. For reasons that will become evident, the 'G' for 'Goals' is given the central position. The premise of MGR is that management consists fundamentally of the methodical or other employment of institutional resources towards the achievement of institutional goals.

Under MGR a clear distinction is made among methods, goals and resources. A corresponding distinction is made among tasks that are primarily method related, goal related and resource related. These tasks, in turn, are broadly defined as planning, implementing, evaluating and documenting. While the focus of any given task may be on one or another method, goal or resource, the nature of these tasks is seen as relatively constant. The traditional distinction between policy and implementation (i.e., the board makes policy; the director and staff implement policy) is not recognized. Policy is envisioned, rather, as one of several methods for employing resources, and policy-making is perceived as an activity that is pervasive throughout the museum.

While the following analysis will focus primarily on the work of senior management, it must be understood that management in its larger sense embraces the sum of every activity performed within the museum and, accordingly, that the board and every member of the staff are to a degree engaged in management. The difference between a museum director and a front-line supervisor lies not so much in the nature of the tasks they perform (planning, implementing, evaluating, documenting) as in the focus of the tasks for which they have immediate responsibility and the scope of the resources under their control.

INSTITUTIONAL GOALS AND GOAL-RELATED TASKS

By definition the general goals of any museum must be those of museums generally. As Joseph Veach Noble has explained, these are to collect, preserve, study, interpret and exhibit.[2]

In every museum these general goals are coupled with particular goals that specify what it is that is to be collected, preserved, studied, interpreted and exhibited (maritime artefacts, Oriental art objects, local history memorabilia) as well, in most cases, as the purpose or purposes for which this work is to be done. A museum's particular goals will customarily be set forth in its charter or other founding document. These goals are the 'givens' of the organization in the pursuit of which substantial resources will already have been assembled and invested. As such, they lie beyond the purview of management and will only rarely be changed. The pursuit of any other goal is improper.

The board of trustees is charged by law with the overall management of the museum. While its authority is ostensibly complete, the highest level of choice it will ordinarily exercise is to set priorities amongst the organization's permitted goals and (as in the case of a museum with several types of collections) within such goals. What is to be emphasized, to what degree, and for how long? Should resources be diverted from a series of scholarly publications to begin an outreach programme? Should a large, unexpected and unrestricted bequest be used to furnish a new conservation laboratory or to endow an acquisitions fund? If there is a shortfall in income, what programme areas should be scaled back or eliminated? How much of a new wing should be devoted to galleries and how much to classrooms? While senior staff may play an advocacy role in setting priorities amongst the museum's permitted goals, this task is essentially one to be performed by the board. Typically, it will do so through its adoption of near-term budgets and long-range plans.

The management tasks of the director and senior staff begin at the level below this. The director's authority to perform such tasks is derived from the board through delegation. Paramount among these tasks is the translation of the museum's priority-ordered general and particular goals into public programmes. Put otherwise, the principal goal-related task of senior management is to convert the institution's skeletal and essentially abstract goals into a concrete and visible form. In this regard it should be noted that both the display and conservation of the museum's permanent collection are considered under MGR to be programmes to exactly the same extent as would the presentation of a special loan exhibition or the preparation of a catalogue.

The translation of goals into programmes is an ongoing management task and cannot be fully accomplished within the lifetime of an institution. The most important of museum goals are basically unattainable. Short of the end of time, there is no point at which the goal of preserving any object will have finally been met. No collection of contemporary art, history or science can ever be brought to completion. In this respect museums differ substantially from other non-profit organizations dedicated to the achievement of such theoretically attainable goals as the eradication of a particular disease or the commemoration of a specific event.

In the performance of its ongoing goal-related tasks, senior staff will typically separate its programme initiatives into a series of discrete components ('objectives') that – together with some further delegation of the authority originally derived from the board – can be assigned to subordinate staff members. At each intermediate level, this process (including the identification of sub-objectives and a further delegation of authority) may be replicated within the narrower compass of these assigned objectives. The sum of accomplished objectives and sub-objectives will constitute the actual programme of the museum.

Under MGR, goal-related tasks are distinguished from resource- and method-related tasks by the directness with which they relate to the museum's public programmes. Thus, to plan or write a collections handbook would be classified as a primarily goal-related task. Selecting a printer for such a handbook would be classified as primarily resource related. The design or implementation of a procurement system through which the museum might regularly purchase its printing would be classified as primarily method related.

INSTITUTIONAL RESOURCES AND RESOURCE-RELATED TASKS

The only purposes for which museum resources may be legitimately expended are those that demonstrably relate either to its governance or directly or indirectly to its goal-related programmes. Any other expenditure – whether of a staff member's time, a sum of money or the use of a gallery – constitutes a waste of resources for which the board may be held accountable.

For the purposes of MGR, the resources that museums employ toward the achievement of their institutional goals are considered as falling into seven clusters. Chief among these, because it is implicit in the definition of the museum, is:

- *Collections*: included here are not only accessioned objects but also any object that may be currently or potentially available for study or exhibition through loan, gift, excavation rights or otherwise

Of the remaining six clusters – all of which (unlike collections) are common to virtually every enterprise – there are three which include resources that are more or less tangible. These, and some of the principal resources within each, are:

- *Human resources*: trustees, paid staff, volunteer staff, independent contractors, consultants, donors, members, vendors;
- *Fiscal resources*: cash, accounts receivable, prepaid expenses, pledges, future interests, investments in securities and similar assets that can be quantified monetarily;
- *Tangible non-collection resources*: land, plant, equipment, tools, supplies, inventory

The remaining three clusters include resources that, while not so tangible, are no less vital. These are:

- *Information*: included here is everything from collections records, photographs, films, tapes and correspondence files to the operating manuals for power tools and a set of telephone books. Also included is the full range of scholarly publications available from both internal and external sources as well as such products of documentation (a basic management task) as the museum's fiscal and personnel records, its plumbing and wiring plans, and the minutes of meetings. Codes of professional conduct and the museum's established operating procedures, while arguably each so distinctive as to constitute a resource of another kind, are also considered forms of information;
- *High public regard*: the totality of positive ways in which the museum is perceived by its various publics, both internal (trustees, staff, volunteers, members) and external (visitors, vendors, collectors, museum professionals, the community, the press, funding sources, local government);
- *Time*: notwithstanding some anomaly in considering time as a resource, it functions as such in the case of planning ('To accomplish X, we will need A people, B dollars and C time'). Moreover, it shares with other resources the quality of being convertible. Thus, the lack of time to complete a specific project in a routine way might be made up by expending dollars (a fiscal resource) for additional help (a human resource). Conversely, the cost of carrying out a specific project might be reduced by deferring the date of its proposed completion and thus, in effect, converting some period of time into dollars

Tasks that are primarily resource related may be divided roughly into those that are performed within the framework of an established method and those for which no method has been prescribed. As a rule, the more routinely that such tasks must be performed, the greater the likelihood that management will have established a method – that is, a 'routine' – to regulate their performance. The more infrequently a task must be performed or the more unanticipated the circumstances that might occasion the task, the less likely it is that any methodical framework will have been provided for its accomplishment.

Most often the level of the museum at which a resource-related task is to be performed will be inversely related to the extent to which a method for its performance has been established. Thus, in a museum charging admission there would commonly be a well-established routine by which the day's proceeds are held in safe keeping overnight and deposited the following morning. Except in unusual circumstances, the daily performance of these tasks would be the immediate responsibility of subordinate staff members. By contrast, the discovery in the museum's lobby of a steamer trunk filled with gold bullion and a note reading 'In gratitude for so many years of pleasure' would inaugurate a series of resource-related tasks that would necessarily involve senior staff and most likely the board of trustees.

Because the resources employed by museums have such widely varying properties, the techniques appropriate for managing them must be equally varied. A malfunctioning typewriter and a depressed and unproductive staff cannot be 'fixed' in the same way, and the criteria for choosing an endowment investment will not be the same as those for selecting and object to be accessioned. None the less, the underlying nature of these resource-related tasks tends to be the same. Once more, they are broadly defined as planning, implementing, evaluating and documenting.

METHODS AND METHOD-RELATED TASKS

> The effective manager does not make many decisions. He solves generic problems through policy.
>
> Peter Drucker[3]

The term 'Methods', as used in MGR, embraces the entire range of policies, procedures, practices, systems, arrangements and routines that may be established, negotiated or permitted to develop for the regular and systematic performance of resource- and goal-related tasks. Management's method-related tasks are planning, implementing, evaluating and documenting such policies, procedures, practices, systems, arrangements and routines.

As Drucker suggests, a principal function of an established policy is to relieve management from the necessity of having constantly to determine how a recurring task is to be performed. To this extent methods operate to conserve management time – a museum resource. The establishment of methods may also be indicated for certain nonrecurring tasks – e.g. the evacuation of the museum in case of fire or the treatment of a stricken visitor – when the brief time available in which to perform the task may preclude making a 'good' decision and when the harm to be anticipated in the absence of such a decision might be very great.

Given the variety of resources employed by museums and the corresponding variety of the techniques that must be used to deal with them, it follows that an equally varied range of methods is also required. A collections management policy will be no more helpful in determining how to pay employees required to work on holidays than will the adoption of an accrual-basis accounting systems assure that an adequate supply of spare light bulbs is kept on hand. Each cluster of resources will require a different and appropriate series of methods for the routine performance of its relevant tasks. A methodical approach to such goal-related tasks as budgeting and long-range planning may require still further methods.

The magnitude of management's task in providing methods for dealing with all of a museum's varied resources may be suggested by listing some of those that might be established with respect to paid staff. In some cases these may be unilaterally prescribed by the board and/or senior management. In others they may have to be reached through negotiation with a collective bargaining agent acting on behalf of the staff:

- A system of delegation (generally reflected in a table of organization) pursuant to which a share of the authority vested by law in the board and originally delegated to the director may be subdivided among those subordinates who will be charged with immediate (but not ultimate) responsibility for the exercise of such authority. Integral to such an arrangement will be a variety of controls as well as procedures for evaluating and documenting the operation of the system;

- Personnel procedures prescribing the manner in which employees are recruited, interviewed and hired; how records are kept of their salaries, benefits and attendance; the documents to be completed on their voluntary or involuntary termination and the records to be retained after such termination;
- A salary and fringe benefits programme;
- A payroll and withholding system;
- A comprehensive set of personnel practices covering such matters as hours of work, overtime, leave policy (including holidays, vacations, sick leave, leaves of absence, jury, voting and military leave), disciplinary and grievance procedures, probationary employment, employee discounts, travel reimbursement and training opportunities;
- A system of job descriptions, performance review and evaluation;
- An equal opportunity policy that may also provide for affirmative action and upward mobility programmes;
- A compilation of health and safety procedures;
- A code of ethics covering such matters as outside employment, private collecting, conflict of interest, dual compensation and the use of privileged information;
- An internal communications system employing such devices as telephones, meetings, memoranda, minutes, newsletters and bulletin boards

The list is by no means complete, and paid staff is only one element in the cluster of human resources that a museum employs toward the accomplishment of its institutional goals. Other methods will be needed to conduct the affairs of the board, to assure that the gifts of donors are promptly and properly acknowledged, and to be certain that museum members receive renewal notices as their memberships expire. Beyond the human resources cluster, the method-related tasks of management require that regular ways be established to do everything from keeping the museum's financial records and maintaining its climate controls to recording its collection and carrying out the trash. In each case, what is involved is again planning, implementing, evaluating and documenting.

POTENTIAL USES OF MGR

How might this schema be useful to museum managers and students of management?

First, MGR could be helpful in avoiding certain confusions endemic to museums. Under MGR, for example, it would appear evident that a museum cannot have as its goal 'to operate in the black' or 'to break even'. Money is a resource, not a goal. While fiscal probity is a necessary precondition to a museum's survival, it is no measure of its success toward achieving its actual general and particular museological goals. A museum may operate with a constantly balanced budget and still, by its failure to generate programmes commensurate with its goals, be an inadequate museum.

Staff morale and museum collections stand in the same condition. Staff is a museum resource, not its purpose for being. A demoralized staff can make it difficult if not impossible for a museum to work effectively toward its goals, but high staff morale would no more indicate a museum's success than would a constantly balanced budget. Collections, too, are a resource, and the measure of museum management lies not in what the institution has historically acquired but in the current programmatic use to which the collection is put.

Methods, too, may be confused with goals. The resulting proposition would be a well-administered museum was a well-managed museum. Administration, however, is no more than the sum of the methods established to employ institutional resources. It is a way of facilitating the work of the museum – a 'how' – but it is in no sense the 'why' for which such resources have been assembled. Sound administration can make a major contribution to the success of a museum. Again, though, it is ultimately by its programmes, not by its administration, that a museum must be judged.

Two further uses of MGR might be to test the 'fit' between a proposed activity and a museum's general and particular goals and to generate such questions as may be necessary to assure that all of the implications of undertaking such an activity have been considered.

The high regard of its various publics is among a museum's most important resources, and this question of 'fit' is important in maintaining this regard. It is not sufficient that these publics understand the museum's underlying goals. It is just as important that as the museum's programmes evolve, all of its publics have a clear understanding of how each of its successive activities relates to these goals. The inability of the museum to demonstrate to its publics (including trustees and staff) that there *is* such a relationship can only raise suspicions that the museum's management is pursuing a proposed activity for reasons that are capricious, of personal rather than an institutional advantage, and/or part of some undisclosed agenda. The damaging effects of such suspicions can spread beyond the proposed activity to reflect negatively on the museum as a whole.

If, however, a proposed activity can be demonstrated to have the requisite 'fit', then the questions generated by MGR might be useful in forecasting how the activity would affect the museum's various resource clusters. The questions are those that an experienced museum manager would instinctively ask:

- What people will be involved?
- What funds will be required, and what offsetting funds might be generated?
- What space will be needed? What supplies and equipment?
- What additional information may be required?
- Will the activity itself produce information of value?
- How will the activity affect the perception of the museum by each of its publics?
- What time periods will be needed for planning and implementation?
- How will the activity be evaluated, by whom, and when?
- What documentation will be necessary?
- Will any new procedures or routines have to be established?
- Which of the resources required will have to be newly obtained and which can be diverted from some prior use?
- For those to be newly obtained, what sources will be looked to?
- For those to be diverted from some prior use, what will this diversion cost the museum's present activities? How does this cost measure against the benefits to be anticipated from the proposed activity?

MGR may also be used as a tool for analysing a museum's overall management. As such it would provoke a different series of questions:

- Have the museum's general and particular goals been clearly articulated?
- To what degree are these goals understood by the museum's various publics?
- Are the museum's public programmes demonstrably consistent with such goals?
- Have these programmes been designed to make optimum use of the museum's available resources?
- To what extent is senior staff engaged in goal-related and method-related tasks? To what extent is it burdened with the performance of routine resource-related tasks that could better be delegated to subordinates? Conversely, has its energy been

misdirected into the establishment and maintenance of a methodical framework larger and more complex than the museum's circumstances in fact require?

- How are energies of the board apportioned among goal-, resource-, and method-related tasks?
- At what organizational levels are planning and evaluation the predominant activities? At what level is the focus on implementation and documentation?

These uses aside MGR could be a crutch for managerial sanity. As a map on which less experienced museum managers might plot the relationship between institutional goals and the seemingly disconnected concerns that bulk so large in their working days, it might help to relieve an intermittent sense of disorientation and discontinuity. Equally, it might be of help to students who need to learn that managing a museum is, in the end, not merely having the skill to handle a particular resource – knowing how to motivate an employee, organize a capital campaign, use time efficiently or select the right word processor. Museum management is, rather, an art that requires the orchestration of all these skills, and more, in support of a museum's basic purpose: to perform an essential public service. MGR might make this clear.

This paper first appeared in S. Weil (1985) Beauty and the Beasts. On Museums, Art, the Law and the Market, *Washington, D.C.: Smithsonian Institution, pp. 69–80.*

NOTES

1 Mintzberg, H. (1975) 'The manager's job: folklore and fact', *Harvard Business Review* 53(4): 49.
2 Noble, J. V. (1970) 'Museum manifesto', *Museum News* 48(8): 16–20.
3 Quoted in Tarrant, J. J. (1980) *Drucker: The Man Who Invented the Corporate Society*, New York: 258.

28

The well-managed museum
Stephen E. Weil and Earl F. Cheit

In this chapter Stephen Weil and Earl Cheit identify factors and attributes that appear essential to managerial excellence in museums. While not a prescription for success, their suggestions offer an invaluable starting-point to the discussion as to what exactly it is that makes a well-managed museum.

Summarizing his twenty-nine-year tenure (1908–37) as director of Cambridge University's Fitzwilliam Museum, the late S. C. Cockerell said, 'I found it a pig sty; I turned it into a palace.' If we assume that Cockerell meant to describe something more than just positive changes in the Fitzwilliam's physical facilities – that he referred as well to improvements in its collections, staff, finances, governance, records and public image – then his remark might serve as a neat shorthand summary of good management. Good management is to move an organization from the 'here' of a less well managed condition to the 'there' of a better managed one – from being something near a pig sty towards being something like a palace. The aim of good management is to have a well-managed museum.

What do we mean by a well-managed museum? The clearest indications that a museum is well managed might be its ability to demonstrate that it makes the most efficient and effective use possible of the resources which it has available. In day-to-day practice, however, it is only rarely that a museum can be measured on so all-encompassing a scale. Most frequently, the degree to which a museum is well managed – or could, at least, be better managed – can only be determined by examining a number of more detailed and specific factors that relate to its programmes, planning capability, governance, staff, finances, facilities, collections, records and outside relationships.

What, then, might some of these factors be? What are some of the attributes of a well-managed museum? The following non-prioritized list (on which a number of entries may overlap) is intended to be suggestive rather than exhaustive:

- A clearly defined mission and set of shared long-term goals and underlying values;
- The ability to formulate and to pursue such strategies as may be necessary to acquire, process and expend the resources that it needs to fulfil its mission, together with an array of ongoing and successive programmes that readily relate to – and demonstrably further – that mission;
- The ability to formulate and to adhere to long-term and short-term budgets, timetables and other operational plans consistent with its various strategies;
- A structure of governance that provides for wise oversight, a long-range institutional view and access to the varied resources that may be necessary to produce its programmes;

- A commitment to develop the managerial and vocational skills and knowledge of its staff;
- A competent, loyal, stable, mutually respectful, well-motivated and well-led staff that is able to work with relative independence in pursuit of a series of agreed-upon and well-understood goals;
- Appropriate physical facilities that are maintained in good repair and provide adequate space for the production of its various programmes;
- A system for implementing each of its functions such as, for example:

   1 Closely followed policies for the acquisition and management of its collections that assure their proper physical care; that provide for the maintenance of appropriate records as to their identification, location, condition and provenance; and that assure their maximum public accessibility consistent with their care;
   2 Information management systems that permit the swift, accurate retrieval of the data necessary to manage its resources and to produce its various programmes;
   3 Financial systems that operate to keep the expenditures of resources within budgeted targets, that keep management accurately advised as to the museum's curent status and that serve as the basis for providing timely reports to various outside individuals and authorities;

- A capacity to resolve issues related to the diversity of its present and potential staff and markets by continually renewing and, where necessary, modifying its practices and programmes;
- A sensitivity to the needs and wishes of its existing and potential patrons and markets sufficiently acute that it can make considered decisions about the extent, if any, to which its programmes will be shaped to meet those needs and wishes;
- The maintenance of a positive public image through which the actions of the institution and its staff are consistently and broadly perceived as related to the pursuit of the institution's mission and goals rather than any undisclosed or self-serving agenda; and
- The maintenance of a favourable legal status pursuant to which the institution will continue to be exempt from federal, state and local income taxes, donors will continue to be able to claim charitable deductions for their contributions, and the museum will continue to enjoy whatever other privileges may be extended by its locality to not-for-profit organizations.

No claim is made that the presence of any or most or even all of these attributes would in itself be sufficient to make a museum an excellent institution. Management, even at its best, is only a single dimension of a museum's overall operation. Excellence in a museum must depend as well on the quality of its educational and other programmes, the importance of its purpose and the disciplinary value of its collection. None the less, it is difficult to conceive that a poorly managed museum would ever be able to achieve and to sustain a level of excellence for any extended time. Good management may not be the measure of a good museum but, in the long run, it would most certainly appear to be one of its critical prerequisites.

This paper first appeared in S. Weil (1985) Rethinking the Museum and other Meditations, *Washington, D.C.: Smithsonian Institution, pp. 69–72.*

Annotated bibliography

Museum management is still a relatively new subject of study, and therefore much of the material is in journal articles rather than books. This particular collection therefore fills an important gap in the literature, by drawing together the more innovative and challenging papers. In this bibliography I have singled out a dozen of the more useful of the existing books in the field, for those new to the subject.

At present we lack a theoretical analysis of museum management to rank alongside those, for example, for history and archaeology curatorship and museum education in the Museum Studies series of Leicester University Press. In the absence of this, Charles Handy's *Understanding Organizations* (Handy 1993) provides an outstanding introduction to general organizational theory. While it is left to the reader to make the connections with the particularities of museums as organizations, this classic work remains an invaluable text for all those with an interest in museum management.

There is no single manual of museum management practice. *The Manual of Curatorship* (Thompson *et al.* 1992) includes some helpful pieces on aspects of management, as does Ambrose and Paine (1993), at an obviously even more basic level. Ambrose (1993), though it has a specific purpose, is also of more general value. The series of guidelines on management issues produced by the Association of Independent Museums in Britain are of value but are inevitably often very specific to the British context. Ambrose and Runyard's *Forward Planning* (1991) is a useful introduction to policy and planning issues. For personnel management, Miller (1980) is a valuable if now dated guide to good practice. Office of Arts and Libraries (1991) is the most useful survey of effective practice in the management and development of volunteers. Tolles (1991) is an interesting if, disappointingly, rather shallow examination of the key question of leadership. Johnson and Thomas (1992) is a model for the study of the economic impact and financial management of any museum. Lord and Lord (1992) contains a wealth of practical information of assistance in managing any kind or scale of museum project, but it lacks an adequate evaluation of the management of people in such creative work. A manual of museum marketing would be a welcome development. Adams (1983) is a useful introduction to discussion in this area, focusing on public relations. Meek (1992) fails to live up to its title. Overall it is rather insubstantial but does contain some marketing case studies of value. (All books are published in the UK unless otherwise stated.)

Adams, G. D (1983) *Museum Public Relations*, Nashville, TN: American Association for State and Local History.
Ambrose, T. (1993) *Managing New Museums: A Guide to Good Practice*, Edinburgh: Scottish Museums Council/HMSO.
Ambrose, T. and Paine, C. (1993) *Museum Basics*, London: Routledge.
Ambrose, T. and Runyard, S. (eds) (1991) *Forward Planning*, London: Routledge.
Handy, C. (1993) *Understanding Organizations*, Harmondsworth: Penguin.

Johnson, P. and Thomas, B. (1992) *Tourism, Museums and the Local Economy: The Economic Impact of the North of England Open Air Museum at Beamish*, Aldershot: Edward Elgar Ltd.

Lord, G. D. and Lord, B. (eds) (1992) *The Manual of Museum Planning*, Manchester: Museum of Science and Industry/HMSO.

Meek, J. (ed.) (1992) *Marketing the Arts. Every Vital Aspect of Museum Management*, London: ICOM.

Miller, R. L. (1980) *Personnel Policies for Museums: A Handbook for Management*, Washington, DC: American Association of Museums.

Office of Arts and Libraries (1991) *Volunteers in Museums and Heritage Organisations. Policy, Planning and Management*, London: HMSO.

Thompson, J. M. A., Lewis, G., Lowell, P. N., Fenton, A. and Bassett, D. A. (1992) *Manual of Curatorship: A Guide to Museum Practice*, London: Museums Association/Butterworth.

Tolles, B. F. (ed.) (1991) *Leadership for the Future: Changing Directorial Roles in American History Museums and Historical Societies*, Nashville, TN: American Association for State and Local History.

291

Index

Tate Gallery, London, England 138
tax exemption, US museums and 15, 19–20, 89, 132
Taylor, Frederick W., on scientific management 4, 121
Taylor, Kendall, on female museum leaders 265–9
Taylor, Lisa, as director of Cooper-Hewitt Museum, NY, USA 269–71
Tea Party Ship, Boston, USA 77–9
teamwork, museum organization and 256–62
theme park, comparability of museum and 109–10, 218
theory: management 2, 4–7, 149; marketing 41–3, 232–3
Thomas, Barry, on assessment of development of Beamish 173–90
Thompson, J. Walter, on planning cycle 221
Thompson, Jon, on cultural entertainment 134–5
time: deadlines 91, 260; goal-setting 37; management 229, 283–4; management and job dissatisfaction 203, 210
title of museum 222–3
tourist attraction, Beamish as 183, 186, 189
Towneley Hall Art Gallery and Museum, Burnley, England 213
Townsend, Robert, on marketing 230
trading companies, museums as 193
training: changes in, as cause of stress 195; customer care 242; directors 278–9; of disabled personnel 129–30; gendered management 267; in-house 214–15, 226–7; in-service 194, 200–2, 209, 210; of managerial groups 171; as necessity 65–7; organizational development

166–7; staff 10, 125, 207, 222; strategic management 60–1; in UK 148–54
trustees: characteristics of 194; defining mission statement 221; planning 253; relationship of curator and 48; role of 15, 234, 236, 241, 263–4, 281
trusteeship, nature of 96–7
Tullie House Museum, Carlisle, England 214
Turner, David, on training 214
turnover of staff 17, 207, 210
typology of museum goals 38

Ulster Folk Museum, Holywood, Co. Down 186
Union Terminal Museum Center, Cincinatti, USA 139
unionization of museums 121
university art museum, defining purpose 115–19
unsocial hours of work and job dissatisfaction 204
updating, planning document 58–9
user-pay, concept of 99–100, 111–12

vacuums, mission 18–19, 31, 33
value: of collection 237–8; definition of 233; of experience 243, 251; of museum point of view 274–8, 288; of reputation 247
value-for-money framework 158–63, 166–7, 170, 243
Van Maanan, J., on qualitative methodology 44–5
Vancouver Public Aquarium, Canada 108
Veblen, Thorstein, on boards 101–2
Victoria and Albert Museum, London, England: admission charges 109, 245; buildings

239–40; catering 138; Chinese Gallery 238; impact of admission charges on attendance 110; Japanese exhibition 213; restructuring 145
videotapes as merchandise 137
visitors: attractions 213; surveys 225–6, 253; tourists as 249, 254; as users 219, 221, 230
volunteer service: dependency on 263; management of 123, 200, 208; as resource 27, 241

Wall Street Journal, on women's careers 268
Walpole, Horace, on trusteeship 96
Ward, James, on concept of museum as educational tool 105
warder, museum attendant as 212–13
Waterman, Robert H., on management theory 5, 149
Weil, Stephen E.: on communication 245; on managerial excellence 288–9; on MGR, a conspectus of museum management 280–7; on specialist or generalist directors 274–9; on trusteeship 96
Welsh Folk Museum, Cardiff, Wales 186
Wernerfelt, B., on resources 141–3
White, Howard, on marketing 133
Wilson, C.H. on concept of public museum 105
Windsor Castle, London, England 213
Winterbotham, Nick, on in-house training 214
work planning and scheduling 205–6

Young, Alan, on museum attendants 213